INFRASTRUCTURAL TIMES

Temporality and the Making
of Global Urban Worlds

Edited by
Jean-Paul D. Addie, Michael R. Glass,
and Jen Nelles

BRISTOL
UNIVERSITY
PRESS

First published in Great Britain in 2025 by

Bristol University Press
University of Bristol
1-9 Old Park Hill
Bristol
BS2 8BB
UK
t: +44 (0)117 374 6645
e: bup-info@bristol.ac.uk

Details of international sales and distribution partners are available at bristoluniversitypress.co.uk

© Bristol University Press 2025

British Library Cataloguing in Publication Data
A catalogue record for this book is available from the British Library

ISBN 978-1-5292-2971-4 hardcover
ISBN 978-1-5292-2972-1 paperback
ISBN 978-1-5292-2973-8 ePub
ISBN 978-1-5292-2974-5 ePdf

The right of Jean-Paul D. Addie, Michael R. Glass and Jen Nelles to be identified as editors of this work has been asserted by them in accordance with the Copyright, Designs and Patents Act 1988.

All rights reserved: no part of this publication may be reproduced, stored in a retrieval system, or transmitted in any form or by any means, electronic, mechanical, photocopying, recording, or otherwise without the prior permission of Bristol University Press.

Every reasonable effort has been made to obtain permission to reproduce copyrighted material. If, however, anyone knows of an oversight, please contact the publisher.

The statements and opinions contained within this publication are solely those of the editors and contributors and not of the University of Bristol or Bristol University Press. The University of Bristol and Bristol University Press disclaim responsibility for any injury to persons or property resulting from any material published in this publication.

Bristol University Press works to counter discrimination on grounds of gender, race, disability, age and sexuality.

Cover design: Lyn Davies Design
Front cover image: Unsplash/ Sawyer Bengtson

Contents

List of Figures and Tables   v
Notes on Contributors   vii
Acknowledgements   xii

1	Time for a Global Infrastructure Turn *Jean-Paul D. Addie, Michael R. Glass, Jen Nelles, and Lauren Marino*	1
2	Rhythmic Infrastructure *Jean-Paul D. Addie*	25

PART I   Infrastructural Pasts, Presents, and Futures

3	Usable Infrastructure Pasts: Mobilizing History for Urban Technology Futures *Timothy Moss*	49
4	Shifting Regimes of Historicity and the Control of Urban Futures through Infrastructures: Continuities, Ambivalences, and Tensions in the Anthropocene *Olivier Coutard*	72
5	Extensions as Infrastructure: The Temporalities between Subjugation and Liberation in Jayapura, West Papua *AbdouMaliq Simone*	95

PART II   Development Times and the Making of Urban Worlds

6	Sequencing Like a State: Ciudad Guayana and the Infrastructures of Arrival *Peter Ekman*	119
7	The Times of Infrastructure Fundamentalism: Future Profits, Slow Operations, Long-Term Impacts *Seth Schindler and J. Miguel Kanai*	140
8	Dissonant Times: The Land–Infrastructure–Finance Nexus in Post-Mubarak Egypt *Dalia Wahdan and Tamer Elshayal*	160

PART III Times of Disruption/Disrupting Times

9	The Multiple Temporalities of Self-Healing Infrastructure: From the F-15 Fighter to the Smart Urban Microgrid *Simon Marvin and Jonathan Rutherford*	185
10	Speed, Suspension, and Stasis: Waiting in the Shadow of Infrastructure *Jessica DiCarlo*	207
11	Desynchronized Infrastructures of Care: Suburban Imaginaries Re-Examined *Samantha Biglieri and Roger Keil*	227
12	Disrupting Infrastructure: Space, Speed, and Street Governance *Amelia Thorpe*	249
13	Urban Infrastructure In and Out of Time *Jean-Paul D. Addie, Michael R. Glass, and Jen Nelles*	270
Index		285

List of Figures and Tables

Figures

2.1	Rhythm as repetition: difference produced through recurrence	30
2.2	Rhythm as cycle: cyclical movement without returning to a previous point of departure	33
2.3	Rhythm as period: dis/continuities between phases of (a) emergence; (b) maturation; (c) decline; and (d) collapse, within and between periods	38
3.1	Berliners fetch water from a public pump during the general strike opposing the Kapp Putsch, March 1920	50
3.2	Transport officials cool off during a heatwave, Berlin, 1931	51
3.3	A street pump for watering trees, Berlin, 2021	52
4.1	The interrelated temporal registers of the modern infrastructural compact	81
5.1	Everything filtered through everything else in Jayapura, West Papua, 2023	100
5.2	The urban extensions of Jayapura, West Papua, 2023	104
6.1	'Order of growth' and 'suggested priority'	124
6.2	The 'firm linear foundation' of an automotive city	126
6.3	'Vision in motion'	127
7.1	The proposed Great Garuda development, Jakarta	151
8.1	The central business district of Egypt in the New Administrative Capital, Cairo, 2023	169
8.2	Map of the Cairo Monorail	171
9.1	Self-healing processes	189
10.1	A home razed below the new Vang Vieng railway tunnel, Vientiane province, 2019	216
10.2	A woman washes materials from a wedding festival in her village's stream, alongside which railway pylons have been constructed, Oudomxay province, 2019	218
11.1	Distribution of COVID-19 infections in Toronto and suburbs on 10 April 2021	234

11.2	Crossing at the median in the Region of Waterloo, Ontario, 2018	241
12.1	"We need a protected bike lane here *now*, not a year from now"	255
12.2	Pedestrian safety 'pilot'	256
12.3	"Hold tight folks, we'll be just a minute!"	259

Tables

9.1	Comparing urban contexts of smart microgrid deployment	200

Notes on Contributors

Jean-Paul D. Addie is Associate Professor at the Urban Studies Institute of Georgia State University. He is a critical urban geographer working on urban and regional governance, urban political economy, and socio-spatial theory, with a specific focus on the politics of infrastructure. He has published widely with recent research on infrastructural regionalism, urban universities, and comparative urban studies appearing in journals including *Cambridge Journal of Regions, Economy and Society*, *CITY*, *International Journal of Urban and Regional Research*, *Regional Studies*, and *Urban Geography*. He is a co-convenor of the Regional Studies Association Research Network on Infrastructural Regionalism (NOIR).

Samantha Biglieri is Assistant Professor in the School of Urban and Regional Planning at Toronto Metropolitan University, and Director of the Health, Access + Planning Lab. Her research as a professional planner uses critical approaches at the intersection of planning and health/wellbeing, making connections with practice to build inclusive and accessible communities. Samantha's research has been published in journals including *Journal of the American Planning Association*, *Journal of Urban Affairs*, and *Cities & Health*. She is co-editor of *Aging People, Aging Places* (with Maxwell Hartt, Sarah Nelson, and Mark Rosenberg, Policy Press, 2021).

Olivier Coutard is CNRS Research Director at the Laboratoire Techniques Territoires Sociétés (LATTS, https/latts.fr). His current research addresses: urban energy and 'energy transition' policies in Europe; the politics of the 'post-networked city'; and the interrelations between infrastructural development, the intensity of *metabolization* processes (i.e., processes of transformation of materials and energy for social purposes), and the collective configuration of social futures. He is a socio-economist with expertise in the governance of urban infrastructure services, reforms in those sectors, and their social, spatial, and environmental implications. He has edited (or co-edited) several books on urban infrastructure including *The Governance of Large Technical Systems* (Routledge, 1999), *Beyond the Networked City* (with Jonathan Rutherford, Routledge, 2015), and *The*

Handbook of Infrastructures and Cities (with Daniel Florentin, Edward Elgar, forthcoming 2024).

Jessica DiCarlo is Assistant Professor of Geography at the University of Utah. Her research focuses on infrastructure, China's global engagements, resource politics, and issues at the environment–society nexus. She is committed to long-term fieldwork with a focus on Asia and uses ethnography to connect ground-level cases with global processes. Her research has been published in *Geoforum, Transactions of the Institute of British Geographers, Ecology and Society, Geopolitics, Area, Ambio*, and multiple books, and she is the co-editor of *The Rise of the Infrastructure State* (with Seth Schindler, Bristol University Press, 2022).

Peter Ekman teaches history and theory in the School of Architecture at the University of Southern California. He is also a postdoctoral fellow of USC's Center on Science, Technology, and Public Life, and of the Berggruen Institute. He is a cultural and historical geographer of urban America who has published in journals including *Planning Perspectives, Journal of Planning History*, and *Journal of Urban History*. His first book, forthcoming with Cornell University Press, is an intellectual history of post-war urbanism that poses a series of questions about the political temporality of what it is to plan the urban future based on knowledge about the past.

Tamer Elshayal is a doctoral student in the Graduate School of Urban Design at Harvard University. He is an urbanist working at the intersection of urban theory, critical geography, environmental anthropology, and science and technology studies. Tamer's research examines the shifting spatialities of mega-engineering in the Middle East through the study of the spatial and cultural politics of large infrastructure projects. He is interested in understanding how large engineering schemes reconfigure territories and landscapes as they take shape materially and discursively, and in turn, how they engender contested socio-spatial formations.

Michael R. Glass is Assistant Professor in Urban Sociology and Director of the Urban Studies Program at the University of Pittsburgh. Michael primarily researches city-region governance and planning, housing, and urban infrastructure, with regional expertise in South East Asia, North America, and Australasia. He is the co-editor of *Performativity, Politics, and the Production of Social Space* (with Rueben Rose-Redwood, Routledge, 2014) and *Urban Violence, Resilience, and Security* (with Taylor Seybolt and Phil Williams, Edward Elgar, 2022) and co-author of *Priced Out: Stuyvesant Town and the Loss of Middle-Class Neighborhoods* (with Lisa Morrison and

Rachael Woldoff, New York Univesity Press, 2016). He is a co-convenor of the Regional Studies Association Research Network on Infrastructural Regionalism (NOIR).

J. Miguel Kanai is Senior Lecturer in the Department of Geography at the University of Sheffield. He is an urban geographer studying the urbanization of the world under contemporary globalized capitalism. His work is specifically concerned with the consequences of intensified inter-territorial competition and the various entrepreneurial strategies adopted by cities and regions in the global South. He has published extensively in international geography and interdisciplinary journals on topics including culture-led regeneration schemes in Buenos Aires, eco-entrepreneurialism in the Brazilian state of Amazonas, and urban entrepreneurial strategies in the United States and Morocco.

Roger Keil is Professor in the Faculty of Environmental and Urban Change, York University in Toronto, Canada. He researches global suburbanization, urban political ecology, cities and infectious disease, infrastructure, and regional governance. Among his recent publications are *Suburban Planet* (Polity Press, 2018) and *After Suburbia* (ed. with Fulong Wu, University of Toronto Press, 2022) as well as *Pandemic Urbanism* (with S. Harris Ali and Creighton Connolly, Polity Press, 2023) and *Turning Up the Heat: Urban Political Ecology for a Climate Emergency* (ed. with Maria Kaika, Tait Mandler, and Yannis Tzaninis, Manchester University Press, 2023). Roger is a Fellow of CIFAR's Humanity's Urban Future programme.

Lauren Marino is an affordable housing professional and graduate of the Urban Studies Master's programme at Georgia State University. Her research interests centre on issues of equity in the built environment with a focus on multi-scalar infrastructures, suburbanization processes, housing policy, and critical urban theory.

Simon Marvin is Professor and Director of the Urban Institute at the University of Sheffield. He is an internationally recognized academic with expertise in the changing relations between socio-technical networks and urban and regional restructuring. His work develops innovative, interdisciplinary perspectives to explore new agendas for urban studies and infrastructural research. Simon has played major roles within urban and planning research towards addressing questions surrounding telecommunications, infrastructure and mobility, sustainability, and systemic transitions. He is the author of numerous research articles and books including *Splintering Urbanism* (with Stephen Graham, Routledge, 2001) and *Urban Operating Systems* (with Andrew Luque-Ayala, MIT Press, 2020).

Timothy Moss is a Senior Researcher at the Integrative Research Institute on Transformations of Human-Environment Systems at the Humboldt University of Berlin. His research and teaching connect historical studies of infrastructure with contemporary debates on socio-technical and urban transitions. Tim is particularly interested in the processes by which energy and water infrastructures reflect and reproduce the multiple geographies, power relations, and socio-materialities of a city. He is author of *Remaking Berlin: A History of the City through Infrastructure, 1920–2020* (MIT Press, 2020).

Jen Nelles is Senior Research Fellow with the Innovation Caucus, Co-Director of the Oxford Regions, Innovation, and Enterprise Lab (ORIEL) at Oxford Brookes Business School, and a visiting research professor at the Networks and Governance Lab at the University of Illinois Chicago. She specializes in innovation and productivity policy, urban and metropolitan governance, regional economic development, infrastructure, and system dynamics. Recent books include *Discovering American Regionalism: An Introduction to Regional Intergovernmental Organizations* (with David Miller, Routledge, 2019) and *Mobilizing the Metropolis* (with Philip Plotch, University of Michigan Press, 2023). Jen is a co-convenor of the Regional Studies Association Research Network on Infrastructural Regionalism (NOIR).

Jonathan Rutherford is a Senior Researcher and Deputy Director of the Laboratoire Techniques Territoires Sociétés (LATTS) – UMR 8134 CNRS, Ecole des Ponts ParisTech, Université Gustave Eiffel (France), and a visiting research fellow at the Urban Institute, University of Sheffield. His research critically analyses the material production of contemporary urban spaces through the technologies and infrastructures (telecommunications, energy, water, and sanitation) that are deployed in and between them. He is author of *Redeploying Urban Infrastructure: The Politics of Urban Socio-Technical Futures* (Palgrave Macmillan, 2020) and co-editor of *Beyond the Networked City* (with Olivier Coutard, Routledge, 2015).

Seth Schindler is Senior Lecturer in Urban Development and Transformation in the Global Development Institute at the University of Manchester. His research examines large-scale urban and regional transformation initiatives that integrate cities into transnational urban systems. Focusing on cities in the global South, he seeks to understand how ordinary cities are impacted by their rapid incorporation into global networks and assess the design of market-oriented territories as a response to the failure of neoliberal reforms. Seth is the co-editor of *The Rise of the Infrastructure State* (with Jessica DiCarlo, Bristol University Press, 2022) and his research has appeared in journals including *CITY*, *Urban Geography*, and *Urban Studies*.

AbdouMaliq Simone is Senior Professorial Fellow at the University of Sheffield's Urban Institute. He works on issues of spatial composition in extended urban regions, the production of everyday life for urban majorities in the global South, infrastructural imaginaries, collective affect, global blackness, and histories of the present for Muslim working classes. AbdouMaliq is author of numerous articles and books on urbanism and infrastructure, including *City Life from Jakarta to Dakar* (Routledge, 2009), *Improvised Lives: Rhythms of Endurance in an Urban South* (Polity Press, 2018), and *The Surrounds: Urban Life Within and Beyond Capture* (Duke University Press, 2022).

Amelia Thorpe is Associate Professor in Law at the University of New South Wales. She works in planning, property, and environmental law, focusing on mobility and urban governance. Her approach is socio-legal and interdisciplinary, drawing on professional experience in planning and urban development and in public interest environmental law. She is author of *Owning the Street: The Everyday Life of Property* (MIT Press, 2020).

Dalia Wahdan is the co-founder of Bureau Gladys, a joint venture for urban and architectural studies based in Egypt, and Associate Professor (adjunct) in the School of Public Policy at the American University in Cairo. She is an anthropologist working on urbanism in India, Egypt, and Saudi Arabia, focusing on new town planning, vulnerability in unplanned settlements, urban subjectivities, insurgent citizenship, and spatial inequities. Her publications include *Planning Egypt's New Settlements: The Politics of Spatial Inequities* (Oxford University Press and Cairo Papers, 2013). She was the head of the Board of Trustees of Greenpeace MENA in 2020.

Acknowledgements

Fittingly, the road to this book has depended on a variety of material, digital, and social infrastructures coming together across multiple time frames. The book, firstly, is a product of the Regional Studies Association Research Network on Infrastructural Regionalism (NOIR) and was made possible by funding and logistical support provided by the Regional Studies Association (RSA). We would like to thank Daniela Carl, Sally Hardy, Alex Holmes, Lesa Reynolds, Klara Sobekova, and Suede Stanton-Drudy at the RSA for supporting NOIR's activities through the RSA Research Network grant scheme.

The idea for a volume exploring infrastructure time germinated, in part, during a panel session organized by NOIR at the 2019 Urban Affairs Association meeting in Los Angeles. Here, in a conversation reflecting on the experiences of Greater Los Angeles, David Abel, Steven Erie, Jeff Kightlinger, and Stephanie Pincetl highlighted that while infrastructural regionalisms evoke complex and contested geographies, they are also built upon and establish a multiplicity of new time frames and temporalities.

Although the COVID-19 pandemic disrupted our original schedule, the RSA's 'Regions in Recovery' e-conference, held virtually in June 2021, provided the platform for an intensive week-long workshop aimed at deeply interrogating how different aspects of time are interwoven with urban and regional infrastructures. We gratefully acknowledge the foundational dialogue and provocative interventions offered by those who presented their work in these sessions. Alongside many of the authors in this volume, we extend our thanks to Michele Acuto, Pushpa Arabindoo, Katreen Boustani, Julie Cidell, Ayona Datta, Hamid Ekbia, Maurico Estrada, Andy Jonas, Rob Kitchin, Fiona McDermott, Jochen Monstadt, Caitlin Morrissey, Nathan Olmstead, Will Payne, Andrea Protschky, John Stehlin, and Alexei Trundle for their insightful and generous contributions. Lauren Marino deserves special thanks for her diligent research work at the project's outset, which provided essential groundwork for our thinking on the intersections of time and infrastructure.

The ideas developed through this volume have further benefited from constructive feedback from Tim Bunnell, Damien Carrière, Jens Ivo Engels,

Daniel Florentin, Anique Hommels, Andrew Karvonen, Colin McFarlane, Sarah Moser, Leonardo Ramondetti, Priyam Tripathy, and Kevin Ward (whether over email, coffee, or a beer or two), as well as comments provided by the anonymous reviewers of the book proposal and draft manuscript.

We greatly appreciate the support and encouragement of Bristol University Press and thank Emily Watt, Anna Richardson, and Inga Boardman for their efforts in bringing the book to fruition.

Finally, we want to acknowledge our gratitude to the chapter authors whose work, intellectual generosity, and collaborative spirit continue to be an inspiration.

1

Time for a Global Infrastructure Turn

Jean-Paul D. Addie, Michael R. Glass, Jen Nelles, and Lauren Marino

Introduction: take your time

We live in infrastructural times. Of course, we always have. Socio-technical systems supplying energy, water, transportation, information, and waste removal have been essential to the development of urban life in its myriad forms, and they continue to be foundational for the remaking of urban and regional worlds. Yet in the first decades of the twenty-first century, infrastructure is having a profound moment in the spotlight. For one, research on urban and regional infrastructure has continued to develop in exciting ways since Susan Leigh Star (1999: 377) implored us to 'study boring things' and unravel the inherent dramas underlying infrastructure's 'singularly unexciting ... lists of numbers and technical specifications'. Indeed, it is difficult to perceive infrastructure as boring or banal as governments around the world embrace massive investments in infrastructure in pursuit of their economic and territorial ambitions at a multitude of scales (Addie, Glass, and Nelles, 2020; Schindler and Kanai, 2021; Shatkin, 2022). At the same time, a global 'infrastructure turn' is compelling scholars in the social and policy sciences (notably in urban studies) to grapple with infrastructures' significance as 'political intermediaries' (Amin, 2014). They have responded by expanding their conceptual and methodological toolkits to interrogate the intersections of infrastructure, urbanization, and urban life in novel and generative ways (Larkin, 2013; Graham and McFarlane, 2015, Wiig et al, 2023). From political-economic critiques of mega-projects that are (re)shaping cities' global competitiveness and intensifying capitalism's crisis tendencies (Jonas et al, 2019; Wiig and Silver, 2019; Schindler and DiCarlo, 2022) to ethnographic explorations of the incremental and improvised ways that infrastructural systems are (re)produced through everyday practice (Lawhon et al, 2018; McFarlane, 2021; Ramakrishnan et al, 2021), the study of infrastructure provides a powerful lens to understand how cities and regions worldwide are being built, governed, and contested.

Contemporary infrastructure scholarship is finely attuned to the geographic imprints of such urban infrastructuring. Roads and rails, cables and containers, pipelines and ports exist in place as specific spatial products, while as networked operating systems they foster all manner of flows across an increasingly urbanized planet. A rich spatial lexicon exists to help us conceptualize infrastructures' central role in connecting, integrating, splintering, and bypassing the material and social geographies of cities, regions, countries, and even continents (Graham and Marvin, 2001; Young and Keil, 2010; Easterling, 2014). We fully embrace the attention paid to space and spatiality in the 'infrastructure turn' yet note that geographic considerations have come to eclipse questions of time and temporality that are paramount to understanding the making of urban worlds through infrastructure. As Timothy Mitchell (2020) bluntly observes, 'the standard way of writing about infrastructure is to start from the question of space and treat time as a consequence ... [even if it] obscures what is often most important in building them'. This imbalance reflects Manuel Castells's (2010: 497) arguments surrounding 'the historical revenge of space' as the rise of networked society '[structures] temporality in different, even contradictory logics according to spatial dynamics'. Yet it is also indicative of time's taken-for-granted banality *and* the sheer multiplicity of its registers, which make it 'extraordinarily difficult to think and talk about' (Adam, 1995: 5).

This volume responds by placing time in the spotlight of the global infrastructure turn, both through foregrounding questions of temporality that need to be accounted for when studying infrastructure and by confronting the complexity and diversity of the time frames and temporal codes that shape our infrastructured worlds. This pressing conceptual and applied task goes beyond simply restating the importance of studying time to understand social issues. Infrastructure systems are not brought into the world fully formed nor are they put into place all at once. They are inherently spatio-*temporal* products, constructed through intersecting times: of planning, of capital flows, of political cycles, of embodied practice, and of the material properties of their organic and inorganic assemblages. The uneven and contested nature of infrastructural space, along with the resources, mobilities, and power it confers, means that urban infrastructure is always in a state of becoming, 'designed to do something, but ... never "finished"' (Smith, 2016: 173). Infrastructures materially, financially, and discursively condition path-dependent futures, lock-ins, and crises yet also offer the potential to reimagine and realize more progressive and sustainable alternatives. They help us understand the past and express how we perceive and live the future in visionary and prosaic terms. As such, the present confluence and uneven experience of grand societal challenges – including fiscal austerity, racial inequity, geopolitical resource conflicts, networked pandemics, and existential ecological crises – demand a rigorous appraisal of why and how time should be further incorporated into the global infrastructure turn, and what possibilities exist to create more equitable infrastructure futures.

Our purpose is a critical engagement with time that can help us grapple with the 'cruelty as well as promise' of infrastructure in exacerbating, or tempering, the environments in which we live (Amin and Thrift, 2017: 6). Focusing on infrastructure's temporalities does not usurp or negate space-centric infrastructure research: time and space are essentially co-constitutive so treating them as somehow analytically separate is neither conceptually nor politically constructive (Massey, 1992). Rather, we aim to reveal how centring time enriches, extends, and challenges spatial narratives by posing questions of infrastructure in alternative registers: disrupting neat teleological narratives; probing the relationship between radical and incremental transformation; interrogating moments of spectacular development and mundane repair; exploring unexpected pathways of urban and technological development; and contextualizing infrastructures' pasts and asking what they signify about possible urban worlds to come.

Of course, issues of time and temporality have not been wholly absent from critical infrastructure studies. Our contributors' arguments occur in dialogue with innovative bodies of scholarship that are taking the problematic and potential of infrastructural time seriously. These fields include foundational work on the philosophy and sociology of time (Nowotny, 1992; Adam, 1995; Lefebvre, 2004) and time geography (Hägerstrand, 1970; Pred, 1981; Thrift, 2005), as well as ongoing scholarship in anthropology (Larkin, 2013; Anand, 2017; Anand et al, 2018), media and communications studies (Hassan, 2003; Sharma, 2014; Velkova and Platin, 2023), science and technology studies (STS) (Graham and Marvin, 2001; Virilio, 2006; Elsner et al, 2019), the history of technology (Schivelbusch, 2014; Engels, 2020; Moss, 2020), and on issues of infrastructural repair, maintenance, and incompleteness (Baptista, 2019; Coss-Corzo, 2020; Guma, 2022). By treating time as a boundary concept, this volume draws together many of these diffuse strands of temporal thinking. In doing so, it aims to overcome some of the siloed perspectives that have characterized this multifaceted literature and illuminate important interconnections between engineering, political-economic, and experiential-affective approaches to infrastructure, as well as between scientific and everyday knowledges. Our collective objective is to examine how temporal experiences, rhythms, cycles, tempos, eras, scales, horizons, and dissonances are conceived, how they can reframe the study of urban infrastructure, and what can be gained by foregrounding notions of temporality within the global infrastructure turn. Chapters in this book therefore:

1) move towards an interdisciplinary synthesis, juxtaposing insights drawn (conceptually and methodologically) from environmental studies, geography, history, law, planning, political science, STS, sociology, and urban studies;
2) broaden and deepen our thinking about infrastructure by expanding the topical, methodological, and geographic scope of research on infrastructural times; and
3) explore emerging themes by applying distinct urban-regional lenses onto infrastructure's temporalities. This informs our broader interest in creating conceptual frameworks that help understand the co-constitution of infrastructure and regions (Addie et al, 2020), although the empirical cases in this book adopt more ecumenical scalar approaches.

In sum, *Infrastructural Times* aims to present a multidimensional (although not exhaustive) perspective that advances our understanding of how time–infrastructure relations are entwined in the production, governance, and lived experience of global urban worlds.

Unpacking infrastructure's temporalities

We anchor this book in the assumption that time and temporality, as with space and spatiality, are socially produced and relational. Time cannot be understood outside of the processes and relations producing it because 'time "dwells" in us – through the biological rhythms to which we are subject, and because we are social beings who are born into a society with changing temporal structures and learn to live in its social time' (Nowotny, 1994: 6). Embracing a heterodox understanding of both time and infrastructure (as socio-technical systems, as power, and as relational) highlights how various elements of urban form and urban life engender differentiated temporalities that themselves inform, and are informed by, a diversity of human experiences. As Besedovsky et al (2019: 581) provocatively contend, we can even conceive of temporalities themselves *as* infrastructure 'that underlie and powerfully shape current forms of social organization and interaction'. What this means for our understanding of the politics of infrastructure in practice, as this volume attests, depends on how we theorize time itself. So let us consider some important ways we might think about the multifaceted manifestations of, and connections between, infrastructure and time.

Time, infrastructure, and the urban experience

Infrastructures, as material and governance technologies, fundamentally shape how we perceive and experience time. The infrastructural rhythms that arise through artefacts, signals, stimuli, and systems enmesh and punctuate the temporal and normative orderings of daily life. These temporalities have deep and often unexpected impacts, as viscerally captured, for instance, in the attempts of urban inhabitants to wrestle with the rapid material, technological, social, cultural, and political transformations ushered into being by modernity (Dennis, 2008; Rosa, 2015; Schivelbusch, 2014). The regulation and standardization of time itself was a key element of the industrial revolution, Taylorist management, and the consequent capitalist imperatives of modernization (Thompson, 1967). This era brought an expanding part of the world under the quantified, abstract conception of a singular (Western) 'clock time' that colonized both qualitative lived perceptions of time and alternative cultural understandings of temporality (Adam, 2004). The emergent primacy of capitalist clock time decoupled the world of work from bodily functions, natural rhythms, and spiritual existence while disciplining individual behaviours and social interactions. Further, in integrating transportation and communication systems, clock time condensed spatial and temporal worlds, with David Harvey's (1989: 260) classic formulation of time–space compression capturing the associated 'radical readjustment in the sense of time and space in economic, political, and cultural life'. Harvey's argument captures the tensions between *modernization* and industrial capitalism (which compelled the standardization of time) and the lived experience of *modernity* (which is marked by ephemerality and change) (see Berman, 1982). Developing communication and transportation technologies continue to restructure the time-based relationships between people and place, providing the foundations for novel, dynamic, and transient forms of 'infrastructural citizenship' (Barak, 2013; Lemanski, 2020; Maharawal, 2023).

For Robert Hassan (2003), the rise of network society has unleashed a qualitatively distinct form of fragmented 'network time' that has changed mechanisms and institutions that were previously conditioned by the abstract standard of modern clock time. The time of the network does not negate that of the clock. Instead, advances in the real-time flow of information now reconfigure how time is signified and made real through logics of 'connected asynchronicity' that colonize other realms of life and align them to postmodern imperatives of flexible accumulation (Hassan, 2007: 51). The splintering of time in network society engenders highly uneven potentialities, enabling 'selected functions and individuals [to] transcend time, while downgraded activities and subordinate people endure life as time goes by' (Castells, 2010: 497). As infrastructural systems are experienced differently by different constituencies, the networked city emerges as one of 'new assemblages of rhythmic practices, new spatio-temporal arrangement and disconnections demanding new forms of urban citizenship, use and, indeed, critical engagement' (Smith and Hetherington, 2013: 9; see also Kitchin, 2019).

Infrastructures as temporal fixes

Investments in infrastructure are a classic example of Harvey's (2007) 'spatial fix' as they both absorb surplus value and facilitate the acceleration of commodities and capital through space. Spatial fixes, though, are always intrinsically temporal, just as financial and fictitious capital are inherently spatialized (Jessop, 2006). Not only do investments in infrastructural fixes need to be viewed in the medium to long term but the vast quantities of capital required by major public works means the production of infrastructure space 'depends heavily on financial instruments and institutions that permit large-scale borrowing and long-term amortization' (Sayre, 2010: 102). As the credit system works to translate the present into long-term future returns, financiers are 'literally graphing the face of the Earth as they translate liquidity into enduring fixed assets essential to our shared future' (Castree and Christophers, 2015: 379). Infrastructural fixes, though, only temporarily offset contradictions in capital's primary circuit, with crisis tendencies of the present set to be amplified down the line given claims made of future profits. The increasing complexity of infrastructure finance may elongate infrastructure timetables. However, the results tend to enable investors to extract quick profits while shifting the financial burden onto taxpayers who may never see any true benefit from such projects, financial or otherwise (Grafe and Hilbrandt, 2019). Spatio-temporal fixes thus exacerbate existing structural inequalities, environmental racism, and unsustainable energy regimes while revealing new insuperable ruptures in late capitalism (Bond, 2019; Silver, 2021; Ponder and Omstedt, 2022).

Temporal imaginaries

Infrastructures exceed their base materiality, functionality, and economic logics. Building from the work of Sara Sharma (2011), we can distinguish between the 'tempo' of capitalist urbanization (the speed of circulation, the expediency of returns on investment, the productivity of urban economies, and the pace of infrastructural fixes) and 'the temporal' (as a form of social power, a relation of difference, and a material struggle that emerges through the practice of urbanism as a way of life). Urban infrastructures perform a vital function in mediating the former abstract yet essential temporal modalities and the latter relations which tangibly shape concrete practices, spatio-temporal perceptions, and lived urban experiences.

In this context, public sentiment surrounding infrastructure projects coalesces around, and is animated by, collective temporal social imaginaries: image-based forms of representation that enable communities to conceive of themselves and their place in the world (Enright, 2022). In 'perform[ing] the future in the present' (Davoudi, 2018: 103), infrastructural imaginaries not only make common practices surrounding the planning, development, and use of infrastructure possible; they also define and enact a claim on the city and its future (Picon, 2018). For example, distinct questions about the tempo and temporality of 'lagging' regions persist in arguments over regional economic development, with political and policy declarations on 'left behind' places that hinge upon infrastructural fixes to surmount structural deficiencies in regions *whose time has passed* (Rodríguez-Pose, 2018). Infrastructural imaginaries, though, are not monolithic, fixed, or immutable. While the road to the infrastructure-enabled future may promise progress, images of failed futures, of paths not taken, and of lingering incompleteness often negate the infrastructural possibilities of the now (Albalate and Bel, 2012; Nielsen and Pedersen, 2015; Carse and Kneas, 2019).

Times of maintenance and repair

While the material and aspirational scope of large-scale infrastructural projects draws much attention, critical infrastructure scholars are also now emphasizing important ecologies of maintenance and repair (Graham and Thrift, 2007; Denis and Pontille, 2015; Ramakrishnan et al, 2021). Shannon Mattern (2018) calls for more consideration of maintenance as a theoretical framework and political cause that straddles scholarship and practice. Engagement with and perceptions of 'defective' or antiquated infrastructures tell us much about the social and political relations of place at the same time as illegal or informal service provision fills in the gaps of absent or unreliable urban systems (Simone, 2004). Logics of repair present a profound reimagining of the temporalities of urban infrastructure and everyday life. These logics stress the immediate restoration of function in the present over longer-term improvement and radical transformation. Yet acts of care and maintenance provide a sense of both endurance *and* aspiration (Bhan, 2019). Embracing repair as an ongoing form of spatio-temporal infrastructural fix highlights the continual application of labour that underpins the 'liveliness' of infrastructure (Amin, 2014) and validates the essential but subtle forms of reparative praxis needed to reproduce both the city and urban life.

Moving infrastructure time forward: an overview of the book

The following chapters develop, expand, and challenge many of these temporal themes as our contributors unpack infrastructural times in their own ways across a variety of geographic and sectoral contexts. The cases they explore illuminate both the multiplicity of infrastructure's temporalities and the diverse strategies we can deploy to analyse 'infrastructure time' as a research problematic, an empirical concern, and a methodological approach. Through their distinct temporal framings, each chapter offers a range of perspectives that address the key questions motivating this volume: is there anything analytically distinct about urban or regional infrastructural times? What are the relationships between time and the production, governance, and experience of urban infrastructure? How do political and technological factors contribute to the evolution of varied infrastructure times? Who can see over what temporal frames? How does the present context help us presage future infrastructure conditions? What lessons can we draw from infrastructural disruptions and their implications for urban and regional decision-making? And what are their social consequences?

The resulting interdisciplinary dialogue allows us to interrogate urban infrastructures as differentiated 'timescapes', created and lived through complex 'clusters of temporal features' including time frames (scaled from seconds to lifetimes and epochs); temporalities (time as process); tempos; timings; time points, patterns, sequences, and extensions; and times past, present, and future (Adam, 2004: 143). As urban society assembles governed, rational, and quantified temporalities alongside intertwined subjective, affective, and irrational experiences of time, 'infrastructure time' comes into focus both as a common element of our urban experience and as a necessarily situated phenomenon that is lived differently by diverse groups, often in partial, fragmented, and conflicting ways. Indeed, different stakeholders perceive urban infrastructures differently because of their relative temporal vantage points. As we shall see, infrastructural lives are constructed and performed in ways that may be differentially splintered in and out of place and time relative to hegemonic or normative ideals (see Hall, 2010; Graham and McFarlane, 2015; Lubitow et al, 2017).

To contextualize the chapters' temporal contributions and their implications, we have organized this book around three key themes: (1) infrastructural pasts, presents, and futures; (2) development times and the making of urban worlds; and (3) times of disruption/disrupting times.

These themes emerge in Chapter 2, where Jean-Paul Addie draws upon Henri Lefebvre's notion of rhythmanalysis to assess how infrastructure sets the pace of urban life. Whereas urbanists frequently use Lefebvre to consider the active production of space, Addie notes the renewed attention being paid to his treatment of space-*time*. Lefebvre's formulation of 'rhythm' was originally deployed to characterize the temporal cadence of capitalism and everyday life, bringing to bear the 'relation of a time to a space, a localized time, or, if one prefers a temporalized space' (2004: 96). While amounting to a formative sketch rather than a complete conceptual framework, Lefebvre's work on rhythmanalysis generatively established that society lives via rhythms, that these rhythms are unconfined by a singular scalar perspective, and that researchers can learn from the aggregated consonant and dissonant rhythms that produce urban life. Addie teases out the implications of a rhythmanalysis framework for infrastructure studies through ideas of repetition, cycle, and period and makes the case for the power and utility of incorporating these temporalities into our understanding of infrastructure time. The chapter concludes by noting the progressive politics of refusal and agency that are part of an infrastructural rhythmanalysis, an intersectional framework that reveals the possibility for defiance and alternative temporalities to linger in the face of infrastructural order, structure, and violence.

Infrastructural pasts, presents, and futures

How might we put infrastructure's temporalities to work to understand the making of urban worlds? And how do infrastructures themselves reshape the spatio-temporal relations of the city and urban life? The chapters in Part I probe how urban infrastructures not only bridge the temporal registers of past, present, and future, but also powerfully reconfigure relations between them. In Chapter 3, Timothy Moss reflects on a century of urban transformation in Berlin, reading its socio-technical systems as 'historicized assemblages' to trace how infrastructural pasts can be made usable for diverse stakeholders attempting to address contemporary and future challenges in the present. Usable infrastructural pasts might lock in normative development trajectories that structure our thinking about possible urban transformation. Yet we can also find them in other forms of provision, operationalized through informal small-scale systems that coexist with, but escape capture by, hegemonic ideas and technologies. Dismissed, devalued, and discarded pasts, Moss asserts, also open alternative approaches in the present and can therefore reorient potential urban futures.

In unpacking usable infrastructure pasts, Moss warns that ideas of continual technological progress can too easily be imported to indicate historical linearity. He highlights the dangers of historical selectiveness when thinking about the past's connections to present-day challenges. As Berlin's infrastructure systems illustrate, actually existing infrastructural pasts are contextual and are usually characterized by unrequited promises, collective amnesia, and points of departure that built upon new technologies in unanticipated ways. Here, what is particularly valuable in Moss's contribution is the emphasis placed on *mobilizing* usable pasts. Understanding the imprints of time and technology upon the built environment necessitates a reflexive approach to historicizing socio-technical systems. Moss animates a vital resource for those looking to rethink the present and establish new infrastructural configurations in productive ways. The past is not a pre-existing external condition but a multifaceted and actively produced social product: something not just to think about, but to think *with*.

Olivier Coutard in Chapter 4 is also concerned about how infrastructures mediate relations between past, present, and future. His chapter begins by bringing three temporal registers into dialogue: the evolutionary life cycles of infrastructure; the experiential dimensions of infrastructure time; and the relations between past, present, and future that shift as infrastructures *materialize* social temporalities via processes of 'infrastructure-based futuring'. This heuristic captures the multidimensional nature of infrastructure time (as perceived, conceived, and lived) and the dialectical tensions within which these temporal registers are ambivalently suspended. Coutard articulates how this temporal ambivalence captures fundamental tensions between two modern 'regimes of historicity': a contemporary *presentism* through which short-termism comes to dominate social time and a modern *futurism* that continues to restate the promise of infrastructure to deliver political, economic, or environmental objectives.

The maturation of the Anthropocene disrupts the logics of both modern temporal regimes. The realities of an existential climate crisis challenge how we envision infrastructural presents and futures – and possible ways to transition between the two. Coutard argues our current infrastructural compact prioritizes forms of adaptation to environmental change rather than radical transformation. The time frames under consideration may vary, but temporality is primarily understood as linear, with the vested interests of 'the present' constraining necessarily radical socio-technical shifts. Yet the ruptures and inequities arising within the Anthropocene also create possibilities for pluralizing time and thus open alternative futures and potentialities for infrastructural change. Here, Coutard provides instructive methodological guidance for researchers interested in operationalizing the study of infrastructure-based futuring, notably advocating for the exploration of experimental *elsewhens* beyond the networked city.

The ability to create and impose hegemonic temporal regimes is a form of power that facilitates the 'control' of the present and the future in direct and indirect ways (Milojević, 2008). Time is a remarkably effective colonizing tool, both through the imposition of particular kinds of time and their associated values and norms (colonization *with* time) and in the social incursion of particular activities and logics *into* time (colonization *of* time) (Adam, 2004: 136–43). But time, as AbdouMaliq Simone argues in Chapter 5, 'is always *extensive*, always outpacing whatever forms that might measure or apportion it'. Simone dwells in the heterodox and incomplete temporalities of the 'perpetual present' in Jayapura, West Papua, to examine 'extensions' as a form of urban infrastructure. Building upon his relational understanding of social infrastructure, Simone points to acts of extension as a complex means by which rule and resistance concretize in built and social environments. Extensions are infrastructural insofar as they open possibilities for encounters, projects, and ultimately ways of life to take place: they accompany and enable a multiplicity of social practices (Simone, 2022: 11). Simone and Coutard therefore both share an interest in how urban infrastructures materialize social and temporal orders (hegemonic and counter-hegemonic) and establish trajectories of change. Each author illustrates how urban infrastructures have their own pace and dynamics that can delineate the parameters of particular practices, experiences, and forms of development. However, because infrastructures are social products, they can be influenced to open alternative ways of *doing* infrastructure time.

Simone encounters Jayapura as a multiplicity unfurling over unruly space and time. Indigenous communities resist capture both by the temporal discipline of the colonial state and from the (modern) future as a teleological yardstick against which liberation is measured. The chapter's account of 'Papuan time' exposes tensions between contracting and protracting temporalities: between modern development narratives portraying indigenous Papuans as 'frozen in time', the lived experience of time as 'broken' with the loss of national self-determination, and the extension of differential infrastructures that attempt to reclaim time amid the uncertainty of an 'interminable present'. Grand infrastructural visions, geopolitical relations, and the prospects of Chinese-led infrastructure development loom in the background (see Schindler and Kanai, this volume). However, these infrastructural futures offer limited prospects for Jayapura's inhabitants to escape a city 'where urban formations seem to have neither discernible past nor future'. Instead, using 'blackness' as an analytical tool, Simone proposes that alternative infrastructural extensions can be developed to reposition Jayapura within an archipelago of cosmopolitan urbanism that refuses capture by the colonial state and the temporal logics of modernity.

The chapters in Part I illustrate how infrastructures produce, and are produced through, multifaceted pasts, presents, and futures. These temporal frames are neither discrete nor immutable and the authors each offer novel analytical and methodological approaches to analyse how the modalities of infrastructure time are constructed, performed, and contested. The past, for example, is mobilized in different registers, offering instrumental lessons for the present or influencing it in unexpected ways via the persistent afterlives of infrastructure. Infrastructural futures, in turn, are ambivalent, even contradictory: locked in but waiting to be unlocked.

The promise of infrastructure unfurls in progressive future-oriented terms (Hetherington, 2014) but our experiential interactions with infrastructures remain bound to the present (Dodgshon, 2008). The present, though, is not simply set by immediate conditions 'in the moment'. It exists as a heterodox uncertainty, from the digital 'perpetual present' of networked society (Coleman, 2020) to the incessant newness of urban inhabitants denied both a past and future trajectories of attainment. We return to these themes in relation to life in the shadows of infrastructure (DiCarlo, this volume) and in the 'forever suburbs' (Biglieri and Keil, this volume). What is clear is that interactions between multiple material infrastructures, their temporal logics, and the ideologies and social practices that they internalize disallows any singular temporality to posit its own course in isolation or in a neatly uniform direction. These chapters reveal how urban worlds are made through a collective experience of simultaneity across multiple temporal registers, whether they be conditioned by linear narratives of modernity and progress or disrupted by non-teleological postcolonial understandings of time.

Development times and the making of urban worlds

The chapters in Part II extend these temporal debates in the context of infrastructure-led development. A common problem with infrastructural systems is that historic infrastructures bring with them financial and functional legacies that are incongruent with current conditions or future visions. The staggeringly long gestation periods for infrastructure projects in most places results from complex and competing 'development times' underpinning their production, an issue which raises obvious questions about the factors (institutional or otherwise) that extend struggles over planning and construction and delay implementation. Project timelines disclose how the temporal horizons of planners, contractors, builders, politicians, users, and opponents assemble, clash, and splinter in the procedural times of environmental and impacts assessments, the developmental winds blown by political cycles, and the time frames set by bonds and other forms of fictitious capital (see Abram, 2014; Arícan, 2020). The two contradicting forces at work here are the promise of space-time contraction via infrastructural modernization, and the problem of time dilation that policy and practice try to solve via new infrastructural fixes.

In Chapter 6, Peter Ekman examines the temporalities of modernist urban planning and the global circulation of socio-technical knowledge as revealed in the intersecting development of Ciudad Guayana, Venezuela, and the Harvard–MIT Joint Center for Urban Studies during the 1960s. The chapter details the modernist imperatives driving the material assemblage of infrastructures – focusing on the 15-mile Avenida Guayana highway – and the temporal rationales that were intended to sequence and stage physical movement through the city. Avenida Guayana represented the ideal of the modern city not as space but as movement: a speed that would reinforce a particular developmental politics of time. Infrastructure constructed the urban as a space of flows, both in the movement of material objects and in the circulation of planning ideas through space and time.

Ekman further shows that infrastructural knowledge, knowledge infrastructures, and the temporality of planning itself have their own situated histories. Expressions of the ostensibly universal 'modern infrastructural ideal' (Graham and Marvin, 2001) cannot be separated from 'the design and execution of specific infrastructural projects: arrangements of material objects, in particular places, positioned so as to impart form, motion and rhythm to everyday life'. The Harvard–MIT Joint Center and Ciudad Guayana were connected by a temporal flow – a history – of ideas, first moving from the former to the latter, and then returning as Ciudad Guayana became an object of analysis and an origin point of critique for planning scholars. The case of Ciudad Guayana therefore offers both a 'usable infrastructural past' (Moss, this volume) and an account (and repudiation) of the modern futurist 'regime of historicity' (Coutard, this volume). By highlighting modern planners' ambivalence to local perceptions and experiences of urban space-time, Ekman also directs us to the lived times of those caught between liberation and subjugation under a different regime of coloniality (Simone, this volume). With this, he ultimately poses the question of who should be able to (or even can) plan the city's future?

In Chapter 7, Seth Schindler and J. Miguel Kanai grapple with infrastructural futures by dissecting how infrastructure is imagined, financed, and produced within an era of infrastructure-led development. Building from Gabor's (2021) argument that the Washington Consensus has been replaced by a new neoliberal regime – the Wall Street Consensus – they trace out the temporal logics of an emergent 'infrastructure fundamentalism'. This captures the present dogma that 'infrastructural connectivity is the single missing ingredient that inhibited growth in earlier rounds of neoliberal restructuring'. To generate the magnitude of capital needed to address states' (real or perceived) infrastructure gaps, infrastructural imaginaries in an age of infrastructure-led development are both monumentally scaled and ambitiously visioned across extended long-term time horizons. Schindler and Kanai (2021) previously cast infrastructure-led development in primarily spatial terms. Here, they demonstrate that it poses questions not only about 'getting the territory right', but also about how to negotiate the temporal horizons of infrastructural imaginaries, the time frames of financial capital, and the management of risk.

Risk is an inherently temporal concept. Whether considered in economic, political, or ecological terms, risk is about mitigating future issues as perceived (and priced) from the present, based on experiences of the past. Schindler and Kanai read infrastructure fundamentalism as driving infrastructure development in ways that attempt to de-risk investment and 'future-proof' profits. Their chapter speaks to the (mis)alignment between long project cycles and grand ambitions and the shorter-term demands of capital that finances them. The temporalities of infrastructure fundamentalism condition infrastructure development to function both as a necessary spatial fix to drive future growth and as an end in themselves as a mode of financialization. Schindler and Kanai conclude by noting the pernicious violence and disconcerting ramifications of the 'slow operations' involved in redesigning transcontinental territories, notably pointing to the absence of *urban* imaginaries even as such large-scale development initiatives profoundly remake urban worlds.

Proponents of infrastructure-led development still see the creation of state-backed infrastructural futures as a legitimate way to respond to disciplinary discourses of infrastructure deficiency. Dalia Wahdan and Tamer Elshayal's case study of the land–infrastructure–finance nexus in Egypt in Chapter 8, however, demonstrates that increasing projects' time horizons and establishing infrastructure as a new asset class are not guaranteed mechanisms to reduce risk or create equitable futures. Rather than neatly de-risking investment, they argue that extending the spatial and temporal horizons of infrastructure development intensifies risk by introducing or increasing uncertainty, making modelling more difficult, or, in attempting to address the proceeding issues, reducing planning documents to vague goals with little by way of substance to support them. Experiences on the frontier of the global infrastructure scramble invoke what Wahdan and Elshayal term a myriad of 'dissonant times'. Their assessment of the Cairo Monorail shows that structural interventions, institutional restructuring, and new revenue streams manifest at different speeds and over differing time frames, with profound implications for the velocity of urban reconfiguration. There is a clear irony in the Egyptian government's adoption of longer-term infrastructural imaginaries to increase the attractiveness of investment while looking to appease shorter-term demands for returns on such investment by disrupting and displacing Cairo residents. Under President Abdel Fattah al-Sisi, Egypt has emerged as an emboldened infrastructure state 'doing what previous regimes dared not' by engaging in widespread neighbourhood demolition, accelerating construction of private real estate developments on evicted plots, and dispossessing citizens for fear of scaring away global investors.

Through examining the making of global urban worlds, the chapters in Part II illustrate how infrastructure's development times unfold unevenly as they are subject to the pushes and pulls of competing temporal incentives. Constituents' demands for a better future in the short term are often surpassed by incremental and radical approaches to change (structured through cycles of power and decision-making) that tend to be adopted by politicians, planners, and others looking to reorient that future, whether through building new cities or looking to engage in infrastructure-based profiteering. These tensions stem from the misalignment between (and erasures of) the lived time of urban inhabitation and the colonizing force of 'project time'. Questions remain regarding how to expand and account for public participation in urban and regional planning decision-making, and how to address community apathy and the constraints on individuals' time that arise in the face of more abstract – yet still vital and lived – infrastructural imaginaries.

The constraints imposed beyond institutions, including technological capabilities and environmental conditions, are also important. There are physical limits to how fast you can dig a tunnel or reclaim desert land for urban settlement and to how tolerant projects are, once initiated, to delays. Bridges, for one, are not designed to be suspended mid-span indefinitely. Delays open opportunities for the spaces needed for infrastructure development to be occupied by competing or incompatible uses as securing and controlling easements, rights of way, or staging lands is itself a lengthy process. In these ways, infrastructure's development times create, and must respond to, physical constraints as time narrows the aperture of possibility for projects as their development paths crystallize. Even then, the extended time frames of our infrastructural imaginaries, and the linear progress of infrastructural 'project time', often fail to align with the pressing needs of urban communities (Koster, 2020). We pick up this theme in Part III.

Times of disruption/disrupting times

By probing how time can be eliminated, disrupted, suspended, accelerated and slowed, and tactically mobilized, the chapters in Part III disrupt notions of time as self-evident, linear, and universal. The form, quality, use, and regulation of infrastructure are not homogeneous across time. Rather, they vary across multiple time frames: household heating and cooling needs vary seasonally; transit systems operate differing schedules on weekdays and weekends; adequate street lighting becomes a concern after dark. These chapters therefore help us grapple with how highly varied infrastructural lives and everyday practices structure, and are structured by, uneven urban landscapes and a plurality of temporal registers.

In Chapter 9, Simon Marvin and Jonathan Rutherford analyse the temporalities of self-healing systems and the capacity of smart microgrids to remove temporal disruptions for critical infrastructures. Building from debates across engineering, STS, and urban studies, their chapter examines the interface of military and urban infrastructures to weave together two major temporal narratives. The first traces the development and circulation of 'self-healing' technologies, imaginaries, and temporal logics from a narrowly averted Israeli military aviation disaster through to the roll-out of urban 'smart microgrid' systems. The other unpacks the temporal capacities of smart grid technologies to respond to increasing security threats and societal vulnerability. Critical assets in military and urban settings require a continuous supply of power to ensure they function during moments of crisis. Ensuring fail-safe power requires multiple temporal adaptations covering immediate transitions, ongoing maintenance, and 'perpetual alert' in the present. The essential functioning of smart microgrids is premised upon the reconfiguration of networked infrastructure around a timescale of microseconds. Such temporal compression not only facilitates near-seamless switching between normal and emergency states but, in detaching instantaneous computational decision-making from human control, also raises questions about how we perceive and govern 'network time' in 'real time' (Kitchin, 2017).

The temporalities of smart microgrids necessitate the socio-technical and political recalibration of infrastructure time. As they splinter from centralized grids, decisions must be made regarding which systems are deemed 'critical assets' and which communities are prioritized during moments of disruption. This highlights new modalities of 'asynchronous resilience', with emerging hierarchies revealing who and what must transcend time through the elimination of temporal interruptions and who and what is left with time to kill during a power outage. The uneven future-proofing of the grid engenders what Tonkiss (2015) terms new 'moral economies of infrastructure' that are played out through the renegotiation of socio-technical configurations in space and time. Marvin and Rutherford suggest such negotiations are fraught because they involve fragmented systems of power generation and a multitude of authorities, agencies, and companies, and they occur through the protracted timelines of procurement, environmental assessments, and regulatory process. Their chapter thus attunes us to wider issues of temporality that connect the need to address future turbulence with infrastructure's role in mediating the development of, and claims to, public space.

In Chapter 10, Jessica DiCarlo explores the experience of living in the shadows of a large-scale infrastructural project. Drawing on an ethnography of people whose lives are disrupted by the construction of the Laos–China Railway, she shows how the material interruptions and abstract imaginaries of infrastructure development remake the social and spatial fabric of everyday life. Her account exposes the disjuncture between the temporalities of 'project time' and the modalities of suspension and stasis that condition the lived realities of this promise. Asynchronicities emerging between the multispeed realities of daily life and urban development at 'China speed' reveal infrastructure time as constructed through dialectics of movement and waiting, progress and stasis, freedom and constraint (see Shin et al, 2020; Moser, 2021).

DiCarlo draws our focus to the everyday experiences of infrastructural lives practised as the complexities and long-term durations of development projects are intermeshed with the rhythms of the day-to-day. Her chapter unpacks multidimensional encounters with waiting to challenge our thinking about the agency of those temporally extracted by and from infrastructure-led development. Waiting does not necessarily connote time wasted (to be filled by productivity) or a passive acceptance of temporal disruption. Waiting is a practice and an experience that is highly affective, incorporating feelings of powerlessness, loss, and annoyance, but also of hope. At once, such thinking speaks to the potential of waiting to be leveraged as a political or emancipatory act (Bissell, 2007). Yet for Laotians existing under the material and imagined presence of the railroad, such hope is more often lived as a form of 'cruel optimism' (Berlant, 2011). Echoing Simone's observations of Jayapura (this volume), it is marginalized ethnic and class groups in Laos who must wait – for compensation, for the ability to farm, for construction to end, and for liberation from an anticipatory future that they are not part of.

Samantha Biglieri and Roger Keil address themes of exclusion and marginalization in Chapter 11 by examining the temporalities of urban disease and public health infrastructures. They present two cases that expose the inequities of time in Toronto's 'sick suburbs': public health responses during COVID-19 and the timescapes of people living with dementia. Biglieri and Keil's analysis engages time both as an infrastructure 'in itself' (that enables certain ways of life and is available to some but not others) and as an analytic that helps us understand how infrastructures materialize structural forms of inequity. They mobilize two key temporal frames to this end. The first draws on Easterling (2014) to illustrate how the temporal 'disposition' of infrastructural space conditions its circuits and operating systems, which tend to crash, become corrupted, or never actually work for those not meeting classed, raced, and ableist norms. The second stresses the experience of 'desynchronization' to capture the sense of being out of sync in general (relative to normative processes and imaginaries) and at specific points of crisis (such as during a global pandemic), both of which profoundly destabilize lived infrastructure time.

Biglieri and Keil's cases not only challenge us to rethink the relationship between time and infrastructure through the temporal politics surrounding who can remove themselves from the rhythms of urban life. They also problematize assumptions about North American suburbia's perceived timelessness and obstinacy as an atomized habitus of automobility, whiteness, and heteronormativity. In critiquing the notion of the 'forever suburb' their chapter shows how infrastructural pasts can influence the present and future in often unforeseen ways. Memory and familiarity, for example, are produced through time, creating persistent emotional and experiential links to place that may be profoundly destabilized by disruptions (intentional or otherwise) to the spatial and temporal ordering of the urban fabric. Importantly, while Biglieri and Keil disclose how infrastructural space-times can rapidly and differentially accelerate and decelerate, expand and shrink for those waiting for vaccination or living with a degenerative disease, they also reveal how 'quotidian agency' can foster innovation in sites of infrastructural disadvantage, provoking us to think differently about illness, dis/ability, and how to manifest more inclusive infrastructure futures.

In Chapter 12, Amelia Thorpe critically assesses the 'speed politics' of street infrastructure (see Hubbard and Lilley, 2004; Virilio, 2006). Temporal orders are secured, legitimized, regulated, and policed in ways that reinforce structural social (dis)advantage but, as Thorpe illustrates, they can also be contested and remade. Her chapter, contextualized by the circulations of infrastructure policy, takes us to San Francisco to examine how transport activists disrupt infrastructure time in the auto-centric city to bring about alternative temporalities and mobilities. Time is of the essence here as the divergent time frames of regulatory procedures, policy implementation, and practices on the street can infringe upon the pace and prospects of urban transformation.

Thorpe asserts that 'the temporalities of street infrastructure are not inevitable, but are instead the result of choices which could be changed – and that change can be fast'. She explores how 'impossible publics' (Harvey and Knox, 2016) – those with the ability (or privilege) to refuse to play the waiting game as defined by the state and other elite actors – attempt to make 'impossible' practices possible. Her analysis focuses on the capacity of two distinct temporal tactics to disrupt the hegemonic flows of the auto-centric city. The first examines unsanctioned do-it-yourself (DIY) interventions that circumvent protracted planning times by materially reshaping street infrastructure to improve safety and amenity for people walking and cycling. DIY infrastructure can accelerate urban transport transitions by 'prefiguring' (potential) permanent installations by the state. In contrast, the second tactic, that of 'heckling', conspicuously disrupts the rhythms of automobility. Activists loudly and visibly slow the pace of the city to 'highlight and challenge the degree to which speed in cars is paid for by slowness outside them'. Thorpe's analysis resonates with scholarship arguing that in the face of repressive social regimes, the ability to exercise a degree of control over infrastructural temporality is fundamentally a political act, whether it be through disruptive cycling events (Sheller, 2018) or blockading critical infrastructure (Crosby and Monaghan, 2016). Struggles to exert power over urban temporalities position infrastructures as both the setting and the stake for social movements remaking urban worlds on the street.

Juxtaposed to shared dreams of frictionless societies, disruptions to the steady flows of infrastructure – via interruption, waiting, impairment, or delay – illuminate jarring instances where infrastructural technologies suspend populations outside the regular rhythms of the city. Sometimes these disruptions capture moments when infrastructure fails and people are thrown out of sync with the expected flows of modernity. At other times, such disruptions are intentional instances of infrastructural violence. The chapters in Part III, however, also illustrate that resisting, opposing, reclaiming, and simply *living* other urban temporalities present opportunities to defy and reimagine the speeds, trajectories, and dispositions of hegemonic infrastructural configurations. The key lesson is that recognizing both the heterogeneous nature of diverse space-times and the capacities of people to usurp dominant temporal orders is vital if we are to imagine and realize alternative, more progressive urban worlds, even if only for a while.

Your time starts now

A complex array of connections exists between infrastructure and the temporalities and time horizons of the city. As this book reveals, we face conceptual, technological, and political challenges regarding what to do with temporal (mis)alignments within and between heterogeneous infrastructure configurations. Bringing time into balance with space within the contemporary global infrastructure turn is an important and necessary step to address the manifold social, political, economic, and environmental challenges confronting urban society. Noting that any conceptual and applied intervention has the capacity to invoke forms of 'temporal othering' that can problematically reproduce racial, patriarchal, or colonial hierarchies (Zeiderman, 2019), our collective efforts here emphasize the value of validating the fluidity and multifaceted nature of time–infrastructure relations. We return to these themes in the book's concluding chapter. For now, we suggest that engaging the interdependencies of such differential infrastructural times – developing 'a sense of being tied together in time' (Sharma, 2013: 314) – can help foster a critical and collective politics to move us towards more cohesive and inclusive urban and regional futures.

References

Abram, S. (2014) 'The time it takes: Temporalities of planning', *Journal of the Royal Anthropological Institute*, 20(S1): 129–47.

Adam, B. (1995) *Timewatch: The Social Analysis of Time*, Cambridge: Polity Press.

Adam, B. (2004) *Time*, Cambridge: Polity Press.

Addie, J.-P.D., Glass, M.R., and Nelles, J. (2020 'Regionalizing the infrastructure turn: A research agenda', *Regional Studies, Regional Science*, 7(1): 10–26.

Albalate, D., and Bel, G. (2012) *The Economics and Politics of High-Speed Rail*, Lanham, MD: Lexington Books.

Amin, A. (2014) 'Lively infrastructure', *Theory, Culture & Society*, 31(7–8): 137–61.

Amin, A., and Thrift, N. (2017) *Seeing Like a City*, Cambridge: Polity Press.

Anand, N. (2017) *Hydraulic City: Water and the Infrastructures of Citizenship in Mumbai*, Durham, NC: Duke University Press.

Anand, N., Gupta, A., and Appel, H. (eds) (2018) *The Promise of Infrastructure*, Durham, NC: Duke University Press.

Arícan, A. (2020) 'Behind the scaffolding: Manipulations of time, delays, and power in Tarlabaşı, Istanbul', *City & Society*, 32(3): 482–507.

Baptista, I. (2019) 'Electricity services always in the making: Informality and the work of infrastructural maintenance and repair in an African city', *Urban Studies*, 56(3): 510–23.

Barak, O. (2013) *On Time: Technology and Temporality in Modern Egypt*, Berkeley, CA: University of California Press.

Berlant, L. (2011) *Cruel Optimism*, Durham, NC: Duke University Press.

Berman, M. (1982) *All That Is Solid Melts into Air: The Experience of Modernity*, New York: Simon & Schuster.

Besedovsky, N., Grafe, F.-J., Hilbrandt, H., and Langguth, H. (2019) 'Time as infrastructure: For an analysis of contemporary urbanization', *City*, 23(4–5): 580–8.

Bhan, G. (2019) 'Notes on a Southern urban practice', *Environment and Urbanization*, 31(2): 639–54.

Bissell, D. (2007) 'Animating suspension: Waiting for mobilities', *Mobilities*, 2(2): 277–98.

Bond, P. (2019) 'Contradictory time horizons of Durban energy piping in an era of looming climate chaos', *City*, 23(4–5): 631–45.

Carse, A., and Kneas, D. (2019) 'Unbuilt and unfinished: The temporalities of infrastructure', *Environment and Society*, 10(1): 9–28.

Castells, M. (2010) *The Rise of the Network Society* (2nd edn), Malden, MA: Blackwell.

Castree, N., and Christophers, B. (2015) 'Banking spatially on the future: Capital switching, infrastructure, and the ecological fix', *Annals of the Association of American Geographers*, 105(2): 378–86.

Coleman, R. (2020) 'Making, managing and experiencing "the now": Digital media and the compression and pacing of "real time"', *New Media & Society*, 22(9): 1680–98.

Coss-Corzo, D. (2020) 'Patchwork: Repair labor and the logics of infrastructure adaptation in Mexico City', *Environment and Planning D: Society and Space*, 39(2): 237–53.

Crosby, A., and Monaghan, J. (2016) 'Settler colonialism and the policing of Idle No More', *Social Justice*, 43(2): 37–57.

Davoudi, S. (2018) 'Imagination and spatial imaginaries: A conceptual framework', *Town Planning Review*, 89(2): 97–107.

Denis, J., and Pontille, D. (2015) 'Material ordering and the care of things', *Science, Technology, and Human Values*, 40(3): 338–67.

Dennis, R. (2008) *Cities in Modernity: Representations and Productions of Metropolitan Space, 1840–1930*, Cambridge: Cambridge University Press.

Dodgshon, R.A. (2008) 'Geography's place in time', *Geografiska Annaler B: Human Geography*, 90(1): 1–15.

Easterling, K. (2014) *Extrastatecraft: The Power of Infrastructure Space*, London: Verso.

Elsner, I., Monstadt, J., and Raven, R. (2019) 'Decarbonizing Rotterdam? Energy transitions and the alignment of urban and infrastructural temporalities', *City*, 23(4–5): 646–57.

Engels, J.I. (2020) 'Technical infrastructures as products and producers of time', *International Journal of History and Ethics of Natural Sciences, Technology and Medicine*, 28(1): 69–90.

Enright, T. (2022) 'The infrastructural imagination', *Journal of Urban Technology*, 29(1): 101–7.

Gabor, D. (2021) 'The Wall Street Consensus', *Development and Change*, 52(3): 429–59.

Grafe, F.-J., and Hilbrandt, H. (2019) 'The temporalities of financialization: Infrastructures, dominations, and openings in the Thames Tideway Tunnel', *City*, 23(4–5): 606–18.

Graham, S., and Marvin, S. (2001) *Splintering Urbanism: Networked Infrastructures, Technological Mobilities and the Urban Condition*, Abingdon: Routledge.

Graham, S., and McFarlane, C. (eds) (2015) *Infrastructural Lives: Urban Infrastructure in Context*, Abingdon: Routledge.

Graham, S., and Thrift, N. (2007) 'Out of order: Understanding repair and maintenance', *Theory, Culture & Society*, 24(3): 1–25.

Guma, P.K. (2022) 'The temporal incompleteness of infrastructure and the urban', *Journal of Urban Technology*, 29(1): 59–67.

Hägerstrand, T. (1970) 'What about people in regional science?', *Papers of the Regional Science Association*, 24: 6–21.

Hall, T. (2010) 'Urban outreach in the polyrhythmic city', in T. Edensor (ed) *Geographies of Rhythm: Nature, Place, Mobilities and Bodies*, Burlington: Ashgate, pp 59–70.

Harvey, D. (1989) *The Condition of Postmodernity*, Oxford: Blackwell.

Harvey, D. (2007) *The Limits to Capital* (2nd edn), London: Verso.

Harvey, P., and Knox, H. (2016) *Roads: An Anthropology of Infrastructure and Expertise*, Ithaca, NY: Cornell University Press.

Hassan, R. (2003) 'Network time and the new knowledge economy', *Time & Society*, 12(2–3): 235–41.

Hassan, R. (2007) 'Network time', in R. Hassan and R.E. Purser (eds) *24/7: Time and Temporality in the Network Society*, Stanford, CA: Stanford University Press, pp 37–61.

Hetherington, K. (2014) 'Waiting for the surveyor: Development promises and the temporality of infrastructure', *Journal of Latin American and Caribbean Anthropology*, 19(2): 195–211.

Hubbard, P., and Lilley, K. (2004) 'Pacemaking the modern city: The urban politics of speed and slowness', *Environment and Planning D: Society and Space*, 22(2): 273–94.

Jessop, B. (2006) 'Spatial fixes, temporal fixes and spatio-temporal fixes', in N. Castree and D. Gregory (eds) *David Harvey: A Critical Reader*, Malden, MA: Blackwell, pp 142–66.

Jonas, A.E.G., Goetz, A.R., and Brady, S. (2019) 'The global infrastructure public–private partnership and the extra-territorial politics of collective provision: The case of regional rail transit in Denver, USA', *Urban Studies*, 56(7): 1426–47.

Kitchin, R. (2017) 'The realtimeness of smart cities', *TECNOSCIENZA Italian Journal of Science & Technology Studies*, 8(2): 19–41.

Kitchin, R. (2019) 'The timescape of smart cities', *Annals of the American Association of Geographers*, 109(3): 775–90.

Koster, M. (2020) 'An ethnographic perspective on urban planning in Brazil: Temporality, diversity and critical urban theory', *International Journal of Urban and Regional Research*, 44(2): 185–99.

Larkin, B. (2013) 'The politics and poetics of infrastructure', *Annual Review of Anthropology*, 42(1): 372–43.

Lawhon, M., Nilsson, D., Silver, J., Ernstson, H., and Lwasa, S. (2018) 'Thinking through heterogeneous infrastructure configurations', *Urban Studies*, 55(4): 720–32.

Lefebvre, H. (2004) *Rhythmanalysis: Space, Time and Everyday Life*, London: Bloomsbury.

Lemanski, C. (ed) (2020) *Citizenship and Infrastructure: Practices and Identities of Citizens and the State*, Abingdon: Routledge.

Lubitow, A., Carathers, J., Kelly, M., and Abelson, M.J. (2017) 'Transmobilities: Mobility, harassment, and violence experienced by transgender and gender nonconforming public transit riders in Portland, Oregon', *Gender, Place and Culture*, 24(10): 1398–418.

Maharawal, M.M. (2023) 'Infrastructural activism: Google Bus blockades, affective politics, and environmental gentrification in San Francisco', *Antipode*, 55(5): 1454–89.

Massey, D. (1992) 'Politics and space/time', *New Left Review*, 196(Nov/Dec): 65–84.

Mattern, S. (2018) 'Maintenance and care', *Places Journal*, https://doi.org/10.22269/181120 (accessed 27 October 2023)

McFarlane, C. (2021) *Fragments of the City: Making and Remaking Urban Worlds*, Berkeley, CA: University of California Press.

Milojević, I. (2008) 'Timing feminism, feminising time', *Futures*, 40(4): 329–45.

Mitchell, T. (2020) 'Infrastructures work on time', *e-flux Architecture*, https://www.e-flux.com/architecture/new-silk-roads/312596/infrastructures-work-on-time/ (accessed 27 October 2023).

Moser, S. (2021) 'Exploring life in the shadows of fast urbanism', *City*, 25(3–4): 556–60.

Moss, T. (2020) *Remaking Berlin: A History of the City through Infrastructure, 1920–2020*, Cambridge, MA: MIT Press.

Nielsen, M., and Pedersen, M.A. (2015) 'Infrastructural imaginaries: Collapsed futures in Mozambique and Mongolia', in M. Harris and N. Rapport (eds) *Reflections on Imagination: Human Capacity and Ethnographic Method*, Burlington: Ashgate, pp 237–62.

Nowotny, H. (1992) 'Time and social theory: Towards a social theory of time', *Time & Society*, 1(3): 421–54.

Nowotny, H. (1994) *Time: The Modern and Postmodern Experience*, Malden, MA: Polity Press.

Picon, A. (2018) 'Urban infrastructure, imagination and politics: From the networked metropolis to the smart city', *International Journal of Urban and Regional Research*, 42(2): 263–75.

Ponder, C.S., and Omstedt, M. (2022) 'The violence of municipal debt: From interest rate swaps to racialized harm in the Detroit water crisis', *Geoforum*, 132: 271–80.

Pred, A. (1981) 'Social reproduction and the time-geography of everyday life', *Geografiska Annaler B: Series B, Human Geography*, 63(1): 5–22.

Ramakrishnan, K., O'Reilly, K., and Budds, J. (2021) 'Between decay and repair: Embodied experiences of infrastructure's materiality', *Environment and Planning E: Nature and Space*, 4(3): 669–73.

Rodríguez-Pose, A. (2018) 'The revenge of the places that don't matter (and what to do about it)', *Cambridge Journal of Regions, Economy and Society*, 11(1): 189–209.

Rosa, H. (2015) *Social Acceleration: A New Theory of Modernity*, New York: Columbia University Press.

Sayre, N. (2010) 'Climate change, scale, and devaluation: The challenge of our built environment', *Washington and Lee Journal of Energy, Climate, and the Environment*, 1: 93–105.

Schindler, S., and DiCarlo, J. (eds) (2022) *The Rise of the Infrastructure State: How US–China Rivalry Shapes Politics and Place Worldwide*, Bristol: Bristol University Press.

Schindler, S., and Kanai, M. (2021) 'Getting the territory right: Infrastructure-led development and the re-emergence of spatial planning strategies', *Regional Studies*, 55(1): 40–51.

Schivelbusch, W. (2014) *The Railway Journey: The Industrialization of Time and Space in the Nineteenth Century*, Berkeley, CA: University of California Press.

Sharma, S. (2011) 'The biological economy of time', *Journal of Communication Inquiry*, 35(4): 439–44.

Sharma, S. (2013) 'Critical time', *Communication and Critical/Cultural Studies*, 10(2–3): 312–18.

Sharma, S. (2014) *In the Meantime: Temporality and Cultural Politics*, Durham, NC: Duke University Press.

Shatkin, G. (2022) 'Mega-urban politics: Analyzing the infrastructure turn through the national state lens', *Environment and Planning A: Economy and Space*, 54(5): 845–66.

Sheller, M. (2018) *Mobility Justice: The Politics of Movement in an Age of Extremes*, London: Verso.

Shin, H.B., Zhao, Y., and Koh, S.Y. (2020) 'Whither progressive urban futures? Critical reflections on the politics of temporality in Asia', *City*, 24(1–2): 244–54.

Silver, J. (2021) 'Decaying infrastructure in the post-industrial city: An urban political ecology of the US pipeline crisis', *Environment and Planning E: Nature and Space*, 4(3): 756–77.

Simone, A.M. (2004) 'People as infrastructure: Intersecting fragments in Johannesburg', *Public Culture*, 16(3): 407–29.

Simone, A.M. (2022) *The Surrounds: Urban Life Within and Beyond Capture*, Durham, NC: Duke University Press.

Smith, M.L. (2016) 'Urban infrastructure as materialized consensus', *World Archaeology*, 48(1): 164–78.

Smith, R.J., and Hetherington, K. (2013) 'Urban rhythms: Mobilities, space and interaction in the contemporary city', *The Sociological Review*, 61(S1): 4–16.

Star, S.L. (1999) 'The ethnography of infrastructure', *American Behavioral Scientist*, 43(3): 377–91.

Thompson, E.P. (1967) 'Time, work-discipline, and industrial capitalism', *Past & Present*, 38: 56–97.

Thrift, N. (2005) 'Torsten Hägerstrand and social theory', *Progress in Human Geography*, 29(3): 337–40.

Tonkiss, F. (2015) 'Economies of infrastructure', *City*, 19(2–3): 384–91.

Velkova, J., and Plantin, J.-C. (2023) 'Data centers and the infrastructural temporalities of digital media: An introduction', *New Media & Society*, 25(2): 273–86.

Virilio, P. (2006) *Speed Politics*, Cambridge, MA: MIT Press.

Wiig, A., and Silver, J. (2019) 'Turbulent presents, precarious futures: Urbanization and the deployment of global infrastructure', *Regional Studies*, 53(6): 912–23.

Wiig, A., Ward, K.G., Enright, T., Hodson, M., Pearsall, H., and Silver, J. (eds) (2023) *Infrastructuring Urban Futures: The Politics of Remaking Cities*, Bristol: Bristol University Press.

Young, D., and Keil, R. (2010) 'Reconnecting the disconnected: The politics of infrastructure in the in-between city', *Cities*, 27(2): 87–95.

Zeiderman, A. (2019) 'Low time: Submerged humanism in a Colombian port', in K. Hetherington (ed) *Infrastructure, Environment, and Life in the Anthropocene*, Durham, NC: Duke University Press, pp 171–92.

2

Rhythmic Infrastructure

Jean-Paul D. Addie

This chapter examines the concept of 'rhythm' as an analytic to illuminate and connect the multitude of times that permeate the city through infrastructure.[1] The study of urban rhythms has a rich history and continues to develop in provocative ways (Edensor, 2010a; Smith and Hetherington, 2013; Crespi and Manghani, 2020; Abdullah et al, 2023). My argument therefore contributes to a growing body of scholarship exploring the city and its infrastructure through 'rhythmanalysis' (see Meyer, 2008; Walker, 2021; Engels, 2022; Monstadt, 2022; Plyushteva and Schwanen, 2022) and is primarily concerned with extending Henri Lefebvre's work on spatio-temporality via an open reading of *Rhythmanalysis* (published in English in 2004). Following Lefebvre, I understand rhythms as regularly occurring sequences of events or processes: not things, but open moving forces that cannot start and stop at any time (Meyer, 2008: 148; Blue, 2019: 937). I build on this idea to unpack three core rhythmic modalities through which infrastructure time unfolds: repetition, cycle, and period. These modalities are valuable because they enable us to dialectically connect the material and affective, organic and mechanical, absolute and relational, and continuous and discontinuous dimensions of urban infrastructure, as well as the quantitatively and qualitatively different time frames through which infrastructural systems and practices of everyday life co-evolve. My goal is to develop a generative framework to conceptualize urban space, politics, and social practice by incorporating a distinct rhythmic temporal analytic into the ongoing 'infrastructure turn'.

Three-dimensional dialectics of space-time

I begin with the assertion that, in the face of time's complexities, neo-Marxist dialectics can help us conceptualize the multiple meanings of infrastructure's spatio-temporality in rigorous, systematic, and productive ways. As a first cut, we can deploy David Harvey's (2006) treatment of space and think about time as a Raymond Williams-esque 'keyword' for critical infrastructure studies. Harvey's famed tripartite division of absolute, relative, and relational space, after all, is founded on the spatial-temporal concerns of, in order, Newton, Einstein, and Leibniz (Harvey, 2006: 272–5; 2009). For Harvey, space is neither absolute, nor relative, nor relational in and of itself, and the same is true for time: the nature of infrastructural space-time is only revealed and resolved through human practice. Understanding and analysing infrastructure time therefore compels a multidimensional exploration of the materiality (absolute/physical properties), connectivity (relative space-time), and contested social meaning (relationality) of infrastructure systems (Fitzpatrick, 2004). Viewing urban infrastructures as multifaceted temporal objects not only highlights new dimensions of their materiality and governance but also exposes how the 'promise of infrastructure' captures a society's self-image and future aspirations (Appel et al, 2018), even if the futures in question lie 'in ruins' (Gupta, 2018) or are manifest through the temporal violence of a 'failure-to-build' (Stamatopoulou-Robbins, 2021).

A second cut reclaims the position of time in Lefebvre's spatial oeuvre by distinguishing the temporal dimensions of his 'trialectic' theory in *The Production of Space* (Lefebvre, 1991; see also Schmid, 2022). Firstly, infrastructure time involves distinct forms of *perceived time* through which spatio-temporal practice is materialized. The daily routines of urban reality are formed by the routes and networks that link the places set aside for 'private life', work, and leisure and the times at which individuals are anticipated to occupy such places. The city is enacted and reproduced through the aggregated uses of time by people in everyday action, revealing a certain cohesiveness if not logical coherence (Lefebvre, 1991: 38). Secondly, the temporality of infrastructure is produced through abstract *representations of time*, captured in schedules, timetables, imagined pasts (Moss, this volume), and anticipated futures (Coutard, this volume) that internalize ideology and seek to shape social action. Thirdly, urban infrastructures mediate and transform *representational time* through the production of images and symbols that render the world understandable and create individual and collective meaning. These are the 'essentially qualitative, fluid, and dynamic' temporal moments through which time is lived (Lefebvre, 1991: 42). The perceived, conceived, and lived dimensions of social time are always co-constituted through their spatial counterparts. We can bring notions of absolute, relative, and relational space-*time* (cut 1) into dialogue with Lefebvre's perceived-conceived-lived schema (cut 2) to construct a multidimensional framework to comprehend the spatio-temporality of urban infrastructures and networked urbanism (Harvey, 2006: 282–3; Addie, 2016a).

A third cut, which I take up in the remainder of this chapter, involves paying attention to how particular temporal abstractions reframe our understanding of infrastructural systems. Space, for Lefebvre, is a social product that must be analysed in its historical context. But as Schmid (2022: 327) notes, Lefebvre 'does not begin his exploration of the history of space with a geographical description of natural space but rather with the study of natural rhythms, their changes, and their inscription into space by human action' – that is, with the specific times and rhythms of everyday life. I build from this assertion to assess three modalities of 'rhythm' developed from Lefebvre and Catherine Régulier's sketches in *Rhythmanalysis* (2004) – repetition, cycle, and period – that I see as useful for differentiating the rationalized abstractions and embodied experiences of infrastructure time. My approach to rhythm (and rhythmic infrastructure) offers an alternative reading of Lefebvre's three-dimensional dialectical articulation in *Rhythmanalysis*, which he frames around a triad of melody-harmony-rhythm. However, I align with Lefebvre's project by developing an open approach to infrastructural rhythms that opposes narrow binaries and connects class politics to the production and experience of urban difference.

Infrastructural rhythms as a temporal analytic

Lefebvre's work on rhythmanalysis is an appealing frame for thinking through infrastructure time because it offers an explicit means to grapple with time and space together: concrete times have/are rhythms and rhythms always 'imply a relation of a time to a space, a localized time, or, if one prefers a temporalized space' (Lefebvre, 2004: 96). While stopping short of a fully realized method or theory to analyse rhythms, Lefebvre's (and Régulier's) sketches for rhythmanalysis establish a disposition for investigations of space-time (Lyon, 2019), what Edensor (2011: 190) terms a 'suggestive vein for temporal thinking'. But what are rhythms, and what are they not? Lefebvre asserts that rhythm is about repetition: 'there is no rhythm without repetition in time and space, without *reprises*, without returns, in short, without measure' (2004: 16). They can manifest in a variety of syncopations, but rhythms cannot start or stop arbitrarily. However, Lefebvre does not present rhythms as monotonous nor as offering a sense that the future will repeat itself intelligibly. Rather, he understands them as fundamentally dialectical, arguing that while rhythms entail 'calculated and expected obligation … there is always something new and unforeseen that introduces itself into the repetitive: difference' (Lefebvre 2004: 18, 16). The concept of rhythm therefore provides a way to think about *both* the disciplinary power of infrastructure to (self-)regulate behaviour (paralleling Foucauldian critiques) *and* direct us to consider the open and transformative potentialities that can be realized within the social, political, and economic interests and institutions that animate them.

As ever, Lefebvre's conceptualization is slippery. He himself notes that while everyone possesses rhythms of various sorts, 'the meanings of the term remain obscure. We easily confuse rhythm with movement, speed, a sequence of movements or objects (machines for example) [and therefore] tend to attribute to rhythms a mechanical overtone, brushing aside the organic aspect of rhythmed movements' (Lefebvre, 2004: 15–16). There is, then, a danger in simply applying a surface-level reading of rhythm when studying contemporary urban life. As Smith and Hetherington (2013: 19–20) urge, we need to 'not only find rhythm (if you look for it you will find rhythm in all things) but think, critically, with that which an attention to rhythm reveals'.

In this context, three points are of note for a Lefebvrian account of rhythmic infrastructure: firstly, rhythmic temporalities bear social norms and normative shifts that 'enforce forms of life, conveying routines, rules and principles' (Coletta et al, 2020: 638). Yet the multiple, divergent, and distinct rhythms of the city defy the idea of a singular, synchronized urban experience (Osman and Mulíček, 2017). Whereas the concept of 'flows' is sufficient for narrow political economic analysis (for example, in capturing the distribution of resources enabled through infrastructure), we 'live' rhythms and experience them subjectively (Lefebvre, 1991: 205–7). Lefebvre therefore calls for 'rhythmanalysts' to pursue an interdisciplinary and multisensory approach to 'listening' to the city 'as an audience listens to a symphony' (2004: 32).

Secondly, rhythmanalysis offers an open frame to investigate everyday life, but as with Lefebvre's predominantly spatial work on urbanization and everydayness, it is not confined to a scalar localism or bodily immediacy. Urban literatures deploying a rhythmanalysis approach have certainly been drawn to the micro-temporalities and the micro-political dynamics of everyday life (notably in mobilities studies and work inspired by Michel de Certeau, Frédéric Gros, and AbdouMaliq Simone, among others) even as they attend to the multiple temporalities of colliding heterogeneous rhythms (for instance, Crang, 2001; Meyer, 2008; Edensor, 2010b). This is not surprising given Lefebvre's positioning of the body and the starting point of rhythmanalysis. But the spatio-temporalities of large-scale social phenomena including demographic change, economic development, and urbanization and micro-practices such as cooking, commuting, and daily labour can be evaluated through the same framework. Rhythms connect the part with the whole, the particular with the general (Smith and Hetherington, 2013: 6). Moving between scales and levels of generality – from 'the *cosmological* in the movement and circling of planets (day/night, seasons, annual cycles), to the *corporeal* in the many rhythms of bodily function (heartbeat, lungs, digestion), and the *social* in the rhythmic ordering work of institutions, conventions, schedules and devices (timetables, festivals, opening hours, eating, travelling times and much more)' (Walker et al, 2022: 574) – is therefore a highly generative practice.

Thirdly, the city is both a product and productive of polyrhythmic phenomena. The heartbeat of everyday urban life is composed of diverse rhythms that may produce a grand symphonic sweep. Here, *eurhythmia* unites the city in a state of health, as in the organization of a healthy living body or a 'normed everydayness'[2] (Lefebvre, 2004: 25). Yet polyrhythmia can also result in misalignments that create discordance and cacophony. *Arrhythmia* captures rhythmic dissonance, attuning us to how things fall apart, ultimately towards a 'fatal disorder' (Lefebvre, 2004: 25). Eurthymia and arrhythmia are not antithetical; each modifies and produces aspects of the other in new rhythms (Blue, 2019: 941). This view is helpful when examining slower, macro-institutional rhythms and modes of infrastructural violence, making sure not to mark these phenomena as being beyond the scope of bundled analyses of social practice.

Reading Lefebvre's *Rhythmanalysis* (2004) alongside work in the global infrastructure turn illuminates the heterodox temporal epistemologies through which networked urbanism is structured and lived. Of course, there are limits, blind fields, and omissions in focusing on spatio-temporal rhythms (and in Lefebvre's work more broadly). Reid-Musson (2018), for instance, notes the need to pay more attention to issues of intersectionality in rhythmanalysis studies (see also Buckley and Strauss, 2016; Peake et al, 2018). However, Lefebvre's rhythmic sketches provocatively connect the notion of rhythm to rational, logical abstractions of time and to visceral and vital embodied experience, finding a 'rhythm' wherever 'there is interaction between a place, a time, and an expenditure of energy' (2004: 25). In the following, I unpack the modalities of repetition, cycle, and period to demonstrate how 'rhythm' can offer an incisive analytic and methodological entry point into the temporal study of urban and regional infrastructure (see also Engels, 2022; Monstadt, 2022).

Repetition: generating difference through repeating

Lefebvre first deploys the notion of rhythm as *repetition* to conceptualize continuity and change within both capitalism and everyday life, bringing forth an order out of background noise. The everyday rhythms of capitalism provide a means to colonize space-time, with repetition establishing the bio-political basis to rationalize and govern social and spatial structures (through wage labour, the working day, and so on). The space-time paths characteristic of time geography, inscribed by repetitious social practice, illuminate the entrenched routines and governance of 'the choreography

Figure 2.1: Rhythm as repetition: difference produced through recurrence

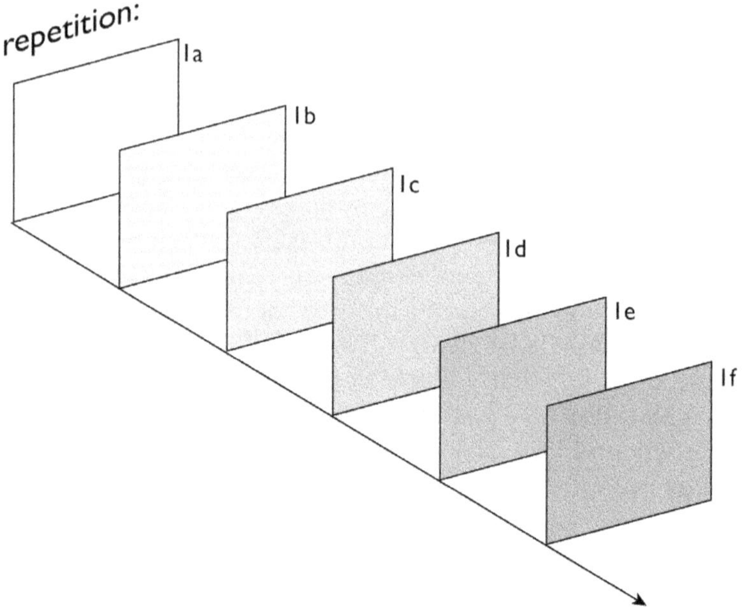

repetition:
1a
1b
1c
1d
1e
1f

Source: Jean-Paul Addie and Lauren Marino

of existence' (Pred, 1977), which both conform to and reproduce the infrastructural geographies of the city. The constructive nature of repetition is also readily apparent in the pulsing flows disclosed in the infrastructural work that establishes the city as a space of circulation (Adams, 2019). Yet the *absolute* repetition of movements, gestures, situations, and actions (as may be structured and governed by infrastructural systems) is a logical fiction (see Figure 2.1). Repetition does not exclude difference but exudes it through the creative and generative act of repeating: a first instance differs from a second because the latter comes after and exists in relation to the former (Lefebvre, 2004: 17). The knowledge necessary to navigate urban and infrastructural systems builds over time through the experience of repetitious practice, whether learning to ride a bike or to master the intricacies of air traffic control. The key proposition, then, is that rhythm as repetition engenders the 'production of the different by the identical' (Lefebvre, 2004: 7–8).

Rhythm as repetition dialectically integrates time's quantitative elements (*chronos*, that is, the sequential ordering and measure of time that distinguishes its moments) and its qualitative aspects (*kairos*, which links moments together and gives them meaning). Repetitious rhythm 'appears as regulated times, governed by rational laws, but in contact with what is least rational in human being: the lived, the carnal, the body' (Lefebvre, 2004: 18). These rhythms are not simple binaries (body/organic rhythms vs technical/mechanical rhythms) but open ways to think through the complexity of the city, infrastructural systems, and urban life as a totality. Moreover, repetitions are performed and overlap, as Edensor (2010b) demonstrates through the multiple physical, cultural, social, and personal dynamics that influence the act of walking. Repetitious bodily rhythms couple and uncouple with other rhythms in the city (of the built environment, weather, infrastructural materiality, and social/political landscapes) to create a polyrhythmia of place that is constantly changing in reactive and formative ways (both harmonious and discordant). Coletta and Kitchin (2017) and Amin and Thrift (2017) both extend such arguments by interrogating how smart city technologies not only employ rhythmanalysis to build an understanding of urban flows, but also act as rhythm-makers that shape the pulse of the 'algorhythmic city'.

Differing urban futures emerge as the performativity and practice of repetitious social relations wax and wane across temporal increments. On the one hand, Anand's (2017) ethnographic study of water infrastructure in Mumbai points to the disciplinary gendered and classed subjectivities produced as the daily rhythms of governmental 'water time' (when and where scarce water resources can be accessed) unevenly colonize the social life of Indian households. On the other hand, Shaw's (2018) work on the city at night points towards the emancipatory potential of the nocturnal city's rhythms that both open time for infrastructural systems to be constructed and repaired and establish recurring liminal space-times where transgressive activities can confront neoliberal governance and commodification. These examples illustrate contradictions in urban everyday life and the capacity of infrastructures to generate 'differential space-times'. As sites and stakes of colonization-resistance, minimal differences in the repetition of infrastructural time can serve as the foundation for realizing maximal, qualitatively different expressions of difference. These may reveal divergent experiences of gender, class, race, and sexuality, and the possibilities of transcending their social inequities (see Simone, this volume).

Rhythmic discordance disrupts repetition, illuminating jarring moments where infrastructural apparatuses discipline behaviours and bodies or suspend populations in time for the practice of governance, for example, holding passengers as they pass through airport security on the basis of socially constructed (often racialized) risk profiles (Salter, 2008; Sheller, 2018), diverting resources to 'critical assets' at moments of crisis (Marvin and Rutherford, this volume), or keeping communities suspended in the shadow of perennially unrealized infrastructure projects (Addie, 2016b). Our collective experiences of the COVID-19 pandemic have offered a clear window to frame the disruptions of lockdowns and social distancing on previous normed everyday routines (James, 2020; Whiteford, 2020). The fitful construction of alternative, retrograde daily repetitions during the pandemic continually threw individuals and communities out of time and place: weeks in lockdown, quarantine, the wait for vaccines. As the space-times of work, play, and rest collapsed into each other, everyday life during pandemic time was experienced by many as an existential arrhythmia, a mundane discordance of rhythms shadowed by the threats of vulnerability to disease and economic insecurity and the nostalgic yearning for a return to normal (normed) time. COVID-19 disruptions also illuminated the vital yet often hidden infrastructures (and the people mobilizing them) that are necessary to reproduce everyday life, from front-line healthcare personnel to logistics workers maintaining the flows of capitalist globalization that support e-commerce and at-home consumption for those privileged enough to pivot to such a pandemic lifestyle (see Biglieri and Keil, this volume). The daily repetitions of lockdown immobilities and the demand for immediate delivery (from the restaurant down the street or the factory in Shenzhen) were essentially dependent upon massive infrastructures of mobility. These differentially exposed people to risk while catalysing major transformations in the urban environment (for instance, the development of new logistics facilities to supply sedentary urban populations) (Ali et al, 2023).

Temporal disruption and infrastructural arrhythmia expose how polyrhythmic social practice splinters urban space and fragments everyday life. Yet in disrupting monotonous routines and challenging hegemonic rhythms, such moments also create opportunities to claim alternative rights to occupy, inhabit, and move through urban space. Here, Bissell (2007) points to moments of emancipation that may be realized when we view waiting as an active and intentional slowing of rhythm, suggesting such liminal periods are latent with anticipation and the freedom of (temporal) removal from the corporal discipline of commodified clock time. Alternatively, disrupting the regular rhythms of urban systems can be a mode of political protest and resistance – for instance, blocking the flows of 'critical' infrastructures or slowing the pace of the auto-centric city (Hall, 2010; Sheller, 2018; Thorpe, this volume) – to expose others to differing temporal experiences of the city.

Cycle: temporal alignment and contradiction

Lefebvre next points to multifaceted modalities of rhythm as *cycle*. His immediate interest in rhythmic cycles emerges in the interactions and interferences of (1) organic *cyclical time* (centred on nature's temporalities: the biological rhythms of the body, the diurnal swings of day and night, the swells of the tides, the weather, seasonal change) and (2) rationalised *linear time* (which emerges from demands placed on human activity as social practice is institutionalized through imposed structures and rhythmic regimes). As with repetition, rhythm-as-cycle contains both sameness and difference, continuity and change, since 'the cycle itself is a repetition ... every cycle is born from

Figure 2.2: Rhythm as cycle: cyclical movement without returning to a previous point of departure

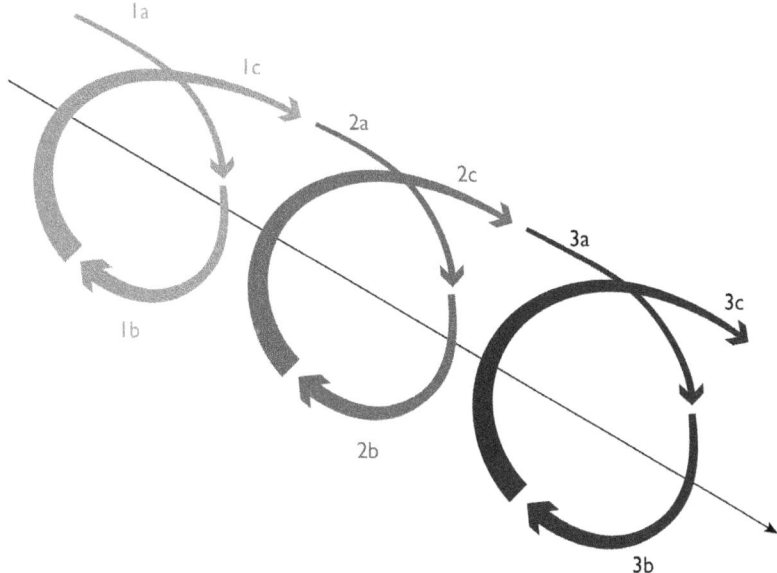

Source: Jean-Paul Addie and Lauren Marino

another cycle and becomes absorbed in other circular movements' but *'[n]o genuine cycle returns exactly to its point of departure or reproduces itself exactly'* (Lefebvre, 2014: 342, emphasis added) (see Figure 2.2). Monotony may arise as one day follows another, but the essential contradictions of everyday life mean that even with this rote reoccurrence, 'everything changes' (Osborne, 1995: 196). Linear time opens to new beginnings by its interactions with the difference marked by the rhizomatic patterns and pulses inherent in everyday life's cyclical rhythms.

Natural rhythms affect which activities are necessary for individuals to survive and for societies to function. Jalas et al engage this problematic by framing engineered infrastructures as interventions intended to isolate us from the cycles of nature:

> If weather is thought of as an infrastructure providing a pervasive rhythmic temporality, technologies of encasement and lighting contribute another layer of infrastructure that lessens and flattens out the cycles of ecosystem services. In general, infrastructures are layered one upon another and partly function to counter the rhythms of one another. (Jalas et al, 2016: 19)

Murphy (2001) foregrounds this temporal understanding in examining the 1998 ice storm in north-eastern North America. In particular, he demonstrates how human intervention in natural systems had led to challenges with predicting risk between Amish communities (where the storm had relatively little impact) versus Canadian society at large (where the impacts of the storm disrupted daily life and safety for weeks, even leading to higher rates of birth complications for pregnant mothers). In Plyushteva and Schwanen's study of flooding in Manila, the rhythms of rising and subsiding floodwaters 'are not simply a sequence of presences and absences' (2022: 4). Rather, they argue that flooding in the city is characterized by frequent uneven and unpredictable 'disruptive rhythms' that permeate a wider, interconnected assemblage of urban infrastructural rhythms – hydrological, social, institutional, technical, political – 'even in dry times' (Plyushteva and Schwanen, 2022: 7). Across these cases, the layering of counter-rhythms (both natural and engineered) underpins instances of infrastructural failure and collapse. Recognizing and internalizing disruption and ultimately failure within rhythmic infrastructural time enables us to 'render visible specific questions on the governance of vulnerable urban systems' (Plyushteva and Schwanen, 2022: 14).

Scholarship on the city at night further discloses the tensions and contradictions between cyclical (natural) and linear (social) rhythms, not least as night work runs counter to the human body's circadian rhythms. The geography of social and economic activity shifts in the city at night, mostly visibly around entertainment districts, bars, and clubs, but also around the healthcare, logistics, and construction industries that undertake essential reparative urban labour (Shaw, 2018). While national and municipal governments approach the provision and regulation of night-time infrastructure in a variety of ways, they are paying increased attention to the distinct demands of nocturnal urban governance (Acuto et al, 2021). Nevertheless, the city at night remains a source of increased vulnerability to temporal forms of violence and exclusion, notably along gender lines (Hadfield, 2015). At the same time, night-based cultural infrastructures offer possibilities for new subjectivities to both coexist with and challenge nocturnal neoliberal governmentalities (Gallen, 2015).

Thinking about infrastructure time through the lens of rhythmic cycles further opens a generative space to explore the applied, material, and political challenges involved in the construction and maintenance of actually existing infrastructure systems, that is, the temporal (mis)alignments of urban infrastructure policy, planning, and governance. Decision-making regarding infrastructural projects often relies on linear, teleological time horizons that drive towards an (idealized) image of the future. Such timelines unfurl through repeated environmental assessments, labour contracts, policy reviews, material degradations and repair, and so on, giving them a nuanced cyclical, rather than simple teleological, logic. Fissures between these cycles frequently disclose how the decades-long planning and consultancy horizons of many projects fail to align with the pressing needs of urban inhabitants who subsequently experience infrastructure time as 'choppy, inconsistent, and unsettling' (Stamatopoulou-Robbins, 2021). The practice and perception of urban transformation evokes its own 'chronopolitics' (Wallis, 1970) that shapes the possibilities for change in the present and the parameters of possible alternative futures.

Project timelines reveal another dimension of infrastructure's (contested) cyclical temporality, captured in the differentiated recurrence of financial boom, bubble, and crisis in infrastructural landscapes and in the institutional scaffolding and processes shaping distinct policy cycles. Abram's (2014: 136) ethnographic planning research documents how '[p]rogression through time is ... ordered into cyclical calendars, each of which must feed into the cyclical calendar of the primary committee, the general municipal council. Municipal council meetings are often seen as ritual formal events where prior work is passed through, but they are not necessarily empty rituals.' Raco et al (2018) stress the importance of the speed of such planning processes, alongside the temporal resources that can be mustered by different actors to realize their interests. Whereas many governments have sought to expedite planning decisions following the 2008 Global Financial Crisis, they argue urban planning should 'be focused on the production of "slow cities", in which decision-making times allow time for proper democratic and judicial-technical oversight of development processes' (Raco et al, 2018: 1176).

Wood's (2015) analysis of the history of bus rapid transit (BRT) initiatives in South Africa reveals another expression of infrastructure planning's cyclical nature, one that discloses the repetitious linear movement of buses on the street and the institutionalized regulatory cycles and temporal politics that put them there. Tracing the temporal aspects of policy circulation through the conceptualization, implementation, and eventual failure that characterize such projects, she posits that slow learning processes form recursive failures foster fertile ground for fast policy transfer. Significantly, Wood problematizes the perceived temporal acceleration of BRT as an infrastructural fix, suggesting that 'while it may seem as though circulated policies shorten the gestation time from policy introduction to policy adoption, gradual and repetitive attempts to implement circulating innovations ensure that when the timing is right, turnover time appears accelerated' (2015: 578). State-led development does not follow a neat linear trajectory, with both frustrating and generative consequences. Indeed, Robin and Nkula-Wenz (2021) note how repeated failures of projects in Cape Town enabled plans to gestate over a longer period, creating diffuse temporal circulations that have subsequently played out at local and global scales.

The studies mentioned earlier are indicative of (1) the non-linear, rhizomatic temporalities that shape the mobility and mutations of urban policy (McCann and Ward, 2011) and (2) how the time horizons of different stakeholders align, clash, and splinter in the political, economic, procedural, and lived times of urban infrastructuring. Bridging such temporal-political interests is challenging, as Elsner et al (2019) illustrate in relation to energy transitions in Rotterdam, because the temporalities of different infrastructure domains are becoming more intertwined but not necessarily aligned. Bond (2019) concurs, asserting that the immediacy of the climate crisis does not readily align with the financial incentives and payback timelines of infrastructural South African mega-projects. It is a question not only of who is going to pay for green infrastructural transformations (Mell, 2021), but also of *when*. The COVID-19 pandemic has further disclosed ongoing splintering in the polyrhythmic city at the intersection of arrhythmic temporal cycles of capitalist accumulation, resource demand, policy design and implementation, and the biological life cycles of global pathogens (Ali et al, 2023; Biglieri and Keil, this volume).

Rhythmic cycles – and the tensions between them – unveil the fitful, contested, and uneven ways in which infrastructure advances and recedes (Appel, 2018), the durability of infrastructure systems themselves, and, ultimately, how urban life functions at the juncture of *linear* 'project time', the *cyclical* lived city (Koster, 2020; Ramakrishnan et al, 2021). Elsner et al (2019: 654) therefore call for greater conceptual and applied attention to be paid to temporal alignment with regard to infrastructures' present or short-term operation and their long-term planning. Yet there is also an opportunity here to consider the progressive potential of protest, imminent critique, and contestation against infrastructures to take root in the aporia of differing legal, political, financial, and administrative systems.

Period: grappling with continuity and discontinuity

Finally, Lefebvre refers to rhythms of 'birth, growth, peak, then decline and end' (2004: 25). Such rhythms immediately capture the organic life cycles of the body and the very materiality of infrastructure. Infrastructures have their own life cycles. They are conceived, planned, constructed, decline, decay, and reach obsolescence, each of which raises distinct questions about funding, maintenance, societal values, and developmental lock-ins. Sometimes concrete crumbles, steel rusts, pipes fracture, and semiconductors burn out because of their natural degradation over time. At other times, different circumstances – social-technical antiquation, natural disasters, or war – can hasten these processes to a premature end.

Yet read through the analytic of rhythm, this temporal modality also restates important questions about the nature of qualitative transformation and how we conceptualize the relationship between continuity and change in infrastructure space as a historical product. This problematic is a central concern for Lefebvre, reflected in his discussions of cyclical and linear time, where he notes that the linear flow of time 'is both continuous and discontinuous. Continuous: its beginning is absolute, and it grows indefinitely from an initial zero. Discontinuous: it fragments into partial time scales assigned to one thing or another according to a programme which is abstract in relation to time. It dissects indefinitely' (Lefebvre, 2014: 342). Lefebvre's response was to grapple with the specificity and contradictions of spatio-temporal configurations by exploring both the historicity of the production of space and 'the grand rhythms of historical time' (2004: 65). This is captured in his attempted periodization of urban development through eras of the political, mercantile, and industrial city to the virtual emergence of urban society in *The Urban Revolution* (Lefebvre, 2003: 15). Rather than making neat cuts into the progress of history, Lefebvre understood the city and the infrastructural forms necessary to produce urban space as particular historical configurations, continually 'see[ing] the historical, the diachronic, the generative past as incessantly written into the present of the spatial' (Schmid, 2022: 327).

With this, I want to extend notions of rhythmic temporality to invoke the logics of periodization as a methodological and conceptual approach to the analysis of infrastructural time. The ontological assumption of periodization rests 'on the paradoxical simultaneity of continuity/discontinuity in the flow of history', with the scope and utility of any given periodization dependent upon (1) the emphasis given to the relations of fixity and fluidity; and (2) the objects and processes under examination (Jessop, 2004: 2). Periodization is a useful tool to analyse key thematic and topical concerns in critical infrastructure studies (Glass et al, 2019), from defining eras of highway planning (DiMento and Ellis, 2014) and framing legislative eras of energy planning/transitions (Silvast et al, 2019) through to projecting the futures of anthropogenic climate change (Koslov, 2019). Indeed, the overarching argument of Graham and Marvin's (2001) *Splintering Urbanism* pivots on a periodization positing the rise and fall of the 'integrated ideal' of the modern networked city. However, the abstractions necessary in systematizing complex social-technical structures into distinct periods also opens the splintering urbanism thesis (and other modes of periodization) to critiques of collapsing geographical and temporal difference within an over-generalized schema (Coutard, 2008).

So in what ways can periods be understood as rhythmic, if their analytic utility presupposes a form of singularity, an incompatibility with other epochs? As a methodology, periodization utilizes multiple temporalities to order actions and events based on analytically noteworthy conjunctures, including the immediate conjunctural significance of events, the institutional setting within which events occur, and each period's past, present, and future significance (Jessop, 2008: 88). Because periodization is dependent upon problems and units of analysis, '[t]here can be no master periodization that captures the essence of a period for all purposes' (Jessop, 2004: 3). The implications here bring questions of radical breaks in urbanization regimes or infrastructural transitions into stark relief, given variations that appear at differing levels of generality. Individual periods, as temporal abstractions, may then encapsulate an analytical singularity in that their boundaries demarcate a discontinuity. But individual periods, of necessity, exist in relation to other periods, both those preceding and following, and those constructed via alternative criteria. In other words, there are continuities that repetitiously link periods together as they succeed each other (as external times) and their internal times of emergence, maturation, decline, and collapse, as illustrated in Figure 2.3. Periodization therefore provides us with times and temporal modalities, but it is vital to understand them as abstractions defined by selective, not absolute, parameters.

We need to engage infrastructural times as they are now and as they evolve across axes of succession and coexistence. Urban infrastructures are useful

Figure 2.3: Rhythm as period: dis/continuities between phases of (a) emergence; (b) maturation; (c) decline; and (d) collapse, within and between periods

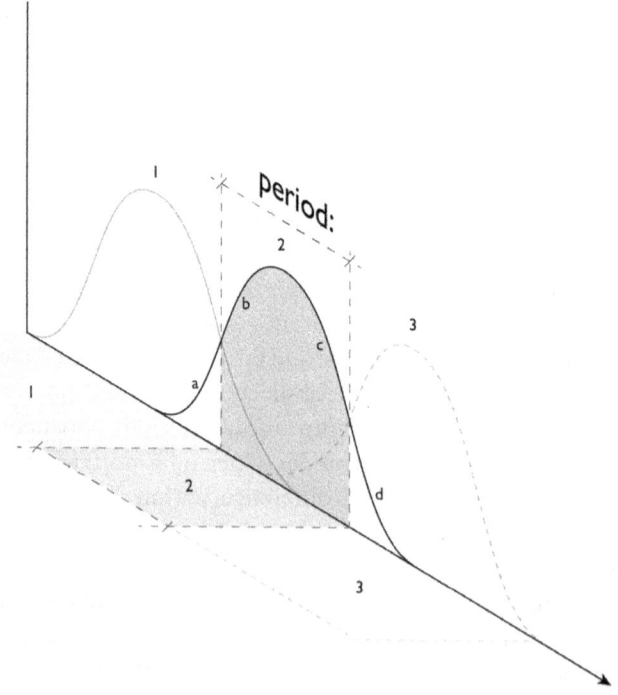

Source: Jean-Paul Addie and Lauren Marino

objects of analysis here as they link periods as temporal scales 'ranging from the *human* (hours, days, years) through the *historical* (decades, centuries) to the *geophysical* (millennia and beyond)' (Edwards, 2003: 194), even as their quantitative and qualitative dimensions have tended to be analysed in isolation. The notion of rhythm helps us shift between micro, meso, and macro temporal scales (in and across geographic contexts) to disclose (1) the myriad ways in which infrastructures are constantly transforming as they erode, degrade, are devalued, updated, and maintained; and (2) how networked urbanism arises through the complex layering, persistence, and erasure of different forms of infrastructure across urban landscapes.

Because the moment of temporal abstraction involves establishing analytical parameters for inclusion/exclusion, periodizing infrastructure time is a fundamentally political process. The challenges of analytical delineation and distinction do not negate periodization's utility (Lieberman, 2001). Rather, periodizing the history of infrastructural space emphasizes the significance of contextualizing our temporal abstractions to avoid reductionist oversimplification. Just as particular spatial scales are never simply given, periodization is informed by specific cases and analyses grounded in distinct empirical and ideological contexts (Wishart, 2004; Ekman, this volume). Periodizing infrastructure time 'as history' brings together people, artefacts, places, and processes, but not everything about them. Further, the simultaneity of continuity and rupture in the flow of history leads periods to blur at the edges, overlap, and be experienced in varying ways by different social groups. Attuning ourselves to how particular periodization strategies establish their parameters for inclusion/exclusion discloses the necessary political moment within the bounding of infrastructure time (Addie, 2020). Yet the distinct methodology of periodization, in contrast to more simplified chronological approaches (Jessop, 2004), ontologically acknowledges the 'simultaneity of multiple normative orderings' (Coletta et al, 2020: 637). Urban infrastructures internalize this complexity, constructing a myriad of hegemonic and insurgent temporalities that shape the historically and geographically varied nature of urban space.

The possibility of rhythmic infrastructure time

By expanding upon the analysis sketched out in Lefebvre's *Rhythmanalysis*, this chapter has presented a series of rhythmic temporal modalities to explore the particular and concrete experiences of urban infrastructure time. Engaging rhythm as a temporal analytic is significant because how we think about space-*time* ultimately shapes our understanding of infrastructure and, with this, urbanization and urban life. Infrastructural rhythms set the pace of urban life. At the same time, they also enable the fragmentation of time that generates repetitious activity, thus connecting the continuous and discontinuous within spatio-temporal configurations. Urban infrastructural rhythms are always multiple. Even as a specific infrastructure may set the rhythm for a particular service of provision (trains, water supply, and so on), these are dependent on other rhythmic activities and orders, thus constituting infrastructure and the city as polyrhythmic bundles of organic, social, and technological temporalities. Approaching urban infrastructure through a rhythmic framework enables us to bring a variety of seemingly discrete or oppositional temporal moments into dialogue: the mechanical and organic, repetition and difference, fast-paced rhythms and slow movement/violence. The aim here is not simply to resolve these tensions but to unpack their contradictions and 'consider what metamorphoses are possible in the everyday as a result of [these] interaction[s]' (Lefebvre, 2014: 343). As a temporal analytic, rhythmic infrastructure time provides a means to address questions regarding the governance and regulation of infrastructures, the interface of natural and socio-technical systems, and the potential to rethink planning regimes for more just and sustainable urban futures (see Elsner et al, 2019; Walker, 2021).

While certain urban rhythms are 'cyclical' in Lefebvre's terms (that is, shaped by biological and physiological processes), the ability to set social rhythms, dissect linear time, and mobilize and manipulate time is a political act. At once, the politics underlying the social production of rhythms directs us towards the colonizing techniques and logics of abstract time under capitalist modernity. The encroachment of rationality, commodification, and control into the temporality of everyday life constitute the alienation of ourselves from time, infringing upon the spontaneity of the festival and the liminal spaces of creativity and transgression. Yet Lefebvre consistently emphasizes rhythms as the foundation of the everyday, and the difference they produce offers opportunities to escape and transform the monotony of daily life. Each rhythm is difference, animated by varied frequencies, intensities, and routines. The temporal modalities of infrastructure shape, and are shaped by, the psychological, social, political, and economic processes involved in reworking the urban fabric and urban society. As infrastructure times may both align (eurhythmia) and conflict (arrhythmia), they encapsulate the values of different groups and different periods (Hope, 2009).

In sum, exploring urban infrastructure as *rhythmic* ultimately draws us to the following. Firstly, the concept of rhythmic infrastructure does not connote something that is mechanical or set. Building on Lefebvre's arguments urges us to see the dialectical tensions between the disciplinary abstraction of capitalist and networked modernity *and* the qualitative transformations emergent in the difference exuded through rhythmic encounters (including their speed, slowness, intensity, scales, and spatiality *and* attending to for whom these matter). Secondly, because the city is polyrhythmic, a three-dimensional dialectic focuses our attention on the contradictions and (a)synchronicity that emerge between different rhythms (social, natural, technical, political, economic, and so on), keeping us suspended within their tensions as rhythmic relations co-evolve at the intersection of infrastructural (re)arrangements and the practice of everyday life. Thirdly, following Lefebvre's dialectical method compels any analysis of rhythm to go beyond simply observing the immediate pulsations of urban life (often a solipsistic exercise in auto-ethnographic empiricism) to question what rhythms (their production and relationality) disclose about urban society. This presents, analytically and methodologically, a robust foundation for the comparison of urban continuities and discontinuities in time and across space, one capable of supporting the analysis of differing groups' abilities to impose temporal orders, structures, speeds, and rhythms onto others and the capacities of others to defy such colonizing times and forge alternative ways of being in the temporal incompleteness of the city (Guma, 2020). Here, it is important to foreground issues of intersectionality that have tended to be downplayed in current conceptions and applications of rhythmanalysis (Reid-Musson, 2018) while also recognizing the potential of the study of rhythms to inform 'cosmopolitan' theorizations that can enrich and extend postcolonial urban and infrastructure studies (Gibert-Flutre, 2021; Plyushteva and Schwanen, 2022). Bringing the infrastructure turn into dialogue with the meanings of rhythm can then not only present a heuristic to examine the production, governance, and experience of urban life, but also establish a conceptual and methodological agenda to identify emergent sites of innovation, empowerment, and collective (re)appropriation latent within and beyond the times of the networked metropolis.

Notes

[1] This chapter expands on a preliminary argument presented in Addie (2022).
[2] An idea subject to critique through the lens of 'crip time' (Biglieri and Keil, this volume).

References

Abdullah, A., Cardoso, R., Dasgupta, S., Pati, S., Plueckhahn, R., Shafique, T. et al (2023) 'Re-arranging the urban: Forms, rhythms, politics', *Transactions of the Institute of British Geographers*, 48(4), 718–44.

Abram, S. (2014) 'The time it takes: Temporalities of planning', *Journal of the Royal Anthropological Institute*, 20(S1): 129–47.

Acuto, M., Seijas, A., McArthur, J., and Robin, E. (2021) *Managing Cities at Night: A Practitioners Guide to the Urban Governance of the Night*, Bristol: Bristol University Press.

Adams, R.E. (2019) *Circulation and Urbanization*, Thousand Oaks, CA: SAGE.

Addie, J.-P.D. (2016a) 'Theorizing suburban infrastructure: A framework for critical and comparative analysis', *Transactions of the Institute of British Geographers*, 41(3): 273–85.

Addie, J.-P.D. (2016b) 'On the road to the in-between city: Excavating peripheral urbanization in Chicago's "Crosstown Corridor"', *Environment and Planning A*, 48(5): 825–43.

Addie, J.-P.D. (2020) 'Stuck inside the urban with the dialectical blues again: Abstraction and generality in urban theory', *Cambridge Journal of Regions Economy and Society*, 13(3): 575–92.

Addie, J.-P.D. (2022). 'The times of Splintering Urbanism', *Journal of Urban Technology*, 29(1): 109–16.

Ali, S.H., Connolly, C., and Keil, R. (2023). *Pandemic Urbanism: Infectious Diseases on a Planet of Cities*, Cambridge: Polity Press.

Amin, A., and Thrift, N. (2017) *Seeing Like a City*, Cambridge: Polity Press.

Anand, N. (2017) *Hydraulic City: Water and the Infrastructures of Citizenship in Mumbai*, Durham, NC: Duke University Press.

Appel, H. (2018) 'Infrastructure time', in N. Anand, A. Gupta, and H. Appel (eds) *The Promise of Infrastructure*, Durham, NC: Duke University Press, pp 41–61.

Appel, H., Anand, N., and Gupta, A. (2018) 'Temporality, politics, and the promise of infrastructure', in N. Anand, A. Gupta, and H. Appel (eds) *The Promise of Infrastructure*, Durham, NC: Duke University Press, pp 1–38.

Bissell, D. (2007) 'Animating suspension: Waiting for mobilities', *Mobilities*, 2(2): 277–98.

Blue, S. (2019) 'Institutional rhythms: Combing practice theory and rhythmanalysis to conceptualise processes of institutionalisation', *Time & Society*, 28(3): 922–50.

Bond, P. (2019) 'Contradictory time horizons of Durban energy piping in an era of looming climate chaos', *City*, 23(4–5): 631–45.

Buckley, M., and Strauss, K. (2016) 'With, against and beyond Lefebvre: Planetary urbanization and epistemic plurality', *Environment and Planning D: Society and Space*, 34(4): 617–36.

Coletta, C., and Kitchin, R. (2017) 'Algorhythmic governance: Regulating the "heartbeat" of a city using the internet of things', *Big Data & Society*, 4(2): 1–16.

Coletta, C., Röhl, T., and Wagenknecht, S. (2020) 'On time: Temporal and normative orderings of mobilities', *Mobilities*, 15(5): 635–46.

Coutard, O. (2008) 'Placing splintering urbanism: Introduction', *Geoforum*, 39(6): 1815–20.

Crang, M. (2001) 'Rhythms of the city: Temporalised space and motion', in J. May and N. Thrift (eds) *Timespace: Geographies of Temporality*, London: Routledge, pp 187–207.

Crespi, P., and Manghani, S. (2020) 'A genealogy of rhythm', in P. Crespi and S. Manghani (eds) *Rhythm and Critique: Techniques, Modalities, Practices*, Edinburgh: Edinburgh University Press, pp 30–54.

DiMento, J., and Ellis, C. (2014) *Changing Lanes: Visions and Histories of Urban Freeways*, Cambridge, MA: MIT Press.

Edensor, T. (ed) (2010a) *Geographies of Rhythm: Nature, Place, Mobilities and Bodies*, Burlington, VA: Ashgate.

Edensor, T. (2010b) 'Walking in rhythms: Place, regulation, style and the flow of experience', *Visual Studies*, 25(1): 69–79.

Edensor, T. (2011) 'Commuter: Mobility, rhythm and commuting', in T. Cresswell and P. Merriman (eds) *Geographies of Mobilities: Practices, Spaces, Subjects*, Farnham: Ashgate, pp 189–204.

Edwards, P.N. (2003) 'Infrastructure and modernity: Force, time, and social organization in the history of socio-technical systems', in T.J. Misa, P. Brey, and A. Feenberg (eds) *Modernity and Technology*, Cambridge, MA: MIT Press, pp 185–226.

Elsner, I., Monstadt, J., and Raven, R. (2019) 'Decarbonizing Rotterdam? Energy transitions and the alignment of urban and infrastructural temporalities', *City*, 23(4–5): 646–57.

Engels, J.I. (2022) 'Rhythm analysis: A heuristic tool for historical infrastructure research', *Technology and Culture,*, 63(3): 830–52.

Fitzpatrick, T. (2004) 'Social policy and time', *Time & Society*, 13(2–3): 197–219.

Gallen, B. (2015) 'Night lives: Heterotopia, youth transitions and cultural infrastructure in the urban night', *Urban Studies*, 52(3): 555–70.

Gibert-Flutre, M. (2021) 'Rhythmanalysis: Rethinking the politics of everyday negotiations in ordinary public spaces', *Environment and Planning C: Politics and Space*, 40(1): 279–97.

Glass, M.R., Addie, J.-P.D., and Nelles, J. (2019) 'Regional infrastructures, infrastructural regionalism', *Regional Studies*, 53(12): 1651–6.

Graham, S., and Marvin, S. (2001) *Splintering Urbanism: Networked Infrastructures, Technological Mobilities and the Urban Condition*, New York: Routledge.

Guma, P.K. (2020) 'Incompleteness of urban infrastructures in transition: Scenarios from the mobile age in Nairobi', *Social Studies of Science*, 50(5): 728–750.

Gupta, A. (2018) 'The future in ruins: Thoughts on the temporality of infrastructure', in N. Anand, A. Gupta, and H. Appel (eds) *The Promise of Infrastructure*, Durham, NC: Duke University Press, pp 62–79.

Hadfield, P. (2015) 'The night-time city. Four modes of exclusion: Reflections on the Urban Studies special collection', *Urban Studies*, 52(3): 606–16.

Hall, T. (2010) 'Urban outreach in the polyrhythmic city', in T. Edensor (ed) *Geographies of Rhythm: Nature, Place, Mobilities and Bodies*, Burlington, VA: Ashgate, pp 59–70.

Harvey, D. (2006) 'Space as a keyword', in N. Castree and D. Gregory (eds) *David Harvey: A Critical Reader*, Malden, MA: Blackwell, pp 270–94.

Harvey, D. (2009) *Social Justice and the City* (revised edn), Athens, GA: University of Georgia Press.

Hope, W. (2009) 'Conflicting temporalities: State, nation, economy and democracy under global capitalism', *Time & Society*, 18(1): 62–85.

Jalas, M., Rinkinen, J., and Silvast, A. (2016) 'The rhythms of infrastructure', *Anthropology Today*, 32(4): 16–19.

James, A.C. (2020) 'Don't stand so close to me: Public spaces, behavioral geography, and COVID-19', *Dialogues in Human Geography*, 10(2): 187–90.

Jessop, B. (2004) 'Recent societal and urban change: Principles of periodization and views in the current period', published by the Department of Sociology, Lancaster University. http://www.comp.lancs.ac.uk/sociology/soc133rj.pdf (accessed 12 December 2022).

Jessop, B. (2008) *State Power: A Strategic Relational Approach*, Malden, MA: Polity Press.

Koslov, L. (2019) 'How maps make time', *City*, 23(4–5): 658–72.

Koster, M. (2020) 'An ethnographic perspective on urban planning in Brazil: Temporality, diversity and critical urban theory', *International Journal of Urban and Regional Research*, 44(2): 185–99.

Lefebvre, H. (1991) *The Production of Space*, Oxford: Blackwell.

Lefebvre, H. (2003) *The Urban Revolution*, Minneapolis, MN: University of Minnesota Press.

Lefebvre, H. (2004) *Rhythmanalysis: Space, Time and Everyday Life*, London: Bloomsbury.

Lefebvre, H. (2014) *Critique of Everyday Life: The One Volume Edition*, London: Verso.

Lieberman, E.S. (2001) 'Causal inferences in historical institutional analysis: A specification of periodization strategies', *Comparative Political Studies*, 34(9): 1011–35.

Lyon, D. (2019) *What Is Rhythmanalysis?*, London: Bloomsbury.

McCann, E., and Ward, K.G. (eds) (2011) *Mobile Urbanism: Cities and Policymaking in the Global Age*, Minneapolis, MN: University of Minnesota Press.

Mell, I. (2021) '"But who's going to pay for it?" Contemporary approaches to green infrastructure financing, development and governance in London, UK', *Journal of Environmental Policy and Planning*, 23(5): 628–45.

Meyer, K. (2008) 'Rhythms, streets, cities', in K. Goonewardena, S. Kipfer, R. Milgrom, and C. Schmid (eds) *Space, Difference, Everyday Life: Reading Henri Lefebvre*, New York: Routledge, pp 147–60.

Monstadt, J. (2022) 'Urban and infrastructural rhythms and the politics of temporal alignment', *Journal of Urban Technology*, 29(1): 69–77.

Murphy, R. (2001) 'Nature's temporalities and the manufacture of vulnerability: A study of a sudden disaster with implications for creeping ones', *Time & Society*, 10(2–3): 329–48.

Osborne, P. (1995) *The Politics of Time: Modernity and Avant Garde*, London: Verso.

Osman, R., and Mulíček, O. (2017) 'Urban chronopolis: Ensemble of rhythmized dislocated places', *Geoforum*, 85: 46–57.

Peake, L., Patrick, D., Reddy, R.N., Tanyildiz, S.G., Ruddick, S., and Tchoukaleyska, R. (2018) 'Placing planetary urbanization in other fields of vision', *Environment and Planning D: Society and Space*, 36(3): 374–86.

Plyushteva, A., and Schwanen, T. (2022) ' "We usually have a bit of flood once a week": Conceptualising the infrastructural rhythms of urban floods in Malate, Manila', *Urban Geography*, 44(8): 1565–83.

Pred, A. (1977) 'The choreography of existence: Comments on Hägerstrand's time-geography and its usefulness', *Economic Geography*, 53(2): 207–21.

Raco, M., Durrant, D., and Livingstone, N. (2018) 'Slow cities, urban politics and the temporalities of planning: Lessons from London', *Environment and Planning C: Politics and Space*, 36(7): 1176–94.

Ramakrishnan, K., O'Reilly, K., and Budds, J. (2021) 'Between decay and repair: Embodied experiences of infrastructure's materiality', *Environment and Planning E: Nature and Space*, 4(3): 669–73.

Reid-Musson, E. (2018) 'Intersectional rhythmanalysis: Power, rhythm, and everyday life', *Progress in Human Geography*, 42(6): 881–97.

Robin, E., and Nkula-Wenz, L. (2021) 'Beyond the success/failure of travelling urban models: Exploring the politics of time and performance in Cape Town's East City', *Environment and Planning C: Politics and Space*, 39(6): 1252–73.

Salter, M.B. (2008) 'The global airport: Managing space, speed, and security', in M.B. Salter (ed) *Politics at the Airport*, Minneapolis, MN: University of Minnesota Press, pp 1–28.

Schmid, C. (2022) *Henri Lefebvre and the Theory of the Production of Space*, London: Verso.

Shaw, R. (2018) *The Nocturnal City*, New York: Routledge.

Sheller, M. (2018) *Mobility Justice: The Politics of Movement in an Age of Extremes*, London: Verso.

Silvast, A., Jalas, M., and Rinkinen, J. (2019) 'Energy governance, risk and temporality: The construction of energy time through law and regulation', in S.M. Beynon-Jones and E. Grabham (eds) *Law and Time*, New York: Routledge, pp 212–28.

Smith, R.J., and Hetherington, K. (2013) 'Urban rhythms: Mobilities, space and interaction in the contemporary city', *The Sociological Review*, 61(S1): 4–16.

Stamatopoulou-Robbins, S.C. (2021) 'Failure to build: Sewage and the choppy temporality of infrastructure in Palestine', *Environment and Planning E: Nature and Space*, 4(1): 28–42.

Walker, G. (2021) *Energy and Rhythm: Rhythmanalysis for a Low Carbon Future*, London: Rowman & Littlefield.

Walker, G., Booker, D., and Young, P.J. (2022) 'Breathing in the polyrhythmic city: A spatiotemporal, rhythmanalytic account of urban air pollution and its inequalities', *Environment and Planning C: Politics and Space*, 40(3): 572–91.

Wallis, G.W. (1970) 'Chronopolitics: The impact of time perspectives on the dynamics of change', *Social Forces,* 49(1): 102–8.

Whiteford, L.M. (2020) 'A room with a view: Observations from two pandemics', *Anthropology Now*, 12(1): 7–10.

Wishart, D. (2004) 'Period and region', *Progress in Human Geography*, 28(3): 305–19.

Wood, A. (2015) 'Multiple temporalities of policy circulation: Gradual, repetitive and delayed processes of BRT adoption in South African cities', *International Journal of Urban and Regional Research*, 39(3): 568–80.

PART I

Infrastructural Pasts, Presents, and Futures

3

Usable Infrastructure Pasts: Mobilizing History for Urban Technology Futures

Timothy Moss

Introduction

If you stroll through the central districts of Berlin, you are bound to encounter, sooner or later, a hand-operated street water pump. Many of these boast an ornate design and clearly date back to the nineteenth century. You would be forgiven for assuming that these street pumps are quaint anachronisms, retained by some curious accident and cultivated today as musealized symbols of a bygone era. But you would be wrong. Berlin's street water pumps did not lose their functionality with the spread of piped water supply in the late nineteenth century. They just began to serve other purposes. Initially, they covered for those households unable to afford water in their own homes and helped put out fires and water draught animals. Then, they proved a life-saving back-up during crises of wartime destruction and political blockade. In the post-war era, they were used to wash cars parked along the street. They have always been a delight for children, playfully designing their own water infrastructures in miniature. Today, Berliners are being called upon to use street pumps to water nearby trees suffering from climate-induced drought. Independent of both the water mains and the electricity grid, these water pumps are kept operational primarily as a valued emergency infrastructure. So, this apparently redundant piece of urban technology has proven remarkably adaptable to changing circumstances (Figures 3.1–3.3 illustrate the diverse uses of Berlin's street water pumps over time). Although itself physically and spatially fixed, its socio-material entanglements have shifted repeatedly over time. Berliners can be glad that these pumps were not removed when their original purpose was fulfilled.

Figure 3.1: Berliners fetch water from a public pump during the general strike opposing the Kapp Putsch, March 1920

Source: Bundesarchiv, Bild 183-R11931/CC-BY-SA 3.0

The repurposing of existing infrastructure is just one instance of making the past usable. The multiple kinds of usable pasts and the various means of making pasts usable for 'progressive infrastructure futures' (Addie, Glass, Nelles, and Marino, this volume) are the subject of this chapter. The purpose of the piece is threefold (1) to define and conceptualize what usable pasts are, based on a wide-ranging literature review; (2) to identify and categorize diverse types of usable infrastructure pasts, illustrated with examples from Berlin's rich history of urban technology; and (3) to explore and suggest ways of mobilizing usable pasts to generative effect today, drawing on the author's own interactions with various publics. Before addressing each of these issues in turn, two common misapprehensions need confronting from the start: that the past is a shackle on the future and that historians should desist from speaking to today's challenges.

It may seem odd – perverse, even – to assert that the past can be a source of inspiration for the future. Past events and the modes of human existence they have engendered are undeniably responsible for the mess we are in. This is nowhere more true than for the infrastructures that provide us with energy, water, mobility, and communication and that dispose of our wastes. These complex socio-technical networks have enabled high living standards with modern comforts in many parts of the world, but at a massive cost to environmental resources, social justice, and the global climate (Melosi,

Figure 3.2: Transport officials cool off during a heatwave, Berlin, 1931

Source: Bundesarchiv, Bild 183-2004-0729-500/CC-BY-SA 3.0

2000; van Laak, 2001; Swyngedouw, 2015). Herein lies the paradox of infrastructure: it is a bearer of both enrichment and deprivation (see Graham and Marvin, 2001; Anand et al, 2018). This poses a particular challenge for enrolling infrastructure histories. Continuing along existing trajectories is clearly not an option if infrastructures are themselves part of the problem. If the world is to inherit a more liveable future (for humans and non-humans) then the infrastructures we know will need to be substantially reconfigured: in institutional and social, as well as technological and material, terms. From this transformative perspective, looking to history for inspiration cannot mean reaffirming continuities or extrapolating from past phenomena but must involve a different kind of engagement across temporalities that uses history as an experiential resource to remind, contextualize, reflect, compare, provoke, and excite.

Figure 3.3: A street pump for watering trees, Berlin, 2021

Source: Timothy Moss

This is where many historians get uncomfortable. The disciplinary mantra to understand the past 'on its own terms' sits uneasily alongside the popular exhortation to 'learn from the past' (Huyssen, 2003; Asdal, 2012; Morin, 2013). Despite the universal claim that history matters, historians are often sceptical of engaging with policymakers and the public over contemporary challenges (Tosh, 2008: 17–19). Few actively strive to render their historical knowledge relevant to modern-day concerns. There are plenty of reasons for this reticence. Historians are justifiably worried about 'presentist' takes on history, involving back-tracing the present; about historical selectiveness, cherry-picking convenient pasts and ignoring uncomfortable ones; about processes of legitimization, using history to justify presents and futures; and about instrumentalism, enrolling historians in acts of historical legitimization.

Yet, in Frank Uekötter's words, '[t]he past lives on in words and laws, in institutions and artefacts, in networks and taboos, and we ignore this legacy at our peril' (2020: 617, author's translation). Intriguingly, historians of technology (and the environment) have been pioneers in exploring ways of drawing contemporary value from the past. Joel Tarr and colleagues have been advocating 'applied history' since the 1970s, explaining how history matters to technology and environmental policy (Stearns, 1982; König, 1984; Hirsh, 2011; Högselius et al, 2016). Many proponents of 'public history' (Tosh, 2008; Guldi and Armitage, 2014), engaging wider communities beyond academia, are 'enviro-technical' historians (for example Radkau, 2008; van der Vleuten et al, 2017; Kirchhof and Meyer, 2021). The concept of 'usable pasts' is the latest in this line of historical research generating productive forms of remembering to inspire change (Huyssen, 2003; Hammersley, 2004; Morin, 2013), recently applied to histories of technology (Schipper et al, 2020; Moss and Weber, 2021).

The aspiration of this chapter is to unpack and systematize knowledge on usable pasts in general, and urban infrastructures in particular, taking up the challenge and acknowledging the risks outlined earlier. The target audience is deliberately diverse. Firstly, I aim to inspire infrastructure scholars of the present to appreciate how the past can provide pointers for their own work beyond hegemonic concepts of path dependence or socio-technical transitions. Secondly, the piece is written for historians of technology and the environment, demonstrating how their research can be made relevant to present-day concerns. Finally, on a broader level, I hope to appeal to practitioners of infrastructure policy, management, and practice who are seeking guidance and inspiration in an uncertain world.

Comprehending usable pasts

Pasts have always been used – and abused. Justifying present actions or future visions through a particular narrative of the past is a familiar repertoire of politicians, business leaders, and opinion makers (Huyssen, 2003: 2). History itself is a form of using pasts, interpreting past events through the scientific methods of the discipline. So, 'usable pasts' may be a rather unfamiliar term, but it is founded on age-old practices. In this chapter, I am interested less in how pasts have been enrolled to justify political agendas in earlier times ('used pasts') than in how they can be rendered valuable to the future ('usable pasts'). Pasts that can be helpful in navigating present-day challenges in ways that are conducive to liveable planetary futures are what is at stake here. First, though, we need a grounded understanding of the usability of the past per se and the value of certain pasts in pursuing particular ends.

The term 'usable past' dates to the early twentieth century, when it was first used in the history of American literature to encourage scholars to revisit past works as sources of inspiration for future writing (Hammersley, 2004: 25; Schipper et al, 2020: 4). It subsequently became associated with the social history of the 1970s and 1980s as a means of challenging master narratives of US history (Morin, 2013: 4). Since the 2000s, 'usable pasts' have been explicitly enrolled to investigate topics ranging from urban memory (Huyssen, 2003), cultural memory (Olick, 2007), and life stories (Aarelaid-Tart, 2010) to transportation (Divall, 2010), prisons (Morin, 2013), and public works agencies (Toussaint, 2016). In applying the lens of 'usable pasts', all these works share a common objective: to challenge popular and convenient histories that legitimize particular presents and futures and to reveal past phenomena capable of inspiring novel and instructive perspectives about the past, the present, and the future (Hammersley, 2004: 24). Put in a nutshell by historian Tony Judt, 'we must learn how to make a better world out of usable pasts rather than dreaming of infinite futures'.[1] Usable pasts, from this perspective, represent a productive form of remembering (Huyssen, 2003). While some authors use the term 'usable pasts' uncritically as a catchphrase (for instance Moeller, 1996), others reflect on its potential pitfalls, echoing some of the concerns voiced by historians wary of speaking to the present. Karen Morin warns about the need to be reflexive, positional, and accountable in discussing usable pasts (2013: 5). She calls on historians to be candid about the presentism of their own accounts, acknowledge diverse interpretations of the past, and attend to the risks of instrumentalization. When considering usable pasts, we should continuously be asking ourselves: 'usable by whom, and for what end or purpose?' (Morin, 2013: 4).

What is striking about the diffuse literature referring explicitly to usable pasts is the absence of either a concise definition of usable pasts or a systematic elaboration of what forms they can take. It is as if the notion is self-explanatory. However, if usable pasts are to develop from a clarion call for historians into a tool for transformative analysis and action, they need grounding in broader debates about the relationship between the past, the present, and the future. In the remainder of this section, I conceptualize 'usable pasts' with reference to pertinent literature from the fields of applied and public history, history of technology, anthropology, and science and technology studies (STS). In doing so, I elaborate the specific relevance of usable pasts to infrastructure studies and develop my own definition of usable pasts, tailored to urban technology.

If the term 'usable pasts' suffers from disparate and unreflective use, the ideas underpinning it enjoy wide-ranging and long-standing advocacy. High-profile books of general history, such as John Tosh's *Why History Matters* (2008) and Jo Guldi and David Armitage's *The History Manifesto* (2014), are testament to a recent upsurge of interest in explicating the value of history to present-day challenges. These and other works deplore the boundaries being drawn between the past and the present by a popular culture that prefers to treat the past as something to celebrate and idealize, rather than to provoke and inspire. They criticize how history is restricted in political discourse to a '"mise-en-scène" of modernity' (Huyssen, 2003: 1) and in the media to nostalgia-tinged heritage consumerism (Tosh, 2008: 11–12). Bringing the past and the present into dialogue is fundamental to their stance, for, in the words of Andreas Huyssen, '[w]e need both the past and future to articulate our political, social, and cultural dissatisfactions with the present state of the world' (2003: 6). Guldi and Armitage reassure us that '[t]hinking about the past in order to see the future is not actually so difficult' (2014: 4). If we want it to, these historians argue, the past can be used to situate the present in long-term processes of change, reveal past choices and thus other possibilities for the future, challenge false myths and apparently immutable assumptions, highlight the transformative power of contingency, and unpack tensions between the enduring and the transient (Tosh, 2008; Guldi and Armitage, 2014). This 'oblique illumination of the present' (Tosh, 2008: 28) enlarges our awareness of contemporary possibilities by evaluating our world from other positions in time.

Scholars of infrastructure have long appreciated the significance of the past in shaping the socio-technical systems we know today. While many general historians are reluctant to turn their knowledge to public account (Tosh, 2008: 17) or to engage with debates on 'grand challenges' (Heßler and Weber, 2019: 3), historians of technology have been far more active in rendering their work relevant to the present day. Joel Tarr pioneered an applied history of technology in the 1970s, encouraging professional audiences beyond the academy to appreciate the contexts of their action and how these can change, using history as analogy, trend assessment, and perspective.[2] He and colleagues have taken their knowledge into town halls and courtrooms to provide historical heft to debates on technology policy and cases of environmental pollution (Melosi, 2000). They have also been instrumental in integrating a socially responsible history of technology into the education of engineers, especially in the US and Germany (Moss and Weber, 2021). Today, many historians of technology openly aspire to make their work more policy-oriented, drawing the attention of practitioners to path dependencies, historical correctives of dominant narratives, process evolution, and discarded alternatives (Hirsh, 2011: 8–13; van der Vleuten et al, 2017; Heßler and Weber, 2019: 4–7). In doing so, they challenge the deep-founded bias of technology science and policy towards the new, revealing how fixation on innovation generates selective timelines of technological 'victors' (König, 1984: 249) combined with ignorance about the value of old or alternative technologies (van Laak, 2001; Edgerton, 2007; Weber and Krebs, 2021) or the many failures of the new (Edgerton, 2007).

Looking beyond the discipline of history, social scientists have long been appreciative of the formative force of past events, processes, and structures on contemporary infrastructures. Transitions research has drawn on multiple historical case studies of past energy, water, and transportation transitions to develop an analytical framework – the Multi-Level Perspective – to explain how socio-technical change happens and can be made to happen (Sovacool and Geels, 2016; Gismondi, 2018). Energy economists and geographers draw on historical analysis to reveal similarities and differences between past and current energy transitions, for instance regarding their speed and duration, the role of path dependence, social injustices, and the strategies of incumbents (Fouquet and Pearson, 2012; Pearson and Foxon, 2012; Barry, 2013). Anthropologists of infrastructure tell their narratives in historically sensitive ways, revealing how infrastructures connect across different eras (for instance, colonial and postcolonial), mediating historical processes and imagery of diverse pasts (von Schnitzler, 2016; Anand et al, 2018). In the words of STS scholar Sheila Jasanoff, '[t]he past is prologue, but it is also a site of memory excavated and reinterpreted in the light of a society's understanding of the present and its hopes for what lies ahead' (2015: 31). How infrastructures shape these futures – whether through legacies from the past or promises of betterment – and thereby span multiple temporalities is central to much of this scholarship (Anand et al, 2018; Mitchell, 2020).

Building on this discussion of relevant strands of literature, I propose the following definition of 'usable pasts' and what they can mean for the field of urban infrastructure: 'usable pasts' refer to the enrolment and critical appraisal of knowledge about the past by researchers, policymakers, opinion makers, and citizens to help address current and future challenges. Applied to urban technology, making pasts usable involves exploring infrastructural change over time, drawing on the past as an experiential resource (for comparison, as a corrective, for inspiration), embracing multiple histories of a city's infrastructure, acknowledging the coexistence of old and new technologies and practices, and revealing path dependencies as well as alternative trajectories in the socio-technical constitution of the urban.

These statements are crafted to capture the meaning and value of usable infrastructure pasts, but they say little about the modes through which pasts are made usable. Here, the work of Kristin Asdal on the future of the past in STS is inspirational. In arguing for greater interaction between historians of science and STS scholars, she makes the provocative case for using actor-network theory (ANT) as 'a historicizing tool'. As she points out, the focus of ANT on processes of making and remaking socio-technical worlds has, to date, privileged the present and largely discarded historical factors (Asdal, 2012), doing scant justice to the *longue durée* (Jasanoff, 2015). Asdal argues, though, that by *not* treating history as context (that is, something external), ANT has the potential to foreground the background, thus rendering historical events integral to any contemporary situation. In this way, STS-inspired research can learn to engage more with how the past manifests itself in an actor-network, while historians can benefit from reading the past in new, socio-material ways, thereby 'undisciplining history' (Asdal, 2012: 397).

This temporal twist to relational thinking resonates with recent ventures to historicize the study of socio-technical configurations as assemblages. The assemblage concept, drawing on ANT, envisages the reconfiguration of infrastructure as an ongoing process of forming and sustaining associations between diverse components (Anderson et al, 2012). Assemblage thinking, like ANT, has generally been used to reveal such associations in the here and now, but its relational and dynamic understanding of (socio)materiality is revelatory from a temporal perspective for providing, in the words of Bakker and Bridge, 'a way to unpack apparent permanencies and stabilities' (2006: 16). Inspired by Stephen Collier's call for a 'historicity of assemblages' (2011: 28), I applied an assemblage approach to my study of Berlin's infrastructure history (Moss, 2020). The 'historicized assemblages' developed in that work are formative behind the ambition of this chapter to explore how traces of the past can be enrolled into contemporary socio-technical configurations to generative effect. In the following section I will elaborate, with illustrations from my research on Berlin, diverse dimensions of usable pasts through this lens of 'historicized assemblages'.

Identifying usable infrastructure pasts

If usable pasts can be so valuable, which pasts are usable for progressive infrastructure futures? Where do we look for such usable pasts? How do we 'distinguish usable pasts from disposable pasts' (Huyssen, 2003: 29)? There are several hints in the literature cited earlier, but no systematization or categorization of usable pasts can be found there. In this section, I propose a typology of usable pasts comprising five categories. I justify their selection and explain their value with reference to existing research and illustrate them with examples from my book on Berlin (Moss, 2020).[3] For Berlin's infrastructure history is littered with lessons – positive and negative – on how to derive utility from an urban utility. Historical knowledge revealed from these five categories cannot provide ready-made solutions, but it can help scholars and practitioners rethink the present, questioning established trajectories, appreciating the political agency of infrastructure, and seeking inspiration from hidden histories of infrastructure.

Embedded pasts

Embedded pasts are legacies of established structures and practices that can enable or constrain options for the future. The strong path dependence of infrastructure systems has been a constant in the history of technology and STS, from early research on large technical systems (Hughes, 1983; Summerton, 1994) to contemporary scholarship on sustainability transitions (Geels, 2002). Past decisions, structures, or circumstances have given rise to infrastructural configurations today that are often hard to change (Melosi, 2000). Infrastructural obduracy can express itself in material form, for instance in Berlin's dependence on fossil fuels for electricity generation as a legacy of energy security concerns during the Cold War (Moss, 2020: 318–19). But it can also be social, as reflected in the persistence of the build-and-supply logic of Berlin's energy and water policy since 1920 across hugely diverse political regimes.

Identifying which components of an infrastructural configuration have a propensity towards path dependence and within which socio-technical assemblage is essential to pinpointing openings for transformation. For historical analysis can reveal that not all components of a socio-technical assemblage prove equally obdurate over time (Moss, 2020: 306–10). It can also show how path dependence can be more assumed than real (Weber, 2019; Moss and Weber, 2021). When Berlin was politically divided after 1948–9, commentators expected the subsequent separation of the electricity, gas, water, and wastewater networks and their reorientation around the new political geographies of East and West Berlin to make any future reunification of these technical networks highly problematic. In fact, the reconnection of the networks after reunification in 1989 proved far more straightforward than the organizational integration of Berlin's utilities (Moss, 2020: 263–4). The power relations embedded in infrastructures can prove more obdurate than physical structures (Engels, 2020: 73). A good example of this is the way infrastructures can function as an 'archive' of colonial capitalism (Jabary Salamanca and Silver, 2022: 122).

Helping prevent such legacies becoming path dependencies is an important objective for usable pasts. For path dependence, recent research teaches us, is not an *a priori* condition of infrastructure systems, but something actively cultivated by system builders and sustained by non-human elements of the assemblage (Engels, 2020: 74). Consequently, it can be countered more readily than is often assumed. The considerable effort put into keeping existing infrastructures going (such as through repair) could be redirected into undoing obduracy (Hommels, 2005) and reconfiguring them to meet new challenges. To this end, Christopher Henke and Benjamin Sims call for a 'distinction between repair as maintenance and repair as transformation' (2020: 131). Recent acknowledgement that the trajectories of infrastructures are far less linear and their histories more prone to disruption and deviation than previously believed also provides encouragement to explore different pathways (Hasenöhrl and Meyer, 2020; Weber and Krebs, 2021; Monstadt, 2022). The notion advanced originally by scholarship on Large Technical

Systems (LTS) that infrastructures follow a common developmental path, from invention and expansion to saturation and even decline (Hughes, 1983; Sovacool et al, 2018), still retains some heuristic value, but it should not blind us to the very different trajectories encountered in practice (Carse and Kneas, 2019).

Adapted pasts

Adapted pasts draw attention to past processes of reconfiguring infrastructures to meet changing circumstances and the openings these imply for the future. For if infrastructures are less obdurate than meets the eye, then adaptation of the socio-technical assemblage – whether deliberate or not – becomes a core characteristic that offers traction for transformative agendas. Growing acknowledgement of the non-linearity of infrastructure trajectories makes critical junctures in their development increasingly significant (Arranz, 2017; Hasenöhrl and Meyer, 2020). Revisiting key decision-making processes or disruptive events in the past can help broaden modern-day perspectives by unpacking debate about the options, risks, and opportunities at moments in time that were to prove critically important. Non-linearity also means leaving behind simplistic notions of one technology or practice being replaced by another without trace.

There is a rich literature today within the history of technology as well as transitions studies on the coexistence of old and new technologies in infrastructure systems (Edgerton, 2007; Geels et al, 2015; Weber and Krebs, 2021). Reinhard Kosseleck's thinking around 'sediments of time' (2018: 6) has been instructive in conceptualizing the layering of the old and the new in constantly changing socio-technical configurations (Weber, 2019; Monstadt, 2022). This work is helping to demystify fascination with (technological) innovation and draw attention to the adaptive work performed by existing infrastructures (Edgerton, 2007). The humble street water pump in Berlin, encountered in the introduction, is a powerful illustration, but examples of wider prevalence are legion. Even the most future-oriented infrastructures are deeply engrained with the past. Smart grids, for instance, draw on the existing power grid, earlier strategies of infrastructure roll-out, past imaginaries of progress through technology, and established norms of how users are expected to respond (Engels, 2020: 85). Understanding these pasts becomes critical for successful socio-technical change.

Following historical instances of repurposing infrastructures is a productive way of rendering such pasts usable. Berlin possesses a massive natural underground gas storage facility that was originally constructed to provide greater energy security for West Berlin during the Cold War (on the following, see Moss, 2020: 241–3, 280). By the time it became operative the Berlin Wall had fallen, and the facility quickly lost its initial purpose. For several years after 1990 it was used to offset seasonal variations in gas prices, enabling cheaper gas to be bought in the summer and stored for winter use. By 2019, with gas prices no longer so volatile, it was being dismantled while options were being pursued for the storage facility to be repurposed as part of a power-to-gas strategy, converting surplus wind- and solar-powered electricity into gas and storing this for use during periods of low renewable energy inputs. This was the status when Russia invaded Ukraine in 2022, revealing suddenly how critical such a redundant storage facility could be to sustain energy security in an unanticipated geopolitical crisis.

Parallel pasts

Parallel pasts refer to coexisting infrastructures that often go unseen yet are revealing of alternative histories. They direct our gaze beyond the hegemonic large-scale technical networks generally associated with infrastructure systems to the small-scale, decentred, and informal technologies and socio-technical practices that can be just as important in providing water or energy services. To seek inspiration from the marginal (following Anna Tsing) calls for 'minor' histories alongside the major narratives. Historical sensitivity is important here to debunk a widespread assumption that alternative technologies emerged only with the environmentalist movement in the 1970s. Historians of technology are today revealing fascinating long-term histories of renewable energies (Hasenöhrl and Meyer, 2020: 298) and 'pockets of persistence' in urban mobility (Schipper et al, 2020: 4) that can be highly instructive for contemporary debates about the interdependence between small-scale and large-scale infrastructures. The layering of the small and the large is proving just as significant as the layering of the old and the new (Edgerton, 2007: xiv) and history can provide pointers for the future here, too.

Exploring modes of infrastructural hybridization in the past is an instructive entry point (Edgerton, 2007: xii; Furlong, 2014). One example from Berlin's history is the coexistence of decentralized rainwater percolation alongside the centralized rain- and wastewater sewer network. Although Berlin's radial sewer system has dominated solutions for wastewater (and rainwater) disposal for 150 years, the system has accommodated artificial groundwater replenishment since 1913 and localized rainwater retention since the 1980s (Moss, 2020: 272). The durable coexistence of district heating alongside coal- and, later, gas-fired heating in the city is another such instance (Moss, 2020: 309). Importantly, these examples dispel notions of perceived incompatibility between large technical systems and small-scale technologies. Revealing the coexistence of hegemonic and vernacular infrastructures is a particular strength of scholarship on colonialism and the global South's 'othered' histories (van der Straeten and Hasenöhrl, 2016). Parallel pasts are not restricted to technologies but can also relate to actors. Scholars are analysing histories of popular and mass movements that targeted urban infrastructures (Gismondi, 2018), for instance comparing protests against nuclear power plants in the 1970s with ones against wind farms since the 2010s (Hasenöhrl and Meyer, 2020). This can encourage us to look beyond entrenched infrastructural discourses and derive novel insight from decentred ideas and practices that often have equally long histories.

Futured pasts

Futured pasts are socio-technical imaginaries from the past that can continue to frame infrastructure presents and futures. Socio-technical imaginaries, as Sheila Jasanoff points out, always link past and future times in their representation of alternative futures (2015: 35). Infrastructures have been described, indeed, as 'the material manifestation of a "past future"' (van Laak, 2001: 368, author's translation). The value of studying earlier imaginaries lies in the ability to unpack the past promises of infrastructure (Anand et al, 2018) and discover what happened to them and why, and what legacies they have left behind (Mahony, 2018: 4). For, as research tells us, history is littered with examples of infrastructure projects that never materialized, many of which have nevertheless had a lasting impact on socio-material worlds (van Laak, 2001; Carse and Kneas, 2019: 15–16).

Following the creation of Greater Berlin in 1920, generating fantastic predictions of a population reaching 7.5 million by 1954, the city's water utility planned a grand water transfer scheme enrolling many distant lakes and rivers to quench the anticipated thirst of this imagined world metropolis (Moss, 2020: 57). The Depression of 1929–32 put an end to these plans, and the division of the city in 1948–9 made them politically unfeasible. However, reunification in 1990 launched a new sense of development euphoria that played out in the emergence of very similar ideas to meet the expected rapid growth in Berlin's water consumption, albeit without a nod to the historical precedent. Once again, the plans were soon dropped as the urban economy took a nosedive and consumption curves defied expectations of growth in the 1990s (Moss, 2020: 280–3). So, tracing futured pasts can help identify how systems designed for generations to come became obsolete over time, but also how stopgap interventions developed a degree of permanence far beyond original intentions. A hire-purchase scheme for electrical appliances, called Elektrissima, was introduced by Berlin's power utility Bewag in 1926 as a temporary measure to boost electrification of households (Moss, 2020: 84–5, 308). Within a few years it had been adapted to promote the night-time use of electricity, via storage heaters, as part of a strategy to balance supply and demand. During the Depression, Elektrissima was used to shore up electricity sales to households to compensate for the massive drop in industrial use. After the war it was rejuvenated to promote West Berlin as a showcase of electricity-powered consumerism in competition with the East. As the city's political economy changed, so too did the rationale of this instrument, enabling it to span multiple eras.

Discarded pasts

Discarded pasts are socio-technical trajectories that are abandoned or forgotten yet hold value in their re-emergence or rehabilitation. The history of technology is full of examples of technologies that appeared outdated or inferior at one time but were reactivated later when circumstances changed (König, 1984; Schipper et al, 2020). Yet contemporaries are often reluctant to acknowledge the historical roots of these technologies, particularly when they are associated in the collective memory with crisis situations, such as a wartime economy, or uncomfortable pasts, such as a dictatorial regime (Moss, 2016; 2020: 120–4, 319).

In Berlin today, the use of sewage gas as a vehicle fuel is being heralded as an innovative contribution to making wastewater utilities greener, while energy utilities are exploring novel ways of flexibilizing electricity supply via energy storage technologies. Similarly, pilot projects are being launched to explore the opportunities for water reuse, using treated wastewater for irrigation and nutrient recycling. Yet no reference is ever made to the fact that all these techniques – albeit in less sophisticated forms – were practised successfully in Berlin during the 1920s and 1930s. Their pasts have been forgotten if they failed to contribute to the master infrastructure narrative or deliberately discarded if they were deemed too closely associated with Nazi or state socialist regimes. Such instances of collective amnesia, or even agnosis, do not apply to technologies alone. Past organizational structures and movements, such as the municipal ownership of infrastructure in the UK (Leopold and McDonald, 2012), can alert us to the need to be open to deviant and discarded configurations beyond the dominant socio-technical system of today. Dismissing alternative pathways as aberrations can deprive us of insight into the culture and politics of transitions. Generating awareness of alternatives is a principal public function of historical debate (Tosh, 2008: 138).

Mobilizing usable infrastructure pasts

How can infrastructure pasts be made usable? What approaches lend themselves to mobilizing histories for the common good? In this final section I propose three modes of mobilization for usable pasts. These I term 're-presenting', 're-membering', and 're-iterating'. They portray three registers for engaging with usable pasts: one discursive, one relational, and one interventionist.

Re-presenting pasts

The first mode involves scrutinizing the many ways in which narratives of the past are, and have been, enrolled to justify ideas and actions in the present and visions for the future. This is about how particular pasts get presented in particular ways again and again (hence re-presenting). As David Edgerton argues, it is often the same kinds of narratives that are retold, reflecting a startling lack of originality in our approach to challenges (2007: xvi). Making pasts usable here means critiquing and correcting historical accounts that are – by accident or design – overly selective, incomplete, or inaccurate. Examples from Berlin's infrastructure history that I have highlighted in earlier work include the repression of memory about reuse technologies of the 1930s and the celebration of municipal enterprises of the Weimar era by West Berlin historians in the 1950s (Moss, 2016; 2020: 61, 134). These two cases draw attention to the value to be derived from challenging collective amnesia over pasts we are embarrassed by and querying analogies that are all too readily drawn from pasts we are proud of. Analogies are not in themselves problematic. They only become so if they are used to suggest complete congruence between the past and the present, rather than to elicit an open-ended comparison (Tosh, 2008: 68–72).

Here, a further meaning of 're-presenting' pasts becomes apparent, as making present (Huyssen, 2003: 10). A fine example of this is the struggle for legitimacy between a private water company and a municipal platform over the future of water services in Barcelona, in which each side is mobilizing its own historical memories to resist or promote 'new municipalism' (Poportan and Ungureanu, 2022). In Berlin, different pasts are being enrolled over the issue of problematically high groundwater levels in low-lying areas of the city. While hydrogeologists are using their monitoring data to argue that groundwater levels in Berlin have a long history of fluctuation, reflecting shifting water consumption patterns, developers and planners prefer to downplay the risks of building in flood-prone areas, dismissing past experiences as exceptional (Moss, 2020: 164–6, 283–4). The many re-presentations of past urban infrastructures need acknowledging and investigating as a preliminary to making them usable.

At the same time, we must speak out when analogies are not being drawn from the past, whether wittingly or unwittingly, as Schipper and colleagues do regarding urban mobility pathways (Schipper et al, 2020: 10). A case in point is the privatization of Berlin's electricity utility Bewag in 1997, which bore an uncanny resemblance to its previous privatization in 1931 in terms of the motives, political process, organizational structures, and impacts on urban governance (Moss, 2020: 92–6, 285–6, 319). Had the hard lessons of 1931 been heeded in 1997, much of the subsequent frustration about loss of municipal influence over the city's energy transition today could have been avoided. The Bewag experience is powerfully illustrative of the failure to seek analogies in the past, underlining how often learning from history does not happen. This first mode of mobilization – targeting used pasts of earlier times – is recommended as an entry point for making pasts usable today.

Re-membering pasts

The second mode of mobilizing usable pasts promotes socio-material learning through history. It encourages us to look beyond just the technical or the social in seeking inspiration for infrastructure futures. I draw here on Bjørnar Olsen's notion of 're-membering things', advancing greater appreciation of things in social and humanist discourses (2003: 100), but I give this a historical twist by highlighting how material pasts become part of contemporary socio-technical assemblages. As Frank Trentmann teasingly remarks, '[t]he material world has too much history in it to leave it to the social sciences' (2009: 307). He argues that the material should be recognized as a 'conduit of political processes that helps shape (and not just reflect) political identities, concerns, and fields of action' (Trentmann, 2009: 307; see also Otter, 2010).

Re-membering infrastructure pasts means, from this perspective, revealing how pasts can be rendered usable through socio-technical assemblages and especially through material things in such assemblages (see Ekman, this volume). The functional flexibility of the physically static street water pump in Berlin is an illustrative case in point. The original socio-material assemblage around water supply that prompted its construction in the nineteenth century has been rearranged to accommodate a succession of emergent components, ranging from thirsty animals, wartime damage, and dirty cars to playful children and strategies of climate adaptation. Repurposing is a form of re-membering. So is politicizing material history. Hitler's desire that Berlin should source its drinking water from distant mountain springs, rather than local groundwater resources, cannot be adequately understood without reference to his idealization of Alpine landscapes and his loathing of the 'degenerate' metropolis (Moss, 2020: 130–2). Making productive forms of re-membering visible through historical research in this way is essential to broaden perspectives beyond those viewed through either a techno-managerial or a social constructivist lens.

Re-iterating pasts

The third mode is about historians facilitating collective learning processes around (infrastructure) pasts. This involves going beyond traditional forms of disseminating historical knowledge in written form to engage more openly and interactively with stakeholders, whether politicians, business leaders, civil society organizations, or individual citizens. Continuous processes of iteration (hence: re-iterating) between historians and non-historians about the past are key to generating wider appreciation of the productive capacity of history. The Dutch Public Works and Water Management Agency, Rijkswaterstaat, has been exemplary in cultivating interactive forms of corporate history-learning (Toussaint, 2016). Having set up its own history unit in 1981, the organization has applied a variety of techniques to explore its usable past, ranging from storytelling in teams, case studies of past decision-making processes, and serious gaming around past critical events to debating historical contexts of action. The result, in Bert Toussaint's analysis, has been to generate both contextual learning, appreciating policy processes in the longer term, and behavioural learning, developing cognitive flexibility through knowledge of corporate history.

I have explored diverse ways of engaging with various publics to draw out the contemporary relevance of my research on Berlin's infrastructure history (on the following, see Moss, 2021). Firstly, a series of short films, commissioned and produced by the Gerda Henkel Foundation, captures my encounters with technology icons, historical documents, and local stakeholders of urban infrastructure. Entitled *Invisible Berlin*, the series seeks to reveal the hidden significance of the city's underground history for its present and future.[4] Secondly, a 'walkshop' (or walking workshop) was held along the border between pre-1920 Berlin and Charlottenburg, passing infrastructures old and new and discussing how they embody and symbolize Berlin's infrastructure politics across time. This live event has been developed into an online version featuring aerial and 360-degree photography, historical photos, and an audio guide.[5] If these two activities address the interested public, the third was targeted at professionals. A stakeholder workshop, involving active and retired local politicians, utility managers, infrastructure planners, and civil society representatives, was held in 2018 to discuss the implications of historical knowledge for the future of Berlin's energy and water infrastructures. Deliberately seeking out usable pasts, the event proved inspirational in thinking through challenges common to the city across the past century. It also revealed, intriguingly, a reluctance to engage with uncomfortable infrastructure pasts from periods of National Socialism and state socialism. This experience underlines the arduous nature of the task in hand, requiring sensitive re-iteration.

Conclusion

While scholars and policymakers alike brood over the opportunities and uncertainties surrounding infrastructure futures, the past provides a rich source of inspiration that is waiting to be tapped. The 'temporal turn' in critical infrastructure studies advocated by this book needs to include new and different histories of urban technology. This chapter has applied the concept of 'usable pasts' to uncover what kinds of history can be used productively and how infrastructure pasts could be rendered valuable in addressing today's global challenges. It began by explicating the meaning of usable pasts, a term widely used but rarely specified or theorized. Drawing on a wider literature on applied and public history, history of technology, anthropology, and STS, I developed a definition of the term, refined for urban technology, and an original approach to historicizing socio-technical assemblages. This approach, together with existing literature and my own research on Berlin, informed the design of a novel typology characterizing five categories of usable past: embedded, adapted, parallel, futured, and discarded. These categories have been designed to direct historians (and others) on where to look for potential usable pasts. To render these usable pasts visible and productive I advocated a three-stage process. The first, 're-presenting', is about scrutinizing and critiquing dominant historical narratives and thus opening the terrain to other people, technologies, ideologies, and practices. The second stage, 're-membering', broadens the perspective further by exploring entanglements of the social and the material over time, revealing lessons in the dynamics of socio-technical assemblages. The third stage, 're-iterating', proposes methods of communicating history's value for contemporary challenges to publics within and beyond the academy.

Throughout this chapter, I have emphasized that deriving value from history is not a straightforward process. If a usable past is a productive form of remembering (Huyssen, 2003), then we must acknowledge that we produce histories, rather than reflect some pre-existing condition of the past. There follow, from this, obligations to be reflexive, positional, and accountable in researching and narrating history, to consider diverse and contested interpretations of the past, and to appreciate different ways of seeing the past from the present, whether instrumental, functional, or causal (Olick, 2007). We should use the past not to draw hard lessons for the present, and certainly not to predict the future, but to understand contexts and processes, exploring tensions between the enduring and the transient (Tosh, 2008: 36). In this way we should be encouraging everyone, following Carl Schorske's exhortation, to think *with* history, rather than just about history.

Acknowledgements

For helpful feedback on this chapter, I am hugely grateful to Rossella Alba, Gretchen Bakke, Dan Durrant, Ignacio Farías, Ute Hasenöhrl, Karena Kalmbach, Ankit Kumar, Jörg Niewöhner, Beril Ocaklı, Joel Tarr, Erik van der Vleuten, Dirk van Laak, and Heike Weber as well as to the book's editors and participants of two online workshops where it was presented ('Doing Energy History in Times of Transition' and 'Planning as Imagineering') and a roundtable on 'Usable Infrastructure Pasts' I co-organized at the annual conference of the European Society of Environmental History in Bristol.

Notes

1. Interview with Peter Jules in *Prospect*, 21 July 2010.
2. Interview with Bruce Stave, in Stave (1983).
3. I acknowledge here the useful typology for analysing the temporalities of unfinished infrastructures developed by Carse and Kneas (2019: 15–22).
4. The films are freely available on https://lisa.gerda-henkel-stiftung.de/das_unsichtbare_berlin?nav_id=8405&language=en.
5. The digital infrastructure tour is freely available on https://www.360.de/remaking-berlin/.

References

Aarelaid-Tart, A. (2010) 'Avoiding uncertainty by making past usable', *Trames*, 1(4): 411–26.

Anand, N., Gupta, A., and Appel, H. (eds) (2018) *The Promise of Infrastructure*, Durham, NC: Duke University Press.

Anderson, B., Kearnes, M., McFarlane, C., and Swanton, D. (2012) 'On assemblages and geography', *Dialogues in Human Geography*, 2(2): 171–89.

Arranz, A.M. (2017) 'Lessons from the past for sustainability transitions? A meta-analysis of socio-technical studies', *Global Environmental Change*, 44: 125–43.

Asdal, K. (2012) 'Contexts in action – and the future of the past in STS', *Science, Technology, & Human Values*, 37(4): 379–403.

Bakker, K., and Bridge, G. (2006) 'Material worlds? Resource geographies and the "matter of nature"', *Progress in Human Geography*, 30(5): 5–27.

Barry, A. (2013) *Material Politics: Disputes along the Pipeline*, Oxford: Wiley-Blackwell.

Carse, A., and Kneas, D. (2019) 'Unbuilt and unfinished: The temporalities of infrastructure', *Environment and Society*, 10(1): 9–28.

Collier, S.J. (2011) *Post-Soviet Social: Neoliberalism, Social Modernity, Biopolitics*, Princeton, NJ: Princeton University Press.

Divall, C. (2010) 'Mobilizing the history of technology', *Technology and Culture*, 51(4): 938–60.

Edgerton, D. (2007) *The Shock of the Old: Technology and Global History since 1900*, Oxford: Oxford University Press.

Engels, J.I. (2020) 'Infrastrukturen als Produkte und Produzenten von Zeit', *NTM Zeitschrift für Geschichte der Wissenschaften, Technik und Medizin*, 28: 69–90.

Fouquet, R., and Pearson, P.J.G. (2012) 'Past and prospective energy transitions: insights from history', *Energy Policy*, 50(1): 1–7.

Furlong, K. (2014) 'STS beyond the "modern infrastructure ideal": Extending theory by engaging with infrastructure challenges in the South', *Technology in Society*, 38: 139–47.

Geels, F.W. (2002) 'Technological transitions as evolutionary reconfiguration processes: A multilevel perspective and a case-study', *Research Policy*, 31(8): 1257–74.

Geels, F.W., McMeekin, A., Mylan, J., and Southerton, D. (2015) 'A critical appraisal of Sustainable Consumption and Production research: The reformist, revolutionary and reconfiguration positions', *Global Environmental Change*, 34: 1–12.

Gismondi, M. (2018) 'Historicizing transitions: The value of historical theory to energy transition research', *Energy Research and Social Science*, 3: 193–8.

Graham, S., and Marvin, S. (2001) *Splintering Urbanism: Networked Infrastructures, Technological Mobilities and the Urban Condition*, London: Routledge.

Guldi, J., and Armitage, D. (2014) *The History Manifesto*, Cambridge: Cambridge University Press.

Hammersley, M. (2004) 'Towards a usable past for qualitative research', *International Journal of Social Research Methodology*, 7(1): 19–27.

Hasenöhrl, U., and Meyer, J.-H. (2020) 'The energy challenge in historical perspective', *Technology and Culture*, 61(1): 295–306.

Henke, C.R., and Sims, B. (2020) *Repairing Infrastructures: The Maintenance of Materiality and Power*, Cambridge, MA: MIT Press.

Heßler, M., and Weber, H. (2019) 'Provokationen der Technikgeschichte: Eine Einleitung', in M. Heßler and H. Weber (eds) *Provokationen der Technikgeschichte: Zum Reflexionszwang historischer Forschung*, Paderborn: Ferdinand Schöningh, pp 1–34.

Hirsh, R.F. (2011) 'Historians of technology in the real world: Reflection on the pursuit of policy-oriented history', *Technology and Culture*, 52(1): 6–20.

Högselius, P., Kaijser, A., and van der Vleuten, E. (2016) *Europe's Infrastructure Transition. Economy, War, Nature*, Basingstoke: Palgrave Macmillan.

Hommels, A. (2005) *Unbuilding Cities: Obduracy in Urban Socio-technical Change*, Cambridge, MA: MIT Press.

Hughes, T.P. (1983) *Networks of Power: Electrification in Western Society, 1880–1930*, Baltimore, MD: Johns Hopkins University Press.

Huyssen, A. (2003) *Present Pasts: Urban Palimpsests and the Politics of Memory*, Stanford, CA: Stanford University Press.

Jabary Salamanca, O., and Silver, J. (2022) 'In the excess of splintering urbanism: The racialized political economy of infrastructure', *Journal of Urban Technology*, 29(1): 117–25.

Jasanoff, S. (2015) 'Future imperfect: Science, technology, and the imaginations of modernity', in S. Jasanoff and S.-H. Kim (eds) *Dreamscapes of Modernity: Socio-technical Imaginaries and the Fabrication of Power*, Chicago, IL: University of Chicago Press, pp 1–33.

Kirchhof, A.M., and Meyer, J.-H. (2021) 'Vielfach nachgefragt: Kernenergiegeschichte', *Technikgeschichte*, 88(4): 391–8.

König, W. (1984) 'Retrospective technology assessment: Technikbewertung im Rückblick', *Technikgeschichte*, 51(4): 247–62.

Koselleck, R. (2018) 'Sediments of time', in S. Franzel and S.-L. Hoffmann (eds) *Sediments of Time: On Possible Histories*, Stanford, CA: Stanford University Press, pp 3–9.

Leopold, E., and McDonald, D.A. (2012) 'Municipal socialism then and now: Some lessons for the Global South', *Third World Quarterly*, 33(10): 1837–53.

Mahony, M. (2018) *Historical Geographies of the Future: Imagination, Expectation and Prediction in the Making of Imperial Atmosphere*. 3S Working Paper 2018–31. Science, Society and Sustainability (3S) Research Group, University of East Anglia, Norwich.

Melosi, M. (2000) *The Sanitary City: Urban Infrastructure in America from Colonial Times to the Present*, Baltimore, MD: Johns Hopkins University Press.

Mitchell, T. (2020) 'Infrastructures work on time', *e-flux Architecture*. https://www.e-flux.com/architecture/new-silk-roads/312596/infrastructures-work-on-time/ (accessed 11 May 2023).

Moeller, R.G. (1996) 'War stories: The search for a usable past in the Federal Republic of Germany', *American Historical Review*, 101(4): 1008–48.

Monstadt, J. (2022) 'Urban and infrastructural rhythms and the politics of temporal alignment', *Journal of Urban Technology*, 29(1): 69–77.

Morin, K.M. (2013) 'Distinguished Historical Geography Lecture 2013: Carceral space and the usable past', *Historical Geography*, 41(1): 1–21.

Moss, T. (2016) 'Discarded surrogates, modified traditions, welcome complements: The chequered careers of alternative technologies in Berlin's infrastructure systems', *Social Studies of Science*, 46(4): 559–82.

Moss, T. (2020) *Remaking Berlin: A History of the City through Infrastructure, 1920–2020*, Cambridge, MA: MIT Press.

Moss, T. (2021) 'Technikgeschichte für heute: Formate der Wissensvermittlung', *Technikgeschichte*, 88(4): 385–90.

Moss, T., and Weber, H. (2021) 'Technik- und Umweltgeschichte als *usable pasts*: Potenziale und Risiken einer angewandten Geschichtswissenschaft', *Technikgeschichte*, 88(4): 367–78.

Olick, J.K. (2007) 'From usable pasts to the return of the repressed', *The Hedgehog Review. Critical Reflections on Contemporary Culture*. https://hedgehogreview.com/issues/the-uses-of-the-past/articles/from-usable-pasts-to-the-return-of-the-repressed (accessed 2 December 2022).

Olsen, B. (2003) 'Material culture after text: Re-membering things', *Norwegian Archaeological Review*, 36(2): 87–104.

Otter, C. (2010) 'Locating matter: The place of materiality in urban history', in T. Bennett and P. Joyce (eds) *Material Powers: Cultural Studies, History and the Material Turn*, London: Routledge, pp 38–59.

Pearson, P.J.G., and Foxon, T.J. (2012) 'A low carbon industrial revolution? Insights and challenges from past technological and economic transformations', *Energy Policy*, 50: 117–27.

Poportan, L.A., and Ungureanu, C. (2022) 'The political ecology of water memory: Contending narratives of past hydraulic infrastructures in Barcelona (2015–2021)', *Political Geography*, 96: 102596.

Radkau, J. (2008) *Nature and Power: A Global History of the Environment*, Cambridge: Cambridge University Press.

Schipper, F., Emanuel, M., and Oldenziel, R. (2020) 'Historicizing sustainable urban mobility', in M. Emanuel, F. Schipper, and R. Oldenziel (eds) *A U-turn to the Future: Sustainable Urban Mobility since 1950*, Oxford: Berghahn Books, pp 1–26.

Sovacool, B.K., and Geels, F.W. (2016) 'Further reflections on the temporality of energy transitions: A response to critics', *Energy Research & Social Science*, 22: 232–7.

Sovacool, B.K., Lovell, K., and Ting, M.B. (2018) 'Reconfiguration, contestation, and decline: Conceptualizing mature large technical systems', *Science, Technology, & Human Values*, 43(6): 1066–97.

Stave, B.M. (1983) 'A conversation with Joel A. Tarr: Urban history and policy', *Journal of Urban History*, 9(2): 195–232.

Stearns, P. (1982) 'Applied history and social sciences', *Social Science History*, 6: 219–26.

Summerton, J. (1994) 'Introductory essay: The systems approach to technological change', in J. Summerton (ed) *Changing Large Technical Systems*, Boulder, CO: Westview Press, pp 1–22.

Swyngedouw, E. (2015) *Liquid Power: Contested Hydro-modernities in Twentieth-Century Spain*, Cambridge, MA: MIT Press.

Tosh, J. (2008) *Why History Matters*, Basingstoke: Palgrave Macmillan.

Toussaint, B. (2016) 'Using the usable past: Reflections and practices in the Netherlands', in C. Divall and J. Hine (eds) *Transport Policy: Learning Lessons from History*, Farnham: Ashgate, pp 15–30.

Trentmann, F. (2009) 'Materiality in the future of history: Things, practices, and politics', *Journal of British Studies*, 48(2): 283–307.

Uekötter, F. (2020) *Im Strudel. Eine Umweltgeschichte der modernen Welt*, Frankfurt/New York: Campus.

van der Straeten, J., and Hasenöhrl, U. (2016) 'Connecting the Empire: New research perspectives on infrastructures and the environment in the (post) colonial world', *NTM Zeitschrift für Geschichte der Wissenschaften, Technik und Medizin*, 24: 355–91.

van der Vleuten, E., Oldenziel, R., and Davids, M. (2017) *Engineering the Future, Understanding the Past: A Social History of Technology*, Amsterdam: Amsterdam University Press.

van Laak, D. (2001) 'Infra-Strukturgeschichte', *Geschichte und Gesellschaft*, 27(3): 367–93.

von Schnitzler, A. (2016) *Democracy's Infrastructure: Techno-Politics and Protest after Apartheid*, Princeton, NJ: Princeton University Press.

Weber, H. (2019) 'Zeitschichten des Technischen: Zum Momentum, Alter(n) und Verschwinden von Technik', in M. Heßler and H. Weber (eds) *Provokationen der Technikgeschichte: Zum Reflexionszwang historischer Forschung*, Paderborn: Ferdinand Schöningh, pp 107–50.

Weber, H., and Krebs, S. (2021) 'The persistence of technology: From maintenance and repair to reuse and disposal', in S. Krebs and H. Weber (eds) *The Persistence of Technology: Histories of Repair, Reuse and Disposal*, Bielefeld: transcript, pp 9–24.

4

Shifting Regimes of Historicity and the Control of Urban Futures through Infrastructures: Continuities, Ambivalences, and Tensions in the Anthropocene

Olivier Coutard

Introduction

Whether 'smart', 'resource-efficient', 'low-carbon', or 'resilient', most of today's imagined, desired, or actively promoted futures seem to rely on infrastructural development. So too do most so-called transition strategies. Arguably, as pervasive and long-lasting apparatuses, networked infrastructures across various sectors – energy, transport, communications, digital, and so on – can be assumed to play a prominent role in shaping individual and collective social futures; and, as I will contend, they have done so over the past two centuries. This raises important questions, both scientific and political, about the ways our futures could, or even should, rely on the development of infrastructure.

In this chapter, I first explore this admittedly broad question by examining infrastructures through three interrelated temporal registers (1) their lifetimes and life cycles; (2) their day-to-day operation, maintenance, and functioning; and (3) the link – both ideal and material – they perform between social pasts, presents, and futures. I hold that, through these three registers, infrastructural environments crucially shape dominant social temporalities by *materializing* them. I then argue that long-industrialized societies have inherited from the modern era a propensity to (seek to) control social futures through infrastructures. Yet predominant forms of 'infrastructure-based futuring', which as any future-oriented action essentially consists in promoting some types of futures and hindering others, entail ambivalent and contradictory implications under contemporary conditions. Indeed, incumbent infrastructure systems tend to simultaneously support contemporary presentism and perpetuate modernist futurism when the challenges associated with the Anthropocene likely call for other, non-modernist forms of futurism, and consequently other infrastructural paradigms. I close with a discussion of some methodological, epistemological, and ultimately political aspects of researching infrastructural, urban-regional, and social futures in the making. In this venture, I rely primarily on observations of, and insights from, Western (European, even) urban contexts in which major energy, transport, communications, and other utility infrastructures are ubiquitous (if unequally distributed across places, groups, and individuals).

The temporalities of modern infrastructures
The infrastructural dimension of modernity

Extensive scholarship emphasizes the connections between the development of infrastructures and the progressive enforcement and expansion of the modern condition since the late eighteenth and early nineteenth centuries.[1] Mann (1984: 212) influentially claimed that the advent of territorialized and centralized societies – 'one of the most decisive aspects of the great modernizing transformations' – essentially rests on *infrastructural power*, 'the power of the state to penetrate and centrally co-ordinate the activities of civil society through its own infrastructure' (Mann, 1984: 189). The advanced capitalist state, he added, 'penetrates everyday life more than did any historical state. Its infrastructural power has increased enormously ... from Alaska to Florida, from the Shetlands to Cornwall there is no hiding place from the infrastructural reach of the modern state' (Mann, 1984: 189).

Supporting this contention, De Swaan (1988) showed the role of (especially) sanitation infrastructures in the development of the welfare state in Europe and the US. Tarr and Dupuy (1988) documented the 'rise of the networked city', while Calhoun (1992) highlighted the central role of information infrastructures in supporting what he regards as a key feature of modernity: the ever-increasing prevalence of indirect social relationships. Mayntz (1995: 15) similarly contended that '[m]odern infrastructure systems and modern nation-states have reinforced one another through their respective development'.[2] Despite substantial variations in analytical, and even normative, perspectives, these authors (among others, notably the seminal works of Breyer, 1982 and Beniger, 1989) have all contributed to flesh out the general idea that large transportation, communications, and energy infrastructure systems are essential to the advent of modern state bureaucracies, productive systems, ways of life, and imaginaries. As Edwards

(2003: 186) puts it, 'infrastructures simultaneously shape and are shaped by – in other words co-construct – the condition of modernity'.

Yet it is striking that up to the 2010s, except for a few environmental historians (for instance, Tarr, 1996 or Melosi, 2000 in the US context), virtually no explorations of modern infrastructures – or 'infrastructured modernity' – significantly addressed issues of how infrastructure systems shape the mutually transformative relations between human societies and the biosphere. Even Edwards (2003) does not thoroughly question the role of infrastructures as quintessential to the modern way of shaping the future and changing natural conditions. Taking inspiration from Latour's discussion of the 'modernist settlement', he does acknowledge that 'to construct infrastructure is simultaneously to construct a particular kind of nature, a Nature as Other to society and technology' (Edwards, 2003: 189). He further notes:

> ... fear of global warming represents the permanent imbrication of industrial infrastructures within the planetary carbon metabolism. This again drives home the falsity of the modernist settlement; technological systems consume carbon, but they rely on nature to cycle it out of the atmosphere and back into the soil. (Edwards, 2003: 196)

Yet Edwards does not elaborate on the ways in which, and the extent to which, modern infrastructuring as a general process plays a crucial role in the transformation of the global environment.

Mukerji takes an important step in that direction by putting forward the notion of 'logistical power', which she defines as 'the ability to mobilize the natural world for political effect' (2010: 402). Based primarily on a study of the construction of the Canal du Midi in the context of seventeenth-century French monarchy, Mukerji masterfully unpacks the political meanings and implications of the 'modernist settlement'. She convincingly demonstrates the role of logistical power and of the 'impersonal rule' exercised by and through the built environment in the rise of the modern territorial state. In particular, her analysis foregrounds how logistical power 'draws attention to the fundamental ways modern states with their obligations of stewardship and their material infrastructures enrol natural forces into political life, and insert risk into politics' (2010: 419).

This chapter explores the implications of the exercise of logistical power in the (late) modern context of increasingly ubiquitous infrastructures of transportation, communication, and energy provision. I pursue what I think is both a heuristic and distinctive (although not unique) approach by reflecting specifically on modern infrastructures from a temporal perspective and, in particular, their intimate relationship with modern futurism. I begin by examining the ways in which social times and rhythms both shape, and are shaped by, three main registers of infrastructural temporality:

1) the lifetimes and lifecycles of infrastructures per se;
2) the day-to-day temporalities and rhythms of operation, maintenance, and functioning of the said infrastructures; and
3) the future-oriented articulation of social past, present, and future through infrastructures.

Let me briefly elaborate on each of these registers and their social significance.

The lifetimes and life cycles of infrastructures in recent history

As a first approximation, we can describe and analyse infrastructure histories in evolutionary terms through dynamics of emergence, growth, maturity, decline, and demise or transformation. This basic model has been sophisticated in various ways, with Thomas Hughes offering the most influential account within historical and social studies of the expansion of 'large technical systems' (LTSs).

Hughes's (1987: 56) 'pattern of evolution' distinguishes a number of phases during which different profiles of 'system builders' have a leading influence (1) *phases of invention and development*, in which 'inventor-entrepreneurs' play a prominent role; (2) *phases of innovation*, and especially of transfer, growth, and competition, in which inventor-entrepreneurs give way to 'manager-entrepreneurs'; and (3) *phases of consolidation and rationalization*, in which 'financier-entrepreneurs' (and associated consulting engineers) have primacy. Hughes insisted that this 'pattern' is not linear: phases 'are not simply sequential: they overlap and backtrack' (1987: 56). While he described a pattern of evolution for expanding systems, 'countless other technological systems in history have arrived at a stage of stasis and then entered a period of decline. ... Historians and sociologists of technology should also search for patterns and concepts applicable to these aspects of the history of technological systems' (1987: 80). Acknowledging these caveats, we can view Hughes's 'pattern' as an evolutionary model for *expanding* systems, thus applicable to many systems originating in the late nineteenth century that followed an expansion trajectory. For this chapter, it is worth noting that, for Hughes, the articulation of time and space is key in the expansion of electricity supply systems and, he speculated, of other LTSs:

> Utility managers ... strove in a purposeful way to expand the territory of their utilities. The objective was not simply size, as crude explanations for the large scale of modern technology and business insist, but expansion to encompass the diversity of loads that brought a fuller round-the-clock utilization of generating equipment. (Hughes, 1983: 463)

Jean-Marc Offner (1993) proposed an alternative, extended evolutionary model that introduced two important addendums. Firstly, in contrast with the concern for expanding LTSs shared by most authors after Hughes, Offner's model encompassed phases of decline and demise, as well as the relations of complementarity or competition that often exist between specific declining and emerging infrastructures. Secondly, he considered the multilayered and spatialized (or territorial) character of large technical (networked) systems, which complicates the general evolutionary pattern. Indeed, a given infrastructure, he argued, consists of several layers (or dimensions): morphological (the layout of the tracks, lines, or conducts), material ('hardware'), functional (services), regulatory (the operating system), and territorial (topology of places, or points in space, connected by the network) (Offner, 1993: 13). Each of these layers has its specific dynamics and temporalities.

Road infrastructures provide a striking illustration of these heterogeneous temporalities. Many of today's French roads, for example, still more or less follow the layout of ancient paths or Roman roads, yet their materiality, functionality, regulation, and territoriality have changed considerably (and repeatedly) over the centuries. From a material perspective, there were no significant changes in road building techniques between Roman times and the late seventeenth and early eighteenth centuries, when more elaborate design techniques were gradually adopted, resulting in major material transformations over the last two centuries (Arbellot, 1973). Road functions and hierarchies changed over time, as combinations of military, commercial (and, more recently, touristic), religious, and territorial administration considerations evolved. Road regulations also changed. This is emblematically illustrated by road maintenance arrangements from slave work in Roman times, through tolls imposed by local lords, bordering communities, or monasteries in exchange for (often minimal) roadworks in the Middle Ages, to the modern 'corvee' introduced in 1738 by the French monarchy. The corvee was itself abandoned in 1787 in favour of a tax system upon which the organization and financing of road maintenance still rests today. Finally, the territoriality of road infrastructure has also evolved, from the spatial mesh extending across the whole territory of the Roman Empire, through the scattered roads of most of the Middle Ages, to the Paris-centred network(s) of the French (absolute) Monarchy, Empire, and Republic from the early eighteenth century onwards. Hence, for example, the section of the contemporary A9 tollway (E15/E80) between Nîmes and the Spanish border at the Perthus pass, which was built in the 1970s, follows nearly exactly the layout of the second-century BC Roman via Domitia that connected Rome with the Iberian Peninsula. In this case, the road's morphology has been preserved while its territoriality (among other dimensions) changed. In contrast, the layout of the horse posthouse infrastructure in modern

France evolved substantially between 1632 (when the Lyons-centred star, inherited from the Roman road network, was salient) and 1708 (when the Paris-centred star and denser network mesh in northern France was clearly established). This Paris-centred star network would last until the termination of the horse postal service in the second half of the nineteenth century (Bretagnolle et al, 2010: 120). In this example, the functions (administrative communications, passenger transport) and (national state) territoriality have persisted while the morphology of the infrastructure has evolved.

Offner's model, which foregrounded the variegated temporalities of multidimensional infrastructures, is echoed in Bowker's (2015: np) reflections on infrastructural temporalities. Indeed, for both authors infrastructures 'do not have clear lifecycles [and] never even [have] the grace to die'. Generally, some of their aspects (or 'dimensions', in Offner's terminology) persist in the 'emergent infrastructural configurations' that they transition into. Bowker, however, adds an important dimension when he writes that infrastructural histories 'are messy stories of making things hook up together, of hopefully continual maintenance' (2015: np; see also Moss, this volume), hence contrasting with prevailing views of infrastructures as stable constructs,[3] and pointing to the now rapidly expanding literature on infrastructure maintenance (Denis and Pontille, 2015).

Within a given territory, modern infrastructures emerge, expand, decline, or undergo transformations depending on the shape, modalities, and intensity of spatio-temporal relationships and, more specifically, on the ways in which interactions between individuals, between activities, and between societies and the wider environment are organized and controlled. As ever more complex, interconnected, and ubiquitous infrastructural systems developed, they fostered the proliferation of networked forms of territoriality in which interactions primarily depend upon (expedient) distant connections rather than geographic proximity, as is the case with traditional, area-based forms of territoriality. In turn, the increasing prevalence of networked territorialities has supported further infrastructural development and profoundly transformed dominant spatio-temporal arrangements.

Infrastructures and the experience of time in everyday life

Infrastructural landscapes – and thus their timescapes (Adam, 2004) – constitute powerful fields of constraint and opportunity for social practices (in everyday life as well as in institutionalized activities). In particular, the day-to-day functioning of infrastructures is strongly associated with the temporalities of social life, especially in two paradigmatic forms (see Lefebvre, 2004). On the one hand, the continuous, predictable rhythms associated with the reproduction of everyday practices are sustained by the 'smooth' functioning of a broad array of essential infrastructure services: energy supply, telecommunications, transportation service, and so on. On the other hand, infrastructural failures are a major cause of disruption in collective and individual rhythms, as any major blackout or public transport strike forcefully demonstrates (also see Addie, this volume). Adopting a historical (and slightly deterministic) perspective, Edwards similarly argues that infrastructures shape our experience of time: 'for example, the telegraph created a sense of simultaneity across huge distances, prefiguring McLuhan's "global village", while electric power extended work hours into the night' (2003: 194–5).

In cities (or larger areas) with long-established ubiquitous infrastructures, it is difficult to grasp the pervasive influence of infrastructural environments on social temporalities and the rhythms of everyday life. But this influence is strikingly revealed, for example, by historical and ethnographic studies of (1) urban life in contexts where infrastructures are temporarily or permanently unavailable to part or all of the population (see Datta, 2019); (2) changes to urban life brought about by the expansion of specific infrastructures (changes that are never fully anticipated, let alone planned) (see Simone, this volume); or (3) the lived experiences of waiting, delay, and suspension associated with repeatedly postponed infrastructure construction works (see DiCarlo, this volume).

These very broad remarks would obviously need considerable further elaboration. In particular, the implications of infrastructure failures are in general strongly differentiated socially and vary considerably according to contexts and to the specific infrastructure(s) at stake. Reciprocally, the rhythms and temporalities of everyday practices and organized activities largely shape operational and maintenance routines and even the design and dimensioning of infrastructural systems, as illustrated by peak management or the scheduling of maintenance works in electricity systems.

Infrastructures and the modern regime of historicity

Foregrounding the infrastructural substratum of the experience of time (and space) in and through everyday practices is essential but misses an important dimension of the ways in which infrastructures relate to the temporalities of modern societies. Indeed, as I will argue, infrastructures also *materialize* modern representations of how the past, the present, and the future relate, and how these relations shape the predominant experience of time in modern societies. More specifically, infrastructural development both sustains and is sustained by what François Hartog (2016 [2003]) has called the modern, 'futurist' *regime of historicity* and its partial and already contested contemporary successor, 'presentism'.

For Hartog, the dominant (or ideal-typical) way in which societies articulate the past, the present, and the future changes over time and from one society, or culture, to another. Regimes of historicity colour how given societies in a given period relate to their future in imagination, in anticipation, or in projection; how they let this constructed future affect their present; and more specifically how specific actors are able (enabled) to deliberately construct a future that conforms to their interest. Expanding on Koselleck (1990 [1979]), Hartog (2016, 2020a) has distinguished four such regimes in Western, especially European, culture (1) a past-oriented heroic regime that prevailed in Ancient times; (2) a Christian regime of 'Apocalyptic presentism' from the Middle Ages to the late eighteenth century; (3) a modern 'futurist' regime up to the middle of the twentieth century; and (4) contemporary presentism.

In the Ancient, 'heroic' regime, the (heroic) past offers examples on which to base present and future action according to Cicero's famous formula (taken up by Koselleck), *historia magistra vitae est*: history (or the past) is the master of (present and future) life. In the modern, 'futurist' regime, the future is seen as an emancipation from the past; it illuminates the past and the present with the light of Progress resulting from scientific 'discoveries' and technological innovations. This futurism is reflected in the elaboration and assertion of grand philosophies (for instance, Hegel) or theories of history (for instance, Marx).

Modern infrastructures that developed from the early nineteenth century onwards have strong links with modern-age futurism in two important ways. On the one hand, as is widely acknowledged, infrastructural development has often been legitimized by promises of modernity or modernization,[4] and (at least in Western countries) it has to a significant extent materialized this promise for more than a century. On the other hand, infrastructures have been essential in *presenting* the future (Rutherford, 2020: 4). Mitchell (2020) importantly argues that as well as, and even prior to, achieving 'faster connections and improved rates of flows', infrastructures are 'an apparatus to capture revenue that lies in the future' (np). Noting that 'prior to the emergence of modern, large-scale infrastructure, there was little value to a claim to revenue that lay far in the future', he contends that two main features of infrastructure projects made this future-proofing possible: 'First, compared to other means of capturing revenue, infrastructures are unusually durable. ... Second, more than many other means of capturing revenues, infrastructures are typically built with another kind of durability, a form of political and legal guarantee' (Mitchell, 2020: np).[5]

This is why, Mitchell argues, the historical development of large infrastructures is directly related to the establishment of some of the most important modern institutions: banks, investment funds, and the modern shareholder company. By presenting future profits, infrastructures are contributing in a crucial way to the hold of the future-oriented regime of historicity that characterizes modernity. To a certain extent, infrastructures can be considered as part and parcel of high-modernist ideology (Scott, 1998). Mitchell could have added a third process through which infrastructures act as a future-proofing apparatus: the mutual shaping of modern infrastructural environments and practices – generally a slow process. Indeed, as Shove et al (2019: 6) note, 'infrastructural arrangements are much more than material artefacts, fixed in the here and now. They cast a shadow on the future, laying the foundations for daily practices in years and decades to come.' Conversely, the reproduction of practices, a social phenomenon of great generality, is a powerful factor of perpetuation of incumbent infrastructures.

The interrelated registers of temporality in the modern infrastructural compact

These remarks suggest that infrastructural imaginaries, rhetoric, and actual projects and apparatuses are mobilized to exercise control not only over space, as is generally acknowledged, but also over time and (the construction of) social futures. This influence upon the future, which I will refer to as *infrastructure-based futuring*, is in part a self-fulfilling prophecy. Indeed, it is largely performed through the establishment of a wide belief in two main promises (1) a promise of future improved material conditions; and (2) a promise of future revenue. Importantly, these promises come with the expectation of immediate political, economic, or financial benefits for key stakeholders (for example, the state, utility companies, investment institutions, and so on). By articulating the three registers of temporalities previously discussed (see Figure 4.1), infrastructural environments *materialize* social temporalities: they inscribe them in space and the built environment, shaping the experience of those temporalities in everyday life, making them tangible and to some extent steerable, and thus creating the conditions for infrastructure-based futuring.

As noted, social change associated with infrastructural development can never be fully anticipated, let alone steered. Yet the materialization of infrastructure-based futuring in actual infrastructure projects shapes the future, opening or reinforcing some possibilities while hindering or closing others.

Infrastructures, modern futurism, and contemporary presentism

Modern infrastructures have contributed in crucial ways to the establishment and perpetuation of the modern regime of historicity by (1) materializing modern narratives and experiences of time and (2) framing how modern societies relate to, and claim to steer, the future. But things have progressively changed in recent decades.

Figure 4.1: The interrelated temporal registers of the modern infrastructural compact

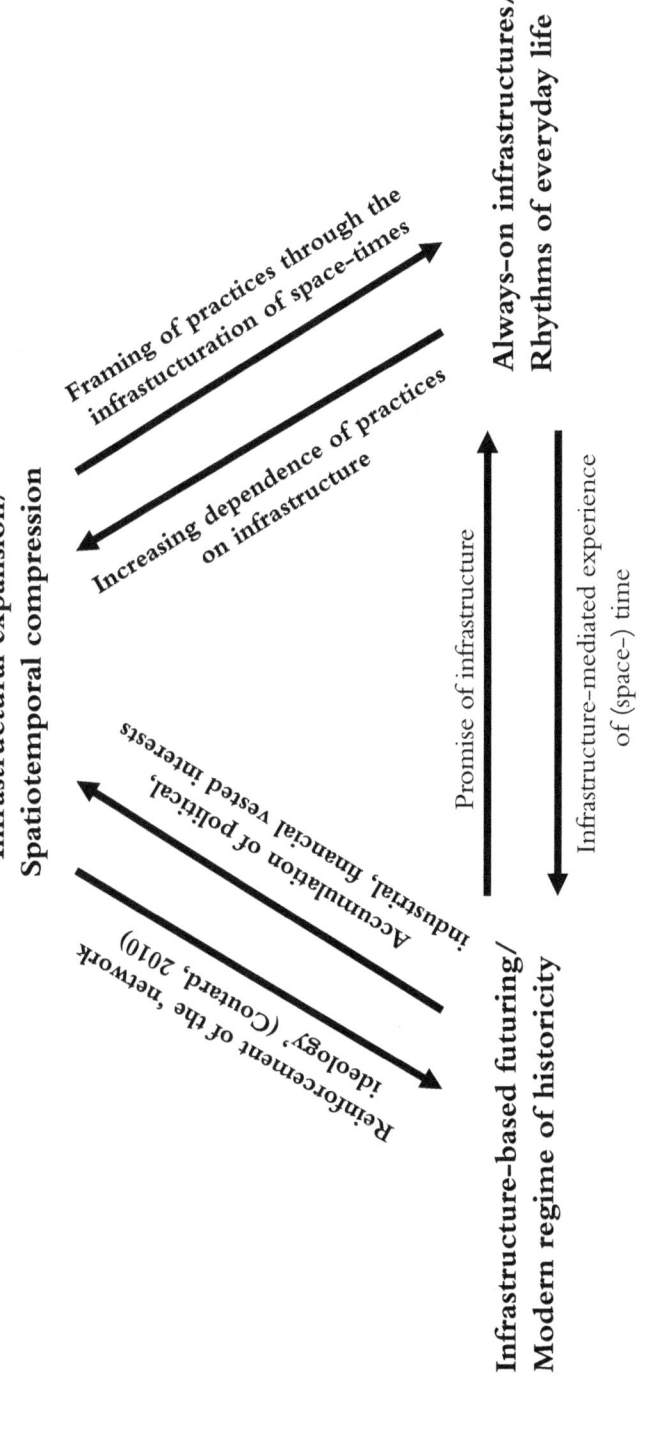

The rise of a presentist experience of time and the digital revolution

According to Hartog (2020b), the modern regime of historicity has been gradually undermined since the early twentieth century as a novel form of presentism emerged that 'continuously fabricates the past and the future it needs' (np). Hartog identifies general factors accounting for the loss of faith in the future and in modern futurism. Precursor events include the two world wars – Hartog (2017: 46) claims that 'the future and progress never recovered from these catastrophes' – as well as the short-termist tyranny of the market and globalization and, crucially, the fall of Soviet communism (Hartog, 2009: 145). Indeed, he cites 1989, the year of the fall of the Berlin Wall, as a key date in the rise of contemporary presentism. Interestingly for our argument, Hartog further points to an infrastructural dimension in this shift, highlighting 'the computer revolution which, I believe, is essentially presentist due to its characteristic features of simultaneity and instantaneity' (2020b: np). Elsewhere, he insists: 'In this novel "digital condition" that many attempt to comprehend, and that can be regarded, as a novel historical condition, it is obvious that the present reigns supreme' (Hartog, 2017: 49).

Kitchin's (2019) discussion of 'the timescape of smart cities' is helpful in elaborating on this idea of 'digital presentism'. In a striking echo of Hartog's reflections (and of the argument developed in this chapter), Kitchin argues that '[a]s well as the temporal rhythms and relations of cities being transformed through the drive to make them smart, a key aspect of how smart city technologies work is how they draw on and reconfigure the relationship between the past, the present, and the future' (2019: 782). Along with Hartog, Kitchin acknowledges the presentist connotation of digital data and communication technologies:

> A significant part of the appeal of smart city technologies is their seeming ability to enable city systems to be used and managed dynamically in real time taking into account present conditions. ... The increasing availability of real-time data seemingly creates an annihilation of space and time to the point where governance is enacted in a 'perpetual present'. (Kitchin, 2019: 783)

Kitchin's observations on the properties associated with smart cities apply to infrastructured environments more generally. Indeed, the 'space-time machine' he describes as characterizing the smart city was to a large extent characteristic of the networked city all along, although in less sophisticated and ubiquitous terms. Consider time-space compression; the increase in, and regulation of, the multiple rhythms of the city; the shift to 'networked times'; or general acceleration (Kitchin, 2019: 777–81): the first expressions of all these trends can be traced back to the early days of modern infrastructure development. However, the development of technologies for the massive storage and the (almost instantaneous) transfer and treatment of digital data has considerably reinforced and accelerated those trends.

Infrastructures between futurism and presentism

The development of digital infrastructures and services thus strongly reinforces a presentist experience of time. On a broader level, signs of weakening of the modernist infrastructural compact have accumulated over the past half-century. In particular, the promise of networked infrastructure was increasingly challenged, both ideally and materially, as a result of the combination of three major factors (1) the liberalization of network industries globally; (2) the environmental critique of large infrastructures, in particular in the global North; and (3) the unfulfilled promise of universalization, in particular in the global South where infrastructure development could not 'keep pace' with dynamics of urban growth (Coutard, 2010). These factors strongly resonate with the loss of faith in the future and in progress identified by Hartog.

Yet modern infrastructures remain crucial ingredients in futurist narratives and future-oriented strategies and actions, as noted earlier with reference to transition rhetoric and strategies. Even digital infrastructures perpetuate to some extent a futurist perspective in the contemporary presentist age, as testified by the many promises of the 'smart city'. In fact, Kitchin also highlights the futurist trope associated with many smart city technologies:

> Smart city technologies, although most often framed around managing the present, are future oriented with respect to plausible and preferable scenarios, dispositions, optimization, and contingency ... Of particular importance [are] the practices of experimental urbanism [through which] innovators are enabled to prototype and trial new technologies in real-world settings to test, learn about and *promote possible and desirable urban futures.* (Kitchin, 2019: 784–5, emphasis added)

Infrastructures thus still materialize a promise of improved future material – now including environmental – conditions, and they still operate as a powerful future-proofing apparatus to *present* future expected financial profits.

This infrastructural ambivalence reflects the broader fact that contemporary presentism has strong roots in modernist futurism and has by no means undermined it entirely. This should come as no surprise as present infrastructural environments materialize elements that are compatible with the two regimes of historicity, in particular:

- technological solutionism;
- the primacy of logics of financial profits in the generation, circulation, and distribution of monetary and material wealth;
- productivism, extractivism, and the increasing concentration of (control over) 'natural' resources; and
- the rise of discipline, control, surveillance, and heteronomy, masked under an apparent 'infrastructural autonomy' that allows every individual (with adequate resources) to create their own 'tailor-made' infrastructural environment.

More fundamentally, I hold that both regimes of historicity share a logic of *control over the future*, albeit a different future. In the futurist regime, this control aims, at least in part, to secure immediate political, economic, or financial profits (Mitchell, 2020). This futurist regime also tends to apply to the development of digital infrastructures. As Mukerji more broadly remarks: 'Modern states ... build their collective futures with scientific infrastructure such as CERN (European Organization for Nuclear Research) and military bases around the world. States continue to define their futures with infrastructures such as the Internet and weapons of war' (2010: 421).

In the contemporary presentist regime, control over the (immediate) future aims to secure immediate benefits in terms of established practices and rooted expectations such as material prosperity, financial wealth, unrestrained mobility and sociality, and permanent and generalized consumption. In particular, 'the current financialized economy rests entirely on forms of anticipation that create a tyranny of immediate future' (Baschet, 2018b: np).

Infrastructures are the apparatus that materialize and effect this control over the future by helping structure social organization, securing and distributing resources, and influencing prevailing practices and dominant cultural values. The 'desirable urban futures' evoked by Kitchin are, for their promoters, *immediate* futures that intensify those among present trends that best serve their current interests, regardless of – or even concealing – the associated risks or negative implications (for instance, pervasive surveillance or environmental collapse; see Schindler and Kanai, this volume). Baschet (2018b) perceptively argues that presentism forbids any future perspective that would not be a prolongation of the present and supports a form of fatalistic lock-in into the present. Undeniably, this is a very strong form of control, and according to Baschet (2018b: np), 'one must carefully examine which types of future disappear in presentism and which prosper'.

Infrastructure-based futuring and the rising concern about the Anthropocene

Our epoch (the early twenty-first century) is characterized by the growing prevalence of a *presentist* experience of time, which is simultaneously rooted in, and undermining, the modern, *futurist* regime of historicity. This dialectical relation is increasingly influenced by concerns regarding the Anthropocene, concerns that have spread from a narrow group of climate and environmental scientists and activists to an ever-wider policy community and the general population, with the potential to change – yet again – the predominant way we experience time and perceive the relationship between past, present, and future. In the first, 'disenchanted' version of presentism, faith in progress and the future has waned. In the second, 'catastrophic' presentism, the future appears primarily as a threat, thus destabilizing in powerful ways the potentially emerging presentist infrastructural compact.

Unsurprisingly, the fundamentally modernist notion of controlling the future is being applied as a first-line approach to planetary environmental changes, the threats associated with them, and possible responses to those threats. Indeed, as already noted, many transition strategies and policies essentially rest on infrastructures. This prompts the question, what does infrastructure-based futuring have to offer regarding these issues? Let us consider two important examples.

Firstly, energy transition strategies promise local metabolic autonomy, enhanced energy efficiency, and carbon neutrality. Yet they are hindered by vested interests in incumbent energy infrastructures and by embedded practices and spatial organizations resting on the virtually unlimited availability of affordable energy. Hence, energy futures largely prove to be locked into the past (and present). Secondly, smart city narratives and promises of 'dematerialized', 'optimized', and 'real-time' urban management (deliberately) ignore the considerable energy and material costs of digital infrastructure. Left unchecked, they will lock urban and social futures into a presentist technological future in radical contradiction with contemporary Anthropocenic challenges.

What, then, is the potential of infrastructure-based futuring to change the rhythms of everyday life in ways favourable to reduced resources consumption (against the increasingly tight grip of the real-time on the predominant contemporary experience of time)? Since their inception, the promise (and, in part, the history) of modern infrastructure systems has primarily been to facilitate ever more regular rhythms of urban life through the continuous and smooth delivery of a wide range of services based on the extensive appropriation of a wide array of resources. The ideal and material inversion of this promise is not the most plausible evolution. In other words, the presentist infrastructural compact in the making tends to prioritize specific forms of *adaptation* to planetary environmental changes that are more compatible with incumbent infrastructures, vested interests, and established practices – and to downplay the more radical transformations that would be required for the mitigation of those global changes. It has a Lampedusian flavour of 'everything must change for everything to remain the same'. But the notion of adaptation is twofold. In its more common acceptance, it refers to the need to adapt, for example, to the effects of climate change. In a subtler acceptance, it points to the need to adapt to the idea that human activities are affecting the global environment in ways that are beyond human steering or restoring capacities, hence returning to notions of mitigation or precaution, and to the need for radical change.

Pluralizing times

I would now like to briefly examine the consequences of the 'shock of the Anthropocene' (Bonneuil and Fressoz, 2016). Various authors, starting with Hartog himself, have noted that it deeply affects both the modern regime of historicity and the contemporary presentist stance (see Hartog, 2017; Baschet, 2018a; Chakrabarty, 2018; Olmstead, 2019; Bonneuil, 2020).

Bonneuil (2020) offers a useful starting point when he notes that the idea of the Anthropocene and the associated knowledge (and, let us add, growing concern) have ambivalent effects on futurist and presentist ideal-typical experiences of time. On the one hand, he contends, they challenge both regimes. Whereas presentism claimed 'the end of history', the exit from the Holocene initiates a new geo-history; and 'the modern [futurist] regime of historicity … is also challenged by the idea of Anthropocene', which leads to reconsidering modern history entirely (Bonneuil, 2020: 14). But, on the other hand:

> … knowledge and discourses about the Anthropocene may also reinforce some features of the modern and presentist regimes. … Isn't the grand narrative foregrounding humanity as a geological force the [negative] side of the modern grand narrative of 'man' improving and planning the globe? … [And] isn't the ambition to steer Earth by articulating the present time of economic prosperity with the deeply remote time of a planet that must be maintained within its 'boundaries' a form of paroxysmal presentism claiming to internalise the most remote future in present action? (Bonneuil, 2020: 14–15)

Escaping this ambivalence requires us to question the modern standards of time. According to Bonneuil (who also relies on Baschet, Haraway, and Bensaude-Vincent), this would imply moving towards an increased 'pluralization' of time so as to 'open up to the plural temporalities that each being generates in the process of its existence' (Bonneuil, 2020: 15). He opposes approaches that rest on 'the return of technocratic practices of foresight, future modelling and planning' and on a reference to a unique universal time 'which would reduce the multiplicity of temporalities of earthly beings and processes to economic rationality' (Bonneuil, 2020: 15).

More generally, Hartog (2017: 48, 49) invites us to 'make room for discordant temporalities in our democratic institutions' and emphasizes the importance of 'paying attention to … the "simultaneity of the non-simultaneous"',[6] to reveal, against the apparent contemporaneity of everything with everything, the different temporalities that cut across or undermine this imperious present. Similarly, Baschet (2018b: np) also invites us 'to reappropriate the notion of duration, i.e., the experience of the concrete temporality of processes … to refute the idea of a unified Time, framework of all things, to give way to the very temporality of beings and things'.

Reopening infrastructural futures

Based on these insights, I now more specifically reflect on these issues from an infrastructural perspective by asking: what role (if any) could infrastructure-based futuring play in an Anthropocenic regime of historicity?

To the extent that they materialize the superimposed modern and presentist regimes of historicity, infrastructures today embody this ambivalence, both perpetuating the promise of ever-increasing material prosperity and attending – or claiming to attend – to the challenges of Anthropocenic change. I have argued that long-industrialized societies have inherited from the modern era a propensity to control social futures through infrastructures, and that they do so now in a specific, more presentist way. Today's predominant forms of 'infrastructure-based futuring' thus entail ambivalent and to some extent contradictory implications. In particular, they do not seem to facilitate emancipation from the prevailing forms of alienation that characterize and plague the contemporary condition, for instance, state and (digital) capitalist control over social (collective and individual) space-times; over resources, landscapes, and local or broader environments; and over practices and imaginaries.

In closing his exploration of the timescape of smart cities, Kitchin (2019) asks: does social desynchronization and the rise of individually tailored temporalities facilitated by digital infrastructures imply an emancipation from the constraints of capitalist production and control? He answers largely in the negative:

> … although citizens might benefit from the deployment of smart city technologies through enhanced optimization and efficiency of services and new apps that facilitate consumption choice and individual autonomy, this takes place within a framework of constraints that prioritize market-led solutions to urban issues, reproduce neoliberal capitalism, enforce technocratic modes of governance, and continue to perpetuate inequalities between communities. (Kitchin, 2019: 788)

On the contrary, recent trends seem to point to an undesirable future (often surreptitiously) perpetuating traditional technological and spatial fixes and traditional patterns of domination, social control, inequalities, and extractivism. More fundamentally, contemporary forms of infrastructure-based futuring seem to perpetuate a 'futurism-tainted presentism' that appears to be in contradiction with the challenges associated with the Anthropocene. What the idea of the Anthropocene suggests is rather that the future is beyond the reach of technological control and that dominant forms of technological development and use must be rejected.

Because infrastructures generally change slowly, infrastructure-based futuring tends to perpetuate established practices; embedded logics of growth, extraction, and social control; and vested industrial, financial, and political interests long into the future. But the social and cultural significance of infrastructure is, and has always been, ambivalent: the future is open. So all hope is not lost (Coutard and Guy, 2007)! We can find seeds of change in contemporary emerging trends or limitations to dominant trends. The future-proofing of carbon-related financial interests through infrastructure is less assured than it used to be, even though it is highly resilient (Mitchell, 2011). Less resource-intensive dietary or mobility practices, especially among younger generations, seem to gain momentum. Attempts at distancing from, or resistance to, contemporary acceleration (and 'acceleration of acceleration', according to Baschet, 2018b) have already been experimented with (Vannini and Taggart, 2015) and may develop further.

The key issue is to be able to reopen futures beyond the resource- and digital technology-intensive script promoted and imposed by dominant vested interests. Infrastructures, in particular energy and digital ones, cannot and should not be a solution in search of a problem. Reopening infrastructural futures first implies reopening futures without presupposing to what extent, and in what ways, infrastructures will be involved in shaping these futures.

How (and why) to research infrastructure-based futuring

I would like to conclude with some reflections on how this temporary zone of *indetermination* can be explored, and why we as researchers and, in my case, as a social scientist should do so. We cannot foretell what role infrastructures will play in an Anthropocenic regime of historicity. What we do know is that it cannot be a perpetuation of the currently dominant patterns of infrastructural development, which close social futures instead of (re)opening them. How, then, can we study the forms of experiencing time that will, could, or even should prevail in an Anthropocenic context, and assess the role evolving infrastructural environments might play in shaping them?

Study initiatives that challenge dominant forms of infrastructure development

Several very diverse initiatives aim to escape, challenge, or disrupt dominant infrastructural *scripts*, from protest movements against fracking, through hacker movements against digital control, to individual or more collective decisions to live 'off the grid'. These initiatives are obvious sites to look for possible alternatives to resource-intensive social futures. An example of such an approach is provided by Wright's endeavour to study 'real utopias' in a book that:

> ... hopes to contribute to rebuilding a sense of possibility for emancipatory social change by investigating the feasibility of radically different kinds of institutions and social relations that could potentially advance the democratic egalitarian goals historically associated with the idea of socialism ... The idea is to provide empirical and theoretical grounding for radical democratic egalitarian visions of an alternative social world. (Wright, 2010: 1)

This approach is also strongly echoed in Baschet's remark that 'there is much to gain in *thinking from* social struggle movements and collective attempts to build other words already' (2018b: np, emphasis added).

Study how futures are actively shaped in the present, and how they were shaped in the past

Seeking to 'account for how the future is made an object of knowledge, practice and ethics, as people from various disciplines, fields and sectors engage with enduring assessments of the "not yet"', Granjou and Salazar (2016: np) recommend foregrounding 'communities of anticipation' by studying 'assemblages of practices, forms of representation and material infrastructures enabling experts and lay people to anticipate, foster, and pre-empt the futures'. This approach echoes recent historical research aiming at 'meditating the unfortunate deviations toward dominations and oppressions of all kinds' (Baschet, 2018b: np). Similarly, reflecting on smart cities, Olmstead calls for more historical reflexivity:

> Whereas the smart city has tried to distance itself from this [i.e., its historical] inheritance, urban governance is in need of a more intentional and transparent acknowledgment of these interconnections and the dissonance that they create in urban living. Rather than hiding from the ghosts of the past, policymakers must account for them. I have argued that this includes replacing the ideal of the smart city with that

of a spectral city – a city more welcoming of the ghosts and ghouls on which it is built. (Olmstead, 2019: 260)

Coutard et al (2023) also foster attempts to account for how dominant forms of infrastructural development became dominant and how alternative forms were marginalized.

Explore elsewheres and elsewhens *beyond the networked city*

Other 'alternative' approaches may be, and often have started to be, mobilized as a complement to mainstream or 'canonical' historical and social science methodologies.[7] Let us consider some candidates:

- *Thought experiments*: science fiction literature is a genre that rests upon thought experiments. Philosophical tradition has long acknowledged the value of such experiments as a reflection technique. Further critical reflection is needed to determine the conditions under which the heuristic power of thought experiments can best be deployed.
- *Speculative design* is a thought experiment equipped by 'fake future objects',[8] which may prove extremely valuable to reflect on the future – and the present – in a more *material*, and ultimately a more open way. Dunne and Raby (2013), for example, approach speculative design as a tool to create not only things but also ideas. Rather than attempting to predict the future, they pose 'what if?' design questions 'to open up all sorts of possibilities that can be discussed, debated, and used to collectively define a preferable future' and contend that as a consequence of speculating more about everything, 'reality will become more malleable' (Dunne and Raby, 2013: 6).
- *Serious games* have a growing importance in education, professional training, and crisis preparedness. They can therefore be considered as a tool to explore possible urban and social futures, the presence of those futures in the present, and associated infrastructural issues, or even as a tool to shape such futures.
- *Counterfactual history*: building on a growing acknowledgement of counterfactual history and the associated body of works (see Ferguson, 1999 for a pioneering contribution), Hartog (2017: 51) invites us to consider 'the possibilities of the past that could not occur' as a way to nourish the future and 'to escape presentism by restoring circulations between the past, the present, and the future'. This also resonates with Baschet (2018b: np), who invites (our) 'worlds always worried about paths to be traced ... to find inspiration in the unaccomplished dreams of the past'.

We can therefore use several relatively novel approaches to explore the processes of construction of urban and social futures, how they operate in the present or have operated in the past, and the part infrastructures play or may play in this process. The main reason why historians, social scientists, and scientists more generally should undertake such exploration is to keep futures open, to open up alternative imaginaries, and to avoid 'impoverished imaginations' (Datta, 2019: 396) or manifestations of the 'violence of imagination' (Simone, 2016: 6).

We need to develop a conversation beyond naive futurism and blind presentism about the most effective, fruitful, and open ways to preserve the plural forms of knowledge and knowledge production on possible futures. This appears as the best strategy to confront the major risks ahead, to escape resignation, and to facilitate the massive changes that will be necessary if contemporary societies are to escape those risks – changes that are so far largely unknown. Infrastructure researchers have a decisive contribution to make to collective efforts to 'maintain the primacy of the processual character of things to come' (Baschet, 2018b: np) and to facilitate the advent of more progressive and liveable futures.

Notes

[1] I use the word 'modern' to refer to what historians usually call 'late modern' (spanning roughly from the mid-eighteenth to the mid-twentieth century) and the word 'contemporary' to refer to the post-Second World War period. These periods, however, are blurred by the fact that there is a lag between a specific epoch-defining event and the realization of full cultural change through which this original event becomes the landmark of a new epoch.

[2] I have translated all quotes from publications in French.

[3] See Edwards's remark that 'infrastructures change too slowly for most of us to notice; the stately pace of infrastructural change is part of their reassuring stability. They exist, as it were, chiefly in historical time' (2003: 194).

[4] Coutard (2001), among others, shows how a 'modernizing imagination' has played a crucial role in programmes of rural electrification in France and the US.

[5] Schindler and Kanai (this volume) highlight a current manifestation of such infrastructure-based future-proofing.

[6] A notion borrowed from Ernst Bloch by Reinhart Koselleck and subsequently Hartog.

[7] The following developments have benefited from presentations by Nathalie Blanc, Martine Drozdz, Céline Granjou, and Carlos López Galviz and the exchanges that followed during a seminar on *The Construction of Urban Futures: Issues for Research*, held at Université Paris-Est on 3 March 2021 (organized by Olivier Coutard).

[8] I am indebted to Nathalie Blanc for this formulation.

References

Adam, B. (2004) *Time*, Cambridge: Polity Press.

Arbellot, G. (1973) 'La grande mutation des routes de France au XVIIIe siècle', *Annales. Economies, sociétés, civilisations*, 28(3): 765–791

Baschet, J. (2018a) *Défaire la Tyrannie du Présent. Temporalités Émergentes et Futurs Inédits*, Paris: La Découverte.

Baschet, J. (2018b) 'Interview by Jean Bastien', *Nonfiction*, 26 June. https://version-imprimable.nonfiction.fr/articlepdf-9443-entretien-avec-jerome-baschet-defaire-la-tyrannie-du-present.htm (accessed 5 September 2022).

Beniger, J.R. (1989) *The Control Revolution: Technological and Economic Origins of the Information Society*, Cambridge, MA: Harvard University Press.

Bonneuil, C. (2020) 'L'historien et la planète. Penser les régimes de planétarité à la croisée des écologies-monde, des réflexivités environnementales et des géopouvoirs'. https://hal.archives-ouvertes.fr/hal-03107193/file/Bonneuil_2020_R%C3%A9gimes%20de%20plan%C3%A9tarit%C3%A9_fr_Gesellschaftstheorie%20im%20Anthropoz%C3%A4n.pdf (accessed 1 September 2022).

Bonneuil, C., and Fressoz, J.-B. (2016) *The Shock of the Anthropocene: The Earth, History and Us*, London: Verso.

Bowker, G. (2015) 'Temporality', The Infrastructure Toolbox. https://culanth.org/fieldsights/temporality (accessed 31 August 2022).

Bretagnolle, A., Giraud, T., Verdier, N. (2010) 'Modéliser l'efficacité d'un réseau. Le cas de la poste aux chevaux dans la France pré-industrielle (1632–1833)', *L'Espace géographique*, 39(2): 117–31.

Breyer, S. (1982) *Regulation and Its Reform*, Cambridge, MA: Harvard University Press.

Calhoun C. (1992) 'The infrastructure of modernity: Indirect social relationships, information technology, and social integration', in H. Haferkamp and N.J. Smelser (eds) *Social Change and Modernity*, Berkeley, CA: University of California Press, pp 205–37.

Chakrabarty, D. (2018) 'Anthropocene time', *History and Theory*, 57(1): 5–32.

Coutard, O. (2001) 'Imaginaire et développement des réseaux techniques: Les apports de l'histoire de l'électrification rurale en France et aux Etats-Unis', *Réseaux*, 19(109): 75–94.

Coutard, O. (2010) 'Services urbains: la fin des grands réseaux', in O. Coutard and J.-P. Lévy (eds) *Ecologies Urbaines*, Paris: Anthropos-Economica (Coll. Villes), pp 102–9.

Coutard, O., and Guy, S. (2007) 'STS and the city: Politics and practices of hope', *Science, Technology and Human Values*, 32(6): 713–34.

Coutard, O., Bothereau, B., and Tarr, J.A. (2023) 'Histories (and stories) of off-grid technologies: A reappraisal', *Flux*, 131: 1–14.

Datta, A. (2019) 'Postcolonial urban futures: Imagining and governing India's smart urban age', *Environment and Planning D: Society and Space*, 37(3): 393–410.

De Swaan, A. (1988) *In Care of the State: Health Care, Education and Welfare in Europe and the USA in the Modern Era*, Cambridge: Polity Press.

Dunne, A., and Raby, F. (2013) *Speculative Everything: Design, Fiction, and Social dreaming*, Cambridge, MA: MIT Press.

Edwards, P.N. (2003) 'Infrastructures and modernity: Force, time, and social organizations in the history of socio-technical systems', in T.J. Misa, P. Brey, and A. Feenberg (eds.) *Modernity and Technology*, Cambridge, MA: MIT Press, pp 185–225.

Ferguson, N. (ed) (1999) *Virtual History: Alternatives and Counterfactuals*, New York: Basic Books.

Granjou, C., and Salazaar, J.F. (2016) 'CFP: Future knowing, future making: What anticipation does for STS', *4S/EASST conference 2016*. https://nomadit.co.uk/conference/easst2016/p/3866 (accessed 21 November 2022).

Hartog, F. (2016 [2003]) *Regimes of Historicity: Presentism and Experiences of Time* (translated by S. Brown), New York: Columbia University Press.

Hartog, F. (2009). 'Sur la notion de régime d'historicité. Entretien avec François Hartog', in C. Delacroix, F. Dosse, and P. Garcia (eds) *Historicités*, Paris: La Découverte (coll. Recherches), pp 133–49.

Hartog, F. (2017) 'Comment rouvrir les futurs? Entretien avec François Hartog, interview by O. Mongin and J.-L. Schlegel', *Esprit*, *431* (January 2017): 44–51.

Hartog, F. (2020a) *Chronos: l'Occident aux Prises avec le Temps*, Paris: Gallimard (Bibliothèque des histoires).

Hartog, F. (2020b) 'Les temporalités de François Hartog, interview by Florian Louis', *Le Grand Continent*. https://legrandcontinent.eu/fr/2020/10/08/francois-hartog/ (accessed 1 September 2022).

Hughes, T.P. (1983) *Networks of Power: Electrification in Western Society, 1880–1930*, Baltimore, MD: Johns Hopkins University Press.

Hughes, T.P. (1987) 'The evolution of large technological systems', in W.E. Bijker, T.P. Hughes, and T. Pinch (eds) *The Social Construction of Technological Systems: New Directions in the Sociology and History of Technology*, Cambridge, MA: MIT Press, pp 51–82.

Kitchin, R. (2019) 'The timescape of smart cities', *Annals of the American Association of Geographers*, 109(3): 775–90.

Koselleck, R. (1990 [1979]) *Le Futur Passé: Contributions à la Sémantique des Temps Historiques*, Paris: Éditions de l'EHESS.

Lefebvre, H. (2004) *Rhythmanalysis: Space, Time and Everyday Life*, London: Continuum.

Mann, M. (1984) 'The autonomous power of the state: Its origins, mechanisms and results', *European Journal of Sociology*, 25(2): 185–213.

Melosi, M. (2000) *The Sanitary City: Urban Infrastructure in America from Colonial Times to the Present*, Baltimore, MD: Johns Hopkins University Press.

Mitchell, T. (2011) *Carbon Democracy: Political Power in the Age of Oil*, London: Verso.

Mitchell, T. (2020) 'Infrastructures work on time', *e-flux Architecture*. https://www.e-flux.com/architecture/new-silk-roads/312596/infrastructures-work-on-time/ (accessed 11 June 2021).

Mukerji, C. (2010) 'The territorial state as a figured world of power: strategies, logistics, and impersonal rule', *Sociological Theory*, 28(4): 402–24.

Offner, J.-M. (1993) 'Le développement des réseaux techniques: Un modèle générique', *Flux*, 13–14: 11–18.

Olmstead, N.A. (2019) 'Data and temporality in the spectral city', *Philosophy & Technology*, 34: 243–63.

Rutherford, J. (2020) *Redeploying Urban Infrastructure: The Politics of Urban Socio-Technical Futures*, Cham: Palgrave Macmillan.

Scott, J.C. (1998) *Seeing Like a State: How Certain Schemes to Improve the Human Condition Have Failed*, New Haven, CT: Yale University Press.

Shove, E., Trentmann, F., and Watson, M. (2019) 'Introduction – Infrastructures in practice: The evolution of demand in networked societies', in E. Shove and F. Trentmann (eds) *Infrastructures in Practice: The Dynamics of Demand in Networked Societies*, London: Routledge, pp 3–9.

Simone, A. (2016) 'City of potentialities: An introduction', *Theory, Culture and Society*, 33(7–8): 5–29.

Tarr, J.A. (1996) *The Search for the Ultimate Sink: Urban Pollution in Historical Perspective*, Akron, OH: University of Akron Press.

Tarr, J.A., and Gabriel, D. (eds) (1988) *Technology and the Rise of the Networked City in Europe and America*, Philadelphia, PA: Temple University Press.

Vannini, P., and Taggart, J. (2015) *Off the Grid: Re-assembling Domestic Life*, New York: Routledge.

Wright, E.O. (2010) *Envisioning Real Utopias*, London: Verso.

5

Extensions as Infrastructure: The Temporalities between Subjugation and Liberation in Jayapura, West Papua

AbdouMaliq Simone

For Papuans, time is literally all over the place: there is the time of constantly deferred national independence, which in each passing year seems less likely to materialize. There is the time of unsettling as a mode of settler colonialism, operationalized by successive Indonesian governments that have accorded a cosmetic measure of self-rule but do not want Papuans to have much infrastructure to work with. There is the time of jettisoning, as many Papuans simply bow out of adherence to any narrative of progression, preferring to live in a 'time without time' rather than be situated on a scale of relative development or underdevelopment. There is the time of continuous and quotidian disjunctions, where Papuan social life follows constantly improvised rhythms and forms of gathering that produce no specific disposition but mark something different than what has transpired before. There is the time of accompaniment, where every context and event is supplemented with a singular sensibility and perception that is not translatable into anything else yet provides a measure of an experience of temporary freedom in the midst of relentless subjugation. Each of these temporalities has a provisional assemblage of materials, sites, protocols – in other words, an infrastructuring – that makes Jayapura, West Papua's largest city, seem perpetually 'new' in the sense of dispositions being constantly deferred in favour of a 'look' where the city seems to be going nowhere. It is as if there are simply too many temporalities at work, pushing and pulling against each other, with no hope of reconciliation.

For many residents of Jayapura, time begins as the famous song by the Papuan group the Black Brothers mark it:

> *In 1965, on 28 July, The Arfai headquarters was attacked by the Papuan Corps*
> *We finished them off, soldiers of The Cassowary Battalion*
> *We vow to keep fighting until independence …*
> *We don't want, and we really do not want*
> *We don't want to be slaves*
> *Regardless whether we will go hungry or full*
> *We will keep fighting*
> *Until we get our independence.* (Author's translation)

The song refers to the beginnings of what is commonly referred to as the 'great awakening', which gradually worked its way across all of West Papua's diverse terrain and populations in an enduring fight against Indonesian colonization/annexation and for national self-determination (Kusumaryati, 2018; 2020). From then on – from highland guerrilla movements to the elaboration of Papuan epistemologies at schools and universities; from ministrations from pulpits to street corners; to everyday subversions and refusals; to the intensive circulation of bodies, marked with all kinds of designations, across the territory and beyond (Chauvel, 2007) – an emerging sense of nation-time (MacLeod, 2015; Lele, 2023) was being constituted within the confines of widespread repression, extraction, militarization, and what has been called 'slow genocide' (Elmslie and Webb-Gannon, 2014).

An important aspect of the struggles for national liberation under conditions of intense military occupation, including targeted killings of Papuan militants, public intellectuals, students, and street gang members, is the way in which growing urban areas are used as platforms for the reciprocal extensions of Papuan households and resources across the entirety of the region: a circulatory force to contrast an occupying one. Lives are less consolidated in place but rather avail to others the possibility of a differentiated positioning, a new angle, a surfeit of relationality. Papuan cities become crossroads in a multiplicity of exchanges that proliferate interfaces and points of contact with an exterior reached through a network of pathways, secret 'highways' and interconnected fields, streams, and backroads leading in and out and towards different towns and settlements. This is not simply the product of a spatial imagination but of a temporal one as well, an ongoing project of 'Papuan time', a time of extending lives to each other as the materialization of a nation not yet realized in terms of the prevailing tropes of sovereignty and recognition (Rutherford, 2003; Kusumaryati, 2018). Even as Papuans are subject to the familiar civilizing missions that lead to little besides dejection, there is a sustained temporality of a refusal to cultivate the self as property even as the Indonesian apparatus tries to divide the Papuan 'body' into increasingly finite micro-units, like that of digital time-keeping.

Many Papuans believe that time does not exist, or at least does not count, before the auspicious date of 28 July 1965. Otherwise, as Elton, a postgraduate student at Walter Post Theological College, indicates, all time is considered "broken" – not in the usual sense of categorization, of clock times, parcels, bits, and units, but broken as an experience of the undulating 'bass lines' that come closest to depicting a Papuan experience of the ebbs and flows of relationalities with all things acting on each other, adjusting to their temperaments. While the subjugation of Papuan lives has been widely reported, often my interlocutors would indicate the greater importance of time itself being broken. The brokenness here does not refer to the abruption of valued ways of life. Rather, brokenness is the occasion for the different facets of human and non-human life to extend themselves to each other, to engage both the familiar and the unanticipated rhythms of how different entities were and could be associated with each other (also see Addie, this volume).

In a seminar on eschatology at Walter Post, 'Papuan time' is deliberated as concretizing the virtual capacities of any location within the ambit of an apparatus of control, one that assigns proportionalities of value and use. Instead, time marks ineffable lines of virtuality, always attempting to recompose lives with others, operating through an imperceptibility indicating their widening to a proliferation of perceivers: different voices, activities, sensibilities, and ontologies. These are lines of formless expression, the making felt of an experience that is always more than what can be identified at any given moment. It is a plenitude of possibility that continuously folds in upon itself as its mode of continuity, rather than being cut in the service of an imaginary or operating logics that enforce its articulation to an economic logic of efficiency with associated forward and backward resonances. Time is always *extensive*, always outpacing whatever forms that might measure or apportion it.

The aim of this chapter, then, is to explore some of the spatio-*temporal* dimensions of urban infrastructure that concretize aspects of such extensionality within a context of brutal colonial rule. Taking Jayapura, West Papua's largest urban area, as its empirical site, the chapter foregrounds the multifaceted notion of *extension* as a modality through which rule, resistance, accommodation, deferral, expansion, and subaltern imagination are both intertwined and detached in materializing built and social environments. Always on the cusp of being something else while often appearing to perpetually remain the same (obdurate, provisional, and unsettled), Jayapura may be a long way removed from the 'normative' urban world. But it has much to say about how multiple instantiations of the urban sit uneasily with each other in often strange patterns of contiguity and separation. What is important here are the ways in which variegated modes of unsettling attempt to unsettle each other. The usual strategic orientation on the part of colonial administrations to speed up instantiating facts on the ground is deferred in a seemingly ironic fashion to Papuan efforts to develop itineraries of circulation that ward off the relinquishing of aspirations for national independence and the divide and rule tactics of the Indonesian military. Whereas Indonesian occupation would seem to emphasize the consolidation of West Papua's integration into Indonesia as an inevitable step-by-step narrative, Papuan time emphasizes multiple extensionalities: time as a means of extending across different regions, vernaculars, and orientations, a means of extending the sense of what Papua might be, in a frame that is not reduced to submission or resistance.

The observations of this chapter are primarily based on walking through almost every street and lane in the metropolitan area over a five-month period, accompanied by an assortment of local 'wise-persons' drawn from local churches, mosques, schools, or customary associations. Collaboratively, through dialogue, we would compose a provisional genealogy of districts and a rudimentary mapping of their important features and operations. For this chapter, materials are definitively not ethnographic, in that they represent a kind of thematic and composite overview of the city as a place of multiple extensions.

While at first glance the notion of extension might be linked and limited to familiar conceptualizations of *extended urbanization*, and indeed draws much of its explanatory valence from it, its use here exceeds the usual parameters to instead act as an infrastructure itself. In other words, extensions are infrastructural not in the sense of expanding or adding on to discernible material forms but in that they entail both spatial and temporal operations that enable the sensing of the varied, virtual articulations among structures otherwise not specified, mapped, or rendered visible in discernible form. Here, extensions intensify, reproduce, or simply sustain the viability of localized operations through articulating them to differentiated exteriors, most elementally as a hedge against entropy, politically (as a manoeuvre to lock in seemingly virtuous co-dependencies) and in urban terms (as a means of exerting particular kinds of claims, rights of access, and spaces of manoeuvre). Extensions become a mode of existence, in the sense both of attempts to saturate the region with the micro-regimens of colonial control and of all the mostly faint efforts to recuperate a time that has been broken. Mediating this antagonism seeks to enable a kind of ontological integrity to function across distances, embedding the endurance of entities or operations within a larger set of nodes, contacts, interfaces, debt relations, and material affordances, or exerting experimental agency across unfamiliar terrain.

West Papua has long sought to be an independent nation. This was an aspiration dutifully expressed according to international law in 1962. It failed in its realization due to the political mechanizations of Cold War politics that saw the United Nations succumb to the complicities between the governments of the US, the Netherlands, and Indonesia to deter the supposed spread of communism (Kirksey, 2012; Viartasiwi, 2018). Indonesia was delegated control until a referendum on West Papua's definitive status could be held. This did not occur until 1969 and even then only involved some 1,025 'tribal chiefs' selected by the Indonesian military, who voted in favour of incorporation at gunpoint. As the 60-year hold of the Indonesian state over West Papua has worked its way through various iterations of military overkill, concessions to gestures of self-rule, and systematic attempts to alter the demographic complexion of the territory, the urban form of Jayapura has also shifted to reflect oscillating centres of economic and cultural gravity.

Extensions reflect not only the territorial expansions of a city always already fragmented, but also the ways in which a sense of 'Papuan time' is being recuperated through the very vernaculars that attempt to enhance control. Here, a simultaneity of diverse authorities, populations, settlement practices, social ontologies, and built and natural environments extend themselves to each other as enabling, constraining, and unsettling functions (see Figure 5.1). Given the large-scale expropriation of Papuan land (often sold as the only means to garner income) and the concurrent ways in which Papuans adamantly hold on to and actively render 'useless' land across the crevices, ravines, swamps, and hilltops of the city, complementarities are spurred among those who tend to the endurance of communities with long histories of self-sufficiency and those who insinuate themselves in the interstices of various terrains across the metropolitan region.

Jayapura is a brutal place of immense beauty, combining extraordinary surveillance and indifference, claustrophobic rule, and the absence of any significant regulation. In a metropolitan region of 700,000 inhabitants, indigenous Papuans are a minority in the face of substantial inflows of largely subsidized migrants from other parts of Indonesia. While much of this inward migration might be understood as a kind of settler colonialism, the intersections of the lives of migrants and what they do to make a living are rarely consolidated or stabilized. There is a constant sense of temporariness and uncertainty that maintains Jayapura in a time of an *interminable present*: a sense that the city is always 'new'.

This chapter will cover several key features of the complexion of the metropolitan area, with an emphasis on how multiple surfaces, sectors, and territories reflect a continuous atmosphere of provisionality. This has less to do with insufficiencies and more to do with the very ways in which territories of operation are being constructed through the folding in of essential components including land, material affordances, a politics of visibility, multiple practices of compliance and disobedience, the highly

Figure 5.1: Everything filtered through everything else in Jayapura, West Papua, 2023

Source: AbdouMaliq Simone

differentiated applications of law, and the multifaceted instrumentalization of religion.

Times of forced autonomy

The urbanization of Papuans has largely proceeded through the incorporation of primarily agrarian lands and activities into an expanding urban region. This has occurred through processes of institutional building, participation in various professional trainings, and the centration exerted through marketing activities. But cities in West Papua remain largely the elaboration of residual colonial towns, centres of administration that have attracted inflows of Papuan migrants from all regions but favoured particular ethnicities, such as the Biak, for specific administrative positions and jobs as teachers, nurses, and social workers. No other vehicle of urban accumulation existed for Papuans. The urban economy, in turn, remains largely ethnically segmented. Javanese migrants – mostly situated in the large, rapidly growing urban hinterlands of Koya where they have had access to subsidized agricultural land – continue to provide most of the foodstuff for the market (Suhartawan et al, 2017). In the Abepura markets, the large-scale wholesale and distributor shops are managed by Chinese and Buginese. On the middle scale, market stalls are controlled by traders from Sulawesi or those of Javanese, Madurese, and Minang backgrounds. Buginese sell clothes, groceries, glassware, and vegetables. Makassarese dominate in the sale of sea products and fish. Butonese sell toys, knock-off products, and second-hand clothes. Madurese offer vegetables and cart services. Minangs sell clothes and electronic devices. Long-standing migrants from Toraja work as drivers and mechanics, while the Ambonese are known for providing security services and run many of the major rackets. At the bottom of the ladder are Papuan women traders (mama-mama), mainly from the highlands, who sell small quantities of garden products such as vegetables, yams, fruits, and betel nuts (Akhmad et al, 2019).

Only with the passage of the Otsus Law 21/2001 (autonomy agreement) – which created two distinct provinces in West Papua, with the trappings of self-rule and reserving the governorship and 80 per cent of civil servant positions for Papuans – was another route opened towards economic advancement (Resosudarmo et al, 2014). In practice, this is precisely the objective of this legislation, which was renewed in 2022 with the creation of three additional provinces: to buy the consent of educated Papuans and provide a pathway to accumulation (Chairullah, 2022). Any significant decisions concerning the disposition of resources, policing, and policy, though, remain de facto the purview of the central government in Jakarta (Chauvel, 2011; Bertrand, 2014).

Attempts to institute and extend a vehicle of urban accumulation to Papuans through the performance of governmentality, while creating a limited vehicle to concretize middle-class status in Papuan cities, has largely had the effect of extending Papuan identity, sensibilities, and affiliations across various registers. While the enduring colonial apparatus seeks to impose a common national identity through establishing itself as the synthesizer of ethnic differences, Papuans increasingly attempt to undermine this manoeuvre by using a highly fungible notion of 'blackness' to institute a different kind of urban modernity (see Kusumaryati, 2021). In Eastern Indonesia, race appeared as a marker of inequality and injustice only after the abolition of slavery and was deployed as a mode of 'sorting' in a population forced into more intensive practices of settlement, rather than circulation across territories. Blackness, as such, indicated something always out of place. Instead of marginality, then, Papuans turn to blackness as a means of living 'out of the emplacement' to which they are subjected, according to a different kind of time. Returning to the discussions at Walter Post, to be out of place then means less the real processes of dispossession but rather a valorized recuperation of the very ebbs and flows that mark 'Papuan time'. Culturally, then, Jayapura is experiencing a wide range of experiments in 'blackness' as a vehicle of interconnection among not only diverse Papuan groupings but also other so-called black or Melanesian Indonesians, such as Ambon, Kei, and Timorese, who make up roughly 15 per cent of Jayapura's population. These interconnections are also extended more broadly across the so-called Black Pacific, whose nations have often been caught between strong sympathies for Papuan national liberation and strong political pressures from Indonesia (Kusumayarti, 2021b).

The register of blackness is increasingly ascendant as a vehicle of organizing articulations among disparate Papuan groupings, pulling orientations towards issues of anti-blackness globally and eastward towards Melanesia, however geographically proximate and virtually inaccessible it remains (all flights from Jayapura are domestic and oriented westwards to other parts of Indonesia). Yet within Jayapura, there is increasing attention to the urban fabric as a series of interconnected nodes of differentiated blackness. While each node may still be ensconced in particular ethnic and religious concentrations, there is increasingly a surfeit of articulation facilitating more expansive circulations of ideas, conversations, and gatherings that introduce new functions and dynamics to the existing environment.

In turn, the state's response to this extended field of everyday transactions, sometimes surfacing as various forms of resistance, is largely centred on increasing the militarization of urban space. As Chauvel (2021) points out, it is estimated that in 2013, there was one soldier or police officer for every 97 residents, and this had only risen by 2023, with increases of 20 per cent and 25 per cent in military and police deployments respectively. True to form, military and police presence assumes the form of both intimate implantation on a neighbourhood level, with significantly sized bases and personnel in every district, and of massive, sprawling installations, with their gated communities and golf courses, situated at high points and strategic crossings.

Large numbers of military officials are involved in land deals and smuggling rackets and exert significant influence over the supply chain of essential commodities. In recent years they have extended their role from 'peacekeeping' and business deals to acting as a 'development arm' of the state, involved in managing infrastructure projects, such as building schools, clinics, and sanitation systems (Kusumayarti, 2021a). Some military personnel are known to enrol Papuan women as concubines, father children that are then abandoned, and shake down local populations for a range of 'services' (Chao, 2022a).

Materializing extensions

In Jayapura, morphological extensions are necessitated by the characteristics of the terrain (coastal, riverine, mountainous), which continuously interrupt the possibility of elongating a seamless and connected urban fabric. A structural disarticulation is instantiated in its place, one which is only partially remediated by extending the road system (see Figure 5.2). As such, Jayapura is many different 'cities'. At the same time, these morphological interruptions permit a range of feral settlement practices, particularly for those who desire to attenuate the intensity of urban connections, who may wish to live off-grid and pursue more traditional subsistence-based livelihoods (Nerenberg, 2021).

Papuan settlements across these 'interruptions' retain a sense of unruliness that continually threatens to engulf large swathes of the urban environment whose proximity to the bush demands large expenditures of time and labour for maintenance and repair. Such is often not forthcoming, since Jayapura residency for many is largely an extension of fundamental attachments elsewhere, in other regions of Indonesia. From any vantage point of the urban tissue, which extends across valleys and coasts, the surrounding mountains are visible and thus also the Papuan settlements which now reach to even higher elevations and are largely inaccessible except by paths generally unknown. This omnipresent visibility, which might normatively be unattended to in day-to-day affairs, nevertheless seems to haunt the imagination of the majority migrant population as something structurally unknowable and to be defended against. For Papuans, those who have long been thoroughly urbanized away from the trappings of rural life, they exist as a necessary historical antecedent and a resource that can be turned to in times of crisis.

For example, the governor's office was occupied for several days by university students during the anti-racist mobilizations of 2019. While the military was mobilized to eventually end the siege, there was some initial hesitancy in terms of moving in with force, not wanting to amplify the weakness of so-called Papuan institutions and temporarily respecting more nuanced mediations on the part of Papuan authorities. When it became clear to the occupiers that the military had lost its patience, they left the headquarters under the cover of darkness, making their way across the short distance to the sea. Here, Papuan fisher folk from the nearby Dock IX – grateful for the distribution of large supplies of rice and other consumables diverted to them by the students from the governor's large warehouse – transported the occupiers in scores of small boats to land north of the city, unreachable by road. From there the students made their way through the

Figure 5.2: The urban extensions of Jayapura, West Papua, 2023

Source: AbdouMaliq Simone

mountains to the outskirts of Cendrawasih University, some 40 kilometres away, hiding away in the bush for nearly two weeks before slipping back into their normal student routines.

Even for those 'migrants' who have been in Jayapura for a long time (some of whom were born there), an affective sense of belonging is usually attached to villages and towns in Sulawesi, Maluku, or Java. As a result, much construction is provisional. This is also a city of *kontraken* and *kos kosan*: boarding houses that resemble cheap American motels providing both short- and long-term accommodation, which house the majority of the city's residents in intensely crowded conditions. These are developed and owned by those able to acquire the long-term use of plots, whose value is maximized through the provision of accommodation, with the owner able to live off the rent. It is not uncommon for entrepreneurs who have migrated to the city to import potential clients from their home areas (usually poor rural residents) and establish them as nearly captured labour in Jayapura, available to extend and diversify not only business activities but also local political power.

While an intended long duration of residence or faith in the eventual success of individual or household effort is commonly marked through curating at least the appearance of residential consolidation or incremental improvement, many residents have no inclination to do so. Sites of residence frequently display the accumulation of everyday survival practices. The debris of inoperable tools and furniture or accumulated waste is strewn across the living space. A lack of either material means or motivation imbues districts with an overarching sense of impending ruination replete with an amassed archive of disparate uses, trials, and errors: all the things that have not worked. Whether this can be attributed to their conviction that they will eventually return home, the ambiguous statuses of their tenure, or the uncertainties about future dispositions for Papua in general cannot be easily distinguished as they blend together to various degrees.

Often such residential settlements are anchored by the construction of a mosque or church that has acquired land beyond its immediate needs or that intentionally uses land acquisition for religious purposes, as a basis on which to install a settlement. For a city quickly approaching one million, there are certainly enough churches and mosques to accommodate a city ten times that size. On one level, the proliferation of religious institutions not only reflects an integral aspect of colonization and disciplinary civility but also addresses the predominance of connections as crucial to livelihood. Neither the Dutch nor the Indonesians have been historically interested in cultivating an urban sensibility based on the responsibilities and affordances of citizenship.

Rather, a 'big man' syndrome pervades almost all aspects of life (Rio, 2014; Reumi and Kationg, 2021). Even the Papuan conventions that have historically favoured the clarity of lineage as the right to rule – and importantly register significant decisions over land disposition and disputes – have largely given way to the consolidation of power through the performance and sometimes violent exertions of toughness and daring. This often occurs through attempts to control space and how it is used, extracting monetary benefit from it, which in turn is distributed in displays of apparent benevolence. To insert oneself into processes that are underway, steering attention to one's potential capacities to deliver unexpected benefits, is a critical manoeuvre in the constitution of local authority. From religion to hip-hop to politics to project development, 'bigness' is often the primary objective. This reinforces the need for everyday social connections in a climate where meritocracy is largely a façade to justify the curtailment of Papuan participation in a broad range of economic and governmental activities.

As such, Jayapura is a city with large numbers of young men sitting idle around barely inhabitable hostels, once intent upon completing some form of advanced education but lacking the means or support to do so. Drug use and alcohol consumption has become a normal routine which affects the temporality of urban life. Large numbers of residents maintain erratic schedules and rely upon theft to meet their daily needs. In contrast, more connected, successfully educated Papuans are then even more determined to counter the stereotypical depictions of collective lassitude with assertive initiatives to achieve, usually in terms of monetary independence and career elevation. In doing so, they often concede the efficacy of maintaining different scales of affiliation with Indonesia despite any nationalist sentiments they might hold (Smith, 2021).

Extending space–time

Despite these emergent class and intra-Papuan ethnic and regional differences of orientation, a key element of everyday urban life is the effort made by Papuan organizations, churches, neighbourhoods, and extended families to arrange various gatherings. It is common to see the roads teeming with pick-up trucks filled to the brim with singing or shouting adults and children on their way to some usually impromptu event. On weekends, the beaches are full of family and associational gatherings that continuously reaffirm the importance of collective life: of people tending to each other through food, dance, music, and palaver.

The aggrandizement and numerical accumulation of big men, the ongoing creation of new political and administrative positions (usually redundant), the sometimes violent clashes among different factions competing for limited resources, and the divergent trajectories of those who have struggled to incorporate themselves in some form of valorized livelihood and those who consider themselves completely dispossessed have all registered a marked sense of fragmentation among urban Papuans. This reiteration of the importance of gathering, of rounding up the multitudes, of using physical mobility to socially link different settlements across a spread-out metropolitan region, is a concrete concrescence of a political culture despite the far-fetched possibilities of independence. It is a way in which this very concrete extension of bodies to each other figures a space of coherence across dispersal. It is a way in which Papuans feel they are already living in a time of liberation but are also free from having to commit themselves to whatever presentist contingencies (that is, the actual work of self-rule) would inevitably present themselves. It is a rehearsal for a way of being 'independent' but without commitment to a specific map or protocol.

Engagements with and withdrawal from other Indonesians and institutions also oscillate. The Biak, the most urbanized of Papuan ethnicities during much of the post-independence period, performed avid engagements with Indonesian institutions, extracting from those engagements a surplus of prestige and status that had local fungibility as a symbolic currency. This did not mean that deep-seated subjective formations were not in accordance with nationalist ideologies – in fact, some of the most militant accentuations of Papuan sovereignty have come from the Biak – rather, it is a strategy of extroversion parlayed into creating space through dissimulation (Rutherford, 2003).

This oscillating shape of engagements is registered on the composition of the Jayapura social body. Perhaps the predominant 'dirty public secret' is how mixed the urban population actually is, with large numbers of *campur* (those of mixed parentage or dual heritage) present, but for whom no clear stable categorization emerges. While the mobilization of 'blackness' as a tentative unifying trope has emerged more frequently and substantially in recent years, there is a residual hesitancy in its use given the long history of negative connotations associated with it. These connotations were very much internalized by large numbers of the indigenous Papuan population while other 'black' Timorese populations (for example, Ambonese, Florese, Kei) simply used them to ward off various cultural and psychological encroachments emanating from the Javanese majority.

The infrastructure of mixing is also fraught with different instances of breakage, that is, the large volume of broken marriages, abandoned children, and the often problematic incorporation of offspring into one racial/ethnic group to the exclusion of significant affiliations with others. In often rigid lines of descent, with implications for accessing land and social connections in particular, there may be instances of exclusion. At the same time, the public secret concerns just how extensive miscegenation may be, whereby territories or communities may have little choice but to readjust their attitudes and practices around it. Sometimes they 'turn to it' as an instrument for smoothing out potential conflicts or use it as a means of imbricating otherwise seemingly divergent lives with each other. Such mixing tends to instigate a continuous tension in boundary making, particularly concerning questions of what might constitute an authentic Papua, which are real considerations for the distribution of reserved civil service positions and usually reconcilable by having at least one parent capable of tracing genealogy to an established indigenous Papuan affinal grouping.

Yet the mixtures are often more complex and even more significant in terms of their implications for the delineation of prospective political mobilizations that seem to inch their way towards both legitimation for locally birthed political parties (separate from those nationally imposed and so far the only legal venues) and the dissipation of the coherence of the so-called Nusantara associations, that is, those with a fairly precise ethnic identification who support Indonesian claims on Papua, and which are well subsidized and extensively armed (Hernawan, 2021).

At the same time, the dispositions of land use and ownership in key districts of the city reflect the tendency of migrants to 'secure the roads', sometimes producing the strange contiguity of large estates abutting shantytowns and historical Papuan villages. The urban tissue is often a jumbled mixture of settlement types, tenures, built environments, and capacities. This is a disposition that is by no means unusual across different urban regions, but it is amplified in particularly sharp ways in Jayapura given the intensity of extortionate measures often applied to force Papuans to sell land (as their only available source of income) and then to retreat further into what for others would be inhospitable or unviable sites and conditions (Mulyadi et al, 2019). Here, they disappear from view, a practice which itself embodies an ambiguous series of advantages and disadvantages. What does local territorial administration come to mean when ways of life so radically diverge, where residents – even among a more heterogeneous set of Papuan communities with different temporal anchorage points in the city – would seem on the surface to have little to do with each other?

Yet these conundrums of adjacency have haunted the structuring of spatial formations ever since the advent of the plantation. Things physically next to each other do not necessarily relate and are not necessarily subsumed under an overarching framework (Chao, 2022b). Intimacies, localities, closeness: all must be figured across different geographies, for it is not simply a matter of distance. As is often the case in urban peripheries, intensely discrepant activities and built environments will stand next to each other, assume the appearance of locality, but entail a different calculus of relations to really connect. Mutual witnessing perhaps takes place, but not necessarily a sense that they have anything to do with each other beyond a factual presence, and therefore a strange relationality is produced.

This entails a temporal dimension as well. If trauma is not history but rather an unrepresentable event or era that gets endlessly repeated and goes nowhere except through its fixation to particular objects or ideals (changing the same), then afterlives (which may function as ghosts, spirits, strange subjectivities) exceed any ideal form. The Angkasa district, for example, in its heterogeneity of settlement dispositions, may have created a small space for a Papuan elite or at least a middle class to enunciate itself in terms of aesthetic and built form. Yet the apparent 'modernization' of the district – proceeding in the face of the extruded, marginalized endurance of the original Papuan inhabitants in deep, recessed gullies and ravines, or the seemingly impenetrable hilltops – cannot erase its haunting by an enduring atmosphere of temporariness and incompletion. Places like Angkasa, then, continue to embody the power of the event of subjugation to be otherwise, to convey what might have been, what might actually be, in ways that move things along, extending things beyond their fixations and enclosures. Entire sections of roads in and out mysteriously disappear. There are constant sightings of multitudes of spirits that spread across the manicured backyards of new middle-class houses. The terrain becomes replete with secrets and absences. What price is yet to be paid for such relative tranquility and success? To what extent is it possible to leave behind the dreams that were promised then destroyed in favour of these new promises of accumulation? As such, these are spaces of incessant speculation, rumour, gossip, and questioning.

Dock IX is a series of coastline settlements that surround a pronounced narrow bay just to the north of the historic centre. It has long been considered the purview of Buton, Bugis, and Makassar (BBM) migrants given their historic domination of fishing, trade, and transhipment. The ways in which they consolidate dense clustering on the water obviates many of the complications and conflicts that come to the fore when migrants attempt to encroach upon so-called native land. These types of settlements are prolific across the port cities of Indonesia. Even though these coastal incursions displaced many Papuan coastal and fishing communities, the incursions of the so-called BBM came from extending their command over navigation of the seas into navigation of commodities across various urban markets, thus cultivating a special kind of resentment.

But coastal Papuans did not simply disappear or move; they established themselves again in various interstitial spaces near the elongating settlements of the Muslim Bugis and Buton. While continuing to eke out some living from fishing, the majority of these Papuans invested in keeping things 'unsettled' through various forms of small daily 'interceptions' of goods and shakedowns, as well as requests for various charitable acts, while building deep along the tributaries and creeks and extending up into the surrounding hills. At the same time, there was a concerted, implicit, and constant performance of restlessness, of young men constantly moving back and forth, constantly congregating quickly and temporarily in various constellations across all different kinds of spaces, making themselves incessantly visible as if they were always up to something, some plan or project that was in the early stages of deployment, constantly provoking a sense of unease and curiosity while at the same time rarely attacking or disrupting head-on. With little money and few services or commodities to sell, there was not much concrete they could do to actually displace BBM consolidation and entrepreneurship.

Rather, this incessant and tacit commitment to demonstrating the possible existence of an entire other substrate or infrastructure of concerted action – an almost magical capacity, beyond words – has gradually worn the BBM down. Many have left for other districts in Abepura or Sentani as Papuans are increasingly 'repatriated' to their former places on Dock IX. Here it was the mobilization of collective performance extending itself beyond anything that could be construed as demonstration, festival, worship, or guerrilla formations into a strange vernacular, resisting clear translation or interpretation, that generated an infrastructural effect on the distribution of materials and affordances. It was an instance of urban life at the extensions.

Perpetually new cities

The 2022 security agreement concluded between the People's Republic of China and the Solomon Islands registered alarm bells throughout the Pacific, perhaps signalling a momentous realignment of regional affiliations and geopolitical dynamics. Imaginations ran wild with speculation about substantial extensions of the Belt and Road Initiative (BRI) apparatus in terms of new maritime corridors, fishing practices, and nascent IT industries. Even as the actual instantiation of BRI projects in the Pacific has been quite limited, and although the Solomons agreement was largely spurred by contentious internal politics, on the ground it is unavoidable to weigh in on the potential implications (Fraenkel and Smith, 2022), especially as the intensity of affiliations with China is increasingly becoming a major fault line of political contestation, not only in the Solomons but also in Papua New Guinea (PNG), Fiji, and Vanuatu. PNG has officially signed on to be a BRI partner, and there are purportedly over 70 state-owned enterprises operating in metallurgy, fibre optics, and construction, as well as the substantiation of a long-existent Chinese presence in retail and distribution, to the dismay of many Papuans (PNG) (O'Dowd, 2021).

While increased Chinese presence has enabled significant sectors across Melanesian political apparatuses to be more overtly committed to issues of regional autonomy, consolidation, and West Papuan aspirations for independence, it also remains a double-edged sword in terms of the often brazen indifference demonstrated to indigenous economic processes. Even as the Chinese increasingly dominate the elaboration of a green extraction economy in Eastern Indonesia (focusing on nickel mining and smelting, as well as lithium, copper, and rare earth metals), the bulk of investments and activities are centred in Sulawesi and Halmahera. Their on-the-ground presence in West Papua has been limited. While it has been reported that the Chinese have financially undergirded the Indonesian stake in West Papua's Freeport, one of the world's largest mines, the security situation has largely limited the scope of foreign investment and presence (Anabarja, 2021).

Nevertheless, in the aftermath of the Solomons accord, there were whispers across some of the backstreets of Jayapura that the Chinese may now be more prepared to assume an activist stance regarding West Papuan aspirations, particularly considering the multiple irritations the Chinese experience with Indonesia's maritime policies and intensifying Islamic ethos. But one rumour was particularly interesting, centring on the intentions of the Chinese to eventually build a 'new city' in Jayapura that would constitute a centre of gravity for its growing Melanesian engagements. Such a rumour is particularly 'bizarre' given how cut off Jayapura is practically for articulations to its Pacific neighbours. Although Indonesia and PNG are incrementally establishing more substantive links – from the symbolic twinning of Jayapura and Port Moseby to the upgrading of road links and the collaborative policing of border smuggling – Jayapura continues to face the Pacific, with few substantive links. As Indonesia is an affiliate member of the Melanesian Spearhead Group (with the United Liberation Movement for West Papua, the region's most prominent nationalist grouping, consigned to observer status), there are few collective forums through which any such articulations can be deliberated. The Jokowi government has even been aggressively arguing that Indonesia is the largest repository of Melanesians across its eastern provinces and thus any specific cultural or racial argument for West Papua independence is largely moot.

Still, many Papuan residents of Jayapura, while always professing the need for independence, increasingly see a more expansive regional role for Jayapura as a potentially Melanesian economic powerhouse as a much more attainable modality of everyday self-determination. Thus, the rumour that the Chinese were preparing to build a 'new city' is not entirely baseless in terms of how urban Papuans think of potential dispositions and trajectories of their social and economic aspirations. Within an urban economy where Papuan routes to accumulation are primarily limited to their usually ambivalent participation in the apparatuses created by the Special Autonomy Law in West Papua, an extension of relations with other Melanesian nations is imagined as a medium of brokerage and entrepreneurship that would be largely unavailable to the *amber* (non-Papuan) residents of the city who have come to dominate almost all economic activity. By attempting to make the rest of the Pacific more intimately 'feel' Papua as something more than a space of victimage, a claim is made on a different socio-political future. There is a strong perception among Papuans that the Makassar and Manado in particular are determined to overwhelm the city with members of their ethnic groups, even at the cost of recruiting thousands of the most marginal and impoverished people to reside in the increasingly vast and crowded 'shanty districts' of the city, with little to sustain them. Without these Melanesian articulations, beyond the widespread affirmation of common cultural orientations (*wabntokisin*), Jayapura remains an incomplete city, something perpetually 'new'. Perhaps ironically then, rumours of a 'new city' are deployed to think about putting an end to this eternal 'newness'.

Conclusion: Extending the eternal present

So just how is Jayapura a 'new city', particularly in a context where there is so much attention to the new urban constructions of the BRI and the development of Nusantara, Indonesia's new capital city in Kalimantan? 'New' primarily does the work of indicating the conceptualization and construction of urban entities that connote a sense of entirety and self-sufficiency: exemplars of interoperability, technological innovation, reduced carbon footprints, and the curation of new modalities of inhabitation that obviate dependencies on automobility and encourage proximity among different domains of everyday life.

But, at the same time, 'newness' points to a temporality where urban formations seem to have neither discernible past nor future. They appear to come out of nowhere and seem to be going nowhere in particular. These are formations not intended for 'settlement' but rather for combinations of extraction, provisional shelter, and population control, instigated by either war, short-term opportunism, punitive sensibilities, colonial scrutiny, or emergencies of various sorts. They neither manifest a clear historical trajectory nor permit residents to work towards cultivating one. Rather, they often reflect a built environment through which a 'history of activity' consists of materials, waste, and items strewn across the landscape with no clear indication of what they were used for and if they have any ongoing use. 'Newness' here is a seemingly interminable present, one devoid of consolidation, incremental change, or trajectories of attainment. It is rather the simple repetition of everyday existence, albeit while recognizing that such repetition will often produce slightly new dispositions and arrangements (see Addie, this volume).

While sometimes referred to as 'sacrifice zones' – repositories of the excluded, the wasted, the ineligible – these can take the shape of 'cities' largely left on their own to figure out the practices and material underpinnings of reproduction, entailing provisional articulations of all kinds to a shifting register of exteriors. They might take the form of encampments, either intentionally designed and administered by national or multilateral organizations or auto-constructed by the vestiges of former work forces in mines, plantations, or factories. Sometimes they assume a shape like that of 'garrison towns', to which populations have been relocated to defend themselves against a range of threats, or from which incursions are launched in surrounding territories, a history entirely dependent upon raiding and warding off raids, for example, the small cities that often appear in the proximity of large extraction zones or those based on illegal economies such as drugs.

Emplaced often on the 'periphery of things', even far beyond the conventional array of informal settlements and suburbs, these cities are sometimes the product of speculation by developers who made promises of affordability to an aspirant middle class, or to residents of urban cores who had been subject to repeated assaults on their livelihoods and living spaces by police, predatory politicians, and businesspersons. When their incomes collapsed, when administrative responsibility was never assumed by any local authority, when developers had long disappeared, these cheaply constructed cities soon fell apart. Residents encumbered with escalating debt often had no choice but to remain in place, shore up the vestiges of the town to ward off total ruination, and depend financially on remittances from elsewhere – again, a sense of 'newness' that entails a never-ending present.

In Jayapura, in the same backstreets where rumours of a Chinese-instigated 'new city' were being proffered, there has also been talk of Jayapura as Indonesia's predominant 'black city'. Blackness is thus extended almost as if it is a gift, a promise: a way for Jayapura to extend itself beyond the implosive character of mundane grinding colonial rule, of all the quotidian brutalities, of everything put on 'hold' as Papuans seem to be actively frozen in time. Here, a mode of urban existence is imagined that pries away its Ambonese, Kei, Timorese, and Alor residents from the status of migrants to enfold them in a speculative deployment of blackness as an infrastructure that both circumvents and exceeds the constraints of either Indonesian or Papuan citizenship, ethnic or regional belonging. It is the imagination of a cosmopolitan urban sensibility that might further establish Jayapura as the key node – the key manifestation – of a Pacific urbanism that in turn might effectively loosen the grip of obdurate coloniality and be freed from both the temporalities of an interminable present and the broken time of Papuans' purported development insufficiencies.

References

Akhmad, R., Tanjung, R.H., Poli, A., Ali, A., and Kumoro, N.B. (2019) 'Ethnicity, identity, and the politics of space in urban society of Jayapura City', *Advances in Social Sciences Research Journal*, 6(2): 383–99.

Anabarja, S. (2021) 'On development and political security nexus', *Tamkang Journal of International Affairs*, 24(4): 119–57.

Bertrand, J. (2014) 'Autonomy and stability: The perils of implementation and "divide-and-rule" tactics in Papua, Indonesia', *Nationalism and Ethnic Politics*, 20(2): 174–99.

Chairullah, E. (2022) *Indonesia's Failure in Papua: The Role of Elites in Designing, Implementing and Undermining Special Autonomy*, London: Routledge.

Chao, S. (2022a) *In the Shadow of the Palms: More-than-Human Becomings in West Papua*, Durham, NC: Duke University Press.

Chao, S. (2022b) '(Un)worlding the plantationocene: Extraction, extinction, emergence', *eTropic: Electronic Journal of Studies in the Tropics*, 21(1): 165–91.

Chauvel, R. (2007) 'Refuge, displacement and dispossession: Responses to Indonesian rule and conflict in Papua', *Dynamics of Conflict and Displacement in Papua, Indonesia, Refugee Studies Centre Working Paper*, 42: 32–51.

Chauvel, R. (2011) 'Policy failure and political impasse: Papua and Jakarta a decade after the "Papuan Spring"', in P. King, J. Elmslie, and C. Webb-Gannon (eds) *Comprehending West Papua*, Sydney: Centre of Peace and Conflict Studies, University of Sydney, pp 105–15.

Chauvel, R. (2021) 'West Papua: Indonesia's last regional conflict', *Small Wars & Insurgencies*, 32(6): 913–44.

Elmslie, J., and Webb-Gannon, C. (2014) 'A slow-motion genocide: Indonesian rule in West Papua', *Griffith Journal of Law & Human Dignity*, 1(2): 142–65.

Fraenkel, J., and Smith, G. (2022) 'The Solomons–China 2022 security deal: Extraterritoriality and the perils of militarisation in the Pacific Islands', *Australian Journal of International Affairs*, 76(5): 473–85.

Hernawan, B. (2021) 'Papua', *The Contemporary Pacific*, 33(2): 548–56.

Kirksey, E. (2012) *Freedom in Entangled Worlds: West Papua in the Architecture of Global Power*, Durham, NC: Duke University Press.

Kusumaryati, V. (2018) 'Ethnography of a colonial present: History, experience, and political consciousness in West Papua'. Doctoral dissertation, Harvard University, Graduate School of Arts & Sciences.

Kusumaryati, V. (2020) 'Adat institutionalisation, the state and the quest for self-determination in West Papua', *The Asia Pacific Journal of Anthropology*, 21(1): 1–16.

Kusumaryati, V. (2021) '#Papuanlivesmatter: Black consciousness and political movements in West Papua', *Critical Asian Studies*, 53(4): 453–75.

Lele, G. (2023) 'Asymmetric decentralization, accommodation and separatist conflict: Lessons from Aceh and Papua, Indonesia', *Territory, Politics, Governance*, 11(5): 972–90.

MacLeod, J. (2015) *Merdeka and the Morning Star: Civil Resistance in West Papua*, Brisbane: University of Queensland Press.

Mulyadi, T., Kamsi K., Surwandono S., and Trisno, R. (2019) 'The legitimacy of Ondoafi in conflict settlement of customary land tenure in Sentani, Papua', *Jurnal Media Hukum*, 26(1): 112–21.

Nerenberg, J. (2021) '"Start from the garden": Distribution, livelihood diversification and narratives of agrarian decline in Papua, Indonesia', *Development and Change*, 53(5): 987–1009.

O'Dowd, S. (2021) 'Bridging the Belt and Road Initiative in Papua New Guinea', in G. Smith and T. Wesley-Smith (eds) *The China Alternative: Changing Regional Order in the Pacific Islands*, Acton: Australian National University Press, pp 397–426.

Resosudarmo, B.P., Mollet, J.A., Raya, U.R., and Kaiwai, H. (2014) 'Development in Papua after special autonomy', in H. Hill (ed) *Regional Dynamics in a Decentralized Indonesia*, Singapore: ISEAS, pp 433–59.

Reumi, F., and Katjong. K. (2021) 'The legal standing of ulayat rights and communal rights of a land based on knowledge and kindship of community system of the Sentani customary law in Jayapura Regency, Papua', *International Journal of Multicultural and Multireligious Understanding*, 8(9): 244–71.

Rio, K. (2014) 'Melanesian egalitarianism: The containment of hierarchy', *Anthropological Theory*, 14(2): 169–90.

Rutherford, D. (2003) *Raiding the Land of the Foreigners*, Princeton, NJ: Princeton University Press.

Smith, A.E.D. (2021) *Crossing the Border: West Papuan Refugees and Self-Determination of Peoples*, London: Balboa Press.

Suhartawan, V.V., Mohammad A.R., and Indyah M. (2017) 'Tolerance of local traders in trading activities at Youtefa Traditional Market, Abepura', *Jurnal Mahasiswa Jurusan Arsitektur*, 5(1). http://arsitektur.studentjournal.ub.ac.id (accessed 29 May 2023).

Viartasiwi, N. (2018) 'The politics of history in West Papua–Indonesia conflict', *Asian Journal of Political Science*, 26(1): 141–59.

PART II

Development Times and the Making of Urban Worlds

6

Sequencing Like a State: Ciudad Guayana and the Infrastructures of Arrival

Peter Ekman

To plan is an inherently temporal proposition: it is to make a series of claims about the future. That temporality has a history all its own, one inseparable from the design and execution of specific infrastructural projects: arrangements of material objects, in particular places, positioned to impart form, motion, and rhythm to everyday life. This chapter routes the history of twentieth-century urban and regional planning – a rich seedbed of 'futures past', despite the field's absence from Koselleck's ([1979] 1985) well-known treatment – through 15 miles of highway that established the central spine of Ciudad Guayana, an industrial New Town purpose-built in the early 1960s along a putative 'resource frontier' in north-eastern Venezuela. That road, Avenida Guayana, became a central political technology and rhetorical touchstone in the broader developmentalist programme put forth by President Rómulo Betancourt. As infrastructure, it at once *indicated* the state-sanctioned course of urbanization and *intervened* to materialize it in three dimensions: it 'promised' a particular technopolitical future (Anand et al, 2018) and, gesturally at least, worked to make it 'present' (Rutherford, 2020). At each stage in its realization, this chapter shows, the city's stewards indexed minute aspects of the highway's physical form – and its visual perception, typically from the window of a moving vehicle – to processes unfolding at regional, national, and transnational scales. Throughout, the chapter argues for the place of transit infrastructures as instruments productive of political temporality. It also demonstrates how certain leading *critiques* of planning and development took shape through encounters with those very same instruments. In equal measure, Avenida Guayana participated in the making and unmaking of global urban futures.

The case of Ciudad Guayana affords perspective on how infrastructures configuring physical *movement* once converged, unstably, with Cold War ideas about social and economic *mobility* – and with American modernization theorists' overwrought ambitions to prescribe the stadial sequences by which other states would emerge into industrial 'maturity'. In that conflict's long aftermath, the episode remains an instructive, if ambivalent, object lesson in how the imposed temporalities of development, seldom if ever linear, can swerve, stall, and break down upon contact with a recalcitrant site. The deferred 'arrivals' of Ciudad Guayana, as seen from the road, afford one rendition of what Van Wyck Brooks (1915, 1918; see also Moss, this volume), writing in a more nationalistic key, once called a 'usable past' (multiplex and cautionary) for planners today concerned with how infrastructures, differently distributed, might disclose better regions and futures than the ones yet envisioned.

Building a future in the other America

The designers of Avenida Guayana were doing their work in the name of the Harvard–MIT Joint Center for Urban Studies, one of the crucial institutions in the post–Second World War United States seeking to codify new approaches to collaborative and interdisciplinary work – 'organized research' (Geiger, 1990) – on urban form, urban life, and their conjunction (see, for example, Vale, 2008; Birch, 2011; Mumford, 2013). It began operations in 1959, seeded with Ford Foundation money and in important respects the prototype for that philanthropy's incursions into 'urban studies', a new field-of-fields codified at the precise moment that Ford and others in its emergent network of self-appointed experts began to pronounce the existence of something called 'the urban crisis', typically stated in the singular (Ford Foundation, 1959). The Joint Center brokered partnerships between physical planning and the social sciences, quickly becoming critical infrastructure in far broader networks of scholarship, policymaking, and public intellect. It encouraged speculation on *The Future Metropolis* (Rodwin, 1961) – the title of its first and most hopeful collective statement – and compelled discussion on the methodologies by which to infer its course. Any institutionally precise history of post-war urban expertise and its temporalities must somehow pass through the Joint Center.

At mid-century, talk of the urban 'future' quickly shaded into debates over Urban Renewal, the federal programme now infamous for top-down schemes of demolition and rebuilding and the dominant style of state-led urban planning in the US from 1949 to 1974. Adjusting for population, Boston, Massachusetts, located just across the Charles River from where the Joint Center convened, was 'by far the busiest of all the big cities' (McQuade, [1964] 1966: 266) when it came to Renewal expenditures. The city's marquee 1950s Renewal project, which levelled the dense West End district, had become a literal textbook case of how *not* to renew, chiefly via sociologist Herbert Gans's popular 1962 account *The Urban Villagers* (see Cohen, 2019). Although some at the Joint Center opined on Urban Renewal (it was difficult not to), the scholars never committed to engaging their surroundings with any degree of seriousness, and as their direct overtures to working-class precincts of Boston and Cambridge met with extreme suspicion, they stepped back, reasoning that, if nothing else, this restraint would allow critical distance from the object of their theorization. By 1961, the Center had by and large opted out of directly building the 'future metropolis' into existence. There was, however, one exception.

Ciudad Guayana, sited where the Caroní River meets the Orinoco, rose in tandem with steel, aluminium, and paper mills; a range of extractive industries; and the hydroelectric Guri Dam, built some 70 miles upstream. Its planners enumerated rich stocks of iron ore; some gold, mined commercially since 1829; the possibility of manganese, nickel, chrome, diamonds, and bauxite; and, nearby, confirmed sources of oil, gas, coal, salt, sulphur, and kaolin (Penfold, 1966: 225, 230). Industrial production made use of nearby clay deposits and bauxite transported from the Caribbean. Access to these resources had justified the formation of the Corporación Venezolana de Guayana (CVG), a regional body constituted on the model of the Tennessee Valley Authority shortly after Betancourt assumed power, in 1958, promising a new look for the oil-rich, freshly democratized petrostate (Betancourt, 1956; Salas, 2009; Velasco, 2015). The CVG was headquartered, without apparent apology, high atop the Shell Building in downtown Caracas, six to eight hours away on rudimentary roads, rather than in the Guayana region or the showpiece city rising at its centre. From 1961 to 1966, the Joint Center was at least as much concerned with this one sliver of Latin America – with a projected population of 650,000, roughly equivalent to Boston proper – as it was with any single square mile of New England. Its urbanism was only ever transnational, and it was along global circuits of its own making that theoretical understandings of planning's time horizons travelled and transformed (Ward, 2002; Sandoval-Strausz and Kwak, 2017).

The Center signed on for five years of official consultation (see Almandoz, 2016; Rots and Fernández Maldonado, 2019; Loss, 2021) following an incidental contact that MIT's Lloyd Rodwin, its co-director, had made, in the context of his own private consulting work overseas, by way of a former student, Luis Lander, now serving as a minister in Betancourt's administration. The CVG's head was also an MIT graduate, the assertive Rafael Alfonzo Ravard, a military man and a survivor of the Pérez Jiménez dictatorship that had ruled from 1948 to 1958. Dozens of faculty and students, representing both institutions and several disciplines, spent a summer or more on site. According to the terms of the agreement, the Joint Center would use this purpose-built city as data from which to make higher-level theoretical generalizations about the nature and future of 'the city' as a settlement type. 'As you say', MIT president Julius Stratton wrote to Rodwin, 'Boston may not be the only laboratory or even the best laboratory for urban research'.[1]

The Guayana project preoccupied the Center. It is also diagnostic of the Betancourt era, both an icon of its political style and one of its constitutive matters of concern in what was called the *ordenamiento* (ordering) of the national territory, region by demarcated region (Almandoz, 2016: 44). 'To plan', Betancourt declared, 'is the unavoidable slogan of our time. … In our days, responsible administrative work is inconceivable without a proper articulation of objectives, coordination of efforts and projections into the future' (cited in Friedmann, 1966: 155). The future, in this sense, came first; it compelled action in the present, drawing it near. The Ford Foundation, for its part, under the leadership of H. Rowan Gaither, was branding itself as a kind of clearing house for knowledge about development. Between 1951 and 1963 it made grants of $141 million to support 'experiments which, if successful, can be adapted for use elsewhere' (Ford Foundation, 1963: 19). Ford came later to Latin America than to other regions (Staples, 1992). Latin America was studiously ignored until 1959, the year that led off with the Cuban Revolution. Ford's thought leaders had begun to theorize one interconnected, global 'urban crisis' joining Northern 'ghettos' with Southern 'slums'. Each pole, improperly managed, seemed to threaten *global* order; on streets everywhere, Ford saw urban opportunities to lose the Cold War (Collings-Wells, 2021).

Guayana had approximated 'Pittsburgh on the Orinoco' (Friedmann, 1966: 157) well before the Joint Center took notice – US Steel and Bethlehem Steel had made incursions during the 1940s, planting small company towns beside gigantic mills – but it had become so, the scholars felt, without any authentically *regional* conception of its infrastructure. The new Ciudad Guayana, by that name, was 'a hybrid of already existing formations' sutured together both physically and symbolically. The land was *not* empty of buildings or bodies: some 50,000 people occupied 'a series of scattered settlements'.[2] It had a past. Yet Ciudad Guayana, wrote the in-house anthropologist Lisa Peattie, 'is a city which lives in the future … It is a city of bulldozers, of engineers who wear boots and dungarees and carry shiny briefcases, of noisy bars and holes in the streets, of new traffic interchanges' (1968: 7). Talk of *el futuro del país*, Peattie noted, peppered daily life. The temporal dimension of urbanization weighed heavily on her research precisely because it weighed on residents themselves (Peattie, 1968: 138).

Perpetually under study, built as the generic laboratory that the Joint Center could never quite find on American soil, Ciudad Guayana belongs within an intellectual history of regional planning and transnational urban studies. Founding co-director Martin Meyerson, of Harvard, citing Diderot, had imagined an entire 'encyclopedia' of urban studies issuing from the project. Rodwin concurred: 'The nature of our field required [such breadth] because it was a horizontal, not a vertical, field.'[3] Much as the Joint Center had sought to broker a higher episcopate of disciplines, the ground-breaking at Ciudad Guayana seemed to be realizing a city-of-cities, a composite *type* to think with. The city was a generator of economic development, but it was also and essentially a generator of *knowledge*, the focal point for a series of books and reports iterated by scholars across the social sciences and environmental-design fields. Guayana knowledge *travelled*, and it often travelled north. Staff were repeatedly instructed that each act of research would be judged by 'the extent to which the resulting volume is likely to qualify as a sociological classic'. Peattie bristled, writing from the field that:

> Although I fully sympathize with the Joint Center's wish to see a series of 'great books' emerge from the present project, and although [I] have every incentive personally to write a 'great book' if within my powers (indeed, the reiteration of this phrase is not comforting), it seems clear to me that the demands of a program such as this on the participants are such as to practically insure that no 'great books' will issue.[4]

This was a 'New Town', one of the period's preferred instruments, along with Urban Renewal, by which to materialize the future in three dimensions (Derthick, 1972; Wakeman, 2016). It was the largest then under construction in the world, claimed Lloyd Rodwin, but it was less gratuitously new than Brasília, the capital city recently completed from scratch in Brazil's interior under President Juscelino Kubitschek (Brillembourg, 2013: 6, 7). Unlike Brasília, Ciudad Guayana eschewed any 'complete "Grand Plan"'. So said Willo von Moltke, the émigré Modernist who served as Ciudad Guayana's chief designer from 1962. Instead, citing the architect Fumihiko Maki, the city would assume a '"master form" which can accommodate future changes'.[5] Rodwin had made his name as a critic of the British programme of New Towns implemented with such purpose after the war. In carrying out that research, he admitted in 1956, he had already been looking ahead to the British model's eventual application and refinement in the US, where national-level planning was historically weak, 'and possibly even [in] overseas development'. Rodwin was perpetually scanning the horizon for examples. He attended a 1964 UN symposium on New Towns held in Moscow and toured several imperfect Soviet attempts.[6] The UK towns, he wrote, lacked 'warmth, sensory delight, surprise, stimulus, drama … like a bad painting, [they] are apprehended too quickly' (Rodwin, 1956: 162, 85). Other New Towns, that is, had been new in the wrong way, entranced by 'the future' as if it had an ontological standing independent of present or past. Social scientists, who more than physical planners set the agenda at the Center, knew it did not.

'Above all', von Moltke wrote, in such planning 'there must be the order of growth, the dimension of time' (1963: 113) (see Figure 6.1). *Order*: in post-war urbanism, this watchword cut two ways. It was a primary category for Corbusian Modernists, who posited 'whole' new cities, with everything visibly in its place, and located those synchronicities, intact, in a future that would *in toto* supersede the current state of affairs. For the Joint Center, however – liberal but never utopian in disposition – the term indicated a consuming interest in *sequence*: an ordered, because *ordinal*, series of temporal

Figure 6.1: 'Order of growth' and 'suggested priority'

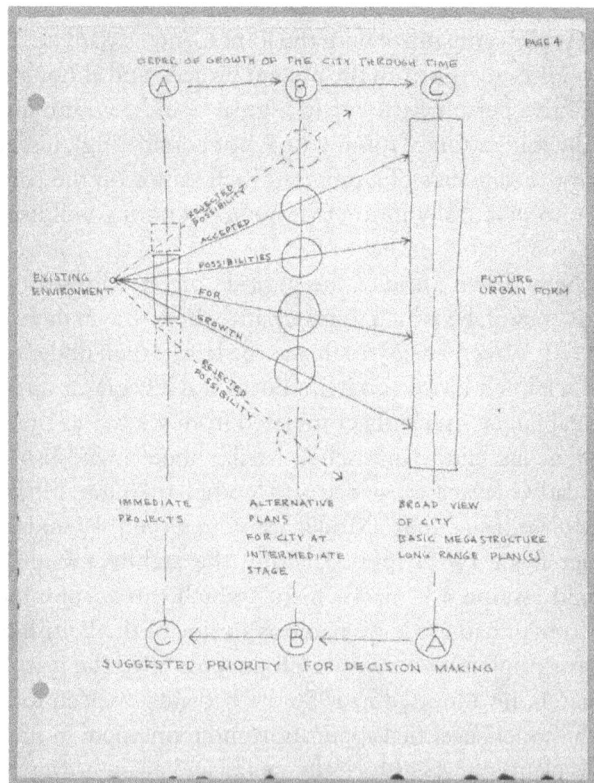

Note: Drawn by a Joint Center planner, this diagram suggests a curious temporality for planning in which future states envisioned for a city take priority over conditions observed in the present.

Source: W. Porter, 'Preliminary Proposal for Planning Process Model for Urban Design Division', 18 January 1963 (Report E70), Box 3, Joint Center for Urban Studies, Records of the Guayana Project, AC 292, Massachusetts Institute of Technology Institute Archives and Special Collections

states (past, present, future) interlinked and constantly cross-referenced. The rhythmic sequencing of urban growth, and the precise manoeuvres by which to think inferentially across the tenses, was the decisive thing. The question then became one of *timing*: when and how fast to make advances towards the horizon without provoking unrest. Still, Ciudad Guayana was, before all else, a built environment – a material assemblage of infrastructures – and the major question soon became how to make these temporal passages perceptible in everyday life. How to sequence urban form? How to stage physical movement through these urban infrastructures in ways that would reinforce this developmental politics of time?

'Intervisible': Avenida Guayana and the temporality of form

Extensive debate attended the question of the new city's physical form. Where would the centre of town be located? *Would* there be just one centre of town? Should it coincide with an existing settlement of Spanish or American provenance, or was it better to construct a new focal point from scratch? MIT's Donald Appleyard, one of the lead designers, weighed in: monocentric and polycentric forms led to different sorts of 'exposure' to the environment, different 'symbolism' of community structure, different 'sensuous impact' as residents and visitors traversed the city, different degrees of formal 'plasticity', intellectual 'challenge' and the possibility of 'withdrawal' from public space.[7] Edmund Bacon, Philadelphia's charismatic director of planning, consulted on the project and proposed a design premised on 'a series of radial axes' that would all intersect by the main waterfall. 'Twin cities' schemes also got a hearing (von Moltke, 1969: 134, 135).[8]

These proposals lost out. Even in presenting Bacon's ideas, the Joint Center had characterized the result as 'a lineal city' with several centres (see Figure 6.2).[9] 'Visual continuity' over the course of a high-speed journey was the desired effect; the proper standpoint from which to assess the city was from a moving vehicle, not via the maps or aerial views that also studded official communication.[10] Ultimately, the central feature of Ciudad Guayana was not any particular point on the map. It was the new Avenida Guayana, a high-speed motorway that extended some 15 miles east to west, joining dispersed nodes of settlement, both the inherited and the imposed, into a new regional unity. One was either on or off Avenida Guayana; it was the sightline to which all questions of cohesion were indexed, and it commanded the lion's share of attention from the city's researchers, designers, and publicists as they sought 'a firm linear foundation on which to develop the city's entity in depth' (Penfold, 1966: 246).

Whereas canonical New Town designs tended to collocate homes and workplaces, binding them into growth-limited pods of settlement and thus enabling short pedestrian commutes, the situation in Betancourt's Venezuela

Figure 6.2: The 'firm linear foundation' of an automotive city

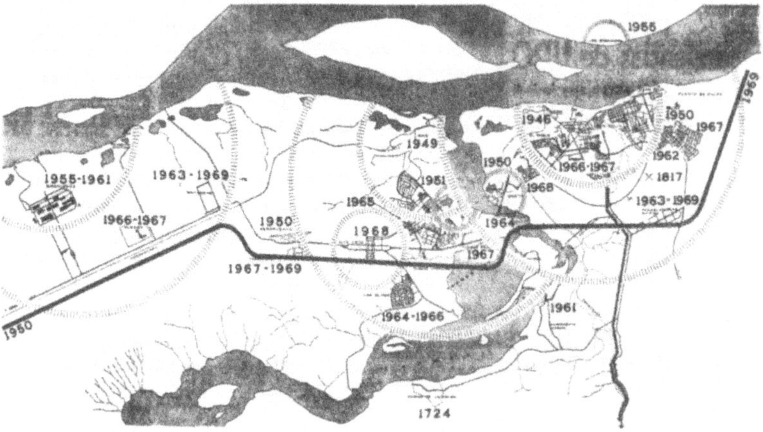

Note: This map spatializes the developmental sequence showing the compresence of Spanish colonial construction (1724, bottom centre), early Venezuelan construction post-independence (1817, upper right), pre-1958 industrial development by US corporations, and, from 1961, the stages of its transformation into 'Ciudad Guayana'.

Source: Appleyard, 1976: 203, Fig 9.18. © 1976 Massachusetts Institute of Technology, by permission of The MIT Press.).

was different. Private autos and public buses were the assumed modes of transport, rail service was not part of the equation, and while planners were thinking constantly of the home–work dyad, they did so in the context of national-level labour laws that obligated all employers to subsidize workers' commutes in full, 'portal to portal', usually at least four miles from work, and often up to ten (Abrams, 1964). The commute was thus no incidental part of a worker's day, and its choreography became central to the CVG's rhetoric and politics of infrastructure. The arts and sciences of movement came to mutually reinforce, and on both fronts the Center reconceptualized 'form' as something that elapses over time and emerges from the experience of motion.

The team referred to Avenida Guayana as the city's 'visual spine'. Appleyard wrote that social researchers' first task concerned vision: to 'discover what is actually seen from the road'.[11] To achieve this, he insisted, a 'visual control diagram' would be necessary – effectively viewshed analysis as featured in his ongoing work with Kevin Lynch and John Myer on Boston's highways in *The View from the Road* (1964) (see Figure 6.3). Appleyard, Lynch, and Myer were convinced that '[t]he problem of designing for vision in motion is everywhere the same' (Appleyard et al, 1964: 83). Nowhere in *View* did Venezuela come up, but it is beyond doubt that Appleyard's proposals for Boston and Ciudad Guayana informed one another. In 1965, to a volume edited by György Kepes called *The Nature and Art of Motion*, he contributed 'Motion, Sequence and the City', a work of theory that extended *View*'s baroque system of notation.

Figure 6.3: 'Vision in motion'

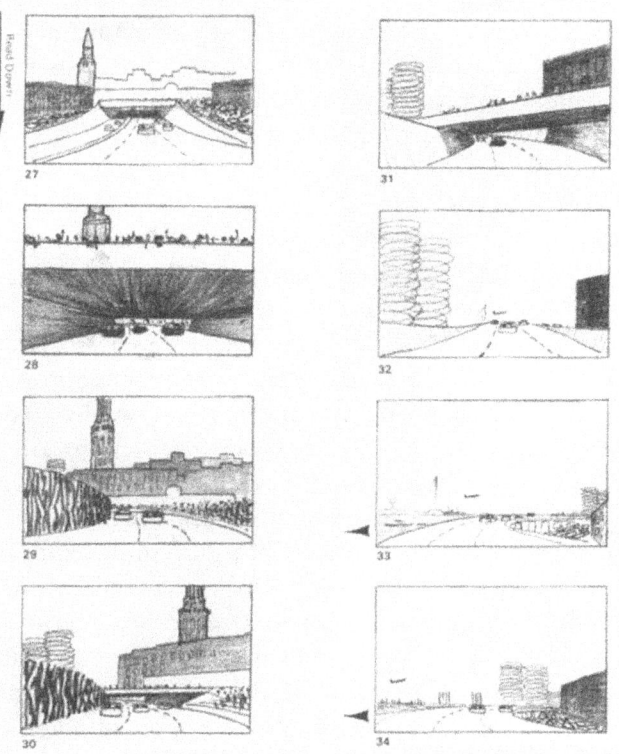

Note: Donald Appleyard, Kevin Lynch, and their collaborator John Myer proposed to diagram drivers' moment-by-moment visual experience along the major circumferential highway proposed to encircle downtown Boston. These panels demonstrate their attempts to conceptualize urban form in terms of an experiential sequence elapsing over time.

Source: Appleyard et al, 1964: 60. © 1964 Massachusetts Institute of Technology, by permission of The MIT Press

Planners needed recourse to a set of 'experiential symbols', he wrote, the better to 'train our senses to the complex delights of "seeing" motion as it is'. The piece glanced in passing at the example of Boston's nascent North East Expressway. On the final page, however, Appleyard shifted course to one lone case study of 'Sequence Design in a New City' (Appleyard, 1965: 189, 185, 190). That new city was Ciudad Guayana.

Among the American visitors, complaints about the town site's supposed 'formlessness' came cheap. The more specific problem, for von Moltke, was the site's traversal: the journey, its 'visual continuity' over time and space, or its lack thereof. These were the criteria, these the terms of debate. Avenida Guayana, he asserted, would rectify the issue: it 'connects all major existing elements, a series of nodes which are intervisible'. A fragmentation of visual experience, he wrote, would surely produce a lack of social solidarity at anything approaching the regional scale. Infrastructure, the Center proposed, did not just serve pre-existing regions; it could suture new ones into existence. In a town populated almost entirely by newcomers, this syncretic dimension of infrastructure had particular force: design could 'go a long way in overcoming the sense of anonymity and isolation'.[12]

The Avenida physically connected older nodes with new ones built from scratch. Alta Vista (or 'El Centro') was the Modernist administrative and commercial district on the western plateau, distant from the river, falls, port, and mill but still the closest thing the linear city had to a downtown. There, in view of the new ziggurat-style CVG headquarters, the road divided into two one-way boulevards, 600 feet apart, and the traveller's attention would inexorably be drawn to the commercial options located in between: 'as he approaches it, he must slow down and turn toward it' (von Moltke, 1969: 142–4; Loss, 2021: 16–18). In so doing, the Avenida would make visible and palpable the passage of historical time itself. By *being seen* from the road, over and over again, each node, rightly composed, was meant to reinforce the city's specific articulation of past with present, present with future.[13] It was infrastructure as exhibition: the Avenida would stage and restage the city's own process of emergence, embedding in the texture of everyday mobilities a stepwise sequence of approaches and arrivals to industrial modernity, as MIT's own W.W. Rostow and many others had lately theorized it (Gilman, 2003). One of these processes operated at the scale of years or decades, the other elapsed in seconds and minutes. Both, they wagered, could be programmed, both brought perceptibly into correlation.

This sequential understanding of infrastructural experience echoed themes that had run through the Joint Center's pre-Guayana output as well. Kevin Lynch, for one, was preoccupied with movement. The dis- and reoriented wanderers who populate *The Image of the City* (1960) – the first entry in the Joint Center's book series – were always potentially on the go, hence the need for the famous cognitive maps he elicited from passers-by on the streets of Boston, Jersey City, and Los Angeles (Sarkis, 2013). Lynch and Appleyard both drew on the work of Philip Thiel, a Joint Center research associate who insisted that urban perception be understood as a 'process involving the consumption of time' and implicating multiple senses at once: 'Architecture may be "frozen music", like a phonograph record; but man is the pickup whose movement realizes the experience' (Thiel, 1961: 33).

Lynch himself paid a visit to Ciudad Guayana in July 1964 to consult on its design. He spent a day and a half touring the city, followed by three days of discussion with colleagues on site, and his reactions point to tensions that the lead designers may have grappled with but preferred not to disclose out loud. Lynch admitted to having no knowledge of Venezuela or the Spanish language. In a report to the design team, he sounded essentially cybernetic themes, ontologies of the built environment that understood its apprehension via the human sensorium as both raw matter and 'information'. 'This fluid situation' unfolding along Avenida Guayana was what most perplexed Lynch. There were two distinct senses in which the *ciudad* could be said to flow – two competing temporalities of urban life. One concerned the planning process. 'Continuous design', transacted in 'liaison' with locals and looping back in 'continuous revision' of its prior assumptions, injected complexity: humans communicating with other humans and working, over time, towards 'two-way accommodation', 'social learning', or what cyberneticians would call feedback.[14] Lynch also, however, used the term 'feedback' to describe the movement of traffic on the Avenida Guayana, of physical *things* hurtling through space and time and interacting with one another. Each car fed back on the other cars, reading their cues and making minute adjustments in speed or spacing. Each driver on the Avenida, moreover, was embroiled in a perceptual feedback loop with the more stationary features of the passing environment: human–object, not human–human, relations. Appleyard (1965: 181, 176), similarly, saw highway drivers perpetually 'engaged in a strategy of search' amid the surfeit of 'unwanted' messages that buildings and landscapes always non-verbally 'emit'. 'The observer', Appleyard (1979: 279) wrote, 'selects and organizes the perceptual world'. The Avenida's designers set out to configure things so that all this feedback would be manageable in real time – so that coherent signals (modernity, progress) would emerge from the ambient noise – at 50 and 60 miles per hour. The task was to sequence the cybernetic highway.

Lynch could sense, however, that durable class and racial segregation was already setting in, with the river acting as the main *cordon sanitaire* between the middle-class west and the eastern 'slums'. He questioned the physical scale of the project, having seen enough of California to know that high-speed roads did not always *feel* like agents of unification. Ciudad Guayana was looking to be 'coarse in grain, even blank and visually somewhat inhuman'. The Avenida was a sound piece of engineering, but its sequencing of experience was off: too many traffic circles, 'several confusions of geometry' in the route, 'ambiguous turns in featureless country' out beyond the airport, and some ill-chosen landmarks to punctuate the trip and compellingly announce 'arrival'. Lynch noted the 'probable inability of the heavy machinery to act as a visual dominant'.[15] Were smokestacks really the future towards which all westbound drivers wanted to be beckoned?

'This is the "natural sequence"', Lynch wrote, the scare quotes marking both distance from and resignation to the sorts of developmental telos that so often underwrote planning and design in the age of high social science.[16] In these privately circulated 'notes' of 1964, he articulated foundational critiques, able to reflect on the Joint Center's and CVG's grandiose performances of competency in ways that Appleyard, von Moltke, certainly Betancourt, and his many agents never mustered the energy (or self-awareness) to air in public. Cambridge and Caracas were imposing new urban rhythms, or trying to, without quite admitting that those housed on site might object. The case of Ciudad Guayana seems to have inflected Lynch's broader thinking on the nature of temporality, regionality, and the sensory dimensions of urban life – concerns that are more pronounced in his later work (Lynch, 1972, 1976). Ciudad Guayana and its central 'spine', domain of the automobiles that for years had been scrambling mental maps up north, helped elicit this turn in his thought.

For Lynch, it was vital that Avenida Guayana 'be considered as a sequence in both directions'. Commutes, he observed, unlike other types of journey, have a 'tidal' quality. To design them holistically, planners needed to think of roads as 'reversible flow devices', not as finite, one-way emplotments with obvious beginnings and ends.[17] Lynch might have said the same of urban history as an elapsing temporal sequence, and of 'development' or 'modernization' as political imperatives. 'The future', as destination, has no existence independent of the past from which it springs; the automotive future would fail if executed in ways ignorant of its forebears. Like those so eagerly and rapidly etching Ciudad Guayana onto the map, Lynch was inclined to relate minute questions of form and design to far broader considerations on the temporality of human existence: the 'intervisibility' of nodes in a three- and four-dimensional urban landscape with the concatenation of past, present, and future as tenses in which to think and live. Lynch came as a critic, however, and his reactions to the Avenida suggest that, in their haste to catalyse development, to bring Venezuela literally and figuratively up to speed, the Joint Center may have timed it wrong.

City as curriculum

Ciudad Guayana was a physical environment, built, inhabited, and visited. Yet it always and already had another life as an object of study. The city was a generator of economic development, but it was also and essentially a generator of knowledge, the focal point for a series of scholarly books and reports (for instance, Soberman, 1966; McGinn and Davis, 1969). It was as a case study in *regional* planning that the place most seamlessly entered academic conversation. Here, the work of John Friedmann, then a young faculty member at MIT, was decisive in converting city into curriculum. His first monograph, the product of two summers spent on site, pronounced on *Regional Development Policy* (1966) as such, but the subtitle gave away its genesis as *A Case Study of Venezuela*. Friedmann would claim in the early twenty-first century that this book was the very first to bring an 'explicit spatial dimension' (Friedmann, 1966: 78) to the question of development. It proposed a general theory of 'growth poles' – a within-nation model of core and periphery that recommended channelling industrial capital only to certain cities – and asserted that 'the spatial structure of its economy has a classical simplicity' (Friedmann, 1966: 160). One could not overstate 'how decisive Latin American experience proved to be for the development of regional planning doctrine', Friedmann would later write (Friedmann and Weaver, 1979: 129). From afar, and well after the fact, Americans had uses for Ciudad Guayana.

Customized development agencies such as the CVG, Friedmann argued, made it plain that institutions based in powerful urban centres did not just happen upon 'remote' regions awaiting capitalization: policy, publicity, investment, discourse, and study all interacted to *produce* regions, to impart 'maximum' but always provisional 'closure with respect to a given problem set' (Friedmann, 1966: 174, 43).

The last official monograph on Venezuela to appear was Donald Appleyard's *Planning a Pluralist City* (1976). Its completion was severely delayed, not least because of Appleyard's 1967 departure for Berkeley. The book did not go to press until a full decade after the Center had ended its contract with the CVG, and six years after the Ford funding dropped off. He had carried out the main body of research, however, in 1964. As published, it was the Joint Center's first avowed, full-scale study of 'urban knowledge' as such.

Planning a Pluralist City remains a highly distinctive piece of scholarship. By 'urban knowledge', Appleyard means primarily sensory perception in and of cities. His debt to Lynch is frankly stated, and at the core of his empirical research stands a body of long-form, exacting interviews with inhabitants of the city-under-construction. Each respondent drew for him a map and narrated, from memory, what it felt like to make a journey down the Avenida. 'Many subjects', Appleyard (1976: 281) noted in an appendix, 'had never drawn a map before and were either reluctant or unable to attempt one. Consequently, ways were developed to assist them.'

Plainly, by 'knowledge' Appleyard does not mean 'expertise'. His is an enquiry into ordinary, vernacular 'styles' of perception and reasoning. The pluralism to which his title refers is a cognitive pluralism. Over and over, Appleyard points out profound incongruities in how different populations (by class, sex, occupation, income, and so on) process the same landscape. 'Ciudad Guayana was many cities in one', Appleyard states on the first page. 'Different people knew it in different ways.' He catalogues these differences and disjunctures out of the conviction that it ought to be possible to bridge them, to integrate this very diversity into the process of environmental design: 'to structure an entity to be comprehended at different levels [at once] and to sustain attention – and affection – after repeated contact'. In the execution, though, Appleyard finds reasons for ambivalence and deep concern. Perhaps designers should *not* be consulting locals for thoughts on the city's future, as 'they might not understand' which options are actually feasible. 'Evidence of individual perceptions' is of course welcome in the name of basic research, but it also 'may reveal a degree of ignorance that may be limiting opportunities … In these cases, policies of changing perceptions and expectations may be justified.' Appleyard proves amenable to a concept of planning understood as 'the diffusion of information about future change' that experts have decided on in advance: 'shift the citizens' perceptions toward … development', he writes, and use 'environmental means' such as fences, plantings, and signs to indicate where the city is headed (Appleyard 1976: 289, 291, 4, 5, 200, 201). The built environment can inhabit the future tense, he suggests, even if its inhabitants do not yet.

Appleyard classifies his respondents' maps into two broad groupings (Appleyard, 1970). One of these he dubs 'sequential' and associates empirically with the city's working and lower classes. A sequential map hangs together by virtue of its paths: it represents a remembered journey through the city, by a moving observer, in which there is one overall directional trend, typically along Avenida Guayana. To this, Appleyard opposes the 'spatial' style of perception (an awkward coinage). If paths, roads, passages, and flows define the former, the latter is grounded in the more static landmarks and district boundaries that tend to register on most official maps in the Western tradition. Appleyard sees 'spatial' maps as 'more objectively' rendered, as if drawn from above the city, not within it. He associates them with the educated, the affluent, and with planners themselves. At this juncture, Appleyard's text becomes visually quite complex, and his will to typologize is apparent: sequential maps have 'fragmented', 'chain', 'branch and loop', and 'netted' variants, while spatial maps can be 'scattered', 'mosaic', 'link[ed]', or 'patterned' (Appleyard, 1976: 158–9, 161, 163). Like any self-respecting typologist, he grants that, in practice, sequential and spatial approaches usually appear in combination. Yet the class coordinates he assigns them (which readily intersect with distinctions of race and nation) stand undisturbed: abstraction belongs to the better off.

Sequence was already a central concept in the planners' understanding of visual experience on the highway, the developmental march from 'backwardness' to 'modernity', and the ways in which these two levels might mutually reinforce. An incautious reading of Appleyard's words cited earlier might suggest that he deemed non-experts and non-planners more systematically attuned to the staged emplotment of urban development. In fact, he took the opposite position, and as the book pivots formally from spatial to temporal perception, Appleyard enters difficult territory, unhappily resonant with Edward Banfield's claims on 'time horizon' as articulated in his arch-conservative, deeply racialized *The Unheavenly City* (1970; see also Reno, 2007). Appleyard's (1976: 210, 211, 205, 206, 221) argument is, in effect, that society's lower registers are by their nature radically present-oriented: 'They seldom inferred beyond their immediate experience, clinging to the known and concrete world ... There was, therefore, a desire for future change but no way of conceiving the future.' Venturing one more binary, he then distinguishes 'inferential' from merely 'responsive', which is to say passive, 'modes' of perception. The educated and the comfortable person will 'begin to infer, extending his action and thought beyond the visible field. His awareness of motivation and choice increases, as does his planning behavior.' The middle classes, in other words, can see into the future. They alone can mentally articulate past with present, present with future. They alone can see the world as planners do.

American pedagogy in planning and urban studies regrouped around the lessons of Ciudad Guayana, embedding it in a network of referents, like and unlike, that spanned the globe. Willo von Moltke taught a 'Case Study Workshop' in 1971 that related Ciudad Guayana to Milton Keynes, the British New Town most adapted to automobility; Fort Lincoln, the federally sponsored 'New Town In-Town' sited in north-east Washington, DC; and James Rouse's Columbia, Maryland.[18] Donald Appleyard's courses at MIT and then Berkeley made routine use of Ciudad Guayana as a case study, almost always alongside examples far better known to the American public, such as Levittown, Canberra, Brasília, and the post-war satellites to London (Appleyard, 1969, 1972, 1979). The Joint Center's entanglements there enabled Appleyard to make his methodologies of visual sequence fully transnational.

At the same time, the project had many critics. Some focused on *un*planned developments: faulty population projections, inadequate provision of housing in the face of rapid rural-to-urban migration, the vast penumbra of shanties surrounding discrete nodes of official order. Others contended that the settlement felt *too* planned, too orderly to encourage the stimulating, urbane existence the designers had imagined.

Some critiques came from within. John Friedmann came to repudiate the programme's intellectual and political substance completely. This meant renouncing positions to which he himself had signed his name. Growth-pole theory, he now held, was an unacceptable 'pursuit of unequal development as a matter of policy'. As far as Friedmann was concerned by the end of the 1970s, 'a good deal of nonsense has been written (including by the present senior author) about the spatial diffusion of economic growth' (Friedmann and Weaver, 1979: 114, 174). Friedmann moved left and openly broke with his colleagues. Failure, however, could be productive, an object lesson of its own kind if anatomized by the right analyst and mobilized in ways that might compel habits of self-criticism. The most lasting of the Ciudad Guayana books, he argued in a memo to architecture student (and future MIT dean) William Porter, would be those committed to asking, 'What went wrong and why?' Answer this question, Friedmann wrote, and 'we could stop teaching the wrong theory to our students'.[19]

One of the ironies of Ciudad Guayana is that, of the many books it spawned, the one plausibly called a classic came from the project's most unsparing critic. Lisa Peattie, the team's lone anthropologist, was mystified from the start by the CVG's 'particularly damaging' decision to remain in Caracas, forfeiting without contest any genuine 'sense of the site'.[20] Her labours ultimately bore fruit as *The View from the Barrio* (1968), an ethnography of the eastern 'slum' La Laja, an informal zone squeezed into a flood-prone triangle of land described by the nearest strip development, the Orinoco, and the outer company fence of Bethlehem Steel. This was not 'research in the conventional sense', she wrote in the preface, 'for I had no "problem", no "research design"' (Peattie, 1968: 27, np). The tone had changed.

Peattie radicalized prodigiously over the course of her research and, to an extent unknown among her colleagues, became an outspoken sceptic of development's administered futures. She was also, it must be said, one of the very few women accorded roles in the overwhelmingly male world of the Joint Center. Full-scale condemnation of the CVG, and by proxy the Joint Center, came in her follow-up book, *Planning: Rethinking Ciudad Guayana* (1987), issued in a climate far more accustomed to 'critical planning' scholarship with Marxian, post-structural, or, in Peattie's case, broadly anarchistic leanings. Yet Peattie held out a dark hope. Futures, she wrote, resulted not from 'economic development', that 'dry technicians' phrase' meaning everything and nothing, but from the thorny process of ordinary, unaccredited citizens 'making the future' for themselves. 'Even as the city grows under the planners' stimulus and direction, it grows only partly according to plan … It is part of planning to realize this' (1968: 134, 143, 4, 3). No Joint Center monograph to date had ontologized urban change in this manner – flexible, negotiated, vernacular, non-linear – and it was Ciudad Guayana, not Boston, that occasioned the break.

Critical avenues

With consequences for urban studies writ large, the Center thus began to retheorize the very temporality of what it is, at root, *to plan*. Its emerging critique was not simply that 'whole' urban visions synchronically promising 'total' spatial scope were brittle and presumptuous; that much was clear from domestic instances of Urban Renewal. The point was that 'feedback' could emerge only *over time*: the concept, imported from MIT's cyberneticians, obligated planners to bend their process back on itself, 'adjusting ends to means', thinking harder about 'sequences' and 'segments of a problem', even 'selecting ends and means simultaneously' (Rodwin, 1969: 482). A usual prospectus for work, one planner at Ciudad Guayana wrote, 'makes each step appear discrete. In fact, overlapping occurs; and a continuous feedback and reappraisal of assumptions blurs the demarcation of each operation' (Penfold,

1966: 245). As was true of earlier, untroubled articulations of 'the future metropolis', the new *critique* of comprehensive planning entailed a specific theory of temporality. By 1966, to oppose the 'view from nowhere' – the much-photographed men in suits looming over scale models and gesturing towards neighbourhoods they would soon anesthetize and cut into – was, in that same act, to introduce a complex, composite sense of timing, by which information gleaned from what had once seemed like the future could circle back and intervene on the principles inherited from history and assumed true on Day One.

What kind of account, then, best captured 'the jigsaw of facts', as Charles Abrams put it on his first visit? How to narrate the recursions by which expertise morphed and self-corrected upon contact with material reality? Were 'instant judgments and adjustments to unforeseen changes' worth converting into narrative, or should they be subordinated in the service of a more authoritative-sounding final analysis? Along uneven transnational circuits that the Joint Center itself established and maintained, these became central questions in planning theory. Abrams called for a daily diary of 'events as they occur'; not moment by moment, perhaps, with planners forever stepping aside to jot down their impressions, but nightly, under cover of darkness and aided by Dictaphone.[21] Could the very temporality of the planning process, however it sputtered or spiralled off, actually be readers' primary topic of interest? And would this infrastructure's promised future ever *arrive*? Fifteen miles of road had forced open, and pointedly materialized, questions that discourses of 'development' might otherwise have left suspended in abstraction.

'The strip is trying to tell us something.' So wrote Grady Clay (1972: 108), the long-time editor of *Landscape Architecture* magazine. Clay joined the Joint Center as a fellow for a year concurrent with the Guayana project, working on a study of architectural competitions that never saw the light of day (Isenberg, 2017: 276–99).[22] He may not have *liked* the highway strip – Clay always equivocated on how completely to embrace the American vernacular – but he defended to the death his contention that it was information-rich, quite possibly the key to any understanding of the American landscape or others created in its image.

From Venezuela, Lisa Peattie would write in one of her transitional memos that a plan is an 'exploratory journey through a territory only incompletely known to science before its exploration by the traveller, to a destination only definitely specified at the time of arrival'.[23] This recurring language of 'path' and 'journey', of the decision process rendered as if it were movement through uncertain infrastructural space and time, came to prevail by the 1970s, when many Americans (grassroots leftists and neo-conservatives alike) turned on urban expertise, questioning whether one could ever realistically produce enough knowledge about 'the future metropolis' to steer its course.

The Joint Center, though, came by this trope honestly; indeed, it was no metaphor. On the highway, from the window of an automobile, a far broader critique of the pacing and spacing of urban development flickered into view.

Notes

1. Julius Stratton to Lloyd Rodwin, 26 February 1964, Box 55, 'Boston Metropolitan Regional Planning, 1961–1965' folder #1, Lloyd Rodwin papers, MC 490, Massachusetts Institute of Technology Institute Archives and Special Collections [hereafter 'LR'].
2. C. Abrams, 'Report on the development of Ciudad Guayana in Venezuela', 25 January 1962 (Report A5), Box 1, Reginald R. Isaacs Files, Special Collections, Frances Loeb Library, Graduate School of Design, Harvard University [hereafter 'RRI'].
3. Interview with Lloyd Rodwin, 11 June 1994, Pioneers in Housing: An Oral History Project, Manuscript Division, Library of Congress.
4. Norman Williams, Jr, to Daniel Lerner, 19 January 1962 (Report C12), Box 1, RRI; Daniel Lerner, 21 May 1962 (Report C8), Box 3, Joint Center for Urban Studies, Records of the Guayana Project, AC 292, Massachusetts Institute of Technology Institute Archives and Special Collections [hereafter 'RGP']; Roderick and Lisa Peattie, 'Some notes on the organization of the Joint Center Guayana project', 19 July 1962 (Report F25), Box 5, RGP.
5. Willo von Moltke, Lecture in Brasília, May 1964, Box 6 (DL24HB), Papers of the Estate of Willo von Moltke, Special Collections, Frances Loeb Library, Graduate School of Design, Harvard University [hereafter 'WvM'].
6. Box 5, 'Round Table Conference on the Planning of New Towns, 1964' folder, LR.
7. Appleyard, 'The future form of Santo Tomé', December 1962, Box 57, Donald Appleyard folder, LR.
8. Frank Martocci to Norman Williams, Jr, 16 March 1962 (Report E38), Box 2, RRI.
9. Norman Williams, Jr, 'Planning the Guayana', address to Fourth International Planning Congress, San Diego, November 1962, Box 1, RGP.
10. Willo von Moltke, 'The Visual Design of Ciudad Guayana' (June 1965), Box 1, Wilhelm von Moltke folder #1, RGP.
11. Donald Appleyard to Lloyd Rodwin, 16 April 1964, Box 57, Donald Appleyard folder, LR.
12. Willo von Moltke, Lecture in Ciudad Guayana, 1972, Box 6 (DL24HB), WvM.
13. 'The Guayana development program', March 1965 (Report B80), Box 1, Joint Center for Urban Studies, Reports of Cuidad Guayana (1960–1965), RRI.
14. K. Lynch, 'Some notes on the design of Ciudad Guayana', 22 July 1964 (Report E90), Box 3, RGP.
15. K. Lynch, 'Some notes on the design of Ciudad Guayana', 22 July 1964.
16. K. Lynch, 'Some notes on the design of Ciudad Guayana', 22 July 1964.
17. K. Lynch, 'Some notes on the design of Ciudad Guayana', 22 July 1964.
18. Case Study Workshop syllabus, 1971, Box 1, Wilhelm von Moltke folder #1, RGP.
19. John Friedmann to William Porter, 20 December 1965, Box 1, John Friedmann folder, RGP.
20. Roderick Peattie and Lisa Peattie, 'Some notes on the organization of the Joint Center Guayana project', 19 July 1962 (Report F25), Box 5, RGP.
21. Abrams, 'Report on the development of Ciudad Guayana in Venezuela'.
22. G. Clay, Draft of *The Competitors* (unpublished book manuscript), Box 11 (DL245F), Grady E. Clay Collection, Special Collections, Frances Loeb Library, Graduate School of Design, Harvard University.
23. Peattie, 'Notes on the concept of "disjointed incrementalism" as applied to regional planning', 7 November 1962 (Report C18), Box 1, RRI.

References

Abrams, C. (1964) *Man's Struggle for Shelter in an Urbanizing World*, Cambridge, MA: Harvard University Press.

Almandoz, A. (2016) 'Towards Brasília and Ciudad Guayana: Development, urbanization and regional planning in Latin America, 1940s–1960s', *Planning Perspectives*, 31(3): 31–53.

Anand, N., Gupta, A., and Appel, H. (eds) (2018) *The Promise of Infrastructure*, Durham, NC: Duke University Press.

Appleyard, D. (1965) 'Motion, sequence and the city', in G. Kepes (ed) *The Nature and Art of Motion*, New York: Braziller, pp 176–92.

Appleyard, D. (1969) *Selected Bibliography: Environmental/Behavioral Factors and Urban Design*, Berkeley, CA: UC Berkeley Department of City and Regional Planning.

Appleyard, D. (1970) 'Styles and methods of structuring a city', *Environment and Behavior*, 2: 100–17.

Appleyard, D. (1972) *The Urban Environment: Selected Bibliography*, Monticello, GA: Council of Planning Librarians.

Appleyard, D. (1976) *Planning a Pluralist City: Conflicting Realities in Ciudad Guayana*, Cambridge, MA: MIT Press.

Appleyard, D. (1979) 'The environment as a social symbol', *Ekistics*, 278: 272–81.

Appleyard, D., Lynch, K., and Myer, J.R. (1964) *The View from the Road*, Cambridge, MA: MIT Press.

Banfield, E.C. (1970) *The Unheavenly City*, Boston, MA: Little, Brown.

Betancourt, R. (1956) *Venezuela: política y petróleo*, Mexico City: Fondo de Cultura Económica.

Birch, E.L. (2011) 'Making urban research intellectually respectable: Martin Meyerson and the Joint Center for Urban Studies of Massachusetts Institute of Technology and Harvard University, 1959–1964', *Journal of Planning History*, 10(3): 219–38.

Brillembourg, C. (2013) 'Sowing the oil: Brutalist urbanism, Ciudad Guayana, Venezuela, 1951–2012', paper delivered to the X Seminário Docomomo Brasil, 15–18 October.

Brooks, V.W. (1915) *America's Coming-of-Age*, New York: Dutton.

Brooks, V.W. (1918) 'On creating a usable past', *The Dial*, 11 April: 337–41.

Clay, G. (1972) *Close-Up: How to Read the American City*, Chicago, IL: University of Chicago Press.

Cohen, L. (2019) *Saving America's Cities: Ed Logue and the Struggle to Renew Urban America in the Suburban Age*, New York: Farrar, Straus & Giroux.

Collings-Wells, S. (2021) 'Developing communities: The Ford Foundation and the global urban crisis, 1958–66', *Journal of Global History*, 16(3): 336–54.

Derthick, M. (1972) *New Towns In-Town*, Washington, DC: Urban Institute.

Ford Foundation (1959) *Metropolis*, New York: Ford Foundation.

Ford Foundation (1963) *About the Ford Foundation*, New York: Ford Foundation.

Friedmann, J. (1966) *Regional Development Policy: A Case Study of Venezuela*, Cambridge, MA: MIT Press.

Friedmann, J., and Weaver, C. (1979) *Territory and Function: The Evolution of Regional Planning*, Berkeley, CA: University of California Press.

Gans, H.J. (1962) *The Urban Villagers*, New York: Free Press.

Geiger, R.L. (1990) 'Organized research units: Their role in the development of university research', *Journal of Higher Education*, 61(1): 1–19.

Gilman, N. (2003) *Mandarins of the Future: Modernization Theory in Cold War America*, Baltimore, MD: Johns Hopkins University Press.

Isenberg, A. (2017) *Designing San Francisco: Art, Land and Urban Renewal in the City by the Bay*, Princeton, NJ: Princeton University Press.

Koselleck, R. ([1979]1985) *Futures Past: On the Semantics of Historical Time*, trans. K. Tribe, New York: Columbia University Press.

Loss, C.P. (2021) '"The city of tomorrow must reckon with the lives and living habits of human beings": The Joint Center for Urban Studies goes to Venezuela, 1957–1969', *Journal of Urban History*, 47(3): 623–50.

Lynch, K. (1960) *The Image of the City*, Cambridge, MA: MIT Press.

Lynch, K. (1972) *What Time Is This Place?* Cambridge, MA: MIT Press.

Lynch, K. (1976) *Managing the Sense of a Region*, Cambridge, MA: MIT Press.

McGinn, N.F., and Davis, R.G. (1969) *Build a Mill, Build a City, Build a School: Industrialization, Urbanization, and Education in Ciudad Guayana*, Cambridge, MA: MIT Press.

McQuade, W. ([1964]1966) 'Urban Renewal in Boston', in J.Q. Wilson (ed) *Urban Renewal: The Record and the Controversy*, Cambridge, MA: MIT Press, pp 259–77.

Mumford, E. (2013) 'From master planning to self-build: The MIT–Harvard Joint Center for Urban Studies, 1959–1971', in A. Dutta (ed) *A Second Modernism: MIT, Architecture, and the 'Techno-Social' moment*, Cambridge, MA: MIT Press, pp 288–309.

Peattie, L.R. (1968) *The View from the Barrio*, Ann Arbor, MI: University of Michigan Press.

Peattie, L.R. (1987) *Planning: Rethinking Ciudad Guayana*, Ann Arbor, MI: University of Michigan Press.

Penfold, A.H. (1966) 'Ciudad Guayana: Planning a new city in Venezuela', *Town Planning Review*, 36(3): 225–48.

Reno, B.J. (2007) 'Rethinking horizon theory: Culture vs. nature', *Perspectives on Political Science*, 36(2): 84–90.

Rodwin, L. (1956) *The British New Towns Policy: Problems and Implications*, Cambridge, MA: Harvard University Press.

Rodwin, L. (1969) 'Reflections on collaborative planning', in L. Rodwin and Associates, *Planning Urban Growth and Regional Development*, Cambridge, MA: MIT Press, pp 467–91.

Rodwin, L. (ed) (1961) *The Future Metropolis*, New York: Braziller.

Rots, S., and Fernández Maldonado, A.M. (2019) 'Planning Ciudad Guayana, an industrial New Town in oil-rich Venezuela', *International Planning Studies*, 24(3–4): 353–68.

Rutherford, J. (2020) *Redeploying Urban Infrastructure: The Politics of Urban Socio-Technical Futures*, New York: Palgrave Macmillan.

Salas, M.T. (2009) *The Enduring Legacy: Oil, Culture and Society in Venezuela*, Durham, NC: Duke University Press.

Sandoval-Strausz, A.K., and Kwak, N.H. (eds) (2017) *Making Cities Global: The Transnational Turn in Urban History*, Philadelphia, PA: University of Pennsylvania Press.

Sarkis, H. (2013) 'Disoriented: Kevin Lynch, around 1960', in A. Dutta (ed) *A Second Modernism: MIT, Architecture, and the 'Techno-Social' Moment*, Cambridge, MA: MIT Press, pp 394–433.

Soberman, R.H. (1966) *Transport Technology for Developing Regions: A Study of Road Transportation in Venezuela*, Cambridge, MA: MIT Press.

Staples, E.S. (1992) *Forty Years: A Learning Curve: The Ford Foundation Programs in India, 1952–1992*, New Delhi: Ford Foundation.

Thiel, P. (1961) 'A sequence-experience notation for architectural and urban spaces', *Town Planning Review*, 32(1): 33–52.

Vale, L.J. (2008) *Changing Cities: 75 Years of Planning Better Futures at MIT*, Cambridge, MA: SA+P Press.

Velasco, A. (2015) *Barrio Rising: Urban Popular Politics and the Making of Modern Venezuela*, Berkeley, CA: University of California Press.

von Moltke, W. (1963) 'Santo Tome de Guayana', *Ekistics*, 15(87): 113–15.

von Moltke, W. (1969) 'The evolution of the linear form', in L. Rodwin and Associates, *Planning Urban Growth and Regional Development*, Cambridge, MA: MIT Press, pp 126–46.

Wakeman, R. (2016) *Practicing Utopia: An Intellectual History of the New Town Movement*, Chicago, IL: University of Chicago Press.

Ward, S.V. (2002) *Planning the Twentieth-Century City*, New York: Wiley.

7

The Times of Infrastructure Fundamentalism: Future Profits, Slow Operations, Long-Term Impacts

Seth Schindler and J. Miguel Kanai

In this chapter, we show how a consensus has emerged among policymakers that infrastructure is a prerequisite for economic growth and development. The 'infrastructure gap' evident in many places is so extensive that it requires an unprecedented amount of private capital. To entice private capital into the infrastructure sector, policymakers have introduced national development plans that extend for two or even three decades into the future. We trace the introduction of this new 'infrastructure time' to the 2008 Global Financial Crisis, which undermined the neoliberal assumption that free markets and 'good governance' institutions were prerequisites for economic growth in low- and middle-income countries. The orthodox Washington Consensus policy framework was under threat from critics long before traders at Lehman Brothers cleared out their offices. Not only had progressive governments in Latin America begun to ignore some of its components (Grugel and Riggirozzi, 2012), but by 2006 closet Keynesians based at the World Bank publicly questioned the wisdom of orthodox neoliberal policy. According to critics of Washington Consensus orthodoxy within the establishment, it had been applied too rigidly and too fast (Rodnik, 2006). But for its defenders, neoliberal restructuring had failed because it was not implemented in earnest.

The collapse of the highly securitized US housing market precipitated a reconciliation between these two groups. At the core of the consensus that emerged in the wake of the 2008 crisis is a fundamental belief that an infrastructure deficit is inhibiting growth and development (Schindler et al, 2022). There was a recognition that private sector investment in infrastructure had failed to keep pace with demand in the three previous decades of neoliberal restructuring. The result was a deficit of infrastructure that inhibited low- and middle-income countries from integrating with global value chains. Since there was widespread agreement that integration with global value chains catalyses productivity gains, structural transformation, and economic growth (Asian Development Bank and World Trade Organization, 2021), it followed that infrastructure was the missing ingredient in earlier rounds of neoliberal reform that prioritized establishing 'free' markets and 'good' governance. The policy implication was that (transnational) connectivity across vast spaces needed to be enhanced through the construction of roads, railways, ports, and transhipment facilities. This was attractive to Keynesians because it offered an opportunity for states to boost demand and create jobs while reasserting their role as agents of development. States had largely relinquished this role to civil society and the private sector during neoliberal restructuring in the 1980s and 1990s, and many governments were eager to reassert a more active role in development policy and planning. Neoliberal hardliners acquiesced to the expanded role of the state in infrastructure provision because this formula did not identify an endogenous flaw in the neoliberal model. Instead, connective infrastructure is portrayed as a precondition for orthodox neoliberal policy to work.

Within a decade, global development institutions went from endorsing spatially blind policy to embracing infrastructural connectivity as the *sine qua non* of global development. An array of global actors mobilized to consolidate this regime of global development, which we have termed 'infrastructure-led development' (ILD) (Schindler and Kanai, 2021). Its primary imperative is to 'get the territory right' by creating investment opportunities through the construction of infrastructure that links historically isolated places to advanced nodes in the global economy. In practice, this means expanding standardized logistics networks and establishing special economic zones. This consensus surrounding infrastructure was animated by a deluge of US dollars as the US Treasury offered direct lines to friendly governments in the immediate aftermath of the crash, while interest rates around the world hit record lows. Governments in low- and middle-income countries welcomed the policy shift that afforded them scope to pursue spatial objectives, and cheap credit made spatial planning financially viable. To its supporters, not only does ILD offer the potential to foster a long cycle of capital accumulation, but also there is simply no alternative to enhancing connectivity to sustain long-term growth. We refer to this faith that infrastructural connectivity is the single missing ingredient that inhibited growth in earlier rounds of neoliberal restructuring as *infrastructure fundamentalism*.

This line of thought was on full display in 2013 when then-Chief Economist at the World Bank Justin Lin advocated a 'global Marshall Plan' (Lin and Wang, 2013). By the mid-2010s a host of transcontinental projects had been announced that were unrivalled in scale and scope. However, their cost was also unprecedented, and one of Lin's objectives was to call attention to the enormous financial cost of ILD. A global growth coalition comprising multilateral development banks, global consultancies, intergovernmental organizations, and powerful governments assembled to mobilize private capital from the OECD for infrastructure projects worldwide. Infrastructure was transformed into an asset class, and institutions such as the Global Infrastructure Hub (GIH) were established to standardize project proposals and link their proponents with potential investors. Despite these efforts, large-scale greenfield infrastructure projects in low- and middle-income countries continued to exceed the risk tolerance of most patient institutional investors such as pension funds.

To make infrastructure more attractive to investors, a host of strategies have been developed to mitigate economic, political, and environmental risks. Most importantly for this volume, these strategies ushered in a new 'infrastructure time' whose horizon stretches into the distant future. This has coincided with a standardization of risk management practices that apportion risk and rewards between the public sector and private investors. Taken together, these efforts amount to an attempt to future-proof the profitability of infrastructure investments in an age of uncertainty and turbulence (Wiig and Silver, 2019).

While only time will tell if de-risked infrastructure investments will buoy the balance sheets of institutional investors, it is undeniable that the enhancement of connectivity has proceeded apace. The result is the incorporation of vast territories into global value chains. The production of such 'operational landscapes' is an ongoing process (Brenner and Katskis, 2020). In contrast to contemporary capitalism's emphasis on quarterly profits, the temporality of ILD is glacial. Since ILD animates national development plans that extend decades into the future, we refer to the redesign of transcontinental territories as *slow operations*. Here we build from Nixon's (2013) notion of 'slow violence' to highlight how 'operations of capital' can unfold slowly, almost imperceptibly, over the course of decades (Mazzadra and Neilsen, 2019). These operations have a profound long-term impact on cities and urbanization, yet the plans that underpin them are largely devoid of an urban imaginary.

In the next section, we show how infrastructure fundamentalism has become rooted in global development policymaking circles. In the third section, we show how it is at the root of the emergent Wall Street Consensus, which serves to distribute risk and rewards between the public sector and private investors in attempts to future-proof profits. In the final section, we turn to the frontier of ILD where slow operations turn lifeworlds upside down. We conclude that the long-term development plans that guide ILD foster urbanization, but they lack an urban imaginary and are geared towards violent resource extraction that may ultimately undermine efforts to future-proof profits.

The means and ends of infrastructure fundamentalism

Neoliberal ideology informed a policy framework that was introduced at the global scale in earnest in the 1980s, and the integration of the global economy accelerated rapidly after the break-up of the Soviet Union and the collapse of the Iron Curtain. States focused their regulatory attention on supply-side issues while simultaneously 'restructuring' the organizational/territorial manifestations of the state itself (Brenner, 2004). Rather than a straightforward 'hollowing out' of the state as some theorists posited, Peck argued that the 'process typically entails a simultaneous roll-back *and roll-out* of state functions' (2001: 447). In this context, state restructuring was not an optional add-on to the neoliberal agenda; rather, the roll-out of neoliberal policy necessitated '*differently* powerful' states that could regulate the supply side of production while disciplining organized labour and introducing fiscal austerity (Peck, 2001: 447).

At the root of institutional reforms and state restructuring was *market fundamentalism*, constituted by an unshakeable belief in the ability of 'free' markets to efficiently allocate the factors of production across space. However, instead of leading to export-oriented economic growth in low- and middle-income countries as its proponents had envisaged, neoliberal reforms imposed by the institutions that comprised the Washington Consensus resulted in economic decline. This led to the inclusion of 'good governance' in the policy grammar of the Washington Consensus. The idea was that markets could not function in the absence of supportive institutions such as an independent legal system that offered protection of private property, so a frenzy of institutional reform was introduced in pursuit of 'good governance'. States that had only recently been dismantled were suddenly being rebuilt, albeit in a form that was meant to offer succour to markets. The 'good governance' regime culminated in the publication of the 2002 World Development Report entitled *Building Institutions for Markets*. According to Rodrik, this amounted to '"[i]nstitutions fundamentalism", to relate it to (and distinguish it from) the earlier wave of "market fundamentalism". Getting the institutions right is the mantra of the former, just as getting prices right was the mantra of the latter' (2006: 979).

Infrastructure-led development emerged in the aftermath of the 2008 crisis with a recognition that for many countries, attempts to get the prices and institutions right had not had the desired results.[1] As previously discussed, it served as the basis for a reconstitution of a consensus among development policymakers. The imperative is to 'get the territory right', and to this end, many governments in low- and middle-income countries go far beyond supply-side interventions. Indeed, national development plans are once again *en vogue* (Chimhowu et al, 2019), while UNCTAD has stated that '[i]n the decade since the global financial crisis, the number of countries adopting national industrial development strategies has increased dramatically. The rate of adoption of both formal industrial policies and individual policy measures targeted at industrial sectors appears to be at an *all-time high*' (2018: 128–9, emphasis added). Furthermore, states are not only regulators but also market participants. This expanded role is underpinned by what we refer to as *infrastructure fundamentalism*. It is an unshakeable belief that enhanced connectivity is an unalloyed virtue that promises to catalyse evolutionary transformation processes that failed to transpire in earlier rounds of neoliberal restructuring.

For proponents of ILD, infrastructure can be a means or an end. For some policymakers it is a means to open commodity frontiers and integrate historically isolated places within global value chains. This viewpoint holds that ILD augments production and tends to be embraced by those advocating industrial policy. For others, infrastructure is an end in itself that promises to generate returns from users (or taxpayers, if demand is insufficient to drive profits). The rate of return is related to circulation (rather than production), and value is extracted through financial arrangements. Governments in the global South tend to belong to the first group, and they have incorporated infrastructure construction and spatial planning more broadly into spatialized industrial policies (Schindler et al, 2022). In this way, ILD is a productivist policy framework that has the potential to catalyse growth in lagging regions. Alternatively, patient investors for whom ILD is an end in itself recognize the potential for infrastructure to catalyse economic activity, but to them infrastructure represents a sink for capital and they hope to generate rent by controlling key points in vast networks through which commodities circulate (Danyluk, 2018). Despite their different motivations, infrastructure's centrality to capital accumulation has become axiomatic to each of these groups. However, the mobilization of private capital remains a challenge because most projects have a risk profile that exceeds the risk tolerance of patient investors. A host of strategies have been developed by the first group (policymakers) to allocate risks in ways that make projects more attractive to the second group (private investors).

The Wall Street Consensus and de-risking infrastructure-led development

There is a consensus that decades of underinvestment have created an 'infrastructure deficit' so large that it cannot be addressed without the mobilization of private capital. This basic principle is at the core of the World Bank's *Maximizing Finance for Development* (MFD) agenda, which was announced in 2017 and whose primary objective is to mobilize private capital for development initiatives including infrastructure projects. The MFD and other similar initiatives recommend 'blended' financing that includes public and private capital. One organization that celebrates blended finance explains it as such:

> Blended finance is the use of catalytic capital from public or philanthropic sources to increase private sector investment in developing countries to realize the SDGs [Sustainable Development Goals]. Blended finance allows organizations with different objectives to invest alongside each other while achieving their own objectives (whether financial return, social impact, or a blend of both). The main investment barriers for private investors addressed by blended finance are (i) high perceived and real risk and (ii) poor returns for the risk relative to comparable investments. Blended finance creates investable opportunities in developing countries, which leads to more development impact. (Convergence, 2021: 8)

As this passage explains, blended finance arrangements include mechanisms to reduce investors' exposure to economic, political, and environmental risks. Daniela Gabor (2021) argues that the institutional reforms designed to mitigate the exposure of private investors to risk constitutes a regime that she terms the *Wall Street Consensus*. In addition to incorporating Washington-based development institutions and global finance in the establishment of risk-distribution mechanisms, Gabor explains that the Wall Street Consensus includes recipient governments which '(a) reorient the fiscal and monetary arm of the state into de-risking development asset classes, to ensure steady cash flows for investors; (b) re-engineer local financial systems in the image of US market-based finance to allow portfolio investors easy entry into, and exit from, new asset classes' (2021: 3).

The notion of risk, of course, is inherently temporal, and it is both articulated and (hopefully) mitigated across a range of temporal vectors. To encourage private investment in infrastructure, a host of mechanisms have been developed to distribute economic, political, and environmental risk among multilateral development banks, governments, and investors. For instance, the World Bank (2017) offers political risk insurance, which may indeed reduce the amount of capital investors stand to lose in the event of a coup. It does not, however, reduce the potential for political instability. This represents an effort to future-proof profits by insulating infrastructure time from alternative temporalities such as global environmental change or election cycles. In the final section, we show how these attempts to de-risk infrastructure projects are undermined by overlapping temporalities that ultimately inhibit ILD.

Economic risk

Most Wall Street Consensus institutions prioritize the distribution of economic risk over other types of risk. Quite simply, this is the risk that borrowing governments will default on a loan, that construction costs will exceed estimates, or that demand for the use of particular infrastructure will fall short of expectations. Multilateral development banks often assume a portion of this risk, while recipient governments typically also assume a significant portion, thereby reducing exposure of private sector investors.

The World Bank's MFD agenda is emblematic of a host of risk distribution initiatives that proliferated in the decade after the 2008 financial crash. Its 'goal is to promote private investments that are economically viable and cost effective; fiscally and commercially sustainable; balanced from a risk–reward perspective; transparent; meet social and environmental safeguards; and aligned with commitments to addressing climate change' (World Bank, 2017: 9). Under this scheme, governments approach the World Bank with proposals that are subjected to a simple set of questions inexplicably referred to as 'Cascade Objective and Algorithm'. It begins by posing the question: 'Is there a sustainable private sector solution that limits public debt and contingent liabilities?' (2017: 2). If the answer is affirmative, then the algorithm ends with the recommendation to 'promote such private solutions', but if it is negative, the next step is to determine if this is due to 'policy or regulatory gaps or weaknesses' (2017: 2). If a private sector solution is unviable due to particular policies, then the World Bank offers assistance in devising regulatory reforms. Alternatively, if risks are inhibiting private sector investment, the algorithm recommends mechanisms to shield investors from said risks. In some cases, the World Bank offers direct financial assistance. According to one article published by the World Bank, it is 'increasingly using guarantees and applying its capital to mitigate key risks in road PPPs [public–private partnerships] and make them more attractive to private investors' (Pulido, 2018: np). In these cases, the World Bank acts as the 'anchor investor' and the capital it provides is meant to reassure private sector investors of the long-term viability of projects.

Several organizations have been established to augment these efforts by linking investors with project proponents. They assist public authorities by helping them standardize projects, from planning to operation, in ways that make projects legible and attractive to investors. One example is Convergence, a network established by the Canadian government in 2015 and launched at the World Economic Forum in 2016. Linking investors with project proponents is one of its main activities, and to this end it operates 'a fundraising deal platform for investors and those seeking capital to connect. As of September 2021, there are live opportunities seeking to raise over $6 billion, representing over $11 billion in aggregate deal value' (Convergence, 2021: 11). The G20 launched a similar initiative, the GIH, and one of its plans is for a 'project pipeline' that 'allows governments to promote public infrastructure projects to a global investor network' (GIH, 2021). It does this by dividing the construction of infrastructure projects into eight discrete steps, from 'initial government announcement' to 'operations phase / construction complete'. Investors can support projects at any stage.

By standardizing project delivery, the GIH seeks to simplify the identification of risk, which is then allocated using a 'Risk Allocation Tool'. This is actually a series of toolkits specific to various types of infrastructure, such as transport, energy, and telecommunications. For each type of infrastructure, the GIH provides a 'risk matrix' for more specific types of projects. A multitude of risks are listed and divided into several categories such as environmental risk, design risk, demand risk, and so on. GIH further subdivides these categories into more specific risks, and the matrix recommends whether the specific risks should be assigned to the public contracting authority, private investor, or both. However, the transport infrastructure risk allocation matrix exposes the limits of standardizing blended finance because, as the report notes, 'PPP project risks vary between projects and the individual characteristics of each project make it inherently problematic to suggest a "one size fits all" risk matrix' (GIH, 2019: 11). For example, it is difficult to forecast future use for many projects, so there is a risk that infrastructure will be un-/under-used. This is called 'demand risk', and in the case of toll roads or airports, it threatens to undermine the profitability of the project. The GIH risk matrix notes that demand risk is typically assumed by the private partner, but this:

> ... is more difficult in less mature markets ... where there is likely to be a lack of relevant comparative market data to begin with. This may involve some level of government revenue support underpinning the risk transfer (such as a minimum revenue guarantee) or result in an availability (or hybrid) payment model being required. (GIH, 2019: 78)

In other words, governments in low- and middle-income countries may have to guarantee their private sector partners a minimum level of profitability. The precise allocation of risk is highly contingent on specific circumstances, and as Gabor (2021) demonstrates, financial systems have been restructured as central banks in many low- and middle-income countries have acquiesced to the demands of investors and assumed significant risk. This was explained by two managers of BlackRock who collaborated with several governments to launch:

> ... a unique blended finance fund structure that seeks to help derisk the opportunity set in emerging markets for institutional investors. In this case, participating governments and philanthropic institutions subordinate their initial economics to provide downside risk and return

protection to the private fund investors, who receive an outsized share of fund outperformance. (McNally and Spoorenberg, 2021: 75)

This acknowledgement that the distribution of risks and rewards is designed to provide investors with an 'outsized share of fund outperformance' demonstrates the power imbalances that animate the Wall Street Consensus. Nevertheless, many governments have embraced the Wall Street Consensus because in contrast to the Washington Consensus it offers considerable policy space. In many cases, its impositions are project-specific, and they pale in comparison with the far-reaching nature of structural adjustments. They also allow – and at times require – governments to play a significant role in the economy, and in this context many governments have outlined ambitious spatialized industrial strategies (Schindler et al, 2022). The achievement of these strategies requires political stability.

Political risk

The formal distribution of political risk poses a challenge given the fact that it covers a broad spectrum of events from a change of law to a *coup d'état*. According to the GIH risk matrices, it does not constitute a separate type of risk, but rather, political risk is included in other risk categories. Many political risks are classified as Material Adverse Government Action (MAGA) risk, which includes things such as nationalization of infrastructure and currency controls that would inhibit international payments. Other political risks are considered *force majeure* events by the GIH (2019: 169), which are defined as 'an event (or combination of events) outside the reasonable control of the contracting parties which prevents one or both parties from performing all or a material part of their contractual obligations'. In many cases, the distinction between MAGA events and *force majeure* depends on the place where the event occurs, rather than the nature of the event itself. Events that might be considered *force majeure* events in OECD countries can be classified as MAGA events in low- and middle-income countries. Thus, the attempted coup in the US in January 2021 might be considered *force majeure*, while Sri Lankans storming the presidential palace could be considered a MAGA event. The difference is significant because '[t]he basic principle of force majeure is that the risk is shared and each party bears its own losses', while 'the underlying principle behind MAGA relief is to put the Private Partner back into the position it would have been in had the MAGA event not occurred' (GIH, 2019: 170, 172).

In most cases, the difference between *force majeure* and MAGA events is outlined in the initial PPP contract. Governments are incentivized to reduce political instability, because then private sector investors are more likely to agree to their classification as *force majeure* events. Governments project stability, firstly, through the centralization of decision-making surrounding spatial planning and infrastructure construction in the executive branch, and secondly, by planning on a long-term time horizon to reassure private investors that the risk of changes in law is minimal (for instance, see Wahdan and Elshayal, this volume).

Many countries have reintroduced national development plans after a decades-long hiatus (Chomhowu et al, 2019). Many of these plans include industrial policies whose spatialized nature necessitates the assembly of large parcels of land. Kenya's national development plan, *Vision 2030*, is essentially a grand national spatial plan that proponents hoped would nearly double manufacturing as a percentage of GDP, from 8.4 per cent in 2017 to 15 per cent in 2022 (Schindler et al, 2022). This reversal in Kenya's industrial fortunes was supposed to happen after a dramatic expansion of logistics infrastructure opened vast territories to foreign direct investment, particularly in agribusiness and resource extraction. The cornerstone of this plan is the Lamu Port–South Sudan–Ethiopia Transport Corridor, which was initially proposed in the 1970s and was recently resurrected with the hope that it would become a vast transnational region centred in northern Kenya geared towards resource extraction, tourism, and logistics. The project has generally been a disappointment (Gillespie and Schindler, 2022), but for this chapter it is important to note that new institutions were created to oversee its realization, such as the LAPSSET Corridor Development Authority and Vision 2030 Secretariat. It is increasingly common for governments to establish new institutions to pursue spatial objectives, while in other cases reforms shield existing institutions that assemble land and determine its use from public oversight. These two trends proceed in tandem; power is centralized in the executive branch while spatial planning is rendered technical and insulated from challenges from civil society (and even other public institutions).

Examples of these trends abound. In Thailand, the military government created the Eastern Economic Corridor Office (EECO) in 2018. In pursuit of the junta's development plan, *Thailand 4.0*, the EECO seeks to attract foreign investment to special economic zones on the eastern borders with Cambodia and Laos. It reports to the highest levels of government, it is empowered to determine land use, and its authority supersedes that of most other public institutions. Similarly, the Kingdom of Saudi Arabia launched a national development plan, *Vision 2030*, designed to diversify the Kingdom's economy in preparation for a post-oil future. This will purportedly be achieved through the construction of a number of 'giga-projects' such as the multibillion-dollar city-region called Neom in the Kingdom's sparsely populated north-west. To fund these extravagant giga-projects, the National Development Fund was established in 2017 by consolidating several public institutions and funds, and it will act as an anchor investor (Arab News,

2020). Meanwhile, the Public Investment Fund, with nearly $1 trillion in assets under its management, was restructured; its powers were expanded as it was tasked with pursuing *Vision 2030* (Habibi, 2019).

The achievement of grandiose national development plans necessitates a level of coordination that justifies political centralization. This is meant to reassure investors that the state has the capability and authority to undertake national development plans. In many cases, state restructuring is undertaken with the aim of concentrating power, but this can precipitate intra-state competition and contribute to political instability rather than forestall it. Pakistan partnered with Beijing in pursuit of spatial objectives and the two countries agreed to create the China–Pakistan Economic Corridor (CPEC) in 2014. A core of China's globe-spanning Belt and Road Initiative, CPEC comprises a host of connectivity-oriented infrastructure projects that promise to deepen Pakistan's economic ties with China and transform its relationship with the global economy. The CPEC Authority was created in 2020 as an autonomous body with immense financial and administrative liberty to oversee infrastructure projects included in CPEC (Pakistan National Assembly, 2020). Predictably, other governmental institutions interpreted the creation of the CPEC Authority as a threat, and this precipitated a power struggle within the Pakistani state. After Prime Minister Imran Khan lost a no confidence vote in the National Assembly in April 2022, it was widely reported that the CPEC Authority will be disbanded, with critics pointing out that its mandate includes activity that falls in the portfolio of the Planning Commission (Yousafzai, 2022). In summary, Islamabad may have been ill-equipped to undertake CPEC, but reforms meant to enhance the capacity and authority of the state actually fostered political infighting and instability.

Another way governments seek to project stability is to make plans with increasingly long time horizons. As noted, Kenya and Saudi Arabia have development plans that stretch to 2030, as does Jamaica, while Buenos Aires recently introduced *Argentina Productiva 2030* and Malaysia embraced the *Shared Prosperity Vision 2030*. Papua New Guinea launched its *Vision 2050* development plan in 2015, with Rwanda and Mongolia following suit in 2020 and 2022, respectively. Not to be outdone, the African Union launched *Agenda 2063*, which is a 'blueprint and master plan for transforming Africa into the global powerhouse of the future' in four decades (African Union, nd). While these visions may guide policy in the medium term, their primary purpose seems to be to project stability by demonstrating commitment to a direction of travel. Yet planning four decades into the future poses serious challenges in a world characterized by uncertainty and turbulence (Wiig and Silver, 2019). Some national development plans accommodate a range of future events by remaining vague, but it is difficult to convince investors to support specific infrastructure projects with vague platitudes.

This is particularly the case in the context of global environmental change. It is difficult to offer certainty of any sort four decades into the future since global environmental change will in part be determined by the extent to which humans reduce emissions in the near future. Nevertheless, investors require a level of certainty, so significant efforts have been made to future-proof profits against future environmental change.

Environmental risk

North Jakarta lies four metres below sea level. Parts of the low-income area owe their existence to ageing water management infrastructure that keeps seawater at bay and drains rainwater. However, as extraction of groundwater has precipitated subsidence, leading to the city sinking approximately 25 centimetres per year (Sherwell, 2016), the area has become increasingly vulnerable to flooding. To address the twin problems of rising sea levels and subsidence, Indonesian authorities embraced a high-modernist scheme to strengthen the sea wall and enclose Jakarta Bay with land 'reclaimed' from the sea (Colvin, 2017). As shown in Figure 7.1, the project calls for the

Figure 7.1: The proposed Great Garuda development, Jakarta

Note: This rendering featured in the Indonesian government's Master Plan for National Capital Integrated Coastal Development along with the caption 'Poised in the middle of the great wing-shaped sea wall will be a new central city area. Positioned as a natural extension of the central spine area of Jakarta, it will provide a spectacular and warm welcome to all who come to the nation's capital' (Ministry of Economic Affairs, 2014: 50).

Source: KuiperCompagnons, reproduced with permission

creation of 17 islands that, from the air, will resemble the mythical *garuda* bird that is a potent national symbol (Wade, 2019). These islands will present opportunities for real estate developers to create 'world-class' cityspace (Salim et al, 2019).

We approach Great Garuda as a case of infrastructure fundamentalism *par excellence*. Faced with the imminent breakdown of existing infrastructure, Indonesian elites have turned to infrastructure planning on a grandiose scale as a solution that promises both to protect Jakarta's residents and built environment from the effects of climate change and to open a new frontier for real estate speculation. Realizing these opportunities is dependent on the Great Garuda scheme insulating Jakarta from the impacts of climate change, and it comes with an estimated cost of $40 billion. This raises questions about the allocation of risk posed by global environmental change. As the climate crisis intensifies, infrastructure will be deployed to shield people and places from its impacts, but this infrastructure will be costly and exposed to severe environmental stress. Who will bear the risk that the infrastructure meant to protect people and places from extreme weather events may crumble in the face of rising sea levels, frequent tropical storms, and intense wildfires? In this case, the Great Garuda proved too risky for private investors, so the state moved in to bear the cost and it seeks to finance the project by selling land reclaimed from the sea to real estate developers.

The Great Garuda has been widely criticized by environmental groups who argue that enclosing Jakarta Bay threatens to trap water run-off and sewage, and therefore, 'the reclamation project will exacerbate, rather than solve, the floods which occur yearly during the rainy season'.[2] It was co-developed by a number of government ministries and Dutch coastline management consultants (Colvin, 2017), and according to the master plan:

> Formed by the laws of nature, flow and efficiency, this elegant foil-shaped waterfront city resembles a great bird, an eagle spreading its great wings to protect the city of Jakarta, the national capital. The national symbol, beloved by everyone, comes to the rescue of the national capital, guarding its people from drowning and providing a grand perspective of the future of Indonesia. (Ministry of Economic Affairs, 2014: 52–3)

We distinguish liabilities that may result from environmental impacts caused by infrastructure from risks to infrastructure posed by climate events. While these are very different types of risks, they tend to be subsumed under the catch-all category of 'environmental risks'. For example, the GIH defines 'environmental risk' for transport infrastructure projects as follows: 'The risk associated with pre-existing conditions; obtaining consents; compliance with laws; conditions caused by the project; external events; and climate change'. Environmental risk is disaggregated in the matrices, and the GIH (2019: 109) notes that '[m]arket practice is [still] developing' in terms of the allocation of risk posed by climate change events to infrastructure itself. At present, however, the GIH advocates either allocating these risks to states or classifying them as *force majeure* events if they are beyond a certain threshold, 'for example, temperatures outside certain ranges'. These thresholds must be agreed upon when the contract is signed, because the GIH is clear that if the project's scope is adapted to reduce vulnerability to climate change events, the cost should be covered by states. The GIH (2019: 109) explains that an 'alternative may be to consider a separate contractual mechanism to address these types of risks over the long-term life of the contract', but it does not explain what this may entail.

The Great Garuda master plan shows how some climate change risks are identified and accounted for in the project's financial structure. First, in line with Wall Street Consensus norms, the plan notes that '[f]inancing flood protection with urban development and other sources of revenues, preferably developed by private enterprises, is one of the project principles. This principle, however appealing from a public budget perspective, transforms a straightforward civil engineering project into a challenging integrated urban development with a complex financing structure' (Ministry of Economic Affairs, 2014: 60).

Furthermore, the business case for the Great Garuda extends to 2050. The project will reclaim land at a cost of $7 billion, which will be sold to real estate developers, and the proceeds will fund the construction of the sea wall and other water management infrastructure. The master plan concludes that 'land reclamation and port expansion are profitable and the components flood protection and transportation are loss making. Over time, the sum of revenues are higher than the total costs, resulting in a positive business case' (Ministry of Economic Affairs, 2014: 64). The business case compartmentalizes the public and private components of the Great Garuda. The infrastructure that will actually protect Jakarta from rising sea levels is a public project, fully financed by the future sale of urban land that the project will produce. Several project-specific risks are identified in the master plan, and the actions taken to mitigate them are explained. They include risks such as the fact that 'real estate prices and land prices might be lower than expected' and land reclamation 'costs might be substantially larger [than anticipated]' (Ministry of Economic Affairs, 2014: 67). However, nowhere in the master plan is the feasibility of the project questioned. It does not countenance the possibility that the sea wall may fail to protect Jakarta from global environmental change despite acknowledging that it 'will be one of the most challenging hydraulic civil works that has been carried out worldwide' (Ministry of Economic Affairs, 2014: 77). The master plan acknowledges that the project's engineers must contend with environmental uncertainties, while they are also constrained by the vagaries of real estate markets because the 'pace and final size of the Garuda should be tuned to the speed of market uptake of real estate' (Ministry of Economic Affairs, 2014: 78). The master plan does not explain whether the sea wall would indeed be built if the business case proves inaccurate and the value of real estate declines, or if there is little interest among real estate developers for land. At the very least, this would inhibit the state from cross-subsidizing the sea wall with the sale of land, and hence, the Indonesian state's attempts to save Jakarta from subsidence and rising sea levels is at least partly influenced by real estate markets.

Global investors assert that '[t]here has never been a better time to invest in climate infrastructure' (McNally and Spoorenberg, 2021: 74), so this raises the question: why is Great Garuda's water management infrastructure fully financed by the public? In this instance, it is because the project was deemed too risky. As human settlements will require larger and more expansive infrastructure in the face of global environmental change in years to come, it remains unclear whether this infrastructure will prove too risky for private investors. Indeed, it appears that the institutions that animate the Wall Street Consensus such as the GIH and Convergence have not figured out how to future-proof investments in the infrastructure that will insulate humans from the ravages of environmental change.

Urban imaginaries of slow operations

Infrastructure was left to the private sector throughout the neoliberal period. Policymakers concentrated on liberalizing markets and then establishing market-supporting governance institutions. The 2008 Global Financial Crisis changed everything. Policymakers began to identify infrastructure as a prerequisite for development. We referred to this as infrastructure fundamentalism and argued that it now underpins global development policy and national development plans. Meanwhile, these plans are animated by increasingly long time spans. As we demonstrated, it is not uncommon for governments to plan two, three, even four decades into the future. One reason policymakers are lengthening the duration of plans is to reassure risk-averse private sector investors. Additionally, a host of risk management strategies have been introduced to encourage private investment in infrastructure. We showed how these strategies are standardized and deal with economic, political, and environmental risks in attempts to future-proof profits decades into the future.

We demonstrated that these strategies are not always able to reduce risk to an acceptable level for private investors. Environmental risks, in particular, are difficult to mitigate given the challenges of modelling global environmental change. Although the amount of private capital mobilized has been insufficient to address the infrastructure gap, vast territories have been moulded into 'operational landscapes' that comprise planetary mines, mega-plantations, and gargantuan warehouses (Arboleda, 2020; Gillespie and Schindler, 2022). These territories are animated by incremental yet inexorable processes that we have referred to as *slow operations*. We conclude this chapter by shifting our gaze to the historically isolated places that are being drawn into the global economy. We focus on the urban space that emerges during slow operations and their inexorable long-term impacts.

We previously introduced the Great Garuda, a high-modernist scheme to save Jakarta from climate change whose success is dependent on its ability to trigger a real estate bonanza. The project is an urban spectacle that promises to create 'world-class' cityspace, and this sets it apart from most ILD schemes that lack an urban vision. Indeed, rather than generating 'world-class' cityspace, ILD tends to catalyse frontier urbanization as new territories are opened for exploitation. According to Moore (2015), capital accumulation requires 'cheap nature' whose production can only be achieved if its custodians are not remunerated. Simply put, resources are cheap when they can be appropriated, but once a place is firmly rooted within certain national (and global) institutional systems, resources become commodified. It is far more difficult (although not impossible) to dispossess owners of commodities than custodians of nature. Hence, there is a tendency for commodity frontiers to expand in a capitalist system, as the powerful rush to appropriate nature and then move on once it is commodified. Moore (2015) argues that contemporary capitalism is in crisis because there is no geographic outside, so it is impossible to produce new commodity frontiers.

The theoretical underpinning of Moore's argument is convincing, but we take issue with its empirical claims that capitalist expansion has run its course (Schindler and Kanai, 2018). Our analysis of risk management strategies demonstrates there is a temporal dimension to infrastructure investment and attempts to future-proof profits are directly related to the expectation that resources will be exploited in the future. Indeed, far from Jakarta's snarled traffic is Kalimantan, an island rich in resources that was transformed into a commodity frontier in the late twentieth century. Anna Tsing documents the complexity of this transformation. She begins by explaining that frontiers do not simply exist; rather, they are 'projects in making geographical and temporal experience' (Tsing, 2005: 29). Tsing shows how the frontier incubates particular human subjects for whom extraction of value is the overriding priority. In Kalimantan, entrepreneurs and armies were able to disengage nature from local ecologies and livelihoods, as global capital took advantage of lax national regulations to fuel the expansion of monocrop plantations in collaboration with the military. She explains how these forces of order unleashed widespread disorder and chaos that 'predict and perform their own reversals. ... Planned communities lead to unplanned settlement; resource nationalization leads to private control; land titling leads to forgery; military protection leads to generalized violence' (Tsing, 2005: 33).

While Tsing's objective was not to focus on the urban spaces that emerged in the wake of the frontier's seemingly unstoppable spread, her ethnographic account provides glimpses of urban life at the interstice of the ancient ecology of the rainforest, the regimented order of plantations, and the wild violence of logging roads. These are 'orderly, blank, anonymous' transmigration villages home to migrant workers whose labour power will animate plantations, called Block A, Block B, and Block C (Tsing, 2005: 36). These anonymous grey villages stand in stark contrast to the temporary settlements of itinerant resource entrepreneurs, be they gold prospectors or loggers, who 'erect camps of bamboo platforms hung with plastic sheets; they have coffee pots, sugar, mackerel cans' (Tsing, 2005: 40). Then there are the 'noisy frontier towns, full of gold merchants, truckers, and hungry, aggressive men' (Tsing, 2005: 36).

These frontier settlements are the flipside of the Great Garuda, and they exemplify the actually existing urbanization effects of ILD. Slow operations engender extensive urbanization processes in which the emerging peri-urban, transitional, and hybrid spaces are devoid of an urban imaginary (Kanai and Schindler, 2022). There is a certain irony that the grand spatial plans that plot the slow operations transforming landscapes the size of entire countries lack even the most rudimentary plans for the new urban spaces that are taking shape. This laissez-faire urbanization, and indeed, the future-proofing of profits on commodity frontiers, turns on faith and erased histories. First, there is faith that people who live near newly built connective infrastructure will recognize the opportunities afforded by roads and railways and self-actualize accordingly (Dye et al, 2021). This view of people as malleable and closet entrepreneurs is related to a second high-modernist faith in the ability of planners to transform places at will on a grand scale (see Coutard, this volume; Ekman, this volume).

These faiths are deeply embedded in the infrastructure time of ILD that looks three or four decades into the future and instantiates slow operations. They also ignore histories of people and landscapes, the age-old ecologies and epistemologies that exist in places inaccessible to large-scale foreign direct investment. In the rare case that the lifeworlds being absorbed into operational landscapes are recognized, there is a paternalistic and naive assumption that populations will be 'improved' through the integration of territory into global value chains (Li, 2007). As Tsing shows, however, the production of a resource frontier did not unleash pent-up entrepreneurialism among the inhabitants of Kalimantan. Instead, the entire region became caught up in a hellish paroxysm of destruction and theft, a 'Wild West scene of rapid and lawless resource extraction'

(2005: 59). Sadly, infrastructure fundamentalism is driving similar events around the world. We predict that in some instances, the failure of slow operations to incorporate and tame existing socialities and ecologies may undermine long-term capital accumulation. In some places, nature will refuse to be tamed and even the most ambitious high-modernist schemes will be undone by global environmental change. In other places, risk mitigation strategies will fail to insulate infrastructure from alternative temporalities, perhaps those of local populations. Surely, in some cases people will defend lifeworlds against slow operations. This defence may be the ultimate *force majeure* that inhibits the future-proofing of profits and disrupts infrastructure fundamentalism.

Notes

[1] The precise goals differed from country to country, but typically included a combination of structural transformation, increased flows of foreign direct investment, export-oriented growth, and industrial diversification and/or upgrading.

[2] This was asserted by the Save Jakarta Bay Coalition in a letter to Netherlands Prime Minister Mark Rutte, available here: https://www.tni.org/files/article-downloads/concern_on_the_gov._of_the_netherlands_support_on_reclamation_of_17_artificial_islands_and_ncicd.pdf.

References

African Union (nd) *Agenda 2063: The Africa We Want*, Addis Ababa: African Union. https://au.int/en/agenda2063/overview (accessed 15 July 2022).

Arab News (2020) 'National Development Fund has $93.33bn capital, mulls new infra fund: Governor', *Arab News*, 23 December. https://www.arabnews.com/node/1781531/business-economy (accessed 4 May 2021).

Arboleda, M. (2020) *Planetary Mine: Territories of Extraction Under Late Capitalism*, London: Verso.

Asian Development Bank and World Trade Organization (2021) *Global Value Chain Development Report: Beyond Production*, Beijing and Geneva: Asian Development Bank and World Trade Organization.

Brenner, N. (2004) *New State Spaces: Urban Governance and the Rescaling of Statehood*, Oxford: Oxford University Press.

Brenner, N., and Katsikis, N. (2020) 'Operational landscapes: Hinterlands of the Capitalocene', *Architectural History*, 90(3): 22–30.

Chimhowu, A., Hulme, D., and Munro, L.T. (2019) 'The "new" national development planning and global development goals: Processes and partnerships', *World Development*, 120: 76–89.

Colvin, E. (2017) 'Understanding the allure of big infrastructure: Jakarta's Great Garuda sea wall project', *Water Alternatives*, 10(2): 250–64.

Convergence (2021) *The State of Blended Finance 2021*, Toronto: Convergence. https://www.convergence.finance/resource/0bbf487e-d76d-4e84-ba9e-bd6d8cf75ea0/view (accessed 2 December 2022).

Danyluk, M. (2018) 'Capital's logistical fix: Accumulation, globalization, and the survival of capitalism', *Environment and Planning D: Society and Space*, 36(4): 630–47.

Dye, B., Schindler, S., and Rwehumbiza, D. (2021) 'The political rationality of state capitalism in Tanzania: Territorial transformation and the entrepreneurial individual', *Area Development & Policy*, 7(1): 42–61.

Gabor, D. (2021) 'The Wall Street Consensus', *Development and Change*, 52(3): 429–59.

Gillespie, T., and Schindler, S. (2022) 'Africa's new urban spaces: Deindustrialisation, infrastructure-led development and real estate frontiers', *Review of African Political Economy*, 49(174): 531–49.

Global Infrastructure Hub (2019) *PPP Risk Allocation Tool 2019 Edition–Transport*, Sydney: Global Infrastructure Hub.

Global Infrastructure Hub (2021) 'Global Infrastructure Hub project pipeline'. https://pipeline.gihub.org/ (accessed 15 July 2022).

Grugel, J., and Riggirozzi, P. (2012) 'Post-neoliberalism in Latin America: Rebuilding and reclaiming the State after crisis', *Development and Change*, 43(1): 1–21.

Habibi, N. (2019) 'Implementing Saudi Arabia's *Vision 2030*: An interim balance sheet', *Middle East Brief*. https://www.brandeis.edu/crown/publications/middle-east-briefs/pdfs/101-200/meb127.pdf (accessed 15 July 2022).

Kanai, M., and Schindler, S. (2022) 'Infrastructure-led development and the peri-urban question: Furthering crossover comparisons', *Urban Studies*, 59(8): 1597–617.

Li, T.M. (2007) *The Will to Improve: Governmentality, Development, and the Practice of Politics*, Durham, NC: Duke University Press.

Lin, J.Y., and Wang, Y. (2013) 'Beyond the Marshall Plan: A Global Structural Transformation Fund', background paper submitted to the High Level Panel on the Post-2015 Development Agenda.

Mezzadra, S., and Neilsen, B. (2019) *The Politics of Operations: Excavating Contemporary Capitalism*, Durham, NC: Duke University Press.

McNally, R., and Spoorenberg, F. (2021) 'Moving from ambition to action: A call for stronger public and private partnerships', in Convergence (ed) *The State of Blended Finance 2021*, Toronto: Convergence, pp 74–5.

Ministry of Economic Affairs (Indonesia) (2014) *Master Plan: National Capital Integrated Coastal Development*, Jakarta: Ministry of Economic Affairs.

Moore, J. (2015) *Capitalism in the Web of Life: Ecology and the Accumulation of Capital*, New York: Verso.

Nixon, R. (2013) *Slow Violence and the Environmentalism of the Poor*, Cambridge, MA: Harvard University Press.

Pakistan National Assembly (2020) 'China Pakistan Economic Corridor Authority Act'. https://na.gov.pk/uploads/documents/1612267873_350.pdf (accessed 15 July 2022).

Peck, J. (2001) 'Neoliberalizing states: Thin policies/hard outcome', *Progress in Human Geography*, 25(3): 445–55.

Pulido, D. (2018) 'Maximizing finance for safe and resilient roads', *World Bank*, 27 March. https://blogs.worldbank.org/transport/maximizing-finance-safe-and-resilient-roads (accessed 15 July 2022).

Rodrik, D. (2006) 'Goodbye Washington Consensus, hello Washington Confusion? A review of the World Bank's "Economic Growth in the 1990s: Learning from a Decade of Reform"', *Journal of Economic Literature*, 44: 973–87.

Salim, W., Bettinger, K., and Fisher, M. (2019) 'Maladaptation on the waterfront: Jakarta's growth Coalition and the Great Garuda', *Environment and Urbanization Asia*, 10(1): 63–80.

Schindler, S., and Kanai, J.M. (2018) 'Producing localized commodity frontiers at the end of cheap nature: An analysis of eco-scalar carbon fixes and their consequences', *International Journal of Urban and Regional Research*, 42(5): 828–44.

Schindler, S., and Kanai, J.M. (2021) 'Getting the territory right: Infrastructure-led development and the re-emergence of spatial planning strategies', *Regional Studies*, 55(1): 40–51.

Schindler, S., Alami, I., and Jepson, N. (2022) 'Goodbye *Washington Confusion*, hello *Wall Street Consensus*: Contemporary state capitalism and the spatialisation of industrial strategy', *New Political Economy*, 28(2): 223–40. https://doi.org/10.1080/13563467.2022.2091534

Sherwell, P. (2016) '$40bn to save Jakarta: The story of the Great Garuda', *The Guardian*, 22 November. https://www.theguardian.com/cities/2016/nov/22/jakarta-great-garuda-seawall-sinking (accessed on 15 July 2022).

Tsing, A.L. (2005) *Friction: An Ethnography of Global Connection*, Princeton, NJ: Princeton University Press.

UNCTAD (United Nations Conference on Trade and Development) (2018) *World Investment Report 2018*, New York: United Nations.

Wade, M. (2019) 'Hyper-planning Jakarta: The Great Garuda and planning the global spectacle', *Singapore Journal of Tropical Geography*, 40: 158–72.

Wiig, A. and Silver, J. (2019) 'Turbulent presents, precarious futures: Urbanization and the deployment of global infrastructure', *Regional Studies*, 53(6): 912–23.

World Bank (2017) *Maximizing Finance for Development: Leveraging the Private Sector for Growth and Sustainable Development*, Washington, DC: Joint Ministerial Committee of the Boards of Governors of the Bank and the Fund on the Transfer of Real Resources to Developing Countries.

Yousafzai, F. (2022) 'Govt likely to dissolve China Pakistan Economic Corridor Authority due to its poor performance', *The Nation*, 21 April. https://nation.com.pk/2022/04/21/govt-likely-to-dissolve-china-pakistan-economic-corridor-authority-due-to-its-poor-performance/ (accessed 15 July 2022).

8

Dissonant Times: The Land–Infrastructure–Finance Nexus in Post-Mubarak Egypt

Dalia Wahdan and Tamer Elshayal

Introduction

In the decade following the Egyptian Revolution in 2011, which saw Hosni Mubarak deposed after nearly 30 years as president, Egypt's state agencies have embarked on a gargantuan scheme to reconfigure the country's territorial and economic geography. Major projects have ranged from the construction of a second navigation canal parallel to the southern section of the Suez Canal to ambitious plans to reclaim 4.1 million acres of land to build 22 new industrial cities, 25 tourist cities, eight airports, and three ports. At the 2015 Egypt Economic Development Conference, Egyptian housing minister Mostafa Madbouly announced a plan to move the nation's capital from Cairo to a new desert city that would host 6.5 million people (reviving proposals floated since the 1970s) and require the construction of over 4,000 kilometres of highways and logistics infrastructure. Infrastructure development and networked connectivity have thus been positioned as central drivers for Egypt's future development. In July 2021, after eight years in office, President Abdel Fattah al-Sisi announced a 'New Republic' and the 'dawn of a modern future', largely premised on economic growth spurred by infrastructure mega-projects, national social infrastructure initiatives, and purportedly democratic principles (see Naucer, 2022). By the year's end – a decade after Mubarak's ouster – construction and building accounted for 7.7 per cent of GDP, and the real estate ownership and services sectors accounted for another 11.4 per cent, superseded only by tourism (54.7 per cent), the extractive sector (37.5 per cent), and revenues from the Suez Canal (23.6 per cent) (Central Bank of Egypt, 2022).

Egypt's rush towards infrastructure-led development needs to be contextualized in relation to the position of the country's economy in the global market. In the financial year (FY) 2021/22, the Egyptian economy was worth 0.02 per cent (US$404 billion) of the world economy, with imports worth US$72.4 billion and a meagre US$40.1 billion of exports. The Economist Intelligence Unit (2022) rated Egypt's economic structure risk factor at 'B' (indicating a high public debt to GDP ratio), rated its sovereign risk at 'B-with negative outlook' (indicating high fiscal deficit as a proportion of GDP), and rated its political risk at 'CCC' (indicating that the tight control over institutions could pose the risk of social unrest). Yet the state continues to build big and quick, tapping into regional and global debt-based financial markets, loans, and direct monetary assistance from international monetary institutions, China, and neighbouring Gulf countries to feed the demand for infrastructure, beyond its already strained budget.

This chapter questions the resurgence of infrastructure mega-projects in Egypt amid dire fiscal, political, economic, and pandemic conditions. We pay particular attention to the temporal relations underpinning the 'territorial moment' of Egypt's infrastructure-led development. These include the historical restructuring of public agencies; the expedited time frames granted to key projects; the temporal extension of credit and risk involved in assetization and the floating of green bonds; and the temporal logics compelling the de-risking functions of the state. Our analysis centres on the case of the Cairo Monorail (CM), a project initiated in 2015 and touted as the world's longest driverless monorail system. It consists of two lines that will connect Cairo's urban core to the New Administrative Capital (NAC) and the city's eastern and western hinterlands. We argue that the CM project is illustrative of a land–infrastructure–finance nexus that has developed since 2015 and continues into the 2020s, albeit abated by the COVID-19 pandemic, the Russia–Ukraine war, and the immediacy of fiscal and financial constraints. This nexus is underpinned by global financial forces, regulatory transformations, and the emergence of infrastructure as a new 'asset class' (Weber et al, 2016), one with distinct associated asset bases, ownership and managerial entities, legal and institutional frameworks, share- and stakeholders, interests, and risk–returns parameters. As Schindler and Kanai (this volume) posit, each element has its own temporal logics, pasts, presents, and futures, and time horizons that have potentially destabilizing effects (also see Kurtiç and Nucho, 2022).

Egypt's land–infrastructure–finance nexus is inherently dissonant. The CM and the NAC are mega-projects that require mega-finance. For these to manifest, they need steady partnering entities, complex risk-interest analyses, risk distribution portfolios, and above all a command-and-control ruling regime that not only stabilizes fiscal and monetary policies but also *primarily* secures sufficient land banks through expropriation and the suppression of social unrest. Excluding technical risks related to constructing and maintaining physical infrastructure, the Egyptian land–infrastructure–finance nexus holds three main temporal, spatial, and scalar dissonances within the mechanisms deployed to (1) de-risk investments, (2) reconfigure urban space, and (3) restructure governmental institutions and operations. These dissonances threaten the viability of infrastructural projects and the stability of the national economy because each presents immediate and future risks to the socio-spatial organization of the city, the legality and legitimacy of the ruling regime, and the capacity of sub-national governments to sustain their functions and mandates.

The chapter begins by assessing the convergent causal pathways shaping the emergence of infrastructure as an asset class. Our analysis explains how financialization processes helped construct the global South as an investment frontier by valorizing land and infrastructure. We locate Egypt within a new global financial hierarchy and review the legal and institutional reforms put in place since the 1990s to facilitate a distinctive land–infrastructure–finance nexus. Building on these foundations, we shift our focus to the Cairo Monorail, paying particular attention to the institutional and temporal restructuring necessitated by the project. The chapter concludes by elaborating on the three key dissonances implicated in the land–infrastructure–finance nexus and suggesting how its temporal dimensions will affect Egypt's urban configurations, governance dynamics, and regime legitimacy.

Converging forces and causal pathways of infrastructure-led development

The current global embrace of infrastructure is situated at the intersection of two converging forces (1) a 'global infrastructure scramble' driven by the surpluses of technologies and the imperatives of financial capital in the global North and China; and (2) shifting multilateral development architectures and the development of new linkages to private financial markets. These two forces are tightly intertwined and shape path-dependent trajectories and discourses of infrastructure deficiency that feed into a mania for mega-infrastructure projects.

Infrastructure as an asset class and the scramble for financing

Kanai and Schindler (2022; Schindler and Kanai, 2021, this volume) trace the emergence of the current global scramble for infrastructure financing to the aftermath of the 2008 Global Financial Crisis, when 'traditional' bank lending slowed down substantially and banks adjusted to tighter regulatory controls, mostly emanating from the stricter Basel III capital and liquidity requirements (see Ouma, 2014). Investing in infrastructure offered a staid and stable option, typically with predictable risk profiles and consistently strong returns. In 2014, the G20 created the Global Infrastructure Hub to monitor infrastructure sectors according to risk/return forecasts and by 2018, a broad policy consensus had emerged around the explicitly stated objective of establishing infrastructure as an asset class (alongside 'traditional' investments in private equity or natural resource extraction) capable of generating trillions of US dollars in bankable investment opportunities (World Bank, 2017; G20/OECD/WB, 2018, see also Gabor, 2021). Linking infrastructure development to the UN's Sustainable Development Goals (SDGs) has further enhanced the perceived robustness of infrastructure investment (Mawdsley, 2018). Global estimates of infrastructure need are forecast to reach US$94 trillion during 2016–2040 with an additional US$3.5 trillion needed to meet SDGs for electricity and water (Oxford Economics, 2017).

Asset management firms have also embraced the viability of infrastructure investments. While acknowledging the potential disruptions presented by digitization and energy and mobility transitions, McKinsey remains largely bullish on the ability of investors to realize strong rates of return from their infrastructure portfolios post-COVID-19 (Brinkman and Sarna, 2022). The investment firm CBRE similarly contends that '[i]nfrastructure earnings are outpacing global equities today. Infrastructure cash flows have also been far more reliable, with less volatility, than global equities over time … *The resiliency of infrastructure should be prized if economic conditions worsen*' (Anagos and Treitel, 2022: 2, emphasis added). Such narratives do not exclusively target individual investors. They also address private institutional investors including multilateral development banks and other non-banking financial institutions across diverse sectors.

Multilateral development convergence with private financial markets

Recent scholarship on asset-manager forms of capitalism and the assetization–finance nexus has driven home the causal pathway from the Global Financial Crisis, through the financialization of the secondary circuit of capital (value extraction from land, infrastructure, and real estate), to the emergence of goal-oriented governing regimes (for example, Christophers, 2009; Dixon and Monk, 2012; Alm, 2015). For Gabor (2021), strategies to 'escort' financial capital into infrastructure investments have built upon the Washington Consensus's 'Holy Trinity' of macroeconomic stabilization, liberalization of capital markets, and the privatization of state-owned assets. Extending the mantra that development is best served by non-state agents, a global revision of the multilateral development paradigm post-Financial Crisis has fostered financial and institutional engineering to ensure core standards of investor protection against expropriation and to set clear policies for land transactions, dispute resolution, and contract renegotiations. Mechanisms utilized to this end include the diversification of project finance vehicles, mezzanine and bridge financing, joint ventures, contractual agreements, and partnerships beyond the common public–private binary, with diverse risk distribution parameters across investment portfolios and partnering entities. In sum, the scramble for infrastructure originated in the financialization of development through strategies of de-risking which reframe the post-Washington Consensus in the language of the SDGs (Gabor, 2021: 430).

Humphrey (2016) provides a granular analysis of the financing models at play, focusing on multilateral development banks (MDBs) including the World Bank, the Inter-American Development Bank, and the Andean Development Corporation. He argues that MDBs' access to private capital markets to secure their core finances establishes a reliance on bond buyers' understanding of what investments are sound. In the process, MDBs make an 'autonomy–resources trade-off', whereby decisions over development projects become less about the real needs of the citizens or governments of the borrowing countries and more about the exigencies of capital markets. When the choice is between 'maintaining rigid adherence to its original mission and securing the resources needed to survive', MDBs frequently choose the latter (Humphrey, 2016: 93). By accessing capital markets and adjusting to the imperatives of bond buyers, MDBs gain leverage in negotiating their mandates with their 'owners' – the shareholding governments. In this arena, Humphrey (2016: 94) states, 'bond buyers are not concerned with economic development or poverty reduction – the stated purpose for which governments created MDBs – but rather the security of their investment'.

Infrastructure deficiency narratives and dependent financialization

This convergence of causal pathways consolidated in global narratives surrounding countries' 'infrastructure gap': the gap between capital (in need of de-risked circulation) and economies (in need of infrastructure). This narrative is one of urgency, not only to save national economies with deficiencies that cannot be addressed by revenues from productive sectors, taxes, or aid alone but also to meet pressing demand in the global North to recycle liquidity 'in countries lower in the global money hierarchy' (Fernandez and Aalbers, 2020: 680). The infrastructure gap is therefore simultaneously a financial and a territorial gap between developed and less developed countries. The scramble to fill such gaps is both spatial (grounded in specific places) and temporal (reflected in the rush to optimize investments in infrastructural assets, to accelerate the flows of surplus capital, and to realize returns within favourable time horizons).

The magnitude of infrastructure gaps purported across the developing world is remarkable. Estache (2010) suggested that in total, developing countries' infrastructure needs for the period 2005–2015 would average 6.5 per cent of their GDP annually, or over US$1.1 trillion per annum. In 2007, the OECD (2007) declared that developing and emerging economies needed an additional US$71 trillion in infrastructure investment beyond current levels during 2010–2030. Globally, McKinsey Global Institute (2014) estimated that infrastructure spending needed to increase from 3.8 per cent to 5.6 per cent by 2020. Focusing on Egypt, the Global Infrastructure Hub (2023) projects that by 2040, the country's total infrastructure investment need will reach US$675.4 billion, with a financing gap of US$230.4 billion, figures second only to those for Ethiopia in Africa. To our knowledge, there has been little verification of those gross numbers nor any released estimates in sector-specific units that would provide a concrete indication of the 'real' demand for mega-infrastructure. Infrastructure is instead financially framed as a normative good with the de facto assumption that economic growth forecasts represent 'real' demand. Infrastructure as an asset class therefore appears as a 'sure bet' and its frontiers as readily expansive (Ouma, 2014).

The Middle East and North Africa (MENA) region has yet to satisfy the appetites of infrastructure financiers. In 2021, MENA invested US$626 million in infrastructure public–private partnerships (PPPs), a figure 90 per cent less than in 2020 and 81 per cent below the previous five-year average. With only 0.05 per cent of the region's total GDP for 2021 directed towards infrastructure PPPs, MENA lags well behind South Asia (0.26 per cent), sub-Saharan Africa (0.31 per cent), and Latin America and the Caribbean (0.46 per cent) (World Bank, 2021: 9). Egypt, though, appears a promising frontier. Quasi-sovereign wealth funds and/or direct monetary assistance from oil-rich Gulf states offer a bailout option when things go awry (Salah, 2022). Moreover, between 1990 and 2021, 58 projects in the country reached financial closure, with total investments of US$15,547 million (World Bank, 2022a). This performance was made possible through a spectrum of reforms that began under the Mubarak regime but which have accelerated since the 2011 uprising.

Egypt as a global infrastructure frontier

Egypt is no stranger to large-scale urban development, massive construction, and land reclamation, yet for most of the twentieth century it suffered from weak institutions (Cuno, 1980). Since 1991, international monetary institutions have imposed several rounds of Economic Reform and Structural Adjustment Programs (ERSAP) to open its national economy to global finance. The Mubarak regime responded by fostering an ecosystem for debt financing through a suite of laws that were intended, in part, to establish and then strengthen the enabling environment for infrastructure investments. Consequently, ERSAPs laid down the foundations for the emergence in

2015 of Egypt's current investment regime and the rise of the infrastructure state. Two sets of reforms are notable for Egypt's land–infrastructure–finance nexus (1) reforms to the banking and non-banking financial services sectors; and (2) reforms to selected public agencies.

Banking and non-banking sector reforms

In 2005, Egypt accepted Article VIII (Sections 2–4) of the International Monetary Fund (IMF), meaning it would not impose restrictions on the making of payments and transfers for current international transactions and would refrain from engaging in any discriminatory currency arrangements without IMF approval. By accepting these obligations, the state signalled to the international community its intention to pursue policies that reduce risks to international finance, or, in Gabor's (2021) terms, to assume the 'de-risking' function. Since then, MDBs have worked with the Government of Egypt (GoE) to reshape the country's economic geography to support more investments in transport, logistics, energy, and ICT infrastructure. The rationales for doing so ranged from improving the ease of conducting business for export-oriented sectors and supporting the country's integration into global supply and value chains to addressing intra-national socio-economic disparities. Nevertheless, some investors continued to see Egypt's banking system as regressive (Hafez, 2022). It was only after the emergence of the new 'investment regime' in 2015 that this domestic and transnational *connectivity* imperative made it to the top of the government's priorities.

Parallel to the banking sector, the GoE passed significant regulations to introduce and expand the scope of non-banking financial services and institutions (NBFIs). This move aligned with global trends towards non-banking credit, partly in the name of achieving the SDGs. Before 2018, NBFIs were only registered non-governmental (charity or development) organizations with micro-lending mandates targeting poor households and/or micro-enterprises. However, a slew of GoE legislations introduced in the early 2000s expanded NBFI operations. Data suggests that a spike in their operations occurred in 2018 with the passing of the Factoring and Leasing law 176/2018, the Consumer credit law 18/2020, and the amendments to the micro-enterprise law extending micro-lending to small and medium enterprises (SME law 18/2020). In June 2021, there were 952 operating NBFIs that doled out EGP£23.6 billion in loan value. The majority (64 per cent) were non-governmental organizations (NGOs) active in social development. By August 2021, they dispensed EGP£10.4 billion directly to beneficiaries. Commercial NFBIs made up 36 per cent but dispensed the lion's share of microfinancing (EGP£13.3 billion).

The rate of NBFI establishment was fast: from June to August 2021, 47 financial leasing companies registered with the Financial Regulatory

Authority (FRA), with a combined portfolio of EGP£75.6 billion. In 2021, leasing to the real estate and property sector was 85 per cent of the market value, up from 75 per cent between 2016 and 2020. The remaining 15 per cent went to other leased assets including production lines, passenger vehicles, heavy machinery and equipment, heavy transport, and office equipment. Assessments of the sector, however, are limited (for an exception, see Rateiwa and Aziakpono, 2017). Further studies are needed on NBFI's relationship to the banking sector; its governance, (de)regulation, accountability/answerability; its contribution to GDP, growth, and economic stability; and importantly for our current argument, its role in supporting demand and returns on infrastructural investments.

Self-financing securitization, economic agency, and opening the infrastructural frontier

In a process started in the 1980s but accelerated by the regime of Abdel Fattah al-Sisi, the state has aggressively transformed over 57 public agencies into economic authorities (*hay'at iqtisadia*). This has entailed self-financing and a phased reduction of public budgetary outlays, as well as changes to auditing and accounting systems, capacity building (through technical assistance programmes funded by international development banks), and the transfer of bankable assets (mostly land and property) to and from those agencies (see Weber et al, 2016). Economic authorities can also establish private funds *(Sanadeeq Khasa)* and engage in financial transactions outside the national budget. The New Urban Communities Authority (NUCA) and the National Authority for Tunnels (NAT) are two such agencies with direct mandates over the NAC and the CM respectively. Their debt portfolios have affected the type and speed of construction of infrastructure and real estate projects and the emergence of a land-property economy as a major source of accumulation in Egypt.

To illustrate, NUCA, established in 1979 under the Ministry of Housing, was mandated with developing new desert cities to limit congestion in core urban areas and reduce urban expansion into agricultural lands (Wahdan, 2013). Prior to the 1990s, the majority of NUCA's income came from the state budget. With substantial land banks, in 2006, the authority became self-financing and evolved from a single revenue stream into a developer, investor, borrower, and debtor. Two reforms streamlined this evolution (1) land auctioning with international competitive bidding, which was part of a government asset management initiative that involved the privatization of other state-held assets started with the 1991 ERSAP; and (2) PPPs in infrastructure investments, which placed land financing at the centre of urban development. The fruits of these reforms surfaced in 2004 when public auctioning was opened for 378,000 km^2 of land at the main entrance to New Cairo, one of the new cities south-east of Cairo. In that year, the administrative price for the sale of publicly owned lands in New Cairo, regardless of location, was EGP£225 per m^2, barely enough to cover the costs of providing internal infrastructure. Four developers participated at a winning price of EGP£625 (US$114) per m^2, almost triple the administrative price.

In May 2007, NUCA auctioned 2,100 hectares of desert land for the establishment of new towns. This secured US$3.12 billion. The proceeds, substantially exceeding the costs of internal infrastructure, went to reimburse those costs, to pay for a new four-lane access highway connecting the new cities to Cairo Ring Road, and for subsidies to provide low-income housing within the new city development areas. The amount was 117 times the total urban property tax collected in that year and equalled approximately 10 per cent of the total national government revenue. The new pricing and auction policy improved NUCA's recovery of all infrastructure costs poured into new cities. Nevertheless, until 2008, land sale policies repeatedly failed to recover the costs of internal infrastructure incurred over the previous 25 years and NUCA recovered less than half its infrastructural investments from land sales (Peterson, 2009: 95–8). NUCA has continued to experiment with other land value capture instruments (World Bank, 2006; 2013), including land-use readjustment fees, leasing, impact charges, and charges to building rights (Walters, 2015). In 2005, the private developer of Madinaty, a new city north-east of Cairo, received free developable desert land from NUCA in return for financing public infrastructure. The developer paid for US$1.45 billion-worth of internal and external infrastructure in addition to turning 7 per cent of serviced land over to NUCA for the construction of moderate-income housing. Other contractual agreements provide a range of urban infrastructure services for more than 3,300 hectares of newly developed land with no financial cost to NUCA.

In 2008, NUCA established Taameer for Securitization, a joint venture with the Bank for Construction and Housing and Al Oula for Non-Banking Financial Services, with 80 per cent paid-in capital. Taameer closed the first securitization deal, worth EGP£4.6 billion over ten years, for another company, Rabwa Real Estate. Then, after a nine-year hiatus, the venture was restructured and two rounds of securitized bonds were issued, with a net value of EGP£20 billion. In June 2019, the Egyptian National Bank announced the success of a fourth round of subsidized securitization worth EGP£10 billion over three tranches (EGP£2.6 billion, EGP£6.2 billion, and EGP£1.2 billion) with maturities of three, five, and seven years, respectively, making it the largest securitization of short and mid-interval financing in Egypt's history. The National Bank of Egypt acted as guarantor and book-runner in association with several MDBs and global financial institutions.

This apparent financial success, though, sits in stark contrast to the rate of project completion, particular in the case of the NAC. Established *ex nihilo* in 2015, the NAC is planned to cover over 700 km^2 (see Figure 8.1).

Figure 8.1: The central business district of Egypt in the New Administrative Capital, Cairo, 2023

Source: Mahan8484, Wikimedia Commons: CC-BY-SA-4.0

With a projected cost of US$300 billion, the city has arguably become the cornerstone in the al-Sisi regime's claim to inaugurate a 'New Republic'. The NAC was recently declared as an investment zone (Prime Minister Decree #2467/2020). This designation not only grants it specific tax and financial incentives but also more importantly defers the development, operation, and governance of the city to the Administrative Capital for Urban Development (ACUD), an entrusted parastatal company formed in 2016 when NUCA partnered (49 per cent) with the National Service Projects Organization and the Armed Forces Land Projects Agency (two military agencies). NUCA's budget has subsequently increased dramatically, from EGP£30.46 billion in FY2013/14 to EGP£172 billion in FY 2021/22. Much of this funding – an estimated EGP£167 billion (US$10.54 billion) by January 2021 – has financed government-led projects in the NAC (Taweel 2023: 18–19). However, despite this accelerated financing, phase I (of three) of the NAC (which was originally expected to be finished by 2019–20) was only 60 per cent complete as of July 2023. Estimated costs have risen from an initial US$45 billion to US$58 billion in 2023 with further increases anticipated (Taweel, 2023: 9). As we illustrate, the NAC is not the only mega-project to experience temporal dissonance between financing and project completion. The Cairo Monorail seems likely to meet the same fate.

The Cairo Monorail

In 2015 – against a backdrop of political turmoil and economic instabilities precipitated by the 2011 uprising and in the aftermath of the reinstatement of political power by the military – the GoE embarked on a massive, state-led scheme to reshape the country's entire transportation and logistics infrastructure. This ambitious plan, requiring unprecedented levels of public investments, became an immediate discursive touchpoint for business and policy analysts, government advisers, and partners in MDBs and international financial institutions. The GoE justified these infrastructural mega-projects through several connected arguments. Firstly, they were deemed necessary to connect Egypt to global supply chains (for instance, China's One Belt One Road initiative) and integrate the country into international value chains, with special economic zones attracting foreign direct investment (for instance, the Suez Canal Economic Zone). Secondly, infrastructure-led development would boost domestic demand for capital and labour. Thirdly, the GoE's plan pressed the development of a new export-oriented industrial policy, which became apparent in a slew of long-term economic strategies announced at the 2015 Egypt Economic Development Conference. After 2015, Egypt's development policies clearly entered a 'territorial moment' (Schindler and Kanai, 2021), the goal of which is no less than the restructuring of the national space economy.

Urbanization (or rather real estate development) occupies a central position within this spatial development framework. While no official data has been released to date, a large proportion of infrastructure projects have been directed towards the valorization of state-owned desert lands. Much attention has focused on a series of over 45 new cities overseen by state agencies and enabled by new financial instruments and PPPs, which themselves have required legal and administrative adjustments. Within this context (and in relation to the parallel, yet older, narrative of the chronic traffic congestion and economic inefficiencies of transit in Cairo), a series of railed public transportation mega-projects have been undertaken, including a light rail transit, high-speed rail, and the CM. All projects converge upon the NAC. Yet these projects have entailed massive capital investments precisely when the GoE faces one of its most acute fiscal crises to date.

The CM is a striking example of the imbrication of the land–infrastructure–finance nexus in contemporary Egypt. Moreover, it is an exemplary case of infrastructural regionalism (Addie et al, 2020) and the temporal dissonances emerging between the imperative of debt-based finances and project completion rates. Initiated in 2015, the project consists of two electric monorail lines with a combined length of 99 km. These lines will connect Cairo's urban core to its eastern hinterlands and the NAC and the new desert cities planned in its western hinterlands at a projected cost of US$4.5 billion (see Figure 8.2). The CM is expected to carry 45,000 passengers per hour in each direction at full capacity. When initially announced, phase I was expected to open in May 2022, while phase II was slated for February 2023. Neither phase is near completion at the time of writing (July 2023).

Figure 8.2: Map of the Cairo Monorail

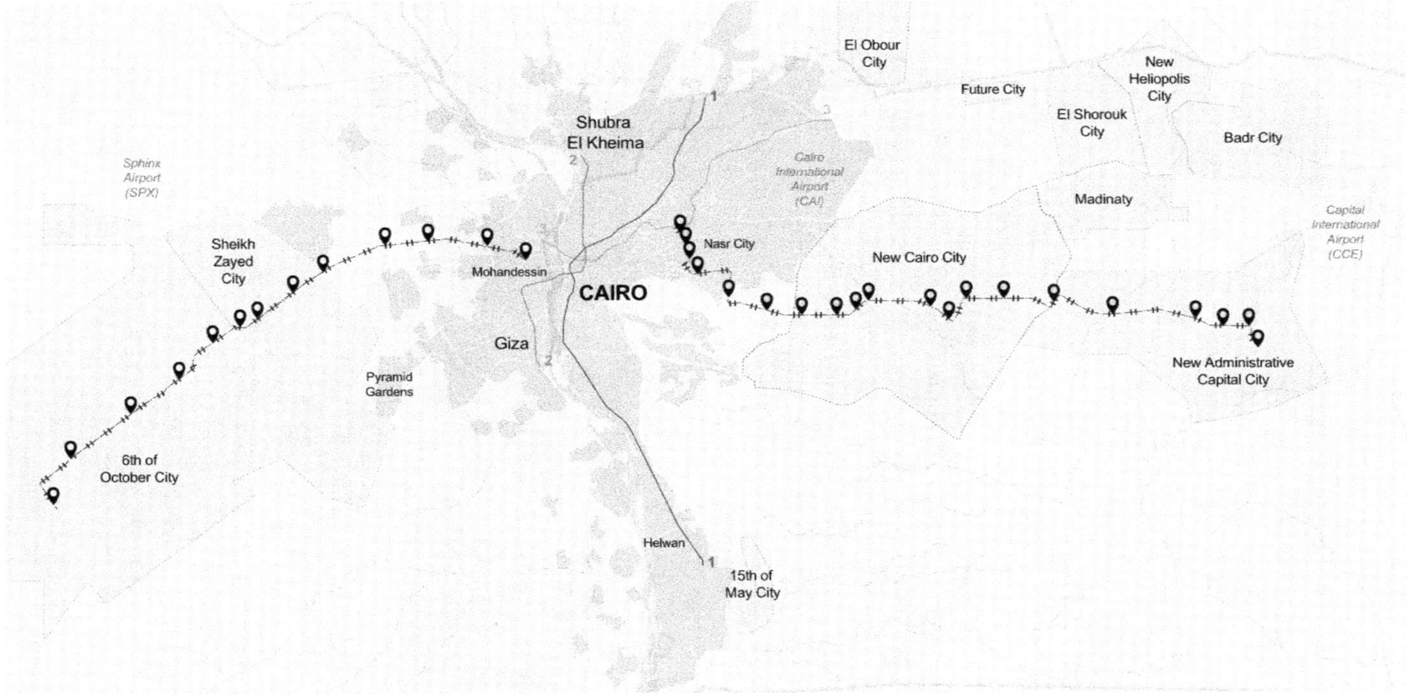

Note: This map shows the 42 km West of Nile line to 6th of October City; the 57 km East of Nile line to the New Administrative Capital, and Cairo's three current Metro lines.

Source: Jean-Paul Addie

As the master developer of the NAC, ACUD oversees the planning and coordination of land use and infrastructure. It does so with the objectives of both ensuring the spatial functioning of the city and maximizing the price of land allotted to the different private real estate developers. As such, the CM is a lynchpin for the economic success of this enterprise, by serving the new city's administrative quarter (its political *raison d'être*) as well as its central business district (phase I and the most lucrative source of revenue).

Given the significance of the CM for the economic prospects of NAC, the GoE expedited the implementation time frame of the project (including all legal and administrative adjustments). In late 2019, a consortium led by Bombardier Transportation was awarded two contracts, a design–build contract, and an operate–maintain contract for 30 years, with a total value of US$4.16 billion. Soon after, the CM was declared a 'public benefit' project. Subsequently, all land plots overlapping with the monorail path were expropriated by eminent domain and their ownership transferred to the National Authority for Tunnels (NAT), a 'public service agency' and a subsidiary body of the Egyptian Ministry of Transport. In 2020, NAT was transformed into an 'economic agency' whose expanded mandate included the right to enter into partnerships and joint ventures with public and private entities, with significant implications for the subsidization of its services and its revenues. The Egyptian Cabinet then moved to declare that the ownership and management of the CM will transfer to a joint stock company – to be established as a partnership between NAT and the Ministry of Finance, NUCA, National Investment Bank, and ACUD – that will be able to issue 'future-flow securitized bonds' and float tradeable debt securities.

In late 2020, the GoE and J.P. Morgan reached a deal whereby the latter led a syndicate of international lenders offering NAT a USD$2.5 billion loan for the construction and procurement phases of the project (to be repaid over 14 years). On a parallel path, the Ministry of Finance issued Egypt's first tranche of sovereign green bonds with a value of US$750 million (World Bank, 2022b). An undeclared portion of their proceeds was earmarked for the financing of monorail construction. In February 2022, the Ministry of Finance revealed pipelined plans to issue the second tranche of sovereign green bonds, which would be the test ground for the Ministry's debt diversification strategy, and part of a larger scheme to issue climate and SDG bonds to finance 'sustainable infrastructure' projects (Mounir, 2022).

The CM thus becomes an asset class predicated on the dual role of the state as an investor/speculative developer and sovereign guarantor, performing the 'de-risking' role for transnational financial capital. Beyond its immediate transit functions, the CM is simultaneously – even primarily – a device for the issuing of new debt instruments, the valorization of land values in state-led new cities, and the acceleration of real estate development. Each one of these revenue streams is a source of rent acting at different speeds and within distinct time frames, lending validity to the statement that 'the financial crisis of capitalism has placed increased premium on land as a means of generating rents for a crony capitalist class, usually well connected to the GoE' (Bush, 2011: 393; see also Wahdan, 2013).

Time, the territorial moment, and the infrastructure state in Egypt

It was the 2015 declaration explicitly setting infrastructure connectivity as an imperative for Egypt's future development that marked the beginning of its 'territorial moment' and the rise of the Egyptian infrastructure state (Schindler and Kanai, 2021). Yet while the forces behind that moment seemed to converge, the Egyptian state's institutional responses and its capacity to complete projects and ensure returns on investments are neither temporally synchronized nor adequately aligned. This becomes clearer when we analyse the transformation of the state's planning institutions as an enabling factor in the task of 'getting the territory right'. Central planning in the sense of a group of experts (civil or military) conducting rigorous studies and designing five- or ten-year comprehensive plans is no longer the case in Egypt. While public organizations mandated with planning, such as the General Organization for Physical Planning and the Ministry of Planning, still stand, the former has been hollowed out with the establishment of the Supreme Council for Planning and Urban Development (Unified Building Law 119/2008) and appears only as a 'participant' in participatory planning initiatives run by international development organizations. The latter, in contrast, has undergone a facelift and now assumes a leading role in orchestrating and monitoring the key performance indicators of global and national frameworks including the SDGs, the New Urban Agenda, *Egypt 2030*, and *Cairo 2025*.

Glossy reports have replaced multi-volume plan documents. What are generally referred to as 'plans' now come in the form of maps plotting out the territorial spread of national development projects. Rarely does anybody raise the question: how did the map come to replace the plan and what is lost along the way? We suggest that through this process, national planning is (re-)colonized by global interests with the support of the Egyptian state. International development organizations have been pouring funds and energies into 'participatory planning', the 'localization' of SDGs, and training on the monitoring and evaluation of key 'good' governance indicators. Yet, we argue, no amount of participatory planning and localization could compensate for the absence of effective and transparent formal democratic institutions that represent 'real' local needs.

The transformations of Egypt's state apparatus cannot be overemphasized. Over time, the state has been restructured such that most, if not all, planning functions now reside within the mandate of the Office of the President. The four supposedly independent national auditing institutions were restructured in 2015 (Law 16) to report to the president. At the urban scale, the Supreme Council for Planning and Urban Development rubber-stamps projects that are decided by the Ministry of Defense and its associated Armed Forces Engineering Authority. Since 2016, several presidential and prime ministerial decrees have been issued to transform public utilities into economic agencies and allow them to avail of financial markets and services. However, those agencies do not have the power to formulate individual or coordinated plans. There is an irony that as planning has been centralized, actual plans are increasingly tethered, temporally and spatially, to global financial and development agendas.

Times of convergence

The present emergence of the infrastructure state in Egypt has coalesced around the desire to 'plug in' the national territory to global markets and networks, a narrative in keeping with Schindler and Kanai's (2021) argument regarding 'getting the territory right'. The Egyptian case, though, brings nuance to this perspective. We suggest that the convergence of a global appetite for assetization, financialization, and de-risking development has proved particularly useful for Egypt's ruling regime for several reasons:

1) These forces justify restructuring and downsizing of large bureaucratic agencies to fit into partnership models. What was previously 'political suicide' in countries such as Egypt and India is now underway, evident in the transformation of public bureaucracies into revenue-generating or NBFI structures, the reduction of state spending on payrolls, the changes of state agencies' mandates and retirement laws, and increasing digitization.
2) The imperatives of financialization require an authoritarian command-and-control ruling regime to both 'stabilize' fiscal and monetary policies and secure lands for infrastructure development. Land-financed infrastructure not only opens diverse revenue streams to the regime in power but also absolves it from the need to further stretch its already strained budgets and provides ready-made symbolic power. In Egypt, the dominance of the military over many economic sectors is consolidated by the fact that it is at once the obligator and guarantor of the financial instruments that make mega-projects including the CM and the NAC possible.
3) The potential of the land–infrastructure–finance nexus to establish ever-changing regional alliances is important in propping up the legitimacy-deficient regime. Born out of financial and institutional modelling, the government can now appeal to a wide range of partners and can

establish investment entities that transcend national jurisdictions. Equally significant are narratives of employment generation, entrepreneurial support, and the ability to build big and quick, which are effectively deployed to support the legitimacy and efficacy of the ruling regime.

4) Land is essential to infrastructure and real estate, yet countries of the global South have chronic inefficiencies in land markets. In Egypt, it is common knowledge that the military and public institutions hold most lands (Sims, 2014). The financial turn in infrastructure drives the state to expand and consolidate land banks and to deploy diverse value capture instruments, some of which have been in use since the 1990s, such as the sale of development rights, while others were dormant or forgotten since the 1950s, such as betterment levies (Walters, 2015). Nationalization and eminent domain are also ad hoc policy instruments utilized by the Egyptian state (PKU-Lincoln Institute Center, 2022).

Dissonant times

Getting the territory right, though, is no easy feat, especially when the land–infrastructure–finance nexus possesses multiple dissonances. We conclude by assessing three of these, suggesting how their temporal and spatial dimensions may affect the future of Egypt's urban configurations, governance dynamics, and regime legitimacy.

Temporal dissonances of de-risking: land- and debt-based financing of infrastructure comes in diverse debt instruments with variable values, rates of return, maturity periods, and risk/interest parameters. These are instruments with variegated timelines and temporalities. They are grouped into portfolios that are substantively different from conventional financing of infrastructure and utilities under state monopolies. To avail of them, state agencies must come into versatile forms of special purpose partnerships with global financial institutions, syndicated banks, and consortia. This renders such institutional arrangements temporary in nature and the viability of each instrument subject to fluctuating market conditions. What does this imply for the nature of the state apparatus and the stability of the regime in Egypt? While this question lies outside the scope of this chapter, the changes discussed earlier imply the palpable collapse of the 'natural monopoly'. The idea that the state is the chief provider of economic infrastructure stresses the importance of a regime that de-risks temporally variegated debt instruments over other state structures and functions (see Schindler and Kanai, this volume). This would render the state apparatus, at least in Egypt, increasingly reactive to debt markets and could render the Egyptian infrastructure state itself increasingly volatile unless a strong autocratic regime is in charge (Soliman, 2011).

There are clear temporal implications concerning state control and ownership of assets. Debt instruments may or may not be collateralized.

The projects financed by those instruments may or may not involve the transfer of asset ownership from public to private hands. Nevertheless, portfolios involve cross leveraging (of instruments against each other), with complex risk/interest distribution models, counter-default measures, and recourse streams. While they may generate instant liquidity, they require state financiers to be extremely experienced and to comply with strict regulatory standards to coordinate revenue streams and manage counter-defaults. In the case of Egypt, where land and property registration is less than optimal and land markets either opaque or dysfunctional, it is highly unlikely that this could happen.

While to global financiers this could be 'business as usual', to us (considering the state structure and capacities), these constitute inherent temporal dissonances that not only affect state structures and functions but also make it extremely difficult for the state to control its monetary and fiscal policies. Few studies have examined these dynamics in Africa or the MENA region (for an exception, see Unruh et al, 2019). In Egypt, the ruling regime must assure investors of its commitment to realize future demand and returns on investments to tap into the temporally variegated debt instruments. It does so, *inter alia*, by orienting its fiscal and monetary policies towards de-risking the emerging asset class and re-engineering local financial systems to allow portfolio investors easy entry and exit from the new asset class. The successive devaluations of the Egyptian pound against the US dollar and other hard currencies since 2016 has had immediate negative impacts on the cost of living, the purchasing power of households, subsidies and social protection programmes, and the viability of small, medium, or even large-scale local businesses (Deboulet, 2016). Counter-intuitively, this temporal dissonance is also causing short-term fluctuations in the values and interest rates of sovereign debt instruments such as Treasury bills, adding volatility to an otherwise safe state-owned instrument.

Urban dissonances: our view of urban dissonances also arises, in part, from investment portfolios. Portfolios are intricately designed to synchronize variegated speculative valuations: booking values, revaluations, depreciation, interest rates, maturity periods, amortization, default risks, and volatile creditworthiness of institutions, countries, and cities. Portfolio management has direct implications for which projects are initiated, where they are located, and when they are completed or turned into ruins (Murray, 2011; Grafe and Hilbrandt, 2019). Judging by the hard currency situation in 2022 in Egypt, it seems that the CM will take longer than its contracted timeline. Nevertheless, it is not only the speed of execution that is tied to the temporalities of finance but also the fate of urban configurations at large (Harvey, 2009). The land–infrastructure–finance nexus in Egypt often compels the state towards land dispossession with direct negative impacts on the poor (Wilhelm-Solomon, 2021). Policies put into practice to meet financial and speculative real estate activities also affect the relatively well off and trigger a cascade of vulnerabilities surrounding employment, healthcare, income, savings, and livelihood across diverse income groups (Ghannam, 2002; Ismail, 2006). Unlike housing (Shawkat, 2020), statements about the mixed outcomes of mega-infrastructure and real estate developments remain anecdotal. We need detailed studies of their impacts on demographic change, mobility, income disparities, and homelessness.

Returning to the CM, although land and property expropriation did not trigger widespread social ire, there are voices opposing the privatization of public lands and the expropriation of private properties for infrastructure development. Prior to the 2011 uprising, successive regimes were wary of any large-scale dispossession of land resources for speculative development. The current regime is different. It prides itself on doing what previous regimes dared not: bulldozing neighbourhoods under the pretext of slum demolition; razing self-built houses for road widening; periodically banning private construction; the military imposing fines on building violations; speedily constructing private real estate on evicted plots; and, with the release of the State Ownership Policy Document in 2023, declaring public assets on offer for speculative developments (Khalifa, 2011; El-Faramawy, 2013; Selim, 2017). When land becomes the primary vehicle for value generation and private finance dictates its temporal and spatial logics, the threat of nationalization is diluted and the power of eminent domain intensifies. The same regime that would dare not scare away private finance would dispossess citizens for the sake of 'public benefit'.

A further urban dissonance concerns access to information about land infrastructure financed projects. The fact that almost all mega-projects – the CM included – are mostly assigned by presidential order (rarely through open public bidding) and operate on contractual agreements with non-disclosure clauses (to ensure best financial practices) means that the 'public' is not a stakeholder in Egypt's infrastructure state. Citizens do not have legal access to those agreements and find it difficult to hold officials accountable or answerable (see comparable experiences in Goldman, 2011; Shatkin, 2017).

Scalar dissonances: our third dissonance brings to the fore issues of creditworthiness and multilevel governance relations. For cities and states to monitor their creditworthiness, they must tread a fine line between making urban development 'investible' for regional and global capital and increasing spatial inequities and economic risks for households and less collateralized enterprises. The valorization of the land, real estate, and infrastructure asset classes is premised on two major leverage points (1) the Egyptian Armed Forces' sustained capacity to capitalize on legal permissibility, discretionary powers, and lack of transparency; and (2) future valorizations that must be seized by a slew of land value capture tools, such as fees, exactions, leveraging of land and property taxes, leases, evictions, and expropriations.

This burden imposes significant political risks that can themselves disrupt future expected gains.

To monitor its creditworthiness, the Egyptian state must continue to consolidate its military-security regime. This is necessary because the military-security regime becomes the sovereign guarantor and lender of its infrastructure asset class while at the same time maintaining tight internal security control by imposing protracted states of emergency and stymying dissent. This control extends to municipal governments. In the absence of decentralization, municipal governments are not permitted to tap into financial markets or borrow from private capital markets via bond issuance, although they might be entitled to extract revenues from land value capture instruments. This failure/absence prevents the possibility of sub-national financialization and creates budgetary tensions that manifest in disparities of urban services and utilities across the national territories. It is ironic, if unsurprising, that a project of the magnitude of the CM integrates dynamic sub-national urban systems along its lines into transnational territories while bypassing, almost impoverishing, others.

The urban lens and the implications for urban forms and dynamics are important to this story. Yet as we have shown, the infrastructure scramble in Egypt is primarily financial. It is the specialized financiers engaging with urban infrastructure – not as a facilitators of urban use values but almost exclusively as a temporally risk-weighted asset – who inform its future urban development. They may score highly on financial standards but, judging by the dire macroeconomic indicators, the discrepancies and the hollowing out of institutional structures, and more importantly, the urban spatial inequities and project incompletion rates, they are ultimately contributing to an increasingly dissonant and inequitable urban future.

References

Addie, J.-P.D., Glass, M.R., and Nelles, J. (2020) 'Regionalizing the infrastructure turn: A research agenda', *Regional Studies, Regional Science*, 7(1): 10–26.

Alm, J. (2015) 'Financing urban infrastructure: Knowns, unknowns, and a way forward', *Journal of Economic Surveys*, 29(2): 230–62.

Anagos, J., and Treitel, J. (2022) *At the Mid-Mark: Infrastructure Steadfast for Investors*, CBRE Investment Management.

Brinkman, M., and Sarna, V. (2022) 'Infrastructure investing will never be the same again', McKinsey. https://www.mckinsey.com/industries/private-equity-and-principal-investors/our-insights/infrastructure-investing-will-never-be-the-same (accessed 2 February 2023).

Bush, R. (2011) 'Coalitions for dispossession and networks of resistance? Land, politics and agrarian reform in Egypt', *British Journal of Middle Eastern Studies*, 38(3): 391–405.

Central Bank of Egypt (2022) *Monthly Statistical Bulletin #308*, Cairo: Economic Research Sector.

Christophers, B. (2009) 'On voodoo economics: Theorising relations of property, value and contemporary capitalism', *Transactions of the Institute of British Geographers*, 35: 94–108.

Cuno, K. (1980) 'The origins of private ownership of land in Egypt: A reappraisal', *International Journal of Middle East Studies*, 12(3): 245–75.

Deboulet, A. (ed) (2016) *Rethinking Precarious Neighbourhoods*, Paris: AFD.

Dixon, A., and Monk, A. (2012) 'Rethinking the sovereign in sovereign wealth funds', *Transactions of the Institute of British Geographers*, 37(1): 104–17.

Economist Intelligence Unit (2022) Egypt. https://country.eiu.com/egypt (accessed on 20 April 2023).

El-Faramawy, A. (2013) Development of informal areas. *Slum Upgrading Blogspot*, 25 February. http://wwwslumupgrading.blogspot.com (accessed 1 February 2023).

Estache, A. (2010) 'Infrastructure finance in developing countries: An overview', *European Investment Bank Papers*, 15(2): 60–88.

Fernandez, R., and Aalbers, M.B. (2020) 'Housing financialization in the global South: In search of a comparative framework', *Housing Policy Debate*, 30(4): 680–701.

G20/OECD/WB (2018) 'Stocktake of Tools and Instruments Related to Infrastructure as an Asset Class', https://www.oecd.org/g20/G20-OECD-WB-Stocktake-of-Tools-and-Instruments-Related-to-Infrastructure-as-asset-class.pdf (accessed 3 November 2023).

Gabor, D. (2021) 'The Wall Street Consensus', *Development and Change*, 52(3): 429–59.

Ghannam, F. (2002) *Remaking the Modern: Space, Relocation, and the Politics of Identity in a Global Cairo*, Berkeley, CA: University of California Press.

Global Infrastructure Hub (2023). 'Country profile: Egypt'. https://www.gihub.org/countries/egypt/ (accessed 3 February 2023).

Goldman, M. (2011) 'Speculative urbanism and the making of the next world city', *International Journal of Urban and Regional Research*, 35(3): 555–81.

Grafe, F.-J., and Hilbrandt, H. (2019) 'The temporalities of financialization: Infrastructures, dominations and openings in the Thames Tideway Tunnel', *City*, 23(4–5): 606–18.

Hafez, T. (2022) 'Egypt's banking sector lures regional suitors', American Chamber of Commerce in Egypt. https://www.amcham.org.eg/publications/business-monthly/issues/204/December-2012/2933/egypts-banking-sector-lures-regional-suitors (accessed 1 February 2023).

Harvey, D. (2009) *Social Justice and the City*, Athens, GA: University of Georgia Press.

Humphrey, C. (2016) 'The invisible hand: Financial pressures and organisational convergence in multilateral development banks', *The Journal of Development Studies*, 52(1): 92–112.

Ismail, S. (2006) *Political Life in Cairo's New Quarters: Encountering the Everyday State*, Minneapolis, MN: University of Minnesota Press.

Kanai, J.M., and Schindler, S. (2022) 'Infrastructure-led development and the peri-urban question: Furthering crossover comparisons', *Urban Studies*, 59(8): 1597–617.

Khalifa, M. (2011) 'Redefining slums in Egypt: Unplanned versus unsafe areas', *Habitat International*, 35(1): 40–9.

Kurtiç, E., and Nucho, J.R. (2022) 'Infrastructural politics in the Middle East and North Africa: Pasts, presents, futures', *Environment and Planning D: Society and Space*, 40(6): 967–74.

Mawdsley, E. (2018) '"From billions to trillions": Financing the SDGs in a world "beyond aid"', *Dialogues in Human Geography*, 8(2): 191–5.

McKinsey Global Institute (2014) 'The future of long-term finance'. http://campus.hec.fr/club_finance/wp-content/uploads/2015/07/HEC_Group-of-30_Long-term-Finance-exhibits-140616-v1.pdf (accessed 2 February 2023).

Mounir, H. (2022) 'Egypt on green, sustainable finance map: Finance Minister', *Daily News Egypt*, 28 February. https://dailynewsegypt.com/2022/02/28/egypt-on-green-sustainable-finance-map-finance-minister/ (accessed 2 February 2023).

Murray, M. (2011) *City of Extremes: The Spatial Politics of Johannesburg*, Durham, NC: Duke University Press.

Naucer, S.P. (2022) 'Al-Sisi's "New Republic": How the real estate frenzy in Egypt sustains the regime's grip on power', Rosa Luxemburg Stiftung. https://rosaluxna.org/publications/al-sisis-new-republic-how-the-real-estate-frenzy-in-egypt-sustains-the-regimes-grip-on-power/ (accessed 1 February 2023).

OECD (2007) *Infrastructure to 2030, Vol. 2: Mapping Policy for Electricity, Water and Transport*, Paris: OECD.

Ouma, S. (2014) 'Situating global finance in the land rush debate: A critical review', *Geoforum*, 57: 162–6.

Oxford Economics (2017) *Global Infrastructure Outlook: Infrastructure Investment Needs 50 Countries, 7 Sectors to 2040*, Sydney: GI Hub.

Peterson, G.E. (2009) *Unlocking Land Values to Finance Urban Infrastructure*, Washington, DC: World Bank.

PKU-Lincoln Institute Center. (2022) *Global Compendium of Land Value Capture Policies*, Paris: OECD.

Rateiwa, R., and Aziakpono, M.J. (2017) 'Non-bank financial institutions and economic growth: Evidence from Africa's three largest economies', *South African Journal of Economic and Management Sciences*, 20(1): 1–11.

Salah, F. (2022) 'Abu Dhabi's ADQ invests $20bn in Egypt over next 10 years: UAE Minister of Economy', *Daily News Egypt*, 27 October. https://dailynewsegypt.com/2022/10/27/abu-dhabis-adq-invests-20bn-in-egypt-over-next-10-years-uae-minister-of-economy/ (accessed 1 February 2023).

Schindler, S., and Kanai, J.M. (2021) 'Getting the territory right: Infrastructure-led development and the re-emergence of spatial planning strategies', *Regional Studies*, 55(1): 40–51.

Selim, G. (2017) *Unfinished Places: The Politics of (Re)making Cairo's Old Quarters*, New York: Routledge.

Shatkin, G. (2017) *Cities for Profit: The Real Estate Turn in Asia's Urban Politics*, Ithaca, NY: Cornell University Press.

Shawkat, Y. (2020) *Egypt's Housing Crisis: The Shaping of Urban Space*, Cairo: American University in Cairo Press.

Sims, D. (2014) *Egypt's Desert Dreams*, Cairo: American University in Cairo Press.

Soliman, S. (2011) *The Autumn of Dictatorship: Fiscal Crisis and Political Change in Egypt under Mubarak*, Stanford, CA: Stanford University Press.

Taweel, S. (2023) *Al-Sisi's Bubble in the Desert: The Political Economy of Egypt's New Administrative Capital*, Washington, DC: Project on Middle East Democracy.

Unruh, J., Pritchard, M., Savage, E., Wade, C., Nair, P., Adenwala, A. et al (2019) 'Linkages between large-scale infrastructure development and conflict dynamics in East Africa', *Journal of Infrastructure Development*, 11(1–2): 1–13.

Wahdan, D. (2013) *Planning Egypt's New Settlements: The Politics of Spatial Inequities*, Cairo: Oxford University Press and Cairo Papers in Social Sciences.

Walters, L. (2015) *Leveraging Land in the Arab Republic of Egypt: The Potential for Increasing Land-Based Financing for Urban Development*, New York: UN-Habitat.

Weber, B., Staub-Bisang, M., and Alfen, H.W. (eds) (2016) *Infrastructure as Asset Class: Investment Strategy, Sustainability, Project Finance and PPP*, Chichester: Wiley.

Wilhelm-Solomon, M. (2021) 'Dispossession as depotentiation', *Environment and Planning D: Society and Space*, 39(6): 976–93.

World Bank (2006) *Arab Republic of Egypt: Egypt Public Land Management Strategy*, Washington, DC: World Bank.

World Bank (2013) *Connecting and Financing Cities – Now: Priorities for City Leaders*, Washington, DC: World Bank.

World Bank (2017) *Maximizing Finance for Development: Leveraging the Private Sector for Growth and Sustainable Development*, Washington, DC: World Bank.

World Bank (2021) *Private Participation in Infrastructure (PPI): 2021 Annual Report*, Washington, DC: World Bank.

World Bank (2022a) 'Country snapshot: Egypt'. https://ppi.worldbank.org/en/snapshots/country/egypt-arab-rep (accessed 28 June 2022).

World Bank (2022b) 'Supporting Egypt's inaugural green bond issuance'. https://www.worldbank.org/en/news/feature/2022/03/02/supporting-egypt-s-inaugural-green-bond-issuance (accessed 2 February 2023).

PART III

Times of Disruption/ Disrupting Times

9

The Multiple Temporalities of Self-Healing Infrastructure: From the F-15 Fighter to the Smart Urban Microgrid

Simon Marvin and Jonathan Rutherford

Introduction

Recognition that the urban context is now the key site of societal vulnerability – and of its management through infrastructural interventions at the nexus of climate, ecological, population, technological, and other security concerns – is claimed to be the 'hegemonic discourse of our time' (Davoudi, 2014: 371; see Braun, 2014; Derickson, 2018; Bulkeley, 2021). Critically, the issue of vulnerability is a matter of strategic and systemic concern for both civil society and the military–security complex. Within the US military, there is now widespread acknowledgement that key operational defence facilities located in North America are also vulnerable to multiple forms of turbulence because *they are reliant on the same centralized electrical grids* as neighbouring cities and communities.

Consequently, there is emerging commensurability between urban resilience and military security. In both sectors, establishing enclaves of critical assets with bespoke infrastructure configurations via the installation of smart microgrids appears to offer protection against both human and climatic threats. The development and roll-out of smart microgrids are being rapidly accelerated in US urban and military contexts to enable a new automated management of interruptions to the central grid (Rutherford and Marvin, 2022). Smart microgrids are energy systems of varying sizes/scales within specific territories that draw on local sources of energy production, increasingly focused on renewables, and storage capacity. Key to their functionality is the way systems are reconfigured to switch in 'microseconds' between 'grid-connected' and 'islanded' modes, thus seamlessly maintaining fail-safe power for a variety of 'critical assets'. Smart microgrids are emerging infrastructural configurations that are always on 'alert'. As such, they aim to secure operational continuity through hardware- and software-enabled adaptive functionalities that operate in 'real time' and that are configured simultaneously for on- and off-grid operations and normal/emergency modes. They operate by removing the temporal interval between the detection of the emergency and the initiation of the response, thus eliminating power interruption for those critical assets connected to a microgrid.

This chapter examines the emergence of the smart microgrid as a logic of grid security that can seamlessly switch between different grid configurations in microseconds. Crucially, this does not provide continued power for everyone because the 'critical assets' whose functioning must be guaranteed are pre-selected, producing a differentiated form of urban resilience (Rutherford and Marvin, 2022). Drawing on a prior logic of business continuity, these systems extend the selective techniques that underpinned the use of standby generation where the most critical commercial, military, or civilian assets are identified in advance to receive emergency power during grid disruption. Key to the operation of this logic is the temporal ability to switch automatically without human intervention between normal and emergency modes.

The chapter makes three contributions to understanding the evolving temporalities of urban infrastructure configurations. Firstly, it illustrates how the '*always-on*' uninterruptible capacity of the smart microgrid is located in a series of concepts, ideas, and strategies from work on 'self-healing systems' that have drawn together networks, power sources, digital control capacities, and social interests into a novel configuration that has transmuted from military to urban contexts of application. Addie, Glass, Nelles, and Marino (this volume) stress the 'unexpected pathways' that urban technologies sometimes take in their development. Here, we trace how the current temporal capacities of urban smart microgrids have their antecedent roots in systems thinking in other domains in which the seamlessness of function and operation have been crucial. Secondly, it traces the development of the smart microgrid in the US military and urban contexts, exploring how it has become central to a logic of urban resilience that seeks to mitigate threats and prepare for future turbulence by pursuing the reconfiguration of grids into *permanent 'alert' mode*. The capacity to switch 'seamlessly' between normal and island mode requires focusing on the forms of socio-spatial selectivity produced (who and where is included and excluded) through addressing temporal questions of how, and for how long, service is maintained. Finally, the chapter outlines the changing implications of the management of microseconds for other, often hidden, *temporal readjustments* that flow from this switching, capturing the inherent varying time frames and what Addie,

Glass, Nelles, and Marino (this volume) call 'heterodox uncertainty' of any infrastructure change. We need to understand both the differential, even asynchronous, experience of seamless transition through which the interval is abolished for some users but exists for others waiting for grid recovery, and the way in which the underlying problematic of turbulence is no longer addressed by this form of 'living with'.

Self-healing systems: Organic, autonomic, and adaptive capacities

We begin our story with a famous incident in the aviation world. An Israeli F-15 fighter was involved in a training accident when it collided with another aircraft, resulting in the loss of one of its wings. It was expected that this damage would make the aircraft uncontrollable and result in a crash. However, the pilot managed to manually find a survivable flight envelope and successfully landed the aircraft. This incident powerfully spurred the funding of self-healing flight control systems by the US military, which invested significantly in research programmes, the development of demonstrations, and the introduction of simple applications (see Tomayko, 2003). These interventions were designed to address the limits of existing techniques used to ensure aircraft safety, including the use of multiple physical/hardware-redundant and backup systems that added significant weight, cost, and performance penalties to aircraft. The use of digital computers in aircraft control systems enabled a new focus on using software to 'replace physical hardware redundancy' (Steinberg, 2005: 263). Researchers subsequently started to develop techniques 'aimed at reconfiguration without pilot intervention and the preservation of normal aircraft flying qualities over an expanded array of fault/battle damage conditions in order to increase the probability of mission success' (Huber and McCulloch, 1984: 477). Although the more advanced adaptive approaches developed in these programmes have not been used in practice due to the problems of certification, this has not diminished the military's interest in self-healing software and materials and their incorporation into body armour, tanks, and aircraft (Cox, 2020).

These military developments need to be placed in the context of a broader shift, examining the potential of self-healing systems taking place across at least three interconnected domains. The first is the literature on self-healing systems that frequently highlights its origins in biological metaphors and concepts, particularly the ability of organisms to immunize themselves from threats. This capacity inspired efforts to design material and computational systems that can move from healthy to unhealthy and back to healthy states (Dreo Rodosek et al, 2009). Natural immune systems that protect animals from pathogens, viruses, bacteria, and toxins are very much 'analogous to the self-healing systems of computers' (Ghosh et al, 2007: 2165).

The second is autonomic computing (AC), which refers to the self-managing characteristics of distributed computing resources that can adapt to unpredictable changes such as overload, technical failure, and power loss while hiding the intrinsic complexity involved from both operators and users (Kephart and Chess, 2003). Although initially complex and expensive, these AC systems have been simplified into accessible packages that are now interwoven into other systems and infrastructures to provide self-managing capacities that do not require the intervention of users.

The third domain centres on the 'adaptive capacity' of socio-ecological systems, a transdisciplinary concept that bridges the natural and social sciences (see Simonet and Duchemin, 2010). This is part of a wider shift to 'self-*' properties' within engineering. This shift focuses on forms of recovery in the management of infrastructure networks in response to internal or contextual failures. In this context, 'self-healing' refers to 'the capability of discovering, diagnosing, and reacting to disruptions. It can also anticipate potential problems, and accordingly take proper actions to prevent a failure' (Salehie and Tahvildari, 2009: 6).

Figure 9.1 illustrates the logic of these self-healing properties. There are two important elements (1) self-diagnosis of errors, faults, and failures; and (2) self-healing capacities that focus on strategies to recover the system. These are applied to large-scale computational systems, infrastructures, and materials that can detect interruption and respond to the problem in order to maintain functionality. The critical challenge is to shorten the 'time to heal' (TTH) so that assets are able to continue to operate effectively. Many critical systems – military control and weapons, cloud service backups, and financial services infrastructures – are required to have fail-safe systems and have emerged as critical markets for these systems. Consequently, in these critical sectors the TTH is required to be in microseconds in order to automatically switch the system between grid-connected and islanded modes, thus ensuring business or operational continuity.

Self-healing systems require the use of digital technologies to monitor and control their physical switching between different system states. They also require the use of physical resources (whether computational and/or power systems) to enable recovery through adaption. Next, we will examine the transmutation of these concepts of self-healing from military aircraft to the civil power grid.

Smart self-healing power grids: The temporal failure of 'standby'

What is important for our story is that this investment in self-healing knowledge and techniques has had wider utilization in the US energy sector. In writing about the history of the smart grid, two researchers

THE TEMPORALITIES OF SELF-HEALING INFRASTRUCTURE

Figure 9.1: Self-healing processes

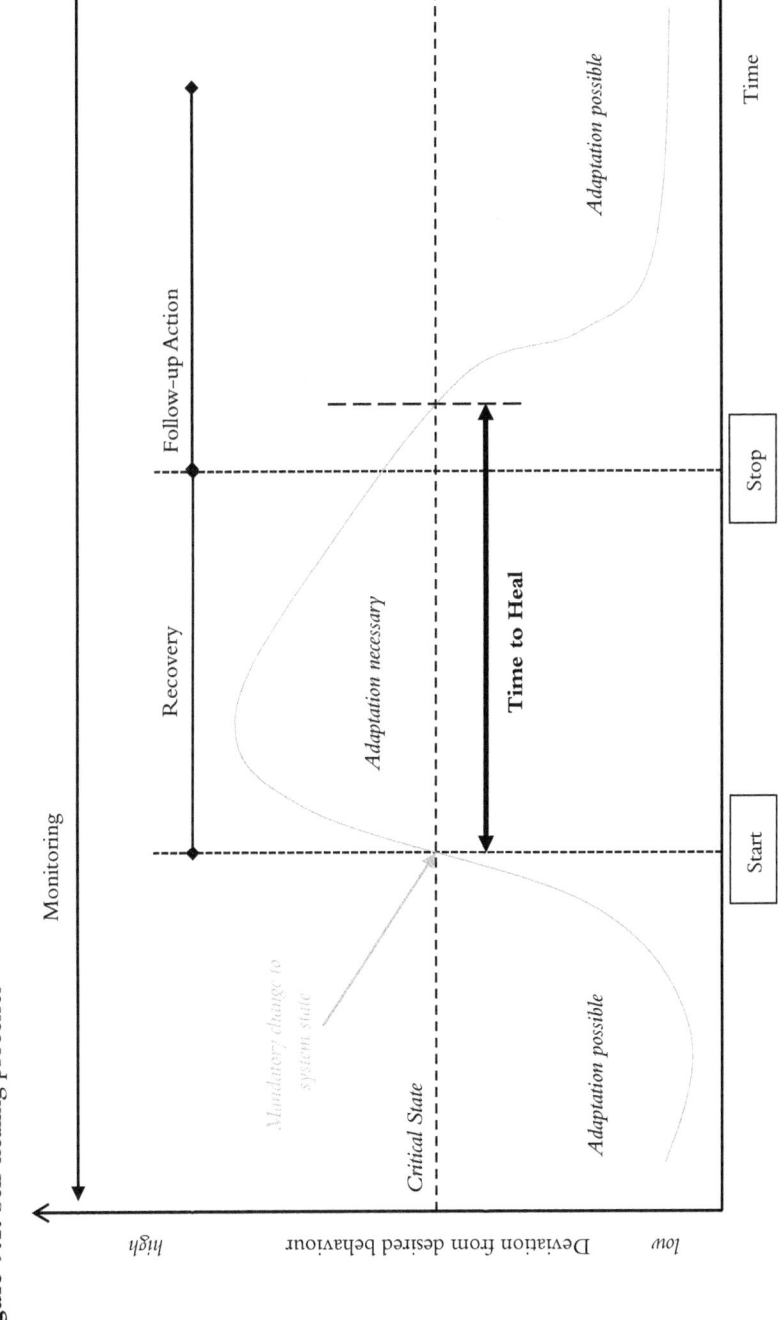

Source: adapted from Dreo Rodosek et al, 2009: 4

who were centrally involved in the programme, Massoud Amin and Bruce Wollenberg, make clear the explicit interconnections with the work sponsored by the Department of Defense on the F-15's reconfigurable aircraft control system in laying the 'conceptual foundations of a self-healing power system' (2005: 35). These smart energy researchers draw the specific analogy between a squadron of aircraft and the many components of an interconnected power system in which system stability and reliability must be maintained under all conditions, including failure and attack. The work on the F-15 provided the knowledge and expertise to launch research on the management of self-healing for energy power systems (Amin and Wollenberg, 2015: 36). Furthermore, the power industry, along with the Departments of Defense and Homeland Security, actually undertook jointly funded programmes of work to develop 'new tools and techniques that will enable large national infrastructures to self-heal in response to threats, material failures, and other destabilizers' (Amin, 2001: 21). Jointly sponsored by the US energy power sector and the civil and military security sectors, these developed the specifications for multilayered self-healing power systems and established a business case analysis to assess the costs and benefits of improved network reliability (Amin, 2001; 2008; Arefifar et al, 2013: 4192). Key to these capacities is the role of high-performance digital infrastructure and software control systems to manage a physical infrastructure network. Three major issues – of central concern to the industry as well as civil and military users – served as drivers for using smart grid technologies for self-healing applications (1) grid vulnerability; (2) problems with standby; and (3) the need to seamlessly restore power without interruption. As we shall see, all of these involved particular forms of temporal problems and solutions.

Increasing vulnerability of the grid

Increasing vulnerability of the grid to technical problems, weather-related failures, and terrorist attacks – as well as the need to reduce the frequency and duration of grid outages given the critical importance of power in supplying digital systems – was a key driver for the uptake of self-healing infrastructures in the energy sector. Critically, we need to understand vulnerability in this context as an interconnected cascading failure problem for the power industry. The power industry itself is under pressure to reduce outages (and deal with their economic ramifications) and faces civil society concerns about public safety, while needing to address potential threats to national security arising from the reliance of domestic military bases on the public grid. The US national electricity grid system is old, increasingly unreliable, and vulnerable to disruption, affecting both military and civil contexts. In New York City, the estimated cost of a single large-scale 29-hour blackout in 2003 was approximately $1.05 billion or $36 million per hour, and an estimated 90 lives (Siegel, 2012).

Fundamental reliance on digital and telecommunications systems for critical financial transactions and military control systems has placed increasing scrutiny on the reliability of the centralized grid. The concept of 'always on power' has become an almost standard business and military requirement, where the duration of any 'downtime' has been viewed as unworkable for critical functions. Because reliance on power for operating IT systems and telecommunications is so fundamental, the (un)reliability of the central grid is of critical concern. Major power outages in the US increased tenfold between 1984 and 2016 and are continuing to increase, with the average household experiencing 470 minutes without power in 2017. Severe weather events cause the most widespread power outages, affecting millions of customers, while electromagnetic events and cyber-physical attacks cause approximately 25 per cent of outages. There were, for example, over 360 'targeted attacks' leading to disruptions in energy provision reported by utilities just between 2011 and 2014 (CNA Military Advisory Board, 2015: 1). Yet rather than focus on the reasons for grid failure (and seeking to systematically address these), attention has increasingly shifted to the development of technological and market-driven solutions for those users that need uninterruptable power when the inevitable grid failure occurs.

The temporal problems of standby and emergency generation

A second key driver was the desire to decrease investment in expensive and unreliable standby capacity. Significantly, as knowledge and techniques for preparedness developed in the Cold War conflict transmuted into both military and civil domains susceptible to disruptions, vital systems security conceived of the management of emergency as an increasingly central part of governing (Collier and Lakoff, 2015). Security mechanisms were developed to reduce vulnerability and increase capacities of control of vital systems within emergency management (see Mayer and Acuto, 2015). Key techniques involved investment in material systems that sought to reduce the vulnerability of infrastructures, including multiple redundant systems and backup and standby generation designed to work in an emergency (see Gissen, 2014; Luque-Ayala and Marvin, 2016; Whitington, 2016). In the US in 2009, an estimated 170GW of backup power is installed, with emergency diesel generators (EDGs) commonly used as backup power for critical loads when the grid fails, 'often deployed as stand-alone generators (<2000 kW) tied to individual buildings for hospitals, emergency services, military bases, ports, airports, industries, and commercial facilities' (Marqusee et al, 2020: 2). The use of EDGs is extremely widespread in both urban and military contexts where a loss of power would 'result in an unacceptable impact to operational capability or present a risk to life, safety, or property' (Marqusee et al, 2020: 2). These systems were configured to start automatically upon grid failure and power essential loads until power is restored. While they have largely been effective and easy to deploy, there are important temporal constraints that have not kept pace with the demand for always-on power.

The first constraint is the reliability of the automated systems for switching on power when the grid fails. Most EDGs run infrequently and sit in what is termed a 'cold state' for much of their lifetimes. Consequently, we know relatively little about their reliability. If properly maintained, regularly tested, and renewed, it is assumed that there is a 95–99 per cent reliability in automatic switching during an emergency. However, this drops significantly if the system is not properly maintained, and human intervention might be required to restart the system. Even the highest level of assumed reliability poses the risk of interruption and the loss of data and/or control capacity and is unacceptable to essential military and civil users.

The second issue is the reliability of the EDG when in actual operation. Clearly, the frequency of grid interruptions is increasing and so is the duration of interruption. EDGs are normally able to cope with interruptions of a few hours, but longer outages cause severe economic costs, increased public risk, and can even threaten national security. Recent research has shown that even well-maintained generators are only 80 per cent likely to provide power for a two-week grid interruption (Marqusee et al, 2020). Additionally, planning for a potential two-week interruption means that power also needs to be provided during this period to ensure essential services for key personnel operating critical functions.

The third constraint is the difficulty of testing the reliability of the EDG in 'real-world' conditions. Although regulations governing the use of these systems often require the generator set to be regularly tested, this is not the same as simply shutting down the grid and testing the efficiency of the automatic control systems. Most users are reluctant to undertake such real-world tests because they do not know if the backup will work effectively. Consequently, there is considerable uncertainty about the reliability of the control systems and whether the generators would come online instantly and dependably in an emergency.

The critical challenge to be addressed was therefore how to maintain critical functions (including vital military control and operating systems as well as public infrastructure such as hospitals) during grid disruption when the EDG system itself might fail. The temporal issues were threefold:

1) How to ensure fail-safe switching between normal and emergency modes in microseconds while retaining power to the most critical assets?
2) How to ensure an extension of the emergency power functioning to enable critical assets to operate for up to two weeks?

3) How to ensure that the reliability of the system could be known in advance across normal and emergency modes?

At this stage, the claim was that the self-healing smart power grid would enable these issues of immediacy/simultaneity, prolongation, and permanent alert to be addressed systematically across the whole national power grid.[1]

The vision of the self-healing power grid

In the face of the previously mentioned temporal issue, the vision of self-healing offered a means to 'deal with unforeseen events and minimize their adverse impact' (Amin, 2008, see also Jackson, 2012: 1). This required a new information, sensing, and control system to be overlaid over existing energy infrastructure in order to enable three sets of new functionalities (Amin, 2008). The first was real-time monitoring to alert grid operators to the precursors or signs of impending faults. The second was to use this data to enable control devices to respond automatically by load shedding and/or increasing power generation to restore balance to the system. A third functionality was created to automatically isolate parts of the system that were failing or about to fail to avoid the spread of disruption and to enable more rapid restoration.

Evidently, 'self-healing' in the event of a problem would then involve decision-making about which loads (of which users) would be 'automatically' shed, and which would then benefit from the maintenance of supply during disruption. These sorts of practical and highly political decisions did not get much of an airing during the development of the smart self-healing policy discourse. Furthermore, the conception of the self-healing grid was not a strongly spatialized or even institutionalized vision that meshed with the socio-technical realities of managing a complex and ageing power system. In the place of competing social interests and place-based demands for reliable power, Massoud Amin used the metaphor of intelligence:

> The self-healing grid can be thought of as having three tiers of intelligence. The bottom layer, closest to devices in the field, is distributed intelligence. It is akin to the reptilian brain, with simple responses to environmental stimuli ... monitors the health of the asset and communicates that to the middle layer, where the validation of incoming data and coordination of various functions takes place in milliseconds. This is similar to a mammalian neocortex that can strategize, act, and be upgraded through experience to higher functionality. The top layer contains the centralized command-and-control functions directed by human operators. (Amin, 2014: np.)

Yet realizing this vision was fraught with many difficulties as the smart grid would need to be layered over a highly fragmented system of power generation, central grid transmission, and local distribution. Moreover, it would involve hundreds of different companies and municipalities using different technologies and sitting across complex state and local jurisdictions. The level of coordination and agreement needed to realize this vision was highly challenging. It was also never clear how software systems would make decisions about which users would be subject to 'load shedding' or how others would be protected. All this, however, became a moot point because as the self-healing vision was subject to review by the industry, the Department of Homeland Security, and the Department of Defense, critical concerns were raised that a new centralized digital control system itself then created potential for new vulnerabilities through technical failure and cyberattack.

Smart urban microgrids: Seamless transition between normalcy and emergency

Just as the vision of the smart self-healing power grid looked like it was going to fail, it became connected to the concept of the microgrid. Microgrids are clearly territorial solutions concerned with infrastructure configurations that relate to place-based priorities and social interests. The capacities of smart self-healing thus increasingly became connected to the limitations of grids in urban and military base contexts. Consequently, a set of issues including grid security concerns, the challenges of ensuring network coordination, and the need to actively manage winners and losers forced a reconsideration of the value of trying to apply these systems across the whole grid. Rather than focus on centrally directed actions, the sector began to experiment with applying smart techniques of control that delegated authority to a lower level in the hierarchy closer to the affected areas suffering from power outages. Key to this was exploring the potential of linking smart self-healing capacities with energy microgrids. This work concluded that 'decentralizing decision-making has unique attributes that make it attractive from a *resiliency perspective*; chiefly because it can avoid the scenario where corruption or failure of the central supervisory node leads to total system collapse' (Colson et al, 2011: 84, emphasis added).

Connecting smart self-healing to microgrids

While there is as yet no detailed history of the smart microgrid, it is clear that when finally written the interrelations between military and civil energy expertise will need to be fully explored. The smart microgrid is distinctive because it seeks to address the 'temporal interval' between the onset of the emergency and recovery by systemically pre-preparing grids and critical assets for islanded operation. Overcoming the timescale of disruption has become an increasingly strategic and systemic priority in both civil and military domains. In decentralizing the notion of the smart self-healing grid and refocusing attention on the microgrid, the concept had to then engage with specific territorial social and political interests: military bases, cities and communities, utilities, and numerous energy users and producer interests. All these interests must be involved in the development of a smart microgrid that involves numerous reconfigurations of their relations to the power system.

Smart microgrids involve the automated restoration of 'island' services in the event of a grid failure. This requires a series of reconfigurations to improve the overall system condition in the resulting 'enclave', involving breaker manipulations, generation start-up or shutdown, load shedding or pickup, or other actions that change system operational 'posture'. Typical performance measures of self-healing may include the speed with which a stable configuration is reached, the quantity of components that remain energized, and the time taken to return to grid connectivity.

We now examine how developments in thinking and practice around infrastructural self-healing systems and seamlessness of power supply have begun to play out at the local level. Here, the smart microgrid is part of an emerging strategic and *in situ* response involving a variety of actors seeking to imbue energy systems with more resilience capacity to withstand greater threats and disturbances to the power grid. The US Department of Energy is quite clear about the benefits of microgrids for 'strengthening grid resilience' and 'supporting a flexible and efficient electric grid' by integrating renewables and reducing transmission losses. These in turn can 'improve reliability and resiliency of the grid, help communities better prepare for future weather events, and keep the nation moving toward a clean energy future' (Office of Electricity, Department of Energy, nd: np). The key point is that military bases and surrounding urban communities are a frontier context in the US for trailing and developing smart microgrids as an operational grid expansion strategy to ensure 'always-on' energy supply across normal and disrupted times.

The failing grid as combined societal and security problematic and response

The historical development of the US grid as a 'patchwork' architecture of individual systems that were joined up incrementally over time, subdivided into three geographical zones but operated and owned by dozens of separate authorities and entities (Suit, 2016: 2; state energy agency interview, November 2019), is an important element in understanding recent smart microgrid projects. In effect, key actors concerned by energy security (for example, the military, the private sector, and municipalities) are seeking system configurations that privilege alternative or concurrent sources of power in times of grid disruption. Grid security concerns are an interconnected security, economic, and social problem. Both the US Departments of Defense and Homeland Security view energy supply as fundamental to national security. Military bases now frame their dependence on the external commercially owned grid as a point of vulnerability that needs to be addressed: 'military installations are only as secure as the communities that neighbor them' (Rickerson et al, 2018: 17). The energy infrastructure upon which Department of Defense bases and installations depend is primarily commercially owned, and 99 per cent of the electrical energy installations consume originates 'outside the fence' (Defense Science Board, 2008). Although many installations have fossil fuel-based backup generators, these, as we have seen, are extremely unreliable, are only designed to function for a few days, and are dependent on fuel supplies (Marqusee et al, 2017: vi). There has been serious concern that the "traditional approach to energy security on bases just doesn't work", with inefficient and unreliable diesel generators and a lack of planning for what happens if critical facilities are turned off (energy security consultant interview, November 2019).

This context has led to an intensive programme of investment in microgrid research and development since 2013, supported through partnerships and coalitions involving military, energy sector, and university actors. As a result, more than 40 military bases in the US have engaged in some form of planning towards microgrid deployment (Alford, 2017: 108). Partnership-based research, planning and investment, and development of expertise in smart microgrids are now spilling over into projects on other sites such as jails, campuses, and business clusters. And of particular interest in this chapter, as we now discuss, they are drawing attention to 'military communities' or 'defense communities' as a key urban area across the US where smart microgrids are reworking base–community relations and grid-based spatial and temporal dynamics. The interrelationships between US domestic military bases and their host communities have become an increasing focus of attention both for the Department of Defense and for the municipalities and states where bases are located (CNA Military Advisory Board, 2015; Defense Science Board, 2016; Rickerson et al, 2018). Both bases and communities frequently share dependence on the same infrastructure networks including transport, waste, water, and the focus of our concern in the following case vignettes, electricity.

Testing the concept: Fort Bliss, El Paso, TX

Crucially, the configuration of a typical base microgrid involves the prior identification of 'critical mission' assets that require secure power both in 'grid-connected' and 'islanded' modes when disengaged from the utility grid during an interruption. Fort Bliss, located near El Paso, Texas, became the first Department of Defense microgrid to be connected to the grid in 2013. This demonstration project, a collaboration between the Army and Lockheed Martin, comprised a modest 120 kW solar array, a 300 kW battery storage system, and existing backup generators managed by an Intelligent Microgrid Control System. An automatic transfer switch connected the local production and storage equipment and base critical loads to allow continuous power supply to the base in the event of the switch sensing a grid outage. Distributed controllers present at critical loads throughout the microgrid configuration could operate autonomously if communication was lost with the centralized controller. The same automatic transfer switch could also revert supply back to the grid when the outage came to an end. The project serviced one of the dining complexes of the base as its primary aim was to test and demonstrate the capability for the continuation of operations through the 'near seamless transition between Grid Tied and Grid Independent modes (Islanding)' (Hall and Fischer, 2014: xii). As a Fort Bliss official stated, "the tactical utility of this technology is its ability to allow us to operate off the grid. This project represents the future of military energy security" (PR Newswire, 2013).

To continue to build energy security and affranchise itself of reliance on backup generators, the base planned to construct a 20 MW solar photovoltaic plant at a cost of $120 million with the local utility El Paso Electric (St John, 2013). However, the project was cancelled in 2015 because the utility was not able to reach an agreement with the Army over the terms of access to the 218 acres needed for the plant (Kolenc, 2015). Although the project failed, the military often supplies unused land – known as 'want-it-in-my-backyard' or WIMBY land – and partners with local utilities or 'energy developers' (Danigelis, 2018). This highlights how reconfiguring connections with the local grid demands protracted negotiations between the military and relevant urban and state governments focused on procurement systems, environmental assessment, and other regulatory processes.

Reconfiguring civil and military energy assets: SUBASE, Groton, CT

Military base projects, it is claimed, can benefit wider communities and states by addressing energy security for military operations and locations while the grid and local communities are "at the same time made more resilient" (energy policy consultant interview, November 2019). The Defense Authorization Act of 2019 (H.R. 5515, 115th Congress) allows military installations to receive state and urban government funding for developing base smart microgrids. This was on the basis that such public investment improved wider energy security and resilience by enabling urban utilities to develop local energy production facilities that displace wholesale purchasers from the grid. However, during a grid disruption municipal power assets are provided to the military to maintain fail-safe service. The Association of Defense Communities (ADC) sought to develop 'defense community partnerships' that are designed to underpin 'policy, planning and resourcing efforts by state and local governments to support energy resilience projects at military bases' (Rickerson et al, 2018: 8). The case of the Naval Submarine Base in New London (SUBASE) was offered by the ADC as an exemplar of the mutual interest of military, state, and urban stakeholders in the development of a microgrid.

In 2005, the SUBASE was selected for closure partly because of the vulnerability of 'the commercial electricity system', with the existing diesel backup generators considered insufficient and a 'high operational risk' (Rickerson et al, 2018: 13–14). Located on a 700-acre site in the city of Groton, Connecticut, the base employed nearly 10,000 personnel and a successful campaign was mounted to prevent its closure. In 2007, the State of Connecticut established the Office of Military Affairs (OMA) and approved a $50 million bond fund for infrastructure upgrades of military value (initiatives designed to retain SUBASE). Furthermore, in 2015 the State authorized the OMA to provide a $1.1 million grant to SUBASE for microgrid design and infrastructure upgrades. This involved SUBASE leasing part of its land for a 7.4 MW fuel cell project that will, under normal conditions, partly supply the power needs of the Connecticut Municipal Electricity Energy Cooperative, displacing power currently purchased on the wholesale market. The agreement is that, in exchange for the lease, SUBASE will receive power from the fuel cells during power outages to maintain critical military facilities. More recently, the municipally owned Groton Utilities has been funded to work on energy resilience planning and microgrid development for its own infrastructure in collaboration with SUBASE (Rickerson et al, 2018: 13). SUBASE provides critical insight into the increasing depth of the policy, planning, and resourcing of interrelationships supporting military microgrid development of wider import through supportive partnerships involving states, urban governments, and localities. We can see how the development of fail-safe energy supplies for military bases requires the active reconfiguration of civilian energy systems and their use by the military during power outages.

Towards wider urban diffusion

These smart microgrid logics and techniques are transmuting into other urban areas and wider initiatives potentially involving more inclusive social interests (on Boston, see Rutherford and Marvin, 2022). Table 9.1 compares the different urban contexts of smart microgrid deployment in the US. The Honnold Foundation, for example, is initiating a solar microgrid project in New Orleans to assist low-income neighbourhoods in recovering from hurricanes. Partnering with a local non-profit, rooftop solar panels and battery storage capability will be installed in restaurants in the city configured as the new 'first responders' to keep refrigerators and charging infrastructure online in any disruption so that local people have access to food and power (Johnson, 2022). This is even more important as the differential infrastructure impacts of recent extreme weather events have powerfully foregrounded the politics of resource distribution and of socio-spatially selective grid management techniques. The February 2021 electricity blackouts in Texas, for example, had a disproportionate impact on minority communities that suffered more and longer rolling power outages to prevent the wider grid from going down (Dobbins and Tabuchi, 2021). At the same time, more affluent Texan residents have been able to set up their own redundant energy systems or domestic microgrids (Webb, 2022). In these ways the military logics of grid development are being selectively transmuted into the diverse contexts of low-income and affluent communities. This creates more highly differentiated experiences of grid failure between those who are protected and those who are unprotected. Moreover, while smart microgrid strategies enable urban utilities to develop local energy production facilities that displace wholesale purchasers from the grid during any emergency, the military base's designated 'mission critical assets' are nonetheless given priority over other users.

In summary, the development of smart microgrids thereby constitutes an important shift in grid expansion strategy, focused now on developing off-grid capacities, islanding, and the integration of renewables and storage in particularly strategic areas that can overcome the temporal problems of standby generation. This works in the following ways:

- enabling fail-safe switching between normal and emergency modes in microseconds through digital control systems that maintain power to the most critical military assets (and potentially to societal assets in community smart microgrids);
- ensuring an extension of the emergency power functioning to enable critical assets to operate for more than a few hours and up to two weeks by actively reconfiguring civil energy assets so that they prioritize servicing military assets during a grid failure;
- ensuring that the reliability of the system is known by operating the system in normal/emergency mode as the usual mode of operation.

Ensuring fail-safe, 'always-on' power then requires several temporal adaptations covering immediacy, prolongation, and permanent alert. Microseconds are vital to enable seamless switching, the potential to maintain power supplies for up to two weeks during a major disruption to

Table 9.1: Comparing urban contexts of smart microgrid deployment

Context	Military base in urban area	Urban communities
Key actors	Military bases and urban infrastructure technical, business, and energy expertise	Urban energy strategies, tech expertise, community groups and non-governmental organizations
Mediating structures	Association of Defense Communities, military energy partnerships, Dept. of Defense and Dept. of Homeland Security	Framework of support from Dept. of Homeland Security, networks of cities (for example, Rockefeller), charities
'Mission critical assets'	An asset whose disruption could result in military mission (or function) failure	An asset whose disruption could result in social, business, or organizational failure
Relationship with context in emergency	Separation: Transcend, exceed, surpass, leave behind, partition *from* context	Linkage: life giving, life support, solidarity, interconnection *with* context
Spatio-temporal reconfiguration	Glo-local Archipelagic Structure: ensuring global continuity of domestic bases in network-centric warfare	Urban Archipelagic Structure: primarily intra-urban focus with permeable boundaries to provide services

the grid, and permanently reconfiguring and operating the system so that it is always configured for normal/emergency operation. Grid expansion in the US is now predicated on a system that prioritizes the expansion of smart microgrid systems rather than central grid development. The claim is that these systems now prevent failures by addressing limits of normal backup and EDG systems because the smart microgrid system itself is always operating in normal/emergency mode. Further research will reveal the glitches and limits of these new systems.

Conclusion: Asynchronous resilience?

Interrogating the application of smart microgrids has revealed their utilization as an increasingly emblematic response to both grid uncertainties and energy securitization rationales in military base communities and, prospectively, in wider urban domains. However, smart grids are not just a response to grid fragility and constraints; they also allow interconnection of more distributed energy resources and new means of transmission and storage of energy, thereby avoiding the wholesale rebuilding of national grids. Smart infrastructure systems and their capacity for near real-time adjustments and modulations are also a technique of dealing *pre-emptively* with increasingly uncertain urban futures. There is a bigger infrastructural temporality issue here of unevenly future-proofing the grid, anticipating the permanent nature and times of disruption and offering a means of dealing with turbulence. These smart microgrid-focused initiatives are specific spatio-temporally differentiated forms of self-healing resilience that sit distinctively and contingently in relation to other parallel efforts at governing and securing urban life (Anderson, 2015).

Crucially, the smart microgrid is an example of a technology of 'event suppression' (Zebrowski, 2019). It does not prevent a disruptive event from occurring, but it works to close down the time of its disruptive effects (the TTH and for up to two weeks), albeit primarily in those spaces endowed with the capacity to do so. It is in this sense that we argue that smart microgrid configurations constitute an emerging political technology that can hold together differing spatio-temporal capacities, relations, and modes of operation that, together, fuse emergency and normal, but in a selective way according to contingent framings of mission critical assets. Smart microgrids thus materialize an extended and deepening, but selective, mode of vital systems security, offering real-time management of everyday and emergency with fast switching between modes. This is nonetheless more about safeguarding connection for and continued functioning of specific critical assets than getting the whole grid working again.

These emerging temporal infrastructure capacities and configurations have crucial socio-spatial implications. They *materialize* a new power for those managing the configuration to control the availability and disposability of assets and people (see Coutard, this volume). Choices must be made about which buildings/sites and groups to prioritize and exclude, with the distinction made through temporal adjustments and switching techniques. The subsequent detachment and attachment of components, assets, and groups are relationally constituted as 'always-on' for a selected few, but at the same time they inherently depend on the capacity to switch off or to place on standby others, reflecting the dialectics of infrastructure time. This spatio-temporal differentiation at work in the smart urban microgrid is fundamentally at odds with the harmonization and synchronization of urban temporal rhythms of the smart city narrative (Coletta and Kitchin, 2017; Kitchin, 2019). The near real-time switching accelerates infrastructure differentiation, producing new divisions between connected and disconnected, divisions forged by/

in microseconds and that can last for two weeks but require modification of the grid in the present. Always-on power requires much spatio-temporal modification of the design and operation of the new grid.

This is a differentiated and selective infrastructure response that furthermore, and crucially, contributes to the emergence of asymmetrical or perhaps even *asynchronous* modes of resilience, shaped by the logics of 'network time' (Hassan, 2007). This means understanding that there is 'an unequal and disproportionate imbalance between actors' in military, urban, and community contexts 'in the level of risk, resources, and consequences' during a grid failure (Oehmen and Multari, 2014: 1) – and, crucially, that this imbalance is constituted through the spatial and temporal capacities of smart microgrids. It is not an attempt at getting the grid functioning again for all, but about keeping certain critical assets online across normal and crisis times irrespective of what happens elsewhere.

We can view smart microgrids, then, as a technique that offers fundamental and disproportionate advantage, through a reworking of infrastructure temporality, to some actors as they seek to defend themselves from turbulence of whatever sort. It differentiates between sites and spaces for access to 'always-on', selectively fuses emergency and normal, and reworks normal infrastructure through crisis functionalities; however, it fails to deal with the longer-term fundamental causes of disruptions, casting further uncertainty over urban infrastructure futures. We begin to see how a particular military-oriented, selective, asynchronous form of resilience not only is only applied in base communities through the smart microgrid but also is increasingly transmuting more widely into the urban arena as local communities attempt to reprioritize public infrastructure provision according to similar rationales and practices.

In an inversion of infrastructure logic to date, this suggests that the key capacity may well now be in creating autonomy and distance from vulnerable, even risky, centralized grids. Value and power are now held in the micro elements of systems and capacity to manage and manipulate fine-grained micro networks/grid time. Increasing self-sufficiency in vital systems such as energy will reproduce and entrench asynchronous resilience. This not only leaves other spaces and groups to rely on vulnerable, slower grid times but also, by further diminishing the case for, or deprioritizing investment in, general grid maintenance and upgrades, the logic of self-sufficiency promotes a secession of responsibility for (and participation in) any longer-term collective action aimed at addressing the original sources of turbulence and upheaval.

Note

[1] It would also solve many other problems including the integration of renewables and microgrids, control of high voltage devices, enablement of new business strategies, maintenance of stability, reliability, and security, and a more efficient grid in a competitive market.

References

Alford, T.J. (2017) 'Off the grid: Facilitating the acquisition of microgrids for military installations to achieve energy security and sustainability', *George Washington Journal of Energy & Environmental Law*, 8(2): 97–120.

Amin, M. (2001) 'Toward self-healing energy infrastructure systems', *IEEE Computer Applications in Power*, 14(1): 20–8.

Amin, M. (2008) 'Challenges in reliability, security, efficiency, resilience of energy infrastructure: Toward smart self-healing electric power grid', *Proceedings of the IEEE Power and Energy Society General Meeting–Conversion and Delivery of Electrical Energy in the 21st Century*, Pittsburgh, PA: IEEE Power and Energy Society, pp 1–5.

Amin, M. (2014) 'A smart self-healing grid: In pursuit of a more reliable and resilient system', *IEEE Power & Energy Society e-News Update*, February. https://site.ieee.org/pes-enews/2013/12/31/a-smart-self-healing-grid/ (accessed 29 November 2022).

Amin, M., and Wollenberg, B.F. (2005) 'Toward a smart grid power delivery for the 21st Century', *IEEE Power Energy Magazine*, 3(5): 234–41.

Anderson, B. (2015) 'What kind of thing is resilience?', *Politics* 35(1): 60–6.

Arefifar, S.A., Mohamed Y.A.-R.I., and El-Fouly, T.H.M. (2013) 'Comprehensive operational planning framework for self-healing control actions in smart distribution grids', *IEEE Transactions on Power Systems*, 28(4): 4192–200.

Braun, B. (2014) 'A new urban dispositif? Governing life in an age of climate change', *Environment and Planning D: Society and Space*, 32(1): 49–64.

Bulkeley, H. (2021) 'Climate changed urban futures: Environmental politics in the Anthropocene city', *Environmental Politics*, 30(1–2): 266–84.

CNA Military Advisory Board (2015) *National Security and Assured U.S. Electrical Power*, Arlington, VA: CNA.

Coletta, C., and Kitchin, R. (2017) 'Algorhythmic governance: Regulating the "heartbeat" of a city using the Internet of Things', *Big Data & Society*, 4(2): 1–16.

Collier, S., and Lakoff, A. (2015) 'Vital systems security: Reflexive biopolitics and the government of emergency', *Theory, Culture & Society*, 32(2): 19–51.

Colson, C.M., Nehrir, M.H., and Gunderson, R.W. (2011) 'Distributed multi-agent microgrids: A decentralized approach to resilient power system self-healing', *4th International Symposium on Resilient Control Systems*, n.p.: IEEE, pp 83–8.

Cox, M. (2020) 'Army researchers dream new self-healing material will lead to "Terminator" technology', *Military.com*, 19 August. https://www.military.com/daily-news/2020/08/19/army-researchers-dream-new-self-healing-material-will-lead-terminator-technology.html (accessed 29 November 2022).

Danigelis, A, (2018) 'US Army targets energy resiliency through microgrid projects', *Energy Manager Today*, 26 March. https://www.energymanagertoday.com/us-army-microgrids-resiliency-0175787/ (accessed 29 November 2022).

Davoudi, S. (2014) 'Climate change, securitization of nature, and resilient urbanism', *Environment and Planning C: Government and Policy*, 32(2): 360–75.

Defense Science Board (2008) *Report of the Defense Science Board Task Force on DoD Energy Strategy: 'More Fight – Less Fuel'*, Washington, DC: Department of Defense.

Defense Science Board (2016) *Task Force on Energy Systems for Forward/Remote Operating Bases: Final Report*, Washington, DC: Department of Defense.

Derickson, K.D. (2018) 'Urban geography III: Anthropocene urbanism', *Progress in Human Geography*, 42(3): 425–35.

Dobbins, J., and Tabuchi, H. (2021) 'Texas blackouts hit minority neighborhoods especially hard', *New York Times*, 16 February. https://www.nytimes.com/2021/02/16/climate/texas-blackout-storm-minorities.html (accessed 29 November 2022).

Dreo Rodosek, G.B., Geihs, K., Schmeck, H., and Stiller, B. (2009) 'Self-healing systems: Foundations and challenges', *Dagstuhl Seminar Proceedings 09201, Combinatorial Scientific Computing*, Leibniz-Zentrum: Dagstuhl, pp 1–6. http://drops.dagstuhl.de/opus/volltexte/2009/2110 (accessed 29 November 2022).

Ghosh, D., Sharman, R., Raghav-Rao, H., and Upadhyaya, S. (2007) 'Self-healing systems: Survey and synthesis', *Decision Support Systems*, 42(4): 2164–85.

Gissen, D. (2014) *Manhattan Atmospheres: Architecture, the Interior Environment, and Urban Crisis*, Minneapolis, MN: University of Minnesota Press.

Hall, T., and Fischer, C. (2014) *Microgrid Enabled Distributed Energy Solutions (MEDES) – Fort Bliss Military Reservation final report. ESTCP Project EW-201140*, Alexandria, VA: SERDP/ESTCP and Lockheed Martin.

Hassan, R. (2007) 'Network time', in R. Hassan, and R.E. Purser (eds) *24/7: Time and Temporality in the Network Society*, Stanford, CA: Stanford University Press, pp 37–61.

Huber, R., and McCulloch, B. (1984) 'Self-repairing flight control system', *SAE Transactions*, 93: 477–96.

Jackson, W. (2012) 'The ability to automatically anticipate, respond to and isolate damage to the Smart Grid could mitigate the impact of power outages', *GCN, The Technology Transforming State and Local Government*. https://gcn.com/cybersecurity/2012/11/7-elements-of-a-self-healing-power-grid/308799/ (accessed 29 November 2022).

Johnson, S. (2022) 'Why Free Solo's Alex Honnold is financing solar power in New Orleans neighborhoods', *Business News*, 19 September. https://biz.crast.net/why-free-solos-alex-honnold-is-financing-solar-power-in-new-orleans-neighborhoods/ (accessed 29 November 2022).

Kephart, J.O., and Chess, D.M. (2003) 'The vision of autonomic computing', *Computer*, 36(1): 41–52.

Kitchin, R. (2019) 'The timescape of smart cities', *Annals of the American Association of Geographers*, 109(3): 775–90.

Kolenc, V. (2015). 'El Paso electric axes Fort Bliss solar plant plans', *El Paso Times*, 21 August. https://eu.elpasotimes.com/story/money/2015/08/21/el-paso-electric-axes-fort-bliss-solar-plant/71993368/ (accessed 29 November 2022).

Luque-Ayala, A., and Marvin, S. (2016) 'The maintenance of urban circulation: An operational logic of infrastructural control', *Environment and Planning D: Society and Space*, 34(2): 191–208.

Marqusee, J, Ericson, S., and Jenket, D. (2020) *Emergency Diesel Generator Reliability and Installation Energy Security* NREL/TP-5C00-76553, Golden, CO: National Renewable Energy Laboratory.

Marqusee, J., Schultz, C., and Robyn, D. (2017) *Power Begins at Home: Assured Energy for U.S. Military Bases*, Restin, VA: Noblis.

Mayer, M., and Acuto, M. (2015) 'The global governance of large technical systems', *Millennium*, 43(2): 660–83.

Oehmen, C., and Multari, N. (2014) *AiR: Asymmetry in resilience – Report on the First Meeting on Asymmetry in Resilience for Complex Cyber Systems*, Richland, WA: Pacific Northwest National Laboratory.

PR Newswire (2013) 'U.S. Army and Lockheed Martin commission microgrid at Fort Bliss', 16 May. https://www.prnewswire.com/news-releases/us-army-and-lockheed-martin-commission-microgrid-at-fort-bliss-207742431.html (accessed 29 November 2022).

Rickerson, W., Wu, M., and Pringle, M. (2018) *Beyond the Fence Line: Strengthening Military Capabilities through Energy Resilience Partnerships*, Washington, DC: Association of Defense Communities & Converge Strategies.

Rutherford, J., and Marvin, S. (2022) 'Urban smart microgrids: A political technology of emergency-normalcy', *Urban Geography*, 44(8): 1794–1815. https://doi.org/10.1080/02723638.2022.2126609

Salehie, M., and Tahvildari, L. (2009) 'Self-adaptive software: Landscape and research challenges', *ACM Transactions on Autonomous and Adaptive Systems*, 4(2): 1–42.

Siegel, K. (2012) 'The true cost of power outages', *Yale Environment Review*, 5 August. https://environment-review.yale.edu/true-cost-power-outages-0 (accessed 29 November 2022).

Simonet, G., and Duchemin, E. (2010) 'The concept of adaptation: Interdisciplinary scope and involvement in climate change', *S.A.P.I.EN.S: Surveys and Perspectives Integrating Environment and Society*, 3(1): 1–9.

St John, J. (2013) 'The military microgrid as smart grid asset', *Greentech Media*, 17 May. https://www.greentechmedia.com/articles/read/the-military-microgrid-as-smart-grid-asset#gs.IpOslVPz (accessed 29 November 2022).

Steinberg, M. (2005) 'Historical overview of research in reconfigurable flight control', *Proceedings of the Institution of Mechanical Engineers, Part G: Journal of Aerospace Engineering*, 219(4): 263–75.

Suit, R. (2016) 'The big potential of microgrids', *Richmond Journal of Law and Technology*, 29 February. https://jolt.richmond.edu/2016/02/29/the-big-potential-of-microgrids/ (accessed 29 November 2022).

Tomayko, J.E. (2003) *Computers Take Flight: A History of NASA's Pioneering Digital Fly-by-Wire Project*, Washington, DC: NASA.

Webb, S. (2022) 'Fed-up Texans are creating their own tiny power grids. Here's how', *Houston Chronicle*, 18 February. https://www.houstonchronicle.com/business/energy/article/Fed-up-with-the-Texas-power-system-residents-are-16928255.php#photo-22080171 (accessed 29 November 2022).

Whitington, J. (2016) 'Modernist infrastructure and the vital systems security of water: Singapore's pluripotent climate futures', *Public Culture*, 28(2): 415–41.

Zebrowski, C. (2019) 'Emergent emergency response: Speed, event suppression and the chronopolitics of resilience', *Security Dialogue*, 50(2): 148–64.

10

Speed, Suspension, and Stasis: Waiting in the Shadow of Infrastructure

Jessica DiCarlo

Introduction

Research on infrastructure – from roads to railways and dams to economic zones – is marked by an interest in space: how projects connect, disconnect, and transform places and regions. However, as this volume attests, infrastructure is inherently spatio-temporal: an assemblage of planning, promise, flows of materials and capital, and embodied experiences. What truly struck me throughout my research on the Laos–China Railway (LCR) were the divergent ways in which interlocutors perceived and expressed time in relation to infrastructure. State officials and planners discussed timelines and project plans, focusing on swift construction completion and successful project operation, emphasizing future potential and profit. In media reports, percentages of project completion took centre stage: Lao Deputy Prime Minister Sonexay Siphandone announced that 'nearly 80 percent of the railway construction was complete' (Xinhua, 2019); and the *Phnom Penh Post* (2021) reported when the Luang Prabang railway station was 'about 45 percent complete.' Alongside promises of connectivity and modernity, temporal framings of the railway position most people in Laos as spectators on the sidelines, waiting to see if the LCR will deliver on promises made by the government: to integrate Laos into the regional and global economy and lift local people out of poverty. This state of anticipation constitutes a broader imagined future for the country, which is not necessarily part of daily life.

In contrast, for residents in the shadow of infrastructure, the railway was ever-present, disrupting their daily lives and generating both anticipation and uncertainty about the future. They navigated between infrastructural 'speeds' and 'suspensions' in relation to railway construction. Rather than awaiting a promised future with no present consequences, those in the path of construction experienced railway time as an intimate state of suspension and stasis as, for example, land, homes, burial areas, and farms were no longer accessible, and residents had to wait for information, some form of redress, or compensation for their losses. Ambiguity in project plans further elongated experiences of suspension, which were compounded by the fact that the railway project had disrupted traditional land use years before the start of construction. This overwhelming sense of stasis sharply conflicted with planners' project visions, pointing to the limitations of relying on project time as the primary mode of understanding the complicated, uneven rhythms and times that surround construction (Addie, this volume).

Infrastructure engenders temporalities that ripple with different implications across a range of landscapes and lives. This chapter unpacks such temporalities – particularly the lived experiences of waiting, delay, and suspension – and examines the differentiations among modalities of waiting for people living in the shadow of the construction of a railway project. In doing so, it identifies variations of waiting, suspension, and stasis as modalities of infrastructure time and contrasts them with notions of speed, progress, and promise, thus disrupting linear notions of 'China speed' and planning or project time. Specifically, I examine this uneven temporal terrain in the villages and homes that have been directly affected by the construction of the railway between 2018 and 2020, as many people in the path of the line were left with limited knowledge or means of redress if they encountered problems or lost access to their land.

This chapter proceeds as follows. The next section surveys three widely held views on infrastructure development: a belief in linear progress leading towards completion, the assumed space-time compression of transportation infrastructures, and the notion of 'China speed'. I rebut and complicate these views to suggest that infrastructure is more productively understood through a critical view on waiting and suspension, which sits in tension with promises of speed and assured outcomes. Drawing inspiration from Carse and Kneas's (2019) notion of the 'suspended present' and literature on waiting, the third section examines multiple modalities of prolonged waiting. Here I am interested in the drawn-out moments and years of railway development through which life is suspended and actively remade as people wait for an unknown and unclear future. I conclude by considering the unevenness of infrastructural temporalities for differently positioned citizens, alongside their changing sense of time and place along the railway line and within the context of rapid development.

From railroad time and 'China speed' to infrastructure time

Since their advent, railroads have engendered a particular temporality, one of tight schedules and precise timekeeping. They were the genesis of the time zone; the introduction of 'railroad time' offered the first regionally standardized time system in 1840 with the Great Western Railway in England. Railroads have also been theorized as shrinking space and time (Lardner, 1850; Geurts, 2019) and conceptualized in terms of time-space compression (Harvey, 1989). Schivelbusch (1978: 40) pronounced the railroad a 'destroyer of experiential space and time' as it reshaped European landscapes and economies throughout the Industrial Revolution. These tropes persist, and today China's railway sector promises a standard of 'China speed' (Xu, 2019) – speed not only of the infrastructure itself but also of its construction.

A key project under China's Belt and Road Initiative, the LCR, is layered with such promises of speed through present construction and projected far into the future. Indeed, many people in Laos have cited a preference for Chinese projects precisely because they are built quickly and will offer Laos a fast track into the global economy. The promises of progress, change, and modernity in which roads, railways, and dams are steeped encourage people to envision a future world and their life possibilities in it (Bear, 2007; Reeves, 2017). Such promise evokes feelings of anticipation and expectation (Anand et al, 2018). Projects such as railways are framed by particular material and temporal visions that aspire towards frictionless flows and signal a politics of the present as constantly restructured by anticipation for the future. To achieve this vision, projects are conceived in a stepwise process. Like development thinking broadly, infrastructure projects are imagined as unfolding linearly towards some state of completion with clear economic ends. In this way, project time is understood as standardized, linear, homogeneous, measurable, and decontextualized (Adam, 1995, 2004): the language of planners.

However, as this volume attests, time is not so straightforward as various conceptions of it intersect, abut, and contradict. While planning and project time remain potent social and political forces, they posit realities that we should not accept at face value, as infrastructure is not always defined by progress, linearity, and forward movement (see Simone, this volume). Instead, these versions of time diverge significantly from the more recent ways in which scholars have begun to theorize infrastructural temporalities and time. Shaped by notions of futurity, relations between people and infrastructure regularly result in deferral, ruination, suspension, abandonment, and repurposing (Stoler, 2013).

Infrastructure time is thus defined by complex temporalities (Appel, 2018) and ongoing delay and decay (Gupta, 2015, 2018) that affect the lives of people living in their very shadows. Yet top-down technocratic processes of infrastructure planning tend to overlook human-scale impacts and what Joniak-Lüthi (2019) calls the 'lifeworlds of infrastructure', particularly during construction. Rather than decay or destruction indicating an endpoint as a project fails or ages, I locate rubble in the very creation of the railway, in supposed moments of 'China speed' and often overlooked spaces and temporalities that transform lives and places, turning a home into a construction site seemingly overnight. Often, lives, social worlds, and livelihoods are held in a liminal state so that infrastructure construction can proceed quickly: here, with the promise of 'China speed'. In this way, the railway is a type of liminal technology (Suboticki and Sørensen, 2018), suspending local contexts and reshaping them to fit project time needs.

This chapter attends to the socio-political and affective dimensions of infrastructure time by bringing often overlooked temporalities of construction to the forefront. I draw inspiration from Carse and Kneas's (2019) typology of the 'suspended present' to illuminate transformations to daily life associated with experiences of infrastructural stasis and suspension. Unlike studies on suspension that look to moments of infrastructural breakdown (Schwenkel, 2015) or ruination (Rippa, 2021), this chapter explores the lives suspended as the result of a mega-project as it starts, stops, and leaves people in the lurch throughout construction. My use of suspension does not refer to a fleeting property or state in-between but rather to a condition, an ongoing state of becoming (Gupta, 2015). When understood as a social and relational process, suspension has distinct rhythms and conditions of possibility and helps us better understand infrastructural temporalities (Carse and Kneas, 2019). The suspended present illuminates the potency of the promise of infrastructure as it holds people's attention. However, there are limitations to thinking only with unbuilt and incomplete projects. In a sense, it cements the orthodoxies of project time, for example, completion and unfinishedness as the two concluding stages of a project. Infrastructure instead entails moments and fits of unfinishedness. In contrast to projects such as the Kaeng Sua Ten Dam in Thailand, which was never built but threatened residents with eviction for four decades (Carse and Kneas, 2019), a different sort of suspension emerges through the railway's swift construction as people are left waiting for information, compensation, and new land.

People living in the shadow of infrastructure have a particular temporal orientation that is organized around waiting. Waiting is often so taken for granted that it has been called the 'neglected Achilles heel of modernity' (Bissell, 2007: 277). However, waiting is not necessarily a uniform or passive act. Rather, it takes various forms: waiting as a form of resistance (Lakha, 2009), a technology of governance (Auyero, 2012), or tool of control and sanctioning (Andersson, 2014). It can thus be conceived as an act, an effect, and a social process (Janeja and Bandak, 2018; Straughan et al, 2020). Multiple and variegated registers of waiting become a central feature of everyday life and of infrastructure time. Waiting persists regardless of whether a project is unfinished or materializes with great fanfare. Literature on waiting, then, opens a theoretical trajectory that complements notions of infrastructural suspension. Understood as an activity, waiting pushes our thinking on suspension as a process to include possibility and agency. More than stagnancy, waiting is 'alive with the potential of being other than this' (Bissell, 2007: 277). Additionally, waiting has relational and political dynamics: 'we wait *for* or *because* of something' (Straughan et al, 2020). Waiting thus yields new perspectives for understanding infrastructure time and its unevenness.

I argue that, together, suspension and waiting sit in tension with *and* make possible the promise of speed and progress. Infrastructure time and experiences of it are the product of this dialectical relationship. Analysing infrastructure and suspension within the literature on waiting opens our thinking to the vacillations between doubt and uncertainty, and hope and expectation on the other, and the power to impose such experiences. A conceptual lens of waiting 'enables us to critically approach the precariousness of existence, made more urgent by current conjunctures of simultaneous waiting and speeding up across scales' (Janeja and Bandak, 2018: 6). Far from waiting offering emancipatory potential (Bissell, 2007), those waiting do not directly benefit from the integrated networked space of the railway. Instead, people experiencing disruptions from construction are unlikely to benefit from the use value of the railroad. However, those who wait do not wait in the same ways and with the same effects, as the following section details.

Suspension on the tracks and variations on waiting

Throughout railway construction, multiple types of suspension emerge, some related to infrastructure planning (those of 'project time') and others embedded in the everyday life of people living in the shadow of construction. Regardless of whether the railway speeds through construction or stalls, other temporalities – of anticipation, suspension, stasis, and liminality – manifest in surrounding social worlds and more aptly capture the temporal tensions and multifaceted on-the-ground experiences of infrastructure. From this view, it becomes clear that construction would not be possible without the very suspension and erasure of the pre-existing lifeworlds. However, this erasure is a highly uneven process.

In 2019, a provincial railway coordinator in Luang Namtha province confirmed that authorities in his districts first informed residents about the project in 2010: "We told people not to carry out any construction or grow crops on land earmarked for the railway corridor to avoid losses" (Vientiane

Times, 2017). However, much of the land that people were instructed to cease farming on had still not been used for the project. In some places, land has sat unproductive for three or more years as those who lived on or used it waited for construction to commence. When construction finally began in 2016, so did another round of waiting, this time for compensation money for homes that were demolished and agricultural land used for construction. As construction neared completion, compensation had not been paid in its entirety to the more than 4,000 families who were directly affected by construction (DiCarlo, 2020; Suhardiman et al, 2021). My interviews as late as March 2020 and again in January 2023 confirmed that across provinces, some people continued to wait for what they considered fair compensation. This, as the Lao planner in the introduction to this chapter lamented, was due to the delayed input of capital from the Lao state, which subsequently stalled the arrival of capital from Chinese policy banks (DiCarlo, 2021).

In addition to compensation, planning and construction have started and stalled multiple times since the early 2000s. Prior to 2016, the project was delayed so many times that many people did not think the expensive and expansive project would ever come to fruition. Even at the time of the ground-breaking ceremony, doubt that it could be completed by the target date of December 2021 was pervasive. Many people in Laos assumed it would be another Lao 'PDR' project – the acronym for the Lao 'People's Democratic Republic' jokingly referred to as Lao 'Please Don't Rush' – reflecting a tendency towards slow-moving bureaucratic processes and projects. However, in the initial years of construction, this epithet was quickly replaced with the notion that the railway was built with 'China speed'. Many of my interlocutors have since looked in awe at the train cars that sit at the site of the future Vientiane station, indicating that this project has finally materialized. Yet in the surrounding countryside, a waiting game persists.

Waiting as death

"We've waited too long for compensation. Three people have already died!" joked Dorn. "They cannot wait. *Bai gon* [so long or goodbye]!" She slapped her knee and laughed heartily at her grim but true joke. Three of her neighbours had indeed passed away since local officials informed her village that a portion of it would be used for railway construction. Dorn is a retired farmer. She made clear that she will no longer engage in the rhythms of her fields because they could be taken at any time; waiting now dominated her day. She was waiting for land compensation and waiting to find out when her family could farm their own land.

As we spent warm afternoons walking the village together, she showed me where local officials told her to expect construction. She was quick to point out that her family was still in the lurch concerning their approximately 2.5 hectares of affected land where they grew teak and another 1.5 hectares of rice fields. "We lost both the rice and teak areas and have not been able to use them for three, almost four years. I have been waiting for compensation that whole time." Her husband, who joined us on that day's walk, added that the construction company had not yet used the land. He continued, "because I don't have a rice field now, I don't have a job. I just stay at home with the family and help with the grandchildren. We must buy rice because we cannot grow it." They lamented that due to the high price of rice, they were not able to buy all the food they needed with their children's low salaries. However, he added, "I will not buy new land once I get compensation because my children work for the government now and they do not have time to do agriculture, and I am getting too old". There is a political economy to waiting. Not only can waiting be a waste of time, but also, in this sense, time is money or food on the table. Here waiting puts pressure on livelihoods and expectations of family labour, especially when families are unable to use their land. As I left Dorn's home that afternoon, I risked a joke, wishing that no one else passes away from all the waiting. She quickly snapped back: "No, no we will get money soon and even travel on the train"; she paused, then reflected, "well, for a few months we can survive the wait … but not years".

Waiting as powerlessness

The next day Dorn and I meandered between gardens dotted with wildflowers to the home of her neighbour, who agreed to talk with me about his farmland. He handed me a short stool, signalling for me to join him on the front stoop of his home. Railway construction affected most of his farmland, a garden and a rice field. "We did not get new land, but we will get money. We have just not received it yet." He echoed Dorn's hope and uncertainty, adding, "I just have to wait. I will accept whatever they offer. It's a government project. There is no choice." Dorn interjected: "This project is very important. If they don't pay you, it's no problem for them. We cannot ask for more money. The land belongs to the government, when they need it, they can get it. When there are no projects, then you can use the land forever. If there are some projects from the government then you have to return the land." Her statement points to a sense that she felt powerless to guide her own life. Indeed, prolonged waiting positions the time and lives of those kept waiting as less valuable than the time and lives of those imposing the wait or not required to wait (Swartz, 1975).

Indeed, residents often described their powerlessness during construction in terms of their lack of choice and incomplete information. "It is the government's plan to develop the country and people should participate. If we have good enough conditions when we move – meaning, we get appropriate compensation and good agricultural land – then people will be happy to move and help the country develop. But we have few details on this", said Dorn's husband. Often, they lacked information on how to engage in bureaucratic procedures, for instance, to obtain information, permits, or permissions, that would allow them to resolve ongoing feelings of suspension. Dorn's neighbour motioned to the other side of the road, saying they had lost much more land there, but they were unsure of how calculations would take place: "Maybe by the trees? But I don't know how much per square metre." He shrugged and concluded: "I do not know what [the government's] real plan is and when they will come, but if they ask us to move, we have to move." The local residents are powerless to end the waiting and increasingly frustrated with the powerful who impose the wait. In this sense, waiting can be punitive when one does not know how long one will be kept waiting.

Waiting between doubt and hope

In response to the waiting, Dorn began to call district offices; she felt this was the most she was able to do. Throughout the railway construction, many residents, along with Dorn, had met with officials about compensation and land loss a handful of times, and all in group meetings. At these meetings, they received partial information on timelines, land values, and construction plans that the provincial offices were still working out. Dorn said that, at first, each meeting felt hypothetical. She did not really believe they would lose their land because the plans were so unclear, and they kept changing. However, with construction came restrictions on land use, so Dorn began to call the railway and land offices in Luang Prabang more frequently. She had done so multiple times to ask for compensation for lost rice cultivation. "We get the same answer, 'please wait'." According to Dorn, the officials she spoke with said little more than this because they likely did not know much more themselves. As often as she called to check in, she did not expect the office to have news. Yet she continued to call. Dorn narrated simultaneous resignation and hope in her waiting: "I have no choice; we have to wait. But I continue to call because they might pay us someday." Her most recent encounter with local railway officials, which took place the day before our walk, gave her hope that compensation might come through soon. She explained that "[the officials] came to the village to ask me to sign compensation papers. I think they were bank documents but I'm not sure. But I think it is good news." She sounded weary, particularly due to the lack of information and the amount of time that had passed without receiving any.

Waiting as annoyance

The affective experience of waiting progresses from hope to helplessness and often to frustration and annoyance. This is particularly true as residents are given information on timelines for compensation and construction that are later delayed. Approximately 150 kilometres south of Dorn's village in a rural part of Vientiane province, Phouthong and I sat on a hill overlooking rail construction. A farmer in his 60s, he pointed out the 1.5 hectares of land that he had gradually lost to the railway. "I watched my rice fields get smaller and smaller through the construction process." Construction halted his ability to farm, and the local government instructed him to wait for more information on when and how he would receive compensation. He explained, "when the local government came to inform us about the project, they only said, 'wait, wait …'. It has been two years without any update." He went on, "I feel very annoyed with waiting now".

In contrast to possible emancipatory qualities of waiting (Bissell, 2007), people do not express comfort in waiting, instead describing it as unpleasant, uncertain, and tedious. Opacity in processes raised additional challenges for many affected people who were unsure which institutions they could communicate with when problems arose. Phouthong did not know how to contact the officials in charge, nor why he had not yet received compensation despite having given up his farmland long ago. He concluded that he could do little else than talk with his village leader. Exasperated by his experience and the little information he was able to provide, he suggested that the next day we visit his family members, who might know more. The next morning, we drove to a neighbouring Hmong village that appeared poorer than Phouthong's village and was next to a new railway tunnel. His cousin was bent over a tub of water, defeathering a chicken, as her three children ran around the hillside. She received compensation for her house two years after construction on the tunnel began. However, she had not yet received redress for the agricultural land where she planted the family garden for sustenance as well as fruit trees from which she sold products at the local market. As these experiences illustrate, not only does making people wait exert power over their lives and time, but also the uneven experiences of infrastructure time lead to frustration and worry.

Waiting as uncertainty

In another Hmong village in rural Vientiane province, the railway tracks had just been laid. I went to visit the site with Foua, who has lived in this village much of his life. He pointed across the tracks to a lone house with walls made of bamboo and an aluminium roof and shared another story of suspension. "The family over there won't clear out, even after the construction and digging began." He looked to the house now perched on a ledge that juts past the retaining walls, hovering 50 feet from the tracks, now disconnected from the village. In the surrounding villages, he explained, most households that moved for the train were ethnic Khmu, many of whom received some compensation, though only a low amount for their houses and nothing for their agricultural land. This Hmong family, Foua explained, cannot move without the compensation that the government promised. Unlike other households, they do not have family land nearby to which to move. "That's why they haven't moved and stayed there even with the construction. But it is very hard to get in their house." To cross the retaining wall, they must travel south to where the wall is low and then walk back up to the house. And if they want to go by motorbike, they have to drive [1 to 2 kms] to the passage for trucks and cars. When I asked how they were able to stay when other households were forced to move, he explained that "when the Chinese came, they said they just wanted enough land for the railway. That's why this family can stay now." The house does not obstruct the tracks. Yet it is a visible form of suspension, perched on an open and dusty ledge that will soon have railway cars rushing past, the family waiting until they are forced to move and waiting for the compensation to be able to do so, whichever comes first (see Figure 10.1).

Figure 10.1: A home razed below the new Vang Vieng railway tunnel, Vientiane province, 2019

Source: Jessica DiCarlo

Agency in waiting

Active waiting among displaced peoples, asylum seekers, and the poor, for example, is well documented (Marcel, 1967; Hage, 2009a, 2009b; Brun, 2010). Hage (2009b: 1) writes: 'Waiting indicates that we are engaged in, and have expectations from, life; that we are on the lookout for what life is going to throw our way.' In the case of the LCR, in contrast to uncertainty and precarity, active forms of waiting also emerged, particularly in communities where multiple families were affected, as I discovered when I returned to several villages located further north within the railway corridor in Oudomxay province. Railway pylons towered over agricultural land on the east side of the community, and construction workers were just starting to connect the pylons to lay the tracks high above the village. It was a dramatic view of construction intersecting with village life and agricultural land. Chickens scurried around the thick grey concrete that dwarfed the small thatch-walled houses. The pylons were stacked tightly together because the track was to be elevated in this section (see Figure 10.2). The railway company claims this will minimize the impact on the community and the environment. However, the villagers say otherwise, as they are acutely attuned to the new dusty concrete landscape of the village and the rhythm of development, a rhythm marked by swift project construction and not-so-swift sharing of information or compensation.

Hong, a 47-year-old man who grew up here, accompanied me on several walks through his village. Even though construction is well underway, and some land was used to build a large nearby labour camp, villagers have yet to be compensated for their lost land. However, waiting does not mean that people are idle (Brun, 2015). Hong explained that every single month they requested a meeting between the provincial railway office, the *naiban*, and affected villagers to discuss and negotiate compensation. "We've done this for two years and still nothing." Rather than a stagnant state, waiting here is both variable and dynamic. Marcel (1967) describes active waiting as consistent monitoring of the likelihood that an event of waiting will pay off based on how long one is prepared to wait. As Dorn explicitly stated earlier: she will wait a few more months, *not* years. Like Dorn, Hong doubts that anything will come of his village's monthly requests for meetings. He instead views them as a means to engage with the project more actively in hopes that it will help him to better calculate his plans. "We keep asking so they don't forget us, and so we know what to do", even though his hope is dwindling after two years of doing this.

Waiting as holding out hope

Waiting, on the one hand, entails a veiled passivity, as Hong and Dorn also demonstrate agency that, while limited, affords them the hope that keeps

Figure 10.2: A woman washes materials from a wedding festival in her village's stream, alongside which railway pylons have been constructed, Oudomxay province, 2019

Source: Jessica DiCarlo

them waiting. My time with Hong highlighted another reason why people hold out hope: there is an important difference between permanent land expropriation and temporary land use during construction. Temporary use of land for construction initially provided many people the assurance that once construction was complete, they could again access their land. Most people with 'temporary use' land lost access to some or all of their agricultural land. Because officials never explained what the land would be temporarily used for, there was an assumption that, when it was returned to the villagers and smallholders, it would be the same as when they left it. However, another man in Hong's village whose land near a tunnel was designated for temporary construction use complained that this was not the case. When local officials came to his village to sign land use and appropriation documents, he agreed to give up one of his three sections of rice paddy land for temporary construction use. However, three months later, when he went to prepare his fields for cultivation, he saw that construction workers had dumped rocks from tunnel excavation on all three parcels of land. He immediately called the district land officer, who instructed him to get paperwork from his village chief to confirm his complaint; only then would they review the case. After weeks, he submitted the correct paperwork and got a response. I asked his wife what they would do with the land when they got it back. She bemoaned, "Oh, there is nothing we can do with it. It does not look like paddy [rice] anymore. It is all big rocks and boulders, and they are too heavy for us to move. No one will move them." After waiting weeks, a local land official visited the village to check on construction and confirm the complaint. The official, upon seeing the land, also asked what they planned to do with the land. Hong responded, "I cannot do anything with the land, I would like to sell it to the project". He has since attempted unsuccessfully to renegotiate his paperwork to include the sale of all three parcels of land.

Partial knowledge about construction and partial compensation exacerbates the challenges of waiting, yet at the same time, the lack of certainty facilitates a sense of hope or expectation. As Bourdieu (2000: 228) explains, the art of 'making people wait, of delaying without destroying hope, of adjourning without totally disappointing, which would have the effect of killing the waiting itself, is an integral part of the exercise of power'. The railway generates hope among the people it holds in suspension. This does not necessarily mean that those living in the shadow of infrastructure are recipients of that hope – of the promises of increased trade and poverty alleviation – yet these visions and promises offer a reason to wait.

For Dorn, Foua, Hong, and Phouthong, their experiences of infrastructure time – promises of speed and modernity in tension with lived experiences of suspension – encouraged them to wait while they held out hope. Hong, for example, understood that the construction workers would only use their land during construction and then would return it. Phouthong's cousin received some compensation, leading her to believe that compensation was being provided as promised, albeit slowly. Dorn continued to make phone calls to local officials, who politely answered and asked her to continue to wait. As is common within bureaucracy, these individuals' waiting involved the expectation of something to come. At the same time, the ambiguity that surrounded their waiting (its duration, rates of compensation, where to move, or when one could use the land) generated feelings of anxiety, ambivalence, and resignation alongside hope. And yet despite a sense of resignation, Dorn and Hong tried to make known their presence and status of waiting. Like Brun's (2015) description of agency-in-waiting, people may feel trapped by present outcomes but are still able to structure their experiences of extended uncertainty and waiting by actively trying to counteract them.

Differentiation and the power of waiting

Literature on waiting and the ethnographic accounts presented earlier encourage reflection on power and highlight what Straughan et al (2020: 639) call the '*durational* dimensions of power-geometrics'. Prolonged waiting has varied implications for citizens differently positioned in relation to infrastructure construction as it fitfully starts, stops, and is suspended. Construction leads to liminal states, with wide-ranging repercussions for people's lives, homes, and livelihoods. Here liminality keeps some people in the dark, unable to ask questions, contest compensation plans, or counter land loss. Time spent waiting is anything but equal (Turnbull, 2015; Foster, 2019). In other words, temporal insecurity is a crucial element in experiences of inequality (Comaroff and Comaroff, 2001; Mains, 2007; Auyero, 2012). Bourdieu (2000: 228) writes that 'absolute power is the power to make oneself unpredictable and deny other people any reasonable anticipation, to place them in total uncertainty by offering no scope to their capacity to predict ... The all-powerful is he who does not wait but who makes others wait.'

Through attention to infrastructural time and waiting, we can critique and account for inequality as people's ability to plan and direct their lives varies across ethnic and class differences. For example, officials outside the village who do not experience delays or displacement easily overlook the concerns of those who do. "Of course, construction can proceed, and compensation can begin later ... if we wait [railway] construction will take too long", said the head of one of the provincial LCR offices in June 2019. His statement demonstrates that waiting is not acceptable for those driving infrastructure projects, and that certain people wait differently. According to Levine (1997), the 'waiting game' determines who waits up front and in the back of the line, and who does not wait at all. He suggests there are rules that dictate the game: the powerful control who waits, time can be given as a gift, waiting can be a method of control, people wait for what they value, the longer people wait for something the greater the status of the waited-upon, and money can buy a spot at the front. On the one hand, waiting and suspension contrast project speeds. On the other hand, there are variations within types of waiting and stasis, as life continues to be actively lived.

A common experience of the less powerful, waiting produces dependency and subordination (Auyero, 2012) as it generates or reinforces precarity and vulnerability. In Laos, people marginalized in terms of ethnicity and class know suspension most intimately. Dorn, Foua, Hong, and Phouthong are all from minority ethnicities, either Hmong or Khmu, rather than the dominant lowland Lao. They all live in small, thatched-walled houses and have spent most of their lives reliant on subsistence agriculture. They also expressly stated a sense of powerlessness in relation to railway construction. In each of their villages, they were instructed not to talk about the project and encountered bureaucratic roadblocks, such as additional paperwork, when they tried to negotiate their position. As Phouthong recapitulated, "I am only an ordinary person, and if the government approved these projects we have to follow".

At the same time, they were all aware that this was not the case for everyone. "Rich people already benefit", said Hong as we sat tucked between yellow backhoes on freshly churned-up red earth with a group of Lao construction workers who kindly indulged my questions on a lunch break. One jumped in to clarify that the real problem is that people will receive different remuneration rates depending on their connections with provincial and district-level officials. "For compensation, if you are rich and have knowledge, then you get maybe 200,000 kip (US$22) per m^2" as opposed to 17,000 kip (US$1.87). He explained that people who are powerful are able and know how to ask for more money. More nods and "*men leo*" (a phrase of affirmation) echoed around the circle. As elsewhere in the world, political, social, and economic capital varies, and elites have an advantage in defining land compensation protocols (Green and Baird, 2016). Many people in Vientiane are part of the dominant Lao ethnic group who, as Petit (2017) shows, often have connections to political elites and, for this reason, have succeeded in opposing other projects. Since the railway land compensation discussions began, spaces of negotiation and contestation have slowly surfaced, but those who have most effectively negotiated their position have done so through individuals with political connections.

A state-run newspaper published on this process in detail (a surprise given the contentious nature of these issues) and reported that in both Oudomxay and Vientiane provinces residents 'have yet to be properly compensated for the loss of their land and other property following the construction of the Laos–China Railway' because they refused compensation on the grounds that the rate was too low or inaccurately accounted. Their refusal results not in resistance to construction or even better compensation, but rather in additional delays in obtaining any compensation at all. A similar case emerged in Vang Vieng as a new city project was put on hold because it affected the land of several local elites. In both instances, people with personal connections to those in power were able to resist the construction of large infrastructure projects.

The uneven ability to contest construction and land compensation is increasingly apparent. For example, on 22 January 2020, members of the Provincial People's Assembly (PPA) in Vientiane Capital raised issues about land compensation for infrastructure projects, including the railway, Vientiane Expressway, and the Mekong Riverbank Erosion Protection project. This area surrounding the capital is largely inhabited by the dominant Lao ethnic group. Vilaysan Phommixay, PPA member from Xaysetta district in the capital, made a public statement on compensation, explaining that "railway construction is near villagers' land, but the compensation rate is very low. For example, the land calculation in Dongmaikhai village, in some areas is calculated to be 5,000 kip [per m^2], while some areas are 10,000 kip. In this case, what should we do? If we ask villagers to move, how can they afford new land as the calculation is very low? How should we find the solution for this issue?"

These are many of the same arguments I heard years earlier in more marginal areas of the country, in the Khmu and Hmong villages that Hong, Dorn, Foua, and Phouthong call home. However, rather than take their issues to the provincial assembly, as ethnic Lao in the capital were able to do (whether they had their demands met is a different question), they were barred from significant interaction with railway construction, leaving them waiting, often resigned and fraught. And yet, so long as waiting is determined to be meaningful or necessary, people wait (Brun, 2015). There is thus a politics to who is to wait, what waiting entails, how to wait, and how to socially organize waiting (Hage, 2009a). As Rundell (2009: 51) puts it, '[w]e all wait for futures – yet not for the same ones, nor in the same way, nor at the same tempo. Modernity, because of its multiple worlds and their temporal horizons, entails that waiting for the future has multiple, clashing and even overlapping effects, affects and modalities.'

Thinking across speed, suspension, and stasis in relation to infrastructure construction reveals an exercise of power over people's lives. Unpacking the politics of waiting and infrastructural suspension as construction speeds ahead draws attention to dynamics and experiences that are often overlooked or homogenized. The unevenness of waiting and the effects of infrastructural suspension expose and further entrench ethnic and class differences that are embedded within a one-party political system that has accepted orthodox framings of infrastructure as development.

Conclusion

This chapter has endeavoured to disrupt linear and teleological notions of project time and infrastructure development to illuminate the temporalities of living in the shadow of the railway. Connecting literature on suspension and waiting with ethnographic insights on infrastructure construction, this chapter exposed the limitations of thinking in terms of project time and 'China speed'. Grand narratives of linear development and future promises mask the lived experiences of infrastructural temporalities. As infrastructure extends far beyond its technical functions, attention to its entangled and uneven temporal terrain illuminates the lived experiences and socio-material relations that discourses of project time and 'China speed' obscure. By bringing the complexity of time to the forefront of railway construction, I highlight the diverse temporalities bound up in the experience of one project and tie them to the social worlds that emerge from and are reshaped by infrastructure.

Infrastructure time and experiences of it are constructed through the dialectics of stasis and speed, as well as suspension and progress. Conceptualizing infrastructure time then means foregrounding not only the temporality of planners but also, as the Introduction to this book advocates, the erasure of 'lived' time by the colonizing force of project time in order to 'grapple with the cruelty and promise of infrastructure' (Addie, Glass, Nelles, and Marino, this volume). As this chapter has shown, waiting and stasis are key modalities of infrastructure time that contrast notions of modernity, progress, and linear development. More than contrasting, the delay and suspension of the social surroundings are the prerequisites for the infrastructural promises of speed and connection. Suspension and waiting sit in tension with *and* make possible the promise of speed and progress.

Analysing infrastructure and suspension alongside the literature on waiting encourages us to hold in tension the feelings of doubt and uncertainty and hope and expectation that accompany infrastructure. It also raises questions regarding who has the power to impose such experiences. Planners, officials, and many observers largely centre their temporal focus on project plans. However, often overlooked temporalities, such as suspension and waiting, are dominant in the eyes of community members. Such perspectives are shaped by long periods of waiting, uncertainty around land, the knowledge that past projects did not materialize, and feelings that participation and redress are not possible. Ethnographic accounts of waiting illuminate the deeply felt experiences of displacement, doubt, and resignation, which are coupled with some form of hope that large infrastructure engenders. Yet the more people waited, felt overlooked, and had bids for help ignored, the more acutely they felt construction in their villages. For Lao residents directly affected by the railroad, hope bleeds into a sort of 'cruel optimism'

(Berlant, 2011) as they anticipate benefits from the object responsible for their dispossession and await a promised future from which they are likely to be excluded.

Foregrounding the intersection of infrastructure and temporality, future work should examine how and why people wait differently. While not the topic of this chapter, the ways people wait for infrastructure in Laos can reveal much about politics and power as well as about how modes of waiting are socially and culturally learned. Future work may also consider what else is suspended when the familiar practices of everyday life cannot be pursued and what this makes possible. Research must attend to the ways that deferral, waiting, and suspension act as means of securing transformation, progress, and speed; in the case of the railway, this entailed securing land for construction without adequate compensation or information. Doing so shows how temporal experiences expand the study of infrastructure by enhancing our understanding of infrastructural displacement as riddled with and a product of tensions from speed and suspension, hope and doubt, and waiting and uncertainty.

References

Adam, B. (1995) *Timework: A Social Analysis of Time*, Cambridge: Polity Press.

Adam, B. (2004) *Time*, Cambridge: Polity Press.

Anand, N., Gupta, A., and Appel, H. (eds) (2018) *The Promise of Infrastructure*, Durham, NC: Duke University Press.

Andersson, R. (2014) 'Time and the migrant other: European border controls and the temporal economics of illegality', *American Anthropologist*, 116(4): 795–809.

Appel, H. (2018) 'Infrastructural time', in N. Anand, A. Gupta, and H. Appel (eds) *The Promise of Infrastructure*, Durham, NC: Duke University Press, pp 41–61.

Auyero, J. (2012) *Patients of the State: The Politics of Waiting in Argentina*, Durham, NC: Duke University Press.

Bear, L. (2007) *Lines of the Nation: Indian Railway Workers, Bureaucracy, and the Intimate Historical Self*, New York: Columbia University Press.

Berlant, L. (2011) *Cruel Optimism*. London: Duke University Press.

Bissell, D. (2007) 'Animating suspension: Waiting for mobilities', *Mobilities*, 2(2): 277–98.

Bourdieu, P. (2000) *Pascalian Meditations*, Stanford, CA: Stanford University Press.

Brun, C. (2015) 'Active waiting and changing hopes: Toward a time perspective on protracted displacement', *Social Analysis*, 59(1): 19–37.

Carse, A., and Kneas, D. (2019) 'Unbuilt and unfinished: The temporalities of infrastructure', *Environment and Society*, 10(1): 9–28.

Comaroff, J., and Comaroff, J.L. (2001) *Millennial Capitalism and the Culture of Neoliberalism*, Durham, NC: Duke University Press.

DiCarlo, J. (2020) 'Mind the gap: Grounding development finance and safeguards through land compensation on the Laos–China Belt and Road corridor', *Global China Initiative Working Paper 013*. Boston University, Global Development Policy Center.

DiCarlo, J. (2021) 'Grounding global China in northern Laos: The making of the infrastructure frontier'. Doctoral dissertation, University of Colorado Boulder.

Foster, R. (2019) '"Doing the wait": An exploration into the waiting experiences of prisoners' families', *Time & Society*, 28(2): 459–77.

Geurts, A.P.H. (2019) 'Trains, bodies, landscapes: Experiencing distance in the long nineteenth century', *The Journal of Transport History*, 40(2): 165–88.

Green, N., and Baird, I. (2016) 'Capitalizing on compensation: Hydropower resettlement and the commodification and decommodification of nature–society relations in southern Laos', *Annals of the American Association of Geographers*, 106(4): 853–73.

Gupta, A. (2015) 'Suspension', Society for Cultural Anthropology. https://culanth.org/fieldsights/suspension (accessed 9 February 2023).

Gupta, A. (2018) 'The future in ruins: Thoughts on the temporalities of infrastructure', in N. Anand, A. Gupta, and H. Appel (eds) *The Promise of Infrastructure*, Durham, NC: Duke University Press, pp 63–79.

Hage, G. (2009a) 'Waiting out the crisis: On stuckness and governmentality', *Anthropological Theory*, 5(1): 463–75.

Hage, G. (ed) (2009b) *Waiting*, Melbourne: Melbourne University Publishing.

Harvey, D. (1989) *The Condition of Postmodernity: An Enquiry into the Origins of Cultural Change*, Oxford: Blackwell.

Janeja, M.K., and Bandak, A. (eds) (2018) *Ethnographies of Waiting: Doubt, Hope, and Uncertainty*, London: Routledge.

Joniak-Lüthi, A. (2019) 'Introduction: Infrastructure as an asynchronic timescape', *Roadsides*, 1: 3–10.

Lakha, S. (2009) 'Waiting to return home: Modes of immigrant waiting', in G. Hage (ed) *Waiting*, Carlton: Melbourne University Publishing, pp 121–34.

Lardner, D. (1850) *Railway Economy: A Treatise on the New Art of Transport, Its Management, Prospects and Relations*, London: Taylor, Walton and Maberly.

Levine, R. (1997) *A Geography of Time*, New York: Basic Books.

Mains, D. (2007) 'Neoliberal times: Progress, boredom, and shame among young men in urban Ethiopia', *American Ethnologist*, 34(4): 659–73.

Marcel, G. (1967) 'Desire and hope', in N. Lawrence and D. O'Connor (eds) *Readings in Existential Phenomenology*, Englewood Cliffs, NJ: Prentice-Hall.

Petit, P. (2017) 'Land, state, and society in Laos: Ethnographies of land policies', *World Food Policy Journal*, 4(1): 83–104.

Phnom Penh Post (2021) 'Luang Prabang railway station nearly 50% done', *Asia News Network*, 23 February.

Reeves, M. (2017) 'Infrastructural hope: Anticipating "independent roads" and territorial integrity in southern Kyrgyzstan', *Ethnos*, 82(4): 711–37.

Rippa, A. (2021) 'From boom to bust – to boom again? Infrastructural suspension and the making of a development zone at the China–Laos borderlands', in M. Chettri and M. Eilenberg (eds) *Development Zones in Asian Borderlands*, Amsterdam: University of Amsterdam Press, pp 231–52.

Rundell, J. (2009) 'Temporal horizons of modernity and modalities of waiting', in G. Hage (ed) *Waiting*, Melbourne: Melbourne University Press, pp 39–53.

Schivelbusch, W. (1978) 'Railroad space and railroad time', *New German Critique*, 14: 31–40.

Schwenkel, C. (2015) 'Spectacular infrastructure and its breakdown in socialist Vietnam', *American Ethnologist*, 42(3): 520–34.

Stoler, A.L. (2013) *Imperial Debris: On Ruins and Ruination*, Durham, NC: Duke University Press.

Straughan, E., Bissell, D., and Gorman-Murray, A. (2020) 'The politics of stuckness: Waiting lives in mobile worlds', *Environment and Planning C: Politics and Space*, 38(4): 636–55.

Suboticki, I., and Sørensen, K.H. (2018) 'Liminal technologies: Exploring the temporalities and struggles in efforts to develop a Belgrade metro', *The Sociological Review*, 69(1): 156–73.

Suhardiman, D., DiCarlo, J., Keovilignavong, O., Rigg, J., and Nicol, A. (2021) '(Re)constructing state power and livelihoods in the Laos–China Railway project', *Geoforum*, 124(2): 79–88.

Swartz, B. (1975) *Queuing and Waiting: Studies in the Social Organization of Access and Delay*, Chicago, IL: University of Chicago Press.

Turnbull, S. (2015) '"Stuck in the middle": Waiting and uncertainty in immigration detention', *Time & Society*, 25(1): 61–79.

Vientiane Times (2017). 'We told people not to carry out any construction or grow crops on land earmarked for the railway corridor to avoid losses', Vientiane Times, April.

Xinhua. (2019). 'Nearly 80 pct of China–Laos railway construction completed', *Xinhua Net*, 22 September.

Xu, D.Y. (2019) 'Chinese speed'. Doctoral dissertation, Massachusetts Institute of Technology.

11

Desynchronized Infrastructures of Care: Suburban Imaginaries Re-Examined

Samantha Biglieri and Roger Keil

Introduction: Time and infrastructure in the sick suburbs

This chapter examines the temporalities of infrastructure at the intersection of health, disease, and urbanization, especially peripheral, or extended, urbanization. At the start of 2020, we were set to study the life of people living with dementia (PLWD) in Toronto's immigrant suburbs. However, when the COVID-19 pandemic made that research temporarily impossible, we pivoted in our collaboration to the effect of COVID-19 on the urban peripheries of Toronto and Milan (Biglieri et al, 2020). This chapter draws from these two disparate research themes to present a rearticulation of our thinking around the 'forever time' that PLWD in suburbs may feel, and the presentism and ad hocism of the pandemic response. To make the connection between people experiencing the chronic, degenerative condition of dementia with those that suffered acute infection from COVID-19, we look at the suburban landscape of care in the Toronto region through a lens of infrastructural temporality.

Our analysis engages the theoretically distinct but intrinsically linked perspectives of understanding infrastructure through a temporal analytic and seeing time itself as an infrastructure. Although neither approach is new per se, we argue that reading across them allows us to examine inequalities across both time and space and to understand the massive differences in how socially constructed times influence and condition the way infrastructures '*materialize*' (Besedovsky et al, 2019; Coutard, this volume). In this chapter, we deploy a temporal analytic to examine how (sub)urban inequalities are created and perpetuated, especially for marginalized populations. Accentuating the temporal exposes structural inequities in regional infrastructures that are often hidden through performative and repetitive political discourses and processes that assign stereotypical roles and expectations to such places as inner cities and suburbs and the actors that inhabit them. Suburban landscapes, for instance, are often seen as lacking in ability to adapt to climate change and other systemic challenges but tend to remain both extensively burdened with infrastructure (from airports to waste dumps) and perpetually infrastructurally ill-equipped to deal with the growing 'urban' problematiques posed by suburban maturation and change.

Seeing time 'as an infrastructure', in turn, helps us critically assess who has time (a non-renewable resource) and how time itself is distributed. For example, people who can afford it may 'purchase time' through hiring service workers to complete everyday tasks (such as house cleaning) or socially reproductive labour (such as childcare and elder care), whereas those who cannot must do such tasks themselves (Dowling, 2021). Time can support and derail everyday life and just like other infrastructures is often allocated inequitably along class, gender, sexuality, race, ability, immigration status, and age lines. We utilize this concept to demonstrate the incompatibility of existing infrastructures on the periphery of Toronto with the needs of people who have fallen out of the 'normal' time frames for which those infrastructures were designed. We argue that in as much as infrastructures determine daily practice, both the immigrant suburban communities disproportionately affected by the COVID-19 pandemic and PLWD in the 'forever present' are left wanting. The infrastructures they have had at their disposal were not constructed and maintained to assist communities under the duress of a pandemic disease, or people who have 'fallen out of time'. Rather, they were built for and constantly reconfirm the 'normalcy' of healthy lives with their associated temporal rhythms and spatial dimensions.

Our cases – the COVID-19 vaccination roll-out in Brampton, Ontario, and the 'forever present' suburbanisms of PLWD – reflect differing sub/urban challenges as well as dichotomies in the temporal nature of disease (acute, fast, primarily affecting bodily functions vs chronic, degenerative, primarily affecting the mind); the scope, scale, and sociality of its impacts (a global pandemic vs private individual/family experiences); and response (global lockdowns and safety measures vs accessing various care services person-by-person). Yet their grounding in the context of Toronto's suburbs enables us to approach them comparatively as 'edge cases' to make our argument. Here, mobilizing a temporal analytic uncovers complementarities that require us to rethink the intersections of everyday life and infrastructure in ways that reveal new theoretical and practical multi-scalar connections.

Guided by Simone's insight that 'as infrastructure configures specific engagements and circuits of exchange and attention, sedentary positions will be unsettled and remade' (2012: np), we challenge the cultural hegemony of the suburban phantasmagoria of being 'frozen in time'. By drawing on literatures including suburban studies, critical geographies, critical dementia studies, disability studies, and the concept of 'crip time',[1] our comparative assessment of infrastructural temporality in Toronto's under-stress peripheries compels a re-examination of such conventional North American suburban imaginaries. We illustrate, for instance, that mobility infrastructures in suburbs were not built for ageing and disability and that health infrastructures in suburbs were not funded like those in the urban core – and we examine the implications of the 'othering' that both engender. However, while infrastructures change slowly and tend to perpetuate established practices (Coutard, this volume), both our cases demonstrate that infrastructural disadvantages can be subject to innovative action by communities and households that counteract the difficulties laid before them through quotidian agency. Conceptually, such counteraction reflects onto infrastructure's often assumed hermetic uniformity and reveals ways in which progressive infrastructure futures of a different kind can manifest.

The forever suburbs: Disposition and desynchronization

Suburbs are often seen to offer the promise of constant renewal and endless futures. Yet, in order to remain promised places of social mobility (an important aspect of the immigrant imaginary), they are written into the North American imagination as an unchanging, eternal place where the ideal life beckons (Keil, 2018). While considered largely stereotypical now, populations in suburbia and the built environments where they reside, shop, work, and play remain normatively frozen in some idealized space and time of eternal sunshine (or *noir*, depending on one's predisposition towards the urban periphery). The notion of the unchanging environment is pronounced in matters of infrastructure, which continue to centre around the private car and roadways. In this idealized space, tropes of whiteness, heteronormativity, family, youth, and health are upheld as the bedrock of community standards (and real estate values).

In reality, the time–space matrix of the suburbs is presenting a new pattern of inequality as more diverse communities have come to populate the periphery and as suburban populations have aged. Life in neoliberal suburbia entails an inequality that 'is more fragmented and invisible, because it takes place within a landscape designed to enhance patterns of private accumulation. The geography of this social dislocation is characterized by a marked absence of both public space and infrastructure' (Quinby, 2011: 51). More precisely, both public space and infrastructure are subservient to the culture of the automobile and the private home, and individuals attempting to move in such restricted landscapes are at a disadvantage if they do not have full access to its predispositions: the car and the tentacled landscape that sustains it.

Infrastructure is also a 'structure of time', and 'the time structures of a given society are inevitably encountered by its members as normative expectations' (Trejo-Mathys, 2015: xix). As such, Rosa argues that '[o]ne decisive advantage of temporal-analytic points of entry to social-theoretical questions [is] the fact that temporal structures and horizons represent one, if not *the*, systematic link between actor and system perspectives' (2015: 4). In our two cases, we see infrastructure-mediated desynchronization of structure and horizon at play (Rosa, 2015: 17). This desynchronization is linked to the destabilization of 'lived time', one of four components that philosopher Max van Manen said were integral to understanding someone's lifeworld (along with lived body, lived others, and lived space; see Ericksen et al, 2020).

Infrastructure spaces are well understood as 'fluid' (Easterling 2014: 241). This fluidity is a temporal dimension of infrastructure as its utility changes over time. It also refers to the subjectivity of infrastructures and the notion of 'mobility' as a complex and diverse amalgam of abilities and disabilities in accessing those structures. This approach is compatible with the now established 'mobilities paradigm' that recognizes the necessity of a 'mobile ontology' in which "*movement is primary as a foundational condition of being, space, subjects, and power*" (Sheller, 2018: 9, original emphasis). The 'specific constellations of uneven mobilities' (Sheller, 2018: 12) that organize mobility are built into the long-term time–space matrix of suburbia. Yet, as we show in the following case studies, they are also upset by the mobility and mutability of viruses as they move through time and space (per Lavau, 2014) and by the impacts of chronic disability on one's ability to navigate social-spatial-temporal worlds.

While it is the very purpose of a road or a sewer to carry expectations of the present into a future of possibilities, our two cases further test the suburbs' 'disposition' for such temporal imaginaries. For Easterling, disposition is:

> the character or propensity of an organization that results from all its activity. It is the medium, not the message. It is not the pattern printed on the fabric but the way the fabric floats. It is not the shape of the game piece but the way the game piece plays. It is not the text but the constantly updating software that manages the text. (Easterling, 2014: 21)

Easterling eventually speaks about the suburb-as-disposition, as 'an unfolding relationship between potentials' (2014: 72). If we insert the notion of time into this understanding of infrastructure disposition, it appears that it is through the agency and movements of 'multipliers, switches, or topologies'

(Easterling, 2014: 239) that infrastructure space is linked to infrastructure time. The metaphors here abound: circuit boards, matrices, operating systems, and so on all suggest movement through time and space that activates such infrastructures. In our cases, we show that some of those circuits are broken, matrices are corrupted, and operating systems are rendered dysfunctional. Indeed, both the ad hocism of the pandemic response and vaccine roll-out and the 'forever present' of life with dementia in the suburbs rebel against the futurist leanings of any infrastructure development. This links back to the notion of temporal structures and horizons and the disconnects of daily life through which infrastructures connect (or not) urban space and society.

Case #1: Brampton and the COVID-19 vaccine roll-out

Brampton is a suburban municipality of 650,000 in Peel Region, west of the city of Toronto. It is sandwiched spatially between a municipality of similar size, Mississauga (pop. 850,000), to its south and a rural municipality, Caledon (pop. 66,000), to its north. The municipality has strong economic and social relationships to Pearson International Airport to its south-east and has become home to many airport-related logistics and manufacturing companies, warehouses, and distribution centres. The Toronto suburbs have become not only the 'reception areas' for many immigrants, predominantly from Asia, but also growth centres for employment in manufacturing and service industries where immigrants find work (Fincher et al, 2019, chapter 4). Employment in Brampton stood at 310,435 in 2016. Manufacturing, transportation, and warehousing (by far the largest employment groups in the city) accounted for 87,000 (28 per cent) of those jobs (Statistics Canada, 2022). A *Toronto Star* article at the height of the first wave of COVID-19 infections laid out the stark realities of racialization in these industries, where they found 'a significant percentage of the South Asian workforce in the trucking sector, moving between hot spots in the U.S. and Canada regularly' (Vohra-Miller et al, 2020: np). The article noted that 'unstable, precarious jobs with limited employee benefits and minimal sick leave' was a common experience among Brampton's racialized workers, especially those from its South Asian communities (Vohra-Miller et al, 2020: np). A large percentage of the workforce in the warehouses and factories of the area is composed of international students from India, who arrive in a steady stream at universities and colleges in the Toronto region and find their home in Peel Region (Bascaramurty et al, 2021a).

In ways, Brampton is the model case for a differentiated post-Fordist suburban community where 'new urban forms on the periphery lead to new mixes and spatial contradictions associated ... with the new era of flexible production or post-Fordism' and where 'conflicting processes of growth and decline can occur synchronically' (Keil and Ronneberger, 1994: 142). It is the synchronicity, non-linearity, and temporal and spatial interconnectivity that are typical not just of communities such as Brampton but also of post-suburban landscapes more generally, where there is always too much and too little infrastructure (Keil and Young, 2014). In the context of this chapter, residents and workers often experience such incongruities as temporal failures: existing needs are not met by current infrastructures, and existing infrastructures (here we think about healthcare) are not just out of place but also don't correspond to the temporal rhythms of suburban life.

The synchronicity of Brampton's economy and society is written into the infrastructural landscape of a new economy powered by tech and e-commerce across North America. This includes 'the right sort of exurban communities to target: wealthy enough to support good schools for employees' kids, but also sufficiently insecure in their civic infrastructure and identity to be easy marks' (MacGillis, 2021: 182). A major logistical hub, Peel Region is also home to several fulfilment centres and expansive warehouses and additional ancillary sites supporting the logistics of modern consumption. Brampton's excellent location in the web of core mobility infrastructures cascading from the airport downward to the local warehouse has made the city a choice site for the burgeoning digital retail and logistics landscape that flourished during the pandemic.

During the pandemic, these often overlooked spaces became viscerally illuminated, both because of the crisis of localized COVID-19 hotspots and the dependency of the rest of the city on the deliveries from its suburban warehouses. The disposition of logistics infrastructures changed as they became visible. It became apparent that '[t]he new decentered space of the postmetropolis is everywhere, reconfiguring both centre and periphery within a new spatial and temporal order' (Quinby, 2011: 15). The post-metropolis (or suburbanized city) is characterized by layered temporalities and spatial interdependencies that reach across the region and into the global economy. It is structured by 'horizontal strategies of surveillance, dispersal and consumption' (Quinby, 2011: 139), with the latter holding it all together as a space 'dispositioned' for constant capital accumulation.

COVID-19 in Brampton

In the late summer of 2020, the urbanized parts of Peel Region west of Toronto (Brampton and Mississauga) emerged as COVID-19 hotspots in the city-region and province. First, the media focused on Brampton as a place of recent South Asian immigration and the cultural aspects of that process: the persistence of family- and business-related international travel, multigenerational households, and social gatherings for cultural or religious holidays were blamed for the high numbers of COVID-19 infections. The community's relationships with India continued to be highlighted in analyses of the high incidence of the Delta variant of the coronavirus (Ibrahim and Dickson, 2021). In Peel Region, 55 per cent of infections affected South Asians, who are just 32 per cent of the area's population (Bascaramurty et al, 2021b), and on the surface, the connections to the subcontinent and cultural factors seemed plausible pathways of infection. But healthcare workers and community leaders in the South Asian community pointed to political and structural factors instead: "You have an area that's under-resourced, under-supported and then you throw a pandemic at it" (Gurpreet Malhotra, executive director of Indus Community Services, cited in Nasser, 2020).

The problem of heightened infection rates in the community was most pronounced in an area of north-eastern Brampton named after its postal code, L6P (see Figure 11.1). In L6P, 89 per cent of residents are racialized, and 66 per cent are South Asian. The median household income is C$102,070, which is 45 per cent higher than the national average, but only because in many homes several workers pool their earnings. The median individual income is just C$26,139. After the first wave of COVID-19, data made clear that race and class were driving forces of the pandemic: precarious employment, lack of paid sick leave, and crowded or multigenerational housing put people at risk for infection and hospitalization. In the third wave, those statistics remained unchanged. L6P has carried an outsized burden. Residents doing essential work could not stay home. As a result, the test positivity rate has hovered above 20 per cent during the time of peak infection in 2020 and 2021 (Bascaramurty and Bhatt, 2021).

The population of this part of Brampton is therefore caught in a debilitating rearrangement of the time–space matrix that usually supports their lives both in the rhythms of the everyday and in their life course. Desynchronization of structures of time and time horizons characterizes all aspects of their existence. While the health crisis compromised the immigrant communities' normal diasporic connectivities (for example, the connections to family and businesses in their countries of origin due to flight cancellations and border closures), it demanded heightened activity for those in the community who are essential workers. Even as the US border was closed for non-essential travel, it remained open (with difficulties) for thousands of long-haul truck drivers in the region who crossed it hauling food and other essential goods from Canada's southern neighbour. The large warehouses and production sites in the region provided a locked down metropolitan region with the supplies it needed. Inside the hotspots, other essential workers, especially those in care fields, scrambled to stay on top of their demanding daily schedules in an environment of weakened healthcare resources. As early as six weeks before the pandemic was declared by the World Health Organization, a local newspaper reported that Brampton was 'lagging well behind Mississauga, Etobicoke in health-care funding' and declared a health

Figure 11.1: Distribution of COVID-19 infections in Toronto and suburbs on 10 April 2021

Source: Map by Chen Wang, published in Bascaramurty and Bhatt, 2021

emergency (Frisque, 2020), a condition that was highlighted and exacerbated by the pandemic (White Coat, Black Art, 2020).

The lack of resources and support for this COVID-19 hotspot, which translated into a systemic infrastructural crisis, had existed before the pandemic but was exacerbated during the health emergency. As early as January 2020, CBC News (2020) reported, 'Brampton council declare[d] health care emergency' and pronounced that patients at Brampton Civic hospital were 'dying in the hallways', all attributed to the gross underfunding of the institution, which is part of a regional health system with the lowest per capita funding in the province, for 'years and years' (Nasser, 2020). This systemic condition demonstrated, in the eyes of many, the area's peripheral status on the immigration and settlement schedule in Canada's largest metropolitan area. We argue that the structural deficiencies in the healthcare infrastructure created the conditions for a perfect storm when coupled with the equally systemic and institutional racialization of the area's workforce in precarious employment, a population that also relied on overcrowded housing and public transportation.

High infection rates were mirrored by unequal vaccine roll-out across the region, which saw the least affected parts of the area served first by vaccinations. Only later were dedicated and targeted programmes put in place to vaccinate essential workers and BIPOC (black, indigenous, and other people of colour) communities in the affected areas, which narrowed the vaccine gap temporarily until it widened again in late May and early June. Starting in January 2021, community actors began to make the case for priority vaccine access for 'hotspot areas'. The provincial government responded by identifying hotspots but without prior consultation or coordination with municipalities.

The vaccine roll-out, with its ad hoc character, was no match for the structural gap between the gravity of the situation in Brampton and the perennial underfunding of the existing public health infrastructure. In this sense, infrastructural times collided in the systems that were available. While there were fundamental deficits in care that had persisted for years, the sudden spurt of pop-up vaccination clinics could not fully solve the problem, although it did have a significant impact and showed once more the dedication of public health staff and community volunteers to make up for gross government failure. Dozens of such clinics were active starting in April but the mayor of Brampton, Patrick Brown, noted that "a hundred more" could be accommodated (although there were not enough vaccines available to do so). Like everywhere in the highly culturally diverse suburban Toronto region, community vaccine ambassadors supported the pop-up effort by providing a popular infrastructure for propagating the vaccination effort in areas that might not respond to information provided in the English mainstream media (Jeyasundaram, 2021). Additionally, workplace pop-up vaccination took place at meatpacking plants (Maple Leaf) and warehouses (Amazon), which added to the overall improvement of the situation in May 2021.

Drawing infrastructural temporalities from the Brampton case

Overall, this experience points to two aspects of infrastructural temporalities. Firstly, the appearance of speed and flexibility implied in the notion of pop-up vaccination ran up against the fundamental inertia of the gross healthcare inequalities and structural socio-spatial inequities permanently baked into the landscape of Brampton and Peel Region. Infrastructures (in this case that of healthcare institutions and delivery) had a disposition that was not conducive to providing an equitable and successful pandemic response. The ultimate reversal of the trend that saw racialized immigrant communities as particularly vulnerable originated in the persistence of community-based organizations. These groups deployed strategies for vaccine roll-out and culturally sensitive educational campaigns that changed the rhythm of service delivery and the temporal and spatial logic of the response overall. Secondly, the mobility of the virus in the community meant that the vaccination response was ultimately in a race against the virus' mutation into different variants (Lavau, 2014). The pop-up infrastructure was the main strategy to stem the spread of the Delta variant. While it appeared to be too little too late, and while some noted that it might lose the race with the variant, others were convinced of the eventual contribution the strategy would make:

> 'At first we were saying the roll-out was too slow and now we're saying "it's just one dose" and it's eroding what is actually a miraculous intervention. No one ever said the vaccines would bring COVID cases down to zero. ... [W]e expect to see small flareups here and there but they will be naturally different with vaccine and a flareup does not mean we have to lock down the community.' (Dr Sumon Chakrabarti, an infectious disease specialist at Trillium Health Partners in Mississauga, cited in Newport, 2021)

The mobility–mutation dynamics brought to light the changed role of Brampton in the imaginary of the COVID-19 response. The once forgotten and ill-understood suburban 'hotspot', rich in mobility infrastructures, logistics, and manufacturing, became recast as the 'vanguard' of the vaccination strategy in the race against challenges brought on by the new variant. Dr Peter Jüni, the former scientific director of the Ontario government's Science Advisory Table, used an explicit temporal frame when noting that Peel Region was "about three weeks ahead" of other parts of Ontario in the spread of the Delta variant in the community on account of having "the most challenging living conditions, working conditions, et cetera" for halting the disease spread (cited in Flanagan, 2021).

The ad hocism of the vaccine roll-out in vulnerable communities is, however, also a clear answer to Simone's (2012) defining question: 'what is that we can do together?' The disadvantages created by the broken spatial matrix of infrastructure and desynchronized operating systems of healthcare and pandemic response were offset by the swift reaction of local communities in providing a different temporal logic in response. Consequently, circuits were restored, matrices fixed, and operating systems fired up when needed at the scale of individual bodies and the community overall. The disconnected rhythms of daily life through which infrastructures connect were rejoined through community action in times of emergency and crisis response.

Case #2: dementia, time, and care

In the idealized suburbanized space of youth, family, whiteness, heteronormativity, and health, living with dementia is not something that people might think 'happens' in the suburbs. Dementia typically occurs in older adults (as well as some people as young as 40), after they have retired and their children have moved out of their houses. Many assume that PLWD live in congregate settings such as specialized care homes and facilities. However, Canadian estimates show that two-thirds live at home in the community. Dementia is an umbrella term describing symptoms including short- and long-term memory loss; issues with navigation, time perception, depth perception, and judgement; and being overwhelmed easily by noise and activity. The impact of these symptoms on people's spatial and temporal perception means that we need to consider how neighbourhood infrastructures support (or stop) people living with dementia from accessing these spaces. Helping PLWD maintain access to their neighbourhood has many benefits: more social interaction, supporting a sense of worth and dignity, and improved mental/physical health (Ward et al, 2022). In this case, we assess these infrastructures through a temporal frame, in addition to examining the intersections of two spatial-temporal imaginaries: (1) a seemingly unchanging image of suburbia (and its rapidly changing demographic and structural reality); and (2) the simultaneous acceleration and deceleration of the 'forever present' everyday lives of PLWD in the suburbs.

Studying the temporalities of PLWD is crucial for understanding their lived experiences and how best to support them 'in terms of enabling people to process and manage the dementia journey' (Ericksen et al, 2020: 451). Lived (experiences of) time is particularly pertinent to PLWD because:

- dementia affects the hippocampus (the body's internal clock), meaning that PLWD might wake up in the middle of the night to go for a walk; not be able to keep track of time passing; and do not know the day, month, or year;
- memory is impacted, affecting one's ability to recall past events and people/places, and/or the chronology of one's life;
- they are more likely to live in a facility or participate in day programmes that are 'ruled' by the clock (for example, lunch at 12:00–12:30 pm) instead of allowing the person to dictate the pace;
- people diagnosed with dementia talk about losing time in the context of the 'typical' lifecourse (Ericksen et al, 2020).

PLWD experience 'lived time' in all three dimensions (past, present, and future) with particular characteristics: identity as rooted in the past; focusing energy on the present; contemplating the future; and experiencing changes in themselves over time (Erickson et al, 2020). In addition, here we see the kinds of processes whereby modernity has led to an 'acceleration of social change ... defined as an increase of the rate of decay of action-orienting experiences and expectations' (Rosa, 2015: 76).

Time, care infrastructures, and the stigmatization of dementia

PLWD face immense stigma of presumed incompetence/incapacity and persistent advocacy using 'dementia as a tragedy' discourse (Bartlett and O'Connor, 2010; Swaffer, 2014). This socio-cultural-political structurization of stigma negatively impacts quality of life (Herrmann et al, 2018), and eliminating it is key to building inclusive communities (PHAC, 2019). Dementia stigma is centred on a normative understanding of time and the socially constructed link between a sense of self and time. PLWD are perceived as 'not being in control' and 'losing oneself' due to their symptoms of short-term and long-term memory loss. This brings with it profound implications for the social acceptability of the disease, reflected in the persistent language used to describe PLWD as sufferers 'doomed, gutted, ravaged, taken over by a beast, and ... the living dead', perpetuating the tragedy discourse (Mitchell et al, 2013: 2).

Hierarchies of disability acceptance have long been challenged by disability studies scholars as socially constructed and harmful to understanding the human condition, which is far more fluid and episodic than the mainstream understanding of what doing and being as human entails. They have questioned normative ableist understandings of time, theorizing *crip time* to complicate these assumptions (Samuels, 2017) and 'unravel the social construction of ability' (Ljuslunder et al, 2020: 36). 'Crip time' can be understood as a way to explain why some tasks take longer compared with ableist time; a way to discuss what society claims is 'wasted time', or unproductive/slow time; and as an analytical tool for examining other temporalities that do not line up with 'fixed' normative temporalities (Baril, 2016; Ljuslinder et al, 2020). We speculate that the stigmatization of dementia is influenced by normative ableist assumptions about linear time, the lifecourse process, and ableist assumptions about what constitutes a sense of self. This also makes sense if we engage time and memory as a form of infrastructure to support 'sense of self' and everyday life and mobility that can be adapted to suit different needs.

Memory and familiarity as infrastructures produced through time

Memories are fluid, temporal, embodied, and emotional. They are often tied to certain infrastructures, be they particular places that evoke smells from childhood or visiting/seeing photos of the neighbourhood they grew up in. Memories (and the complex aspects that make them) can also be considered a form of infrastructure that supports us in making sense of the past, present, and future. These examples of 'cueing' memory are types of therapeutic interventions that are used with PLWD. Such familiar supports are a type of infrastructure and can teach us about how memory-as-infrastructure is heterogeneous and can be experienced, remembered, and used in different ways.

Familiarity is the factor most often cited by PLWD for feeling comfortable in their own neighbourhoods. It is produced through time and actively embodied through everyday experiences of moving within neighbourhood space. PLWD in suburban neighbourhoods talk about how they have lived in the same place for decades, or grew up in a similar suburb, and how that influences their sense of familiarity today (Biglieri and Dean, 2021). Familiarity is practised through repetitive actions and routines (visiting the same café on multiple days of the week) and experienced as a whole (knowing the neighbourhood) (Margot-Cattin et al, 2021). A form of supportive infrastructure, the production of familiarity through time (past, present, future) in place for PLWD is also precarious. To use our metaphor, it is an example of a circuit board of supportive infrastructure rendered vulnerable to dysfunction and corruption: familiarity may be challenged through minor alterations in the built environment (Brorsson et al, 2011) and exacerbated by risky situations or unsupportive built infrastructures (Biglieri and Dean, 2022), resulting in inhibited mobility for PLWD.

Conceptualizing familiarity and memory as produced through 'time as infrastructure' must also acknowledge the relationship between our bodies' sensorial capacities and space because this process is much quicker than the time it takes for our cognitive selves to comprehend (Andrews et al, 2013). This is a relationship between bodies and human and more-than-human others, but it also acknowledges that these relationships can be different for each individual. This gut feeling is how we relate to the world, and this concept of affect is particularly salient for someone living with dementia. Current research demonstrates that even with the progression of the condition, and the loss of specific memories of events, PLWD continue to remember how a person or place makes them feel. The fact that our relationships with spaces and places are shaped by our own histories and experiences means that studies need to continue to be done that examine PLWD's gut reaction to space and infrastructures, as it can tell us more about how to build accessible and inclusive communities.

(Re)making spaces to adapt to daily bodily rhythms

Dementia is a degenerative set of symptoms, meaning that they change and become more pronounced over time. PLWD have good and bad days, but they also experience an increased sense of vulnerability, for instance, in the outdoors (Bartlett and Brannelly, 2019). PLWD experience a 'shrinking world' effect (Duggan et al, 2008), meaning that their literal and metaphorical communities and neighbourhoods get smaller as the symptoms progress. This is caused by both individual (changing abilities, reduced confidence) and structural factors (unsafe community design and physical infrastructures; stigma and fear of mental illness). However, PLWD have been found in small-scale studies to be actively resisting this 'shrinking world' effect by changing their everyday practices in neighbourhoods, such as building new friendships, joining organizations, and walking in their communities (Odzakovic et al, 2021). PLWD are also actively (re)making spaces to adapt to their changing daily bodily rhythms in a variety of ways (Bowlby, 2012; Biglieri, 2021). This is in response to a realization that their daily rhythms no longer 'adhere' to ableist understandings of time and mobilities of everyday life (Addie, this volume). This changing nature of time (condensing, expanding) when living with degenerative disease makes it more difficult to build, maintain, and change one's multi-scalar care infrastructures of support to enable one to continue to move within one's neighbourhood.

This (re)making of spaces to suit one's new-found realities is a true example of the capacity of the human condition to inform our design of infrastructures (Biglieri, 2021). A temporal frame plays a key role, and understanding how diverse 'bodyminds' experience infrastructures can tell us about whom they were built for and whom they actively exclude. Take mobility. It is important to understand mobility not just as getting from A to B, but also as the time that it takes to get there. *Crip time* explains how travel that takes an able-bodied person X amount of time requires more time for a disabled person, because infrastructure is inaccessible. An oft-cited example is encountering a broken lift at your subway stop when you use a mobility device and having to figure out an alternate route. This is a way of seeing time as infrastructure, something that able-bodied people tend to have more access to than disabled folks. For PLWD, more time is required to accomplish things that they used to do without thinking or without conscious effort. A trip to the grocery store for a PLWD requires planning out every step carefully, and with reminders: making a shopping list, remembering keys, remembering how to get there, shopping, and carrying the items home/remembering how to navigate there (Brorsson et al, 2011). PLWD also take more time when crossing a street or intersection as they can feel overwhelmed by the noise and activity and must break down the steps of crossing into smaller parts in order to feel safe (Biglieri and Dean, 2021).

Suburban landscapes are made to prioritize the movement and time of cars and the infrastructures that enable their movement (see also Thorpe, this volume). Even when pedestrians are thought of, ableist notions of 'normate' space-time predominate and consequently create barriers to using infrastructure for disabled populations, for instance, an all-way intersection with signalized lights for cars and pedestrians, including a zebra crossing and a countdown for pedestrians to cross the street. I (Samantha) thought PLWD might prefer this signalized, protected intersection, but the opposite was true. PLWD talked about how they preferred to cross at medians farther up the road because it enabled them to only have to pay attention to one 'input' at a time (cars travelling in one direction) before resting and doing it again (see Figure 11.2). This contrasted with crossing at the intersection where they had to negotiate cars zooming past, cars turning right and left, the red/yellow/green lights, the pedestrian symbols and flashing countdown, staying inside the zebra crossing zone, and not running into people crossing from the other direction. It was their way of controlling the spatial-temporal environment to suit their abilities (Biglieri and Dean, 2021, 2022). By using a temporal analytic frame, we can think of infrastructures as working for some, but not all. It helps us slow down to think about what would make those journeys less stressful and easier. Perhaps it is better signage for wayfinding, less overwhelming intersections with indicators that prioritize pedestrians without being complicated, and prioritizing accessibility (and meaningful engagement with disabled people) in infrastructure investments. Infrastructures must be viewed from the

Figure 11.2: Crossing at the median in the Region of Waterloo, Ontario, 2018

Source: Samantha Biglieri

perspectives of the most marginalized because all too often they are built for the 'normate' (Garland-Thompson, 1996).

Conclusion: Suburban landscapes of care through time

Our studies of suburban landscapes of care in Toronto underline both how infrastructures '*materialize*' and how they entail 'normative expectations' (Trejo-Mathys, 2015) that are linked to particular uses of time and space. The response to the COVID-19 pandemic and realities of living with dementia illustrate the ways in which some people and communities have 'fallen out' of the time regimes associated with the infrastructures that were ostensibly there to serve and care for them. These cases demonstrate the need to recognize the multiplicity of temporalities, reject universalistic notions of time, and re-examine the study of everyday life and infrastructure across diverse urban settings.

Our cases speak to different but colliding understandings of time in a multitude of respects, from disease type and speed to mobilities, temporalities, disposition, and desynchronization. There are marked differences between the two groups whose lives have been affected by dementia and COVID-19. For instance, chronic conditions such as dementia are usually seen as frozen in time, with afflicted persons as deteriorating and tragic, while the (emerging) infectious disease response (through vaccination) is cast as dynamic and, in terms of responses to it, hopeful, especially after widespread vaccination took hold early in 2021. Yet there are similarities as both conditions have potentially increased the marginality of impacted individuals and communities through scapegoating and racism, ageism, and ableism. Those with both dementia and COVID-19 are found predominantly among older individuals. Those racialized as non-White and those who are immigrants are unlikely to be involved in research (leading to critical gaps and to these populations being underserved), while the virus infected predominantly BIPOC individuals – often tied to essential industries – in the suburbs we studied. Dementia 'others' people to the point of systematic exclusion from everyday life. COVID-19 has found most of its victims in economically and socially vulnerable communities in the social, spatial, and institutional peripheries of the urban area, and it has contributed to the further destabilization of poor, immigrant, racialized communities across the Toronto region (Biglieri et al, 2020).

Engaging the concept of 'infrastructure time' not only enables us to expose the role of infrastructure itself in identifying and transforming structural inequities but also allows us to rethink the study of everyday life and infrastructure(s). Firstly, conceptualizing 'time as infrastructure' shows how building pop-up healthcare infrastructure(s) in high infection risk areas (warehouses, essential workplaces) aided workers to be protected against the virus when they could not access other community clinics due to their jobs. For PLWD, suburban landscapes of memory and familiarity are cited as significant supports enabling them to continue to effectively live in their community: a form of infrastructure produced through time. Secondly, in using time to measure inequities in society, Brampton shows starkly inequitable living conditions of essential workers and just-in-time producers compared with the white-collar workers who could 'work from home' during the pandemic and needed online ordering and products to stay safe. The temporal analytic of *crip time* further enables us to expose caring and uncaring infrastructures in terms of access to communities for people living with dementia. These cases therefore exemplify that it is 'normate' privileged people that can access more time infrastructure because of how we have structured society.

Time in the sick suburbs challenges the imaginary of suburbia as an unchanging, heteronormative phantasmagoria through the experience of desynchronization. Infrastructural times are produced and lived in heterodox, desynchronized ways across suburban landscapes. Dementia and COVID-19 disclose infrastructural space-times that are rapidly being accelerated and decelerated. The life of PLWD tends to decelerate and slow down as their symptoms progress, but it also accelerates as the typical lifecourse and sense of 'time left' shrinks. Similarly, life under COVID-19 accelerated for many, as essential workers had to meet the demand on their services and were unable to transition to home-based work or move out of hotspots, temporarily or for good. The different pace and direction of acceleration is mirrored by the kinds of treatments that are administered: slow (or lack of) investment and provision of health and social care services and accessible infrastructures for PLWD compared with a 'rush' towards vaccines for the communities affected by SARS-CoV-2. But the sense of temporality shifted most pronouncedly for the communities under COVID-19, as what was first seen as an 'event' rather than a permanent affliction dragged on through three consecutive 'waves' of infection, each one worse and longer-lasting than the last, with an uncertain environment of pandemic response governing the way those changes were experienced. This contrasts with the slow, changing notions of (crip) time for PLWD.

The suburbs' infrastructural 'disposition' reveals itself to be characterized by the need for continuity and stability in the face of growing disconnection while being marked by change, instability, and connectivity. Yet as our cases reveal, its infrastructures tend to leave out bodies that do not fit the 'normate'. On the one hand, we have shown that the tempos of everyday lives that suburban infrastructures have been 'dispositioned for' are out of sync with the needs of vulnerable populations during a pandemic and those of PLWD. On the other hand, our cases also include interventions by users and providers of infrastructure services (vaccination, care, and so on) that have made a difference. There is the potential to reconcile the dispositions of infrastructures with the demands of the rhythms of life of the affected communities: circuits of infrastructures can be broken and corrupted, but it is possible to work together to repair and care for them. Infrastructural agency matters. Here we see the confirmation of Rosa's (2015: 4) idea that a temporal lens might provide '*the* systematic link between actor and system perspectives'. This is evident in how the dispositions of infrastructural pasts influence the future, showing how familiarity is (re)produced by PLWD through emotional, embodied, and experiential linkages to place that continue to shape their lifeworlds and cognitive maps long after that person's abilities have changed or the infrastructure itself is deteriorated or gone. Paying attention to memory as infrastructure(s) through time (past, present, future, and constantly changing) allows us to think about diverse everyday experiences of infrastructure, upending classic 'modernist' views of infrastructure and showing both the limits and the potential of what Coutard (this volume) terms 'infrastructure-based futuring'.

In concluding, we suggest that one way to materialize infrastructures in support of excluded communities is to engage with 'crip near-futures' (Ignagni et al, 2019). This way of 'futuring' infrastructure in the near term *with* the people most likely to be excluded by it has transformative potential:

> It is a future close enough for our individual experience to be and remain directly relevant, yet distant enough that the boundaries of our experience could be 'cripped' – expanded, revised or ruptured – by technological trends. Crip near futures also promise our survival and reference our resilience in the face of past and present ableist violence. Our presence in a crip near future suggests that we have somehow disrupted the current normative order. (Ignagni et al, 2019: 292–3)

This framing acknowledges how people can experience infrastructures in diverse ways based on a variety of factors and recognizes that our infrastructural lives are not fixed in time but rather are fluid throughout our varied lifecourses. Crip near-futures can also illuminate how people often at the social and spatial peripheries are forced to reshape their own everyday spaces and rhythms due to structural barriers created by infrastructures. In response, animating an ethic of care lens (Biglieri, 2021) can enable time and infrastructural issues to bubble to the surface through an understanding of how individuals reshape/hack their worlds. With this, we can work to centre the infrastructural pasts, everyday lives, and futures of those living at the peripheries of society within the processes of making urban worlds.

Note

[1] Crip has been used as a pejorative term to stigmatize and oppress disabled people. However, there are disabled folks who have reclaimed the word to assert social power (Hutcheon and Wolbring, 2013).

References

Andrews, G.J., Evans, J., and Wiles, J.L. (2013) 'Re-spacing the re-placing gerontology: Relationality and affect', *Aging & Society*, 33(8): 1339–73.

Baril, A. (2016) '"Doctor, am I an Anglophone trapped in a Francophone body?" An intersextional analysis of "trans-frip-t time" in ableist, cisnormative, anglonormative societies', *Journal of Literary & Cultural Disability Studies*, 10(2): 155–72.

Bartlett, R., and Brannelly, T. (2019) 'On being outdoors: How people with dementia experience and deal with vulnerabilities', *Social Science Medicine*. https://doi.org/10.1016/j.socscimed.2019.05.041.

Bartlett, R., and O'Connor, D. (2010) *Broadening the Dementia Debate: Towards Social Citizenship*, Bristol: Policy Press.

Bascaramurty, D., and Bhatt, V. (2021) 'Impossible choices: How this Brampton community explains Canada's COVID-19 crisis like no other', *The Globe and Mail*, 20 May. https://www.theglobeandmail.com/canada/article-l6p-brampton-english/ (accessed 13 December 2022).

Bascaramurty, D., Bhatt, N., and Rana, U. (2021a) 'Canada's international student recruiting machine is broken', *The Globe and Mail*, 4 November. https://www.theglobeandmail.com/canada/article-india-canada-international-student-recruitment/ (accessed 13 December 2022).

Bascaramurty, D., Grant, K., and Nouser, M. (2021b) 'Vaccine hesitancy raises alarms as COVID-19's highly contagious Delta variant spreads in Brampton', *The Globe and Mail*, 7 June. https://www.theglobeandmail.com/canada/article-vaccine-hesitancy-raises-alarms-as-covid-19s-highly-contagious-delta/ (accessed 13 December 2022).

Besedovsky, N., Grafe, F.J., Hilbrandt, H., and Langguth, H. (2019) 'Time as infrastructure: For an analysis of contemporary urbanization', *City*, 23(4–5): 580–8.

Biglieri, S. (2021) 'Examining everyday outdoor practices in suburban public space: The case for an expanded definition of care as an analytical framework', in A. Gabauer, S. Knierbein, N. Cohen, H. Lebuhn, K. Trogal, T. Viderman, and T. Haas (eds) *Care and the City: Encounters with Urban Studies*, London: Routledge, pp 88–100.

Biglieri, S., and Dean, J. (2021) 'Everyday built environments of care: Examining the socio-spatial relationalities of suburban neighbourhoods for people living with dementia', *Wellbeing, Space and Society*, 2: 100058.

Biglieri, S., and Dean, J. (2022) 'Fostering mobility for people living with dementia in suburban neighborhoods through land use, urban design and wayfinding', *Journal of Planning Education and Research*, https://doi.org/10.1177/0739456X2211137

Biglieri, S., De Vidovich, L., and Keil, R. (2020) 'City as the core of contagion? Repositioning COVID-19 at the social and spatial periphery of urban society', *Cities & Health*, 5(sup1): s63–s65.

Bowlby, S. (2012) 'Recognising the time-space dimensions of care: Caringscapes and carescapes', *Environment and Planning A: Economy and Space*, 44(9): 2101–18.

Brorsson, A., Öhman, A., Lundberg, S., and Nygård, L. (2011) 'Accessibility in public space as perceived by people with Alzheimer's disease', *Dementia*, 10(4): 587–602.

CBC News (2020) 'Patrick Brown, Brampton council declare health care emergency', 22 January. https://www.cbc.ca/news/canada/toronto/brampton-health-emergency-declaration-1.5436518 (accessed 13 December 2022).

Dowling, E. (2021) *The Care Crisis: What Caused It and How Can We End It?*, London: Verso.

Duggan, S., Blackman, T., Martyr, A., and Van Schaik, P. (2008) 'The impact of early dementia on outdoor life: A "shrinking world"?', *Dementia*, 7(2): 191–204.

Easterling, K. (2014) *Extrastatecraft: The Power of Infrastructure Space*, London: Verso.

Fincher, R., Iveson, K., Leitner, H., and Preston, V. (2019) *Everyday Equalities: Making Multicultures in Settler Colonial Cities*, Minneapolis, MN: University of Minnesota Press.

Flanagan, R. (2021) 'The coronavirus "delta variant" that could spark a fourth wave', CTV News, 2 June. https://www.ctvnews.ca/health/coronavirus/b-1-617-the-coronavirus-delta-variant-that-could-spark-a-fourth-wave-1.5453176 (accessed 13 December 2022).

Frisque, G. (2020) 'Brampton lagging well behind Mississauga, Etobicoke in health-care funding', *Brampton Guardian*, 2 February. https://www.bramptonguardian.com/news-story/9835772-brampton-lagging-well-behind-mississauga-etobicoke-in-health-care-funding/ (accessed 13 December 2022).

Garland-Thomson, R. (ed) (1996) *Freakery: Cultural Spectacles of the Extraordinary Body*, New York: New York University Press.

Herrmann, L.K., Welter, E., Leverenz, J., Lerner, A.J., Udelson, N., Kanetsky, C. et al (2018) 'A systematic review of dementia-related stigma research: Can we move the stigma dial?', *The American Journal of Geriatric Psychiatry*, 26(3): 316–31.

Hutcheon, E., and Wolbring, G. (2013) '"Cripping" resilience: Contributions from disability studies to resilience theory', *M/C Journal*, 16(5). https://doi.org/10.5204/mcj.697

Ibrahim, E., and Dickson, J. (2021) 'Flight ban leaves travellers from India, Pakistan in limbo', *The Globe and Mail*, 9 June. https://www.theglobeandmail.com/politics/article-flight-ban-leaves-travellers-from-india-pakistan-in-limbo/ (accessed 13 December 2022).

Ignagni, E., Chandler, E., Collins, K., Darby, A., and Liddiard, K. (2019) 'Designing access together: Surviving the demand for resilience', *Canadian Journal of Disability Studies*, 8(4): 293–320.

Jeyasundaram, B. (2021) 'Community ambassadors are the link to Toronto's unvaccinated populations', *Next City*, 14 June. https://nextcity.org/daily/entry/community-ambassadors-are-the-link-to-torontos-unvaccinated-populations?utm_source=Next+City+Newsletter&utm_campaign=e4065fedf5-Issue_482_COPY_01&utm_medium=email&utm_term=0_fcee5bf7a0-e4065fedf5-43829985 (accessed 13 December 2022).

Keil, R. (2018) 'Paved paradise: The suburb as chief artefact of the Anthropocene and terrain of new political performativities', in H. Ernstson and E. Swyngedouw (eds) *Urban Political Ecology in the Anthropo-obscene*, London: Routledge, pp 165–83.

Keil, R., and Ronneberger, K. (1994) 'Going up the country: Internationalization and urbanization on Frankfurt's northern fringe', *Environment and Planning D: Society and Space*, 12(2): 137–66.

Keil, R., and Young, D. (2014) 'In-between mobility in Toronto's new (sub)urban neighborhoods', in P. Watt and P. Smeets (eds) *Mobilities and Neighborhood Belonging in Cities and Suburbs*, London: Palgrave Macmillan, pp 201–21.

Lavau, S. (2014) 'Viruses', in P. Adey, D. Bissell, K. Hannam, P. Merriman, and M. Sheller (eds) *The Routledge Handbook of Mobilities*, London: Routledge, pp 298–305.

Ljuslinder, K., Ellis, K., and Vikström, L. (2020) 'Cripping time – understanding the life course through the lens of ableism', *Scandinavian Journal of Disability Research*, 22(1): 35–8.

MacGillis, A. (2021) *Fulfillment: Winning and Losing in One-Click America*, New York: Farrar, Straus and Giroux.

Margot-Cattin, I., Ludwig, C., Kühne, N., Eriksson, G., Berchtold, A., Nygard, L. et al (2021) 'Visiting out-of-home places when living with dementia: A cross-sectional observational study', *Canadian Journal of Occupational Therapy*, 88(2): 131–41.

Mitchell, G.J., Dupuis, S.L., and Kontos, P. (2013) 'Dementia discourse: From imposed suffering to knowing other-wise', *Journal of Applied Hermeneutics*, Article 5: 1–19.

Nasser, S. (2020) 'Brampton has emerged as one of Ontario's COVID-19 hotspots, but experts urge caution on where to lay blame', *CBC News*, 14 September. https://www.cbc.ca/news/canada/toronto/brampton-coronavirus-covid-19-south-asian-1.5723330 (accessed 13 December 2022).

Newport, A. (2021) 'Vaccines will blunt impact of new variant, says infectious disease specialist in Mississauga', *insauga*, 5 June. https://www.insauga.com/infectious-disease-specialist-in-mississauga-hopeful-about-future-says-vaccines-will-blunt-impact-of (accessed 13 December 2022).

Odzakovic, E., Hellström, I., Nedlund, A.-C., and Kullberg, A. (2021) 'Health promotion initiative: A dementia-friendly local community in Sweden', *Dementia*, 20(6): 1971–87.

PHAC (Public Health Authority of Canada) (2019) *A Dementia Strategy for Canada: Together We Aspire*, Ottawa: Public Health Authority of Canada.

Quinby, R. (2011) *Time and the Suburbs: The Politics of Built Environments and the Future of Dissent*, Winnipeg: ARP.

Rosa, H. (2015) *Social Acceleration: A New Theory of Modernity*, New York: Columbia University Press.

Samuels, E. (2017) 'Six ways of looking at crip time', *Disability Studies Quarterly*, 37(3). https://dsq-sds.org/article/view/5824 (accessed 29 February 2022).

Sheller, M. (2018) *Mobility Justice: The Politics of Movement in an Age of Extremes*, London: Verso.

Simone, A.M. (2012) 'Infrastructure: Commentary', *Cultural Anthropology*. https://journal.culanth.org/index.php/ca/infrastructure-abdoumaliq-simone (accessed 29 February 2022).

Statistics Canada (2022) 'Brampton Census profile, 2016 Census'. https://www12.statcan.gc.ca/census-recensement/2016/dp-pd/prof/details/Page.cfm?Lang=E&Geo1=CSD&Code1=3521010&Geo2=PR&Code2=35&Data=Count&SearchText=Toronto&SearchType=Begins&SearchPR=01&B1=All (accessed 13 December 2022).

Swaffer, K. (2014) 'Dementia: Stigma, language, and dementia-friendly', *Dementia*, 13(6): 709–16.

Trejo-Mathis, J. (2015) 'Translator's introduction: Modernity and time', in H. Rosa (ed) *Social Acceleration: A New Theory of Modernity*, New York: Columbia University Press, pp xi–xxxii.

Vohra-Miller, S., Brar, A., and Banerjee, A.T. (2020) '"It's not Diwali, it's precarious employment and less health care resources." South Asian medical experts on Brampton's rising, COVID-19 cases', *Toronto Star*, 19 November. https://www.thestar.com/opinion/contributors/2020/11/19/its-not-diwali-its-precarious-employment-and-less-health-care-resources-south-asian-medical-experts-on-bramptons-rising-covid-19-cases.html (accessed 13 December 2022).

Ward, R., Rummery, K., Odzakovic, E., Manji, K., Kullberg, A., Keady, J. et al (2022) 'Taking time: The temporal politics of dementia, care and support in the neighbourhood', *Sociology of Health and Illness*, 44(9): 1427–44.

White Coat, Black Art (2020) 'COVID-19 hotspot Brampton, Ont., chronically underfunded in community health services, local advocate says', CBC, 4 December. https://www.cbc.ca/radio/whitecoat/covid-19-hotspot-brampton-ont-chronically-underfunded-in-community-health-services-local-advocate-says-1.5823815 (accessed 13 December 2022).

12

Disrupting Infrastructure: Space, Speed, and Street Governance

Amelia Thorpe

If the temporalities of infrastructure are socially produced and relational, how might alternative temporalities be brought into being? The intimate connections between speed and power and between power and automobility mean that street infrastructure is typically allocated and regulated to prioritize speed for those in cars, and in doing so tends to produce slowness for others. Yet these claims and connections are not fixed. This chapter explores a range of activities designed to rework the temporalities of infrastructure on the streets of San Francisco, California. I focus on two practices: prefiguring, in which activists quietly and anonymously make unsanctioned 'improvements' to city streets in an effort to speed up the provision of protected infrastructure for walking and cycling; and heckling, in which activists loudly and comically redirect traffic so as to highlight and challenge the degree to which speed in cars is paid for by slowness outside them. While heckling is often controversial, I use this loaded term deliberately to emphasize the power relations at stake. Like hecklers, protests disrupting traffic are frequently frowned upon, and successful interventions must be skilful and sophisticated. The central claim in both sets of practices is the same: the temporalities of street infrastructure are not inevitable but are instead the result of choices that could be changed – and that change can be fast.

Infrastructure and automobility

The control of infrastructure connects to the control of time, enabling the powerful to be fast, and rendering the powerless slow (Wajcman and Dodd, 2016). The intimate connections between infrastructure, time, and power are clearly apparent on streets, making these a frequent site of conflict (Hubbard and Lilley, 2004; Cresswell, 2006; Norton, 2011). Streets are ubiquitous, encompassing a third of all developed urban land worldwide (Southworth and Ben-Joseph, 2013: 5). Far beyond the journey, differential access to speed on streets results in vast differences in social and economic opportunities, from access to employment and education, to health and life expectancy (Sheller, 2018). Much of the conflict over streets centres on the place of cars, recognizing that the emphasis on speed and mobility for those inside cars has produced slowness and immobility for others.

Globally, there is growing recognition that automobility comes at a high price. This includes direct costs like infrastructure budgets, but also costs such as air and water pollution – transport is the second biggest emitter of greenhouse gases (23 per cent globally and predicted to double by 2050, with 72 per cent from road vehicles; UN Environment Programme, 2020) – as well as deaths and injuries (car crashes have long been the leading killer of children and young people in the US and internationally; WHO, 2019), plus a vast array of indirect costs borne by governments and communities (Böhm et al, 2006; Culver, 2018; Henderson, 2020). With the recognition of these costs, cities and states are adopting policies and programmes aimed to reduce the dominance and impact of cars on city streets. Vision Zero is increasingly prominent among these and involves a commitment to eliminate traffic deaths and serious injuries within ten years (Shahum, 2017). Other policy frameworks include Complete Streets (Smart Growth America, 2019), Transit Oriented Development (Dittmar and Ohland, 2004), and Link and Place (Jones et al, 2007, also known as Movement and Place), as well as the commitment to sustainable transport systems in the UN Sustainable Development Goals (11.2). Vision Zero was adopted by San Francisco in 2014, shortly after New York became the first US city to commit to the programme (Shahum, 2017).

Commitments to policies like Vision Zero suggest that pedestrians, cyclists, transit riders, and others not travelling by car have in some sense won the policy debate, and that infrastructure to support safe walking and cycling will indeed be provided. Conditions on the ground, however, are quite different.

To take effect, policies need physical and regulatory changes: new planning and engineering standards, reduced speed limits, revisions to road rules and driver training, changes to enforcement practices, and the reallocation and repricing of parking spaces. Perhaps most crucially, a move away from automobility requires infrastructural change. Numerous studies have documented the central role of infrastructure in increasing the share of trips made by walking, cycling, public transport, and other forms of open-air mobility (Schoner and Levinson, 2014; van Goeverden et al, 2015; Aldred and Dales, 2017; Buehler and Pucher, 2021; Zhu et al, 2022). Far more than weather, speed, or personal fitness, the lack of physical protection from cars is a key barrier to walking and cycling.

There is a wide spectrum of possible street infrastructures, from 'sharrows' (painted images of bicycles and arrows to indicate a road should be shared by cars and cyclists) and painted lines (delineating lanes to be used by bicycles, alongside motor vehicles), to protected infrastructure (for instance, physically separated cycle lanes with more substantial materials like concrete bollards and kerbs, and pedestrian crossings with level changes and 'bulb outs' forcing cars to slow down). While paint offers very little protection – and sharrows may actually make streets more dangerous (Ferenchak and Marshall, 2019) – physical separation improves both actual and perceived safety for all road users (Buehler and Pucher, 2021). The benefits of infrastructure improvements are especially significant for racialized and other vulnerable communities, who bear the greatest burdens in the current system of automobility (Sheller, 2018; Lusk et al, 2019; Raifman and Choma, 2022).

Infrastructure is accordingly a key part of policies and strategies to reduce the dominance of cars. San Francisco's Vision Zero Action Strategy, for example, states: 'Vision Zero San Francisco commits City agencies to build better and safer streets, educate the public on traffic safety, enforce traffic laws, and adopt policy changes that save lives' (City of San Francisco, 2021: 5). Despite this clear mandate, the allocation and regulation of street infrastructure remains contested. Proposals for cycle lanes, pedestrian upgrades, and other infrastructure for active and open-air transport can attract fierce opposition (see Vreugdenhil and Williams, 2013; Wild et al, 2018; Roberts, 2020; Ferster et al, 2021; Leyendecker and Cox, 2022 among others). These projects are replete with what Akhil Gupta (2015: np) describes as suspension, in which 'completion is not the only possible outcome'. While infrastructure that is not yet in place tends to be deemed incomplete, infrastructure projects are not always completed. Projects can be suspended indefinitely; they can also be cancelled. Even projects that have been constructed may not be secure, as built works can be dismantled, torn down, or removed.

Implementation can be delayed in many ways: studies, consultation, and testing that draw-out construction time frames; competition for funding that pushes projects from short to medium and medium to long term; electoral cycles that require pauses and revisions. The conflict over street governance then can be understood as less about content and more about time: when will physical infrastructure shift in line with policy shifts?

This question connects to literature exploring the suspended, deferred, delayed, and unfinished (Lombard, 2013; Carse and Kneas, 2019; Stamatopoulou-Robbins, 2021). A key point highlighted in this literature is the significance of temporality to power. While many studies trace how spatial transformation projects are 'decided upon' and what happens when they are 'completed', projects do not always follow clear-cut trajectories, and results are not always certain (Arícan, 2020). Through a study of construction projects in Istanbul, Alize Arıcan shows how delays can be used to reshuffle who controls and who benefits from projects. As Arıcan argues, 'it is specifically through delays that economic and political power is exerted, navigated and negotiated' (2020: 482).

Power often works in predictable ways, deployed by already powerful groups to maintain and extend agency. But this is not always fixed. As Simone Abram explains, notions of progress implicit in plans for infrastructure suggest a modern, linear conception of time, 'yet close attention to planning practices indicates that such temporalities are doubted, contested, and mediated' (2014: 129). Gupta makes a similar point: 'The bridge to the future is always under erasure, and we do not know where it will lead' (2015: np).

With respect to street infrastructure in particular, Hubbard and Lilley's (2004) study of road engineering in post-war Coventry highlights the differential and conflictual production of space and time. The efficient city that planners laid out on paper was never fully brought into being. Mobilities were not produced as planned; efforts to construct new highways instead created an uneven and contested 'speed politics'. Emphasizing the performative and contingent nature of cities, Hubbard and Lilley show how high modernist plans were disrupted to generate new temporalities. Particular groups can channel the energies of the city in particular directions, they explain, 'alert[ing] us to the human creativity that might otherwise be papered over in accounts that emphasize the colonization of everyday life by the forces of capitalism, technology, and science' (2004: 291).

In the very different context of contemporary Peru, Harvey and Knox (2015) show similarly that the politics of road infrastructure is enacted, anticipated, and understood in diverse ways. In explaining this, they set out a schema that is helpful in thinking about the politics of street infrastructure in San Francisco. This begins with two groups familiar in political theory: publics whose engagement consists in large part in practices of cooperation and community engagement, and counter-publics driven by oppositional logics. Alongside these two, Harvey and Knox identify a third group: impossible publics. Impossible publics refuse to play the game, to follow the processes set by the state. For Harvey and Knox, impossible publics 'respond to state projects in ways that fail to either accommodate or oppose them in ways that fit the expectations of the engineering professionals. … they follow alternative, uncooperative, or spontaneous possibilities … refus[ing] to behave responsibly [and] manifest[ing] a troubling creativity and imaginative response to regulation' (2015: 16–17).

In the sections that follow, I explore 'impossible' practices through which activists in San Francisco interrupt the temporalities of street infrastructure. I begin with a brief sketch of the context for open-air transport activism in San Francisco, noting the length and breadth of activities before discussing two in more depth. First, DIY (do-it-yourself) infrastructure, in which participants place official-looking objects on the street to 'pilot' or prefigure faster action on infrastructure by the City. Second, the JAM (just a minute), in which participants challenge or heckle the social and legal norms that enable car drivers to colonize infrastructure allocated to other road users. Despite their very different tactics, both practices show that the rhythms of street infrastructure are not fixed and could – quite quickly – be shifted such that speed and slowness are more equally shared among all road users.

Speed politics in San Francisco

> 'Why are we waiting and doing one block at a time and lobbying and ... [having] all these meetings and conversations? It's stupid. We need to get things going more quickly ... our Vision Zero [death toll] is going up, not down and I am done [waiting]'. (Interview, 6 July 2022)

As with many other progressive causes, there is a long history of advocacy and activism around the governance of streets in San Francisco and the Bay Area. There is a committed activist community, leading well-established (and internationally influential) activities such as Critical Mass, which recently celebrated its 30th year (Carlsson, 2002), and PARK(ing) Day, which is approaching its 20th (Thorpe, 2020). There is also a strong culture of engagement in formal processes, including large and long-running advocacy groups such as Walk San Francisco and the San Francisco Bicycle Coalition, which have played significant roles in the adoption of Vision Zero (Schneider, 2014; Stehlin, 2015; Vision Zero Coalition, 2015).

While progress has been made in securing these commitments, there remains a long way to go. Even with political will and budget allocations, building the infrastructure necessary to protect pedestrians and cyclists involves consultation and approval processes that can extend for many years. In the words of Mayor London Breed, 'layers of bureaucracy ... have historically slowed progress toward achieving the City's Vision Zero goal' (Breed, 2019: np).

Frustration with those processes has prompted some to look for alternative forms of engagement. Instead of participating in state-led processes (for example, engaging in activities like writing letters, collecting signatures, speaking at public meetings, making submissions, or filling out surveys and online forms), some have pursued more direct options. Participants expressed frustration not only with the length of city processes, but also the power imbalance. In their approach to safe infrastructure, one explained, the City sends a clear message: "[They] say non-verbally: people, mind your place. We are the ones who put this infrastructure in. You will wait. You will wait for the process to trickle down and mind your place" (interview, 23 June 2022).

Rejecting that message, activists have developed practices of engagement that work to interrupt those trickle-down processes. Building on informal, unsanctioned activities such as Critical Mass and PARK(ing) Day, these practices are wide-ranging. Some are very serious, such as vigils in which participants gather to commemorate pedestrians and cyclists killed by cars, often extended symbolically for a few days or weeks by handmade signs stating 'a driver killed our neighbor here'. Others are more playful and celebratory, such as cycle parties, and 'slow rides', in which people travel by walking, jogging, roller skating, and a range of other non-car means, followed at the back by a line of slow-riding cyclists who stop cars moving at anything more than a pedestrian-friendly pace. In contrast to organized groups like Walk San Francisco and the San Francisco Bicycle Coalition, organization of these activities is loose, with participants dropping in and out. Coordination has largely been through social media, with some participants known to each other not by name, but merely by Twitter handle. These oppositional publics are also part of a larger ecosystem, sharing ideas and strategies with activists and more conventional advocacy groups (publics and counter-publics) working in other cities and other countries.

In the remainder of this chapter, I focus on two of these practices: DIY infrastructure and JAMs. Both pursue speed and space, calling for more protected cycle lanes, pedestrian crossings, and other infrastructure necessary to support safe and efficient travel outside of private cars. They do this in quite different ways. With DIY infrastructure, participants work to accelerate the introduction of infrastructure by installing objects directly onto city streets. Acceleration is thus sought in both city processes and travel speeds for those outside of cars. Objects are placed anonymously, as if by the City. In this way, I argue, they can be understood as prefigurative efforts to bring about change by acting as if that change has already taken place. JAMs take a very different approach. Instead of acting quietly and attempting to blend in or pass as official, participants use cowbells, megaphones, signs, and bright clothing to attract attention. JAMs highlight the slowness cars impose on other road users, and the unequal governance processes that allow this. JAMs, I argue, can be likened to heckles: interventions that disrupt an expected sequence of events by highlighting its flaws, forcing a rethink and perhaps a reset.

Prefiguring speed

The cones, posts, and flowers depicted in Figure 12.1 were installed in 2016 by the San Francisco Municipal Transformation Agency (SFMTrA), a loosely organized group of transport activists (Thorpe, 2022). As the sign explains, the installation followed the death of Kate Slattery. Slattery had been cycling in the cycle lane when a motorist drove their car out of its

Figure 12.1: "We need a protected bike lane here *now*, not a year from now"

[Photo of street with memorial sign reading: "IN MEMORY OF KATE SLATTERY KILLED HERE ON JUNE 22nd 2016 SFMTA: WE NEED A PROTECTED BIKE LANE HERE NOW, NOT A YEAR FROM NOW"]

Source: SFMTrA

allocated space and into hers. Another young woman, Heather Miller, was killed in a similar hit and run in San Francisco that same day.

The SFMTrA followed that intervention with others across San Francisco, adding orange cones and other objects to painted lines to increase visibility and separation between cars and more vulnerable road users. As in the example in Figure 12.1, cones and posts were added to places where pedestrians and cyclists had been killed. Interventions were also made in other sites, identified using sources including the City's High Injury Network (a map prepared in 2016 to support the City's commitment to Vision Zero). The SFMTrA also created its own online map, inviting people to identify areas in need of infrastructure improvements. Members of the SFMTrA, who were often white men, recognized the importance of site selection, and the need to involve others in this process. As one member commented:

> 'I don't think everyone in our city would be as comfortable doing these things, as we did, and I think I increasingly reflect on some form of privilege that allowed me to feel comfortable borrowing cones and standing in the street and fixing things the City couldn't fix ... We made a conscious point to select locations that were socio economically and racially diverse as best we could and bring in more voices to participate.' (Interview, 17 June 2022)

Figure 12.2: Pedestrian safety 'pilot'

Source: SFMTrA

Instead of calling for a reprioritization of walking and cycling infrastructure, these interventions are deployed as if that change has already taken place, as if cities and states do indeed see their responsibilities to provide safe spaces for walking and cycling as urgent and immediate. They act as if citizens are already entitled to streets that are safe for walking and cycling (see Figure 12.2). In doing so, DIY infrastructure works prefiguratively to enact a different temporality. As one participant explains: "We experimented with lots of materials; we experimented with paint, we experimented with posts, we experimented with the cones ... We could exercise prototyping and design ideas in a different way ... where can we learn and share with the community and the City new prototyping ideas" (interview, 17 June 2022).

Commonly attributed to Carl Boggs, prefiguration describes 'the embodiment, within the ongoing political practice of a movement, of those forms of social relations, decision-making, culture, and human experience that are the ultimate goal' (1977: 100). Prefiguration joins 'ends' and 'means'. Instead of imagining or lobbying for the implementation of alternative urban forms at some point in the future, prefigurative strategies work performatively to put those alternatives into practice now (Maeckelbergh, 2011). As Cohen and Morgan (2023: 1053–4) explain, prefigurative strategies pursue a form of social change which 'does not entail a great rupture miraculously coordinated from above or a revolutionary ground swelling from below. Rather, it entails the accumulation of millions of everyday practices that presuppose current socio-economic structures and yet call forth new social worlds.'

The SFMTrA does not call for a shift in what the City is and is not responsible for, or what citizens can and cannot expect. Instead, they assume that shift has already taken place. Interventions are designed to support existing City policies and commitments, to assist the City to fulfil promises and comply with obligations already undertaken. The members of the group remained anonymous, letting the infrastructure speak for them. As their founding member explains: "[I made] a very specific point of not naming myself. I didn't want to be a leader, I wanted this to be [that] we are San Francisco, and we are doing this" (interview, 14 June 2022). The emphasis is on the infrastructure, and on the official-looking objects used to construct it. Because street infrastructure is increasingly constructed from materials produced by and purchased from the private sector, and installed by private contractors, making installations appear official can be quite simple. One participant advised:

'If somebody was going to do that, I would advise, one: check the Internet. All this stuff is available online, you can buy safe hit posts, and you can buy the sticky stuff and safety vests ... And be smart where you put it. You know, make it look like it's just like the regular city stuff.' (Interview, 23 June 2022)

Acting anonymously through infrastructure adds to the prefigurative power of the SFMTrA's installations, their capacity to disrupt and reshape rights and rhythms by acting as if the City is responsible for providing streets that are safe for everyone:

'We could borrow cones from construction sites and make a real difference there, and also really see how it would change the behavior of automobile drivers instantaneously. There's some psychological effect of an orange cone that me standing there with my bicycle doesn't have. An orange cone says don't do this, you can't drive here, to people. It has authority.' (Interview, 17 June 2022)

The SFMTrA acts as if city and state authorities take their commitments to reduce pedestrian and cyclist deaths seriously and are indeed responsible for improving safety for people who walk and ride on city streets right now. Interventions often used orange cones and posts found around the city, which participants told me they 'borrowed' for the duration of the installation. When I queried the use of this term, one explained:

'We were essentially saying in the physical environment, [to] the City of San Francisco ... let us help you, and so we would be borrowing cones from other City departments, so we were being civic minded, but we were essentially re-prioritizing where orange cones should go in San Francisco ... And they often got taken back by those Departments, so, in effect, we did return them, but it was an official prototyping [using] materials from the City and County of San Francisco.' (Interview, 17 June 2022)

The SFMTrA works not to shift, but to speed up state action. Their name is a play on that of the official body, the San Francisco Municipal Transportation Agency. It was inspired by a similar group in New York City, the New York Transformation Department. The replacement of 'transportation' with 'transformation' was intended to convey this temporal change. As the New York activist who coined their group's name explains:

'We wanted something clever that seemed official, that had a little bit of joy and magic to it, and also conveyed this idea of change ... We could transform a street instantly. It also speaks to this idea, if just the City agency would change its thinking, literally by just one letter, right, that we could change the city much faster.' (Interview, 21 May 2019)

Heckling slowness

DIY infrastructure is quiet, anonymous, and can last for days or weeks; JAMs are quite different. JAM stands for just a minute, another play on words, this time a double reference. First, to the drivers who park in cycle lanes saying they will be "just be a minute" and, second, to the traffic jam that a JAM temporarily creates. Brief, noisy, and tongue-in-cheek, JAMs involve a small group of people, a megaphone, signs, and safety vests (see Figure 12.3). Participants block the car lane until the car obstructing the cycle lane is driven away, using the megaphone to explain this to people passing: "the bicycle lane is obstructed, we'll just be a minute"; "this car will be just a minute". They hold signs reading 'Just a Minute' and 'Sorry'. Cyclists are welcomed through the blocked vehicle lanes. Motor vehicles are told to wait for just a minute while the driver of the illegally parked car completes their "important business".

Whereas DIY infrastructure centres on the form of street infrastructure, JAMs challenge its governance. JAMs critique behaviours that are already illegal (parking in a cycle lane) but are rarely enforced. Many JAMs have been held on Valencia Street, a key corridor between downtown and the Mission and a site of extensive activism. While plans for protected infrastructure along Valencia have long been in place, progress in implementation has been slow. The painted cycle lane has frequently been used as a parking space, forcing cyclists to ride around cars into traffic, and causing injuries regularly (Rudick,

Figure 12.3: "Hold tight folks, we'll be just a minute!"

Source: @SafeStreetRebel

2020). JAMs call out the behaviour of the drivers involved. They also call out the social norms that have supported those drivers in failing to police such transgressions and, more fundamentally, in accepting infrastructure that can so easily be driven over.

Slowness and speed are at the heart of the JAM. Participants challenge the slowness forced upon cyclists by cars that take up space beyond their allocated lanes. They reclaim space for cyclists to travel faster, and temporarily force cars to accept the slowness their fellow drivers create. As one commentator explains, JAMs 'force motorists to wait and experience first-hand what cyclists go through every time someone blocks the bike lane for "just a minute"' (Rudick, 2022: np). Speed is central also to the conduct of a JAM: it lasts for just a minute, and participants must move quickly.

> 'Once the bike lane is clear, you need to run back onto the sidewalk and ... you have the potential for colliding with bicyclists or such like that. For the JAMs, you need to be very nimble. You say "oh there's a car run, run and run and go. No dilly-dallying." It's definitely the action for people who are fit.' (Interview, 23 June 2022)

JAMs make no attempt to pass as official, and participants do not hide their identities. While members of the SFMTrA have been careful to preserve their anonymity (a key condition in agreeing to speak to me), participants in JAMs are more open. The idea was conceived by Maureen Persico, a prominent transport activist spurred into action some years ago when she started trying to cycle with her young son to school. JAMs are coordinated by Safe Street Rebel, another loosely organized group of activists who engage in JAMs and several other activities. As the name suggests, Safe Street Rebel is more oppositional than the SFMTrA and pursues change not by prefiguring alternatives but by challenging the status quo.

As well as traffic jams, the JAM also invokes other practices. The name echoes culture jamming, in which 'a range of tactics [are] used to critique, subvert, and otherwise "jam" the workings of consumer culture' (DeLaure and Fink, 2017: 6). While Safe Street Rebel's JAMs are not oriented towards advertising and consumer culture, they share with culture jamming an emphasis on disruption, on 'scrambling the signal, injecting the unexpected, jarring audiences, provoking critical thinking, inviting play and public participation' (DeLaure and Fink, 2017: 6). In this emphasis on interruption, JAMs operate as a form of *heckling*.

Heckling is defined as a social drama, which is evaluated by its watchers as judges (Kádár and Ran, 2015). In theatre, comedy, or politics, where heckling is more common, this social drama centres on the heckled person, who has an institutionalized right to speak or perform on stage, and the heckler, the unauthorized public speaker who interrupts the public performer. Hecklers are impossible publics, undermining established hierarchies by refusing to observe social norms about who can speak and when.

Through counter-performance, hecklers aim to affiliate themselves with the audience, encouraging that audience to shift their allegiance away from the planned performance. Hecklers interrupt and challenge, but they can also be constructive, enabling onlookers to see more than one position at a time. Hecklers can thus make vital contributions to democratic exchange, as Mel Jordan explains:

> Institutions of public speech inscribe the heckler as anti-social, but I want us to consider her in quite the opposite way, as the very embodiment of becoming-social. Let's ... think of the heckler as heroic, a kind of public speech superhero, with the ability to suspend rhetoric, preserving the right to speak out of turn. The violence, awkwardness and embarrassment of the heckle are signs of its political courage, fearlessness and agency. The heckler's interruption opens up a space for public discourse. Deprived of the heckler we would have one less method of turning passers-by into assembled publics. (Jordan, 2011: 118)

Car drivers do not have a legal right to park in a cycle lane, even for just a minute, but social norms and enforcement practices have allowed this to become a common practice. In this context, JAMs ask onlookers to switch their affiliation from double-parking drivers to cyclists. Just as Jordan argues hecklers undermine established hierarchies by refusing social norms about who can speak and when, JAMs disrupt social norms about who and what streets are for. For JAMmers as for hecklers, humour is an important tool for disruption:

> … we need more fun in advocacy. There's a lot to be angry about. And I do think you can channel that anger into all kinds of protests. But sometimes just taking and making your point with humor breaks through. Especially, you know, that's a viral tweet, right? And was shared by lots of people, and there's something really fun and funny about it. But it still makes the point that, like, this shit has to stop. You're endangering people's lives. And so my hat is off to the advocates in San Francisco who came up with this. (Goodyear et al, 2022: np)

JAMs are oppositional, but they share with DIY infrastructure – and with heckling at its best – a commitment to make the city better. While interruptions are often portrayed as negative and impolite, they can be effective in opening power relations, and in provoking participation (Campbell, 2017). Commentators have described JAMs as 'defending the city' and praised the power that comes from their joyful elements:

> … in so many ways, city government is failing us, and even when we pass laws and make things happen, [when] we turn the wheels of government. We take three years to pass the Reckless Driver Accountability Act, or take 10 years to pass congestion pricing, it still doesn't happen. Government seems like it's not doing a very good job of implementing these days, and in some ways that forces citizens to go out and do direct action. (Goodyear et al, 2022: np)

Safe Street Rebel can be understood as a kind of heckle itself, with the suggestion that rebellion is necessary to achieve safety. The group is more diverse than the SFMTrA, with more women and more people of colour. This is a conscious choice, as participants explain:

> 'All my actions, especially the JAMs, if you see my Twitter feed, they're all about, we want to mentor you. We're going to tell you exactly what we learned … we break it down, we mentor people through DMs. It's all about reproducing it as far and as wide as it possibly can go.' (Interview, 23 June 2022)

Some members of Safe Street Rebel are fearless, bravely and loudly standing up to cars and officials. Others are more cautious, working behind the scenes on things like signs and social media. The group recognizes the different capacities of certain people to engage in activism and advocacy, and the relationship between this and street infrastructure. Protected infrastructure is needed most urgently by those that are already marginalized and vulnerable, as participants explain:

> 'It's infrastructure that keeps the inner police officer out of my head. It's infrastructure that supports people whose job it is to deliver food or drive people and often those are people of colour or people who have lower economic means. So, give them what they need to do their jobs and support their families, which is loading zones and clear signage and safe places to pull over, and give pedestrians and bicyclists space. The flaw [in my earlier advocacy] was thinking "oh, we can just keep it clear and demand that police come and ticket". It took me a while, but I finally learned something about police interactions with people of colour and I finally learned about the need for real infrastructure.' (Interview, 23 June 2022)

JAMs challenge – heckle – established norms about who speaks and when, about slowness, and especially about slowness for women and others who have been marginalized for too long. They interrupt the established car-based order, calling out the inequities this creates and the implication not just of officials but of passers-by in sustaining them. JAMs show that cars already exceed their authority, and that change is both possible and potentially very fast.

Shifting speed politics

'We need to keep this momentum up.' (Wiener, 2022: np)

Official responses vary. Participants report only limited police engagement with their interventions on the street, and several examples where that engagement was positive. Engagement with city planners has been less direct, but there is some evidence to suggest that these interventions have had an impact. It is important to note that both DIY infrastructure and JAMs took place alongside a wider ecosystem of advocacy and were given substantial impetus by COVID-19 (Flynn and Thorpe, 2021). But speed politics is shifting.

With respect to DIY infrastructure, official engagement has been with the objects rather than the groups deploying them, consistent with the anonymous, quiet nature of the interventions. Much of this engagement has followed publicity on social media. While some see this as an important part of the process, others would rather let the objects blend in with official infrastructure. As one participant explains:

'What was so infuriating is that they [others in SFMTrA] would post it. And the City would say, "Oh, we can't put infrastructure, oh it will take so much time", but the very next day, they would have crews to scrape off the safe infrastructure, they would come the very next day.' (Interview, 23 June 2022)

In many instances, posts and cones have been removed by City authorities. But sometimes the unofficial infrastructure proved stickier. Participants described several locations where their interventions were initially removed but then, following media reports and public support, the City would install their own posts and protected infrastructure.

Perhaps the most celebrated of these is JFK Drive in Golden Gate Park, the site of one of the SFMTrA's first interventions. Unusually, the SFMTA allowed the DIY posts along the painted cycle lane to remain in place. The rationale for this, the SFMTA explained, was that the City was planning to install their own posts there (Bialick, 2016). The SFMTA replaced the SFMTrA's posts a few weeks later. DIY infrastructure also prompted shifts extending beyond their particular locations. One participant described a change in the rules regarding buffer space requirements around protected infrastructure, which had previously prevented the installation of soft-hit posts by the City:

'The City said, "I'm sorry there's just not enough space". And so we put some on … where cars were double parking. We put them in there, and now I think the City essentially changed their policy as a result of it. … they now don't require that extra space, they changed their policy because we proved that their policy was entirely academic.' (Interview, 17 June 2022)

With respect to JAMs, engagement with officials has been more direct, but also quite limited. In one example that was filmed and shared online, participants in a JAM explain their actions to passing police and ticket inspectors. Both are immediately convinced; one says, "I'm totally behind you guys" (Bike Lane Protest on Valencia St, 2022).

Police have even been the object of a JAM. Seeing a police car parked in the cycle lane, the group decided to hold a JAM as they would for any other car. When I asked how the police reacted, I was told:

'They talked amongst themselves, I was on the megaphone at the time, so I said Important Cop Business. Sorry to block, sorry to hold you all up. This is Important Cop Business. So, they chatted amongst themselves, probably wondering what to do, and then they drove away.' (Interview, 23 June 2022)

In June 2019, the SFMTA introduced a new policy: Quick Build. In the words of Mayor London Breed, Quick Build was intended 'to allow the Agency to cut through the layers of bureaucracy that have historically slowed progress toward achieving the City's Vision Zero goal' (Breed, 2019: np). Two legislative amendments supported Quick Build (California Senate Bills 743 and 288), which changed the way transport projects are assessed under the California Environmental Quality Act. Guidelines implemented under SB 743 in 2018 shifted the focus from traffic congestion to reducing vehicle miles travelled, and in 2020 SB 288 exempted transit, cycle, and pedestrian projects from the lengthy reviews required for more substantial infrastructure for a two-year trial period. The focus of this exemption was on lightweight, reversible projects – very much like those installed by the SFMTrA.

The reversible nature of these projects meant they could be treated as pilots or experiments, and accordingly given much less consultation prior to their installation. As SFMTA transportation director Jeffrey Tumlin explains:

> 'Because the Quick Build projects are so cheap and reversible, we can take any feedback and make adjustments … our intention is to tinker around until we get it right. Then that becomes the blueprint for a later, much more expensive construction project that will involve concrete and curb work and streetscaping.' (Harrison-Caldwell, 2021: np)

Advocacy groups have welcomed Quick Build, but they have also highlighted areas in need of improvement, including expanding the range of projects exempted (Tolkoff and Anzai, 2022). Some activists have been more critical:

> 'It sounds wonderful and if it were done as named, it would be wonderful [but] the Quick Build program in San Francisco is: "we're going to have a series of meetings with the people that are on this block, most of them who drive, and we're going to ask them how they feel about it and then maybe within six months we'll get some soft posts or something". The money that we spend, the time that we spend on negotiating human safety, is morally reprehensible.' (Interview, 6 July 2022)

While far from ideal, the Quick Build programme shows progress in raising the profile of temporality. In developing a policy specifically focused on speed, we can see evidence of an official recognition that policy commitments are not enough, that timely implementation is also required. In October 2022, with the initial two-year trial approaching its end, new legislation was passed to make the exemption permanent (SB 922). Introducing the new bill, Senator Scott Wiener emphasized the critical importance of speed:

'We cannot allow sustainable transportation projects to get bogged down in years of unnecessary and expensive administrative delays when we could be revitalizing California's transportation landscape now … we need to get these projects going much faster than we have in the past. We've seen just how successful SB 288 has been in jumpstarting sustainable transportation projects – we need to keep this momentum up.' (Wiener, 2022: np)

Conclusion

'It has to change. It's not sustainable for people that are involved and angry, it's not sustainable, for a city it's not cost effective to do things one block at a time. [I don't want] to start here and … build from here … I want all of that now! … make all this stuff happen now!' (Interview, 6 July 2022)

Activists and advocacy groups have fought hard to secure policy commitments like Vision Zero, which promise to redistribute speed and slowness more equally among those in cars and those outside them. The progression from policy to plans to change on the ground, however, has proved elusive. The long association between power and automobility is reflected in the apparent obduracy of the myriad norms, rules, and practices through which street infrastructure and its temporalities are sustained. In the face of that obduracy, some activists have shifted their emphasis from contribution to disruption.

DIY infrastructure and JAMs sit outside of state-led processes; they neither accommodate nor oppose the City's plans and proposals. Participants work instead as impossible publics, setting their own terms for engagement. These unruly citizens trouble both the temporalities that exist on car-oriented streets and the temporalities of official efforts to rework them. With DIY infrastructure, citizens prefigure a different approach to speed, one in which people outside cars are provided with the infrastructure necessary to travel safely and efficiently. DIY infrastructure also prefigures an alternative approach to governance, in which city agencies responsible for that infrastructure act with urgency. With JAMs, citizens heckle car drivers who, in their own pursuit of speed, impose slowness on others. JAMs also heckle the officials who allow drivers to colonize cycle lanes in that way and, more fundamentally, the wider social norms and expectations that sustain this. Together, they help to disrupt the connections between speed and cars, and slowness and other forms of transport.

DIY infrastructure and JAMs challenge the temporalities of urban governance, and particularly the idea that change is unavoidably slow. These practices reveal the degree to which slowness for pedestrians, cyclists, and others outside cars is not inevitable, but the product of choices about infrastructure and its governance. While highlighting significant inertia, both DIY infrastructure and JAMs show also that these choices can be overturned. Speed for those in cars need not be prioritized and, without the social norms that have sustained car dominance, the allocation and regulation of streets can shift quickly.

References

Abram, S. (2014) 'The time it takes: Temporalities of planning', *Journal of the Royal Anthropological Institute*, 20(s1): 129–47.

Aldred, R., and Dales, J. (2017) 'Diversifying and normalising cycling in London, UK: An exploratory study on the influence of infrastructure', *Journal of Transport & Health*, 4: 348–62.

Arícan, A. (2020) 'Behind the scaffolding: Manipulations of time, delays, and power in Tarlabaşı, Istanbul', *City & Society*, 32(3): 482–507.

Bialick, A. (2016) 'Beyond safe-hit posts: Tackling the challenges of engineering safer streets'. https://www.sfmta.com/blog/beyond-safe-hit-posts-tackling-challenges-engineering-safer-streets (accessed 14 December 2022).

Bike Lane Protest on Valencia St (2022) available at: https://www.youtube.com/watch?v=kDboYpYvT2o (accessed 14 December 2022).

Boggs, C. (1977) 'Marxism, prefigurative communism and the problem of workers' control', *Radical America*, 6(Winter): 99–122.

Böhm, S., Jones, C., Land, C., and Paterson, M. (eds) (2006) *Against Automobility*, Malden, MA: Blackwell.

Breed, L. (2019) 'Building safer streets faster: Our new "Quick Build" policy'. https://londonbreed.medium.com/building-safer-streets-faster-our-new-quick-build-policy-92012487ce76 (accessed 22 July 2022).

Buehler, R., and Pucher, J.R. (eds) (2021) *Cycling for Sustainable Cities: Urban and Industrial Environments*, Cambridge, MA: MIT Press.

Campbell, L. (2017) 'Collaborators and hecklers: Performative pedagogy and interruptive processes', *Scenario: A Journal of Performative Teaching, Learning, Research*, 11(1): 33–71.

Carlsson, C. (ed) (2002) *Critical Mass: Bicycling's Defiant Celebration*, Edinburgh: AK Press.

Carse, A., and Kneas, D. (2019) 'Unbuilt and unfinished: The temporalities of infrastructure', *Environment and Society*, 10(1), 9–28.

City of San Francisco (2021) 'Vision Zero SF Action Strategy'. https://www.visionzerosf.org/about/action-strategy/ (accessed 25 July 2022).

Cohen, A.J., and Morgan, B. (2023) 'Prefigurative legality', *Law & Social Inquiry*, 48(3): 1053–82. https://doi.org/10.1017/lsi.2023.4

Cresswell, T. (2006) *On the Move: Mobility in the Modern Western World*, New York: Routledge.

Culver, G. (2018) 'Death and the car: On (auto)mobility, violence, and injustice', *ACME*, 17(1): 144–70.

DeLaure, M., and Fink, M. (eds) (2017) *Culture Jamming: Activism and the Art of Cultural Resistance*, New York: New York University Press.

Dittmar, H., and Ohland, G. (eds) (2004) *The New Transit Town: Best Practices in Transit-Oriented Development*, Washington, DC: Island Press.

Ferenchak, N.N., and Marshall, W.E. (2019) 'Advancing healthy cities through safer cycling: An examination of shared lane markings', *International Journal of Transportation Science and Technology*, 8(2): 136–45.

Ferster, C., Laberee, K., Nelson, T., Thigpen, C., Simeone, M., and Winters, M. (2021) 'From advocacy to acceptance: Social media discussions of protected bike lane installations', *Urban Studies*, 58(5): 941–58.

Flynn, A., and Thorpe, A. (2021) 'Pandemic pop-ups and the performance of legality', in B. Doucet, R. van Melik, and P. Filion (eds) *Global Reflections on COVID-19 and Urban Inequalities. Volume 3: Public Space and Mobility*, Bristol: Bristol University Press, pp 25–35.

Goodyear, S., Gordon, D., and Naparstek, A. (2022) 'They paved paradise and put up a parking lot', *The War on Cars, New York*. https://www.google.com/url?sa=t&rct=j&q=&esrc=s&source=web&cd=&cad=rja&uact=8&ved=2ahUKEwi_jticz-f7AhWjzzgGHe5aBjAQFnoECA0QAQ&url=https%3A%2F%2Fthewaroncars.org%2Fepisode-84-they-paved-r-place-and-put-up-a-parking-lot-final-web-transcript%2F&usg=AOvVaw0mxI16FaFQ_6TcdWs-l0iA (accessed 14 December 2022).

Gupta, A. (2015) 'Suspension', Theorizing the Contemporary, *Fieldsights*, 24 September 24. https://culanth.org/fieldsights/suspension (accessed 11 June 2021).

Harrison-Caldwell, M. (2021) 'How SF's Quick Build program works around bureaucratic obstacles', *The Frisc*, 5 November. https://thefrisc.com/how-sfs-quick-build-program-works-around-bureaucratic-obstacles-9ca899eb7ed7 (accessed 14 December 2022).

Harvey, P., and Knox, H. (2015) *Roads: An Anthropology of Infrastructure and Expertise*, Ithaca, NY: Cornell University Press.

Henderson, J. (2020) 'EVs are not the answer: A mobility justice critique of electric vehicle transitions', *Annals of the American Association of Geographers*, 110(6): 1993–2010.

Hubbard, P., and Lilley, K. (2004) 'Pacemaking the modern city: The urban politics of speed and slowness', *Environment and Planning D: Society and Space*, 22(2): 273–94.

Jones, P., Boujenko, N., and Marshall, S. (2007) *Link & Place: A Guide to Street Planning and Design*, London: Local Transport Today.

Jordan, M. (2011) 'Heckle, hiss, howl and holler', *Art & the Public Sphere*, 1(2): 117–19.

Kádár, D.Z., and Ran, Y. (2015) 'Ritual in intercultural contact: A metapragmatic case study of heckling', *Journal of Pragmatics*, 77: 41–55.

Leyendecker, K., and Cox, P. (2022) 'Cycle campaigning for a just city', *Transportation Research Interdisciplinary Perspectives*, 15: 100678.

Lombard, M. (2013) 'Struggling, suffering, hoping, waiting: Perceptions of temporality in two informal neighborhoods in Mexico', *Environment and Planning D: Society and Space*, 31(5): 813–29.

Lusk, A.C., Willett, W.C., Morris, V., Byner, C., and Li, Y. (2019) 'Bicycle facilities safest from crime and crashes: Perceptions of residents familiar with higher crime/lower income neighborhoods in Boston', *International Journal of Environmental Research and Public Health*, 16(3): 484.

Maeckelbergh, M. (2011) 'Doing is believing: Prefiguration as strategic practice in the alterglobalization movement', *Social Movement Studies*, 10(1): 1–20.

Norton, P.D. (2011) *Fighting Traffic: The Dawn of the Motor Age in the American City*, Cambridge, MA: MIT Press.

Raifman, M.A., and Choma, E.F. (2022) 'Disparities in activity and traffic fatalities by race/ethnicity', *American Journal of Preventive Medicine*, 63(2): 160–7.

Roberts, C. (2020) 'Into a headwind: Canadian cycle commuting and the growth of sustainable practices in hostile political contexts', *Energy Research & Social Science*, 70: 101679.

Rudick, R. (2020). 'Another crash on Valencia as City drags feet on safety', *Streetsblog San Francisco*, 27 October. https://sf.streetsblog.org/2020/10/27/another-crash-on-valencia-as-city-drags-feet-on-safety/ (accessed 14 December 2022).

Rudick, R. (2022) 'Valencia Street 'Just a Minute' pilot protest', *Streetsblog San Francisco*, 26 January. https://sf.streetsblog.org/2022/01/26/valencia-street-just-a-minute-pilot-protest/ (accessed 14 December 2022).

Schneider, N. (2014) *Vision Zero, SF*, Berkeley, CA: Institute of Transportation Studies, UC Berkeley.

Schoner, J.E., and Levinson, D.M. (2014) 'The missing link: Bicycle infrastructure networks and ridership in 74 US cities', *Transportation*, 41(6): 1187–204.

Shahum, L. (2017) 'Safe Streets: Insights on Vision Zero policies from European cities', German Marshall Fund of the United States. http://www.jstor.com/stable/resrep18873 (accessed 14 December 2022).

Sheller, M. (2018) *Mobility Justice: The Politics of Movement in the Age of Extremes*, London: Verso.

Smart Growth America (2019) 'What are complete streets?' https://smartgrowthamerica.org/program/national-complete-streets-coalition/publications/what-are-complete-streets/ (accessed 14 December 2022).

Southworth, M., and Ben-Joseph, E. (2013) *Streets and the Shaping of Towns and Cities*, Washington, DC: Island Press.

Stamatopoulou-Robbins, S.C. (2021) 'Failure to build: Sewage and the choppy temporality of infrastructure in Palestine', *Environment and Planning E: Nature and Space*, 4(1): 28–42.

Stehlin, J. (2015) 'Cycles of investment: Bicycle infrastructure, gentrification, and the restructuring of the San Francisco Bay Area', *Environment and Planning A: Economy and Space*, 47(1): 121–37.

Thorpe, A. (2020) *Owning the Street: The Everyday Life of Property*, Cambridge, MA: MIT Press.

Thorpe, A. (2022) 'Prefigurative infrastructure: Mobility, citizenship, and the agency of objects', *International Journal of Urban and Regional Research*, 47(2): 183–99.

Tolkoff, L., and Anzai, K. (2022) 'Accelerating sustainable transportation in California', SPUR. https://www.spur.org/sites/default/files/2022-04/SPUR_Accelerating_Sustainable_Transportation_in_California.pdf (accessed 29 July 2022).

UN Environment Programme (2020) *Share the Road Programme Annual Report 2019*, Nairobi: UNEP.

van Goeverden, K., Nielsen, T.S., Harder, H., and van Nes, R. (2015) 'Interventions in bicycle infrastructure: Lessons from Dutch and Danish cases', *Transportation Research Procedia*, 10: 403–12.

Vision Zero Coalition (2015) 'Vision Zero: Where San Francisco stands in achieving Vision Zero: One Year Progress Report'. http://sfbike.org/wp-content/uploads/2015/02/Vision-Zero-Report-2014-web.pdf?org=451&lvl=100&ite=7046&lea=3362887&ctr=0&par=1 (accessed 14 December 2022).

Vreugdenhil, R., and Williams, S. (2013) 'White line fever: A socio-technical perspective on the contested implementation of an urban bike lane network: White line fever', *Area*, 45(3): 283–91.

Wajcman, J., and Dodd, N. (2016) 'Introduction: The powerful are fast, the powerless are slow', in J. Wajcman and N. Dodd (eds) *The Sociology of Speed: Digital, Organizational, and Social Temporalities*, Oxford: Oxford University Press, pp 1–12.

WHO (World Health Organization) (2019) 'Global status report on road safety 2018'. https://www.who.int/violence_injury_prevention/road_safety_status/2018/en/ (accessed 14 December 2022).

Wiener, S. (2022) 'Senator Wiener introduces SB 922 to expedite sustainable transportation projects'. https://sd11.senate.ca.gov/print/967 (accessed 29 July 2022).

Wild, K., Woodward, A., Field, A., and Macmillan, A. (2018) 'Beyond "bikelash": Engaging with community opposition to cycle lanes', *Mobilities*, 13(4): 505–19.

Zhu, M., Li, H., Sze, N.N., and Ren, G. (2022) 'Exploring the impacts of street layout on the frequency of pedestrian crashes: A micro-level study', *Journal of Safety Research*, 81: 91–100.

13

Urban Infrastructure In and Out of Time

Jean-Paul D. Addie, Michael R. Glass, and Jen Nelles

The central contribution of the book is making new space for time and temporality in the global 'infrastructure turn'. Contemporary infrastructure scholarship is highlighting the significance of infrastructural systems to the production and reconstruction of urban and regional space, yet we and our contributors argue it is the combination of temporalities and infrastructures that infuses cities and regions with rhythm and meaning. The book's chapters demonstrate the complex and multifaceted ways that time pervades the city through infrastructure and shapes the infrastructures of cities themselves. We have encountered the evolving materiality of water pipes and pumps, of concrete and rails, of electrical microgrids and global pathogens, and the resultant speeds and time frames through which financial value unevenly flows across time and space. The chapters' empirical investigations have revealed a wealth of formal and informal social infrastructures that enable, produce, and replicate socio-technical configurations, from unfurling forms of financialization and state de-risking to the regulatory regimes shaping our ability to access urban space. We have also seen how time can be put to work (pasts mobilized, futures engaged, the present contested and claimed) to understand our current infrastructural worlds and foster their potential alternatives. What we hope emerges from these temporal adventures in infrastructure is a renewed appreciation of 'infrastructure time' as a social construct whose plurality – that is, the co-presence of multiple temporalities – informs, and is informed by, diverse, overlapping, and sometimes paradoxical human experiences (Nowotny, 1994).

The challenge for future infrastructure studies is to create geographically contextual accounts of these pluralistic temporal modalities, considering empirical detail about both the microseconds involved in self-healing systems and the epochal transformations of the Anthropocene. As we have seen from the streets of San Francisco to the fields of Laos, infrastructural times are embodied as people navigate their temporal and spatial worlds and are tempered by their individual agency and social constraints. Studying infrastructure's temporalities thus hinges on incorporating multiple knowledge systems (academic and lived) and requires us to recognize multiple ways of knowing and doing infrastructure time.

The organization of this book into three parts reflects some of the constituent complexities with which an enlivened sense of infrastructure time should engage. Part I addressed how researchers can conceptualize infrastructure time through notions of past, present, and future. We then added the contingencies of how overlapping temporalities shape infrastructure development and the making of particular global urban worlds in Part II. We confronted the dialectical challenges of disrupting times and times of disruption in Part III and considered what these mean for thinking about infrastructure time in practical and conceptual terms. We use this concluding chapter to reflect on these provocations and to highlight the key themes and contributions emerging from the book. This stands as a call to action to reassert the essential co-constitution of time and space when it comes to infrastructural research at multiple scales. We illustrate how these investigations into infrastructure's temporalities collectively advance knowledge at the intersection of urban, infrastructure, and time studies and assert how this volume has established 'infrastructure time' as a generative conceptual and methodological analytic. We conclude by charting out future terrains, trajectories, and questions to motivate a 'temporal turn' in critical infrastructure studies.

Infrastructure studies of/with time: Cases and comparison

Infrastructural Times is defined by an embrace of the interdisciplinary imperative underpinning the global 'infrastructure turn' (Addie et al, 2020). While some of our contributors are primarily scholars of time, many are urban and infrastructural researchers who used their chapters to grapple with how temporal frames and experiences of time inform their wider work. By using time and temporality as boundary concepts, we have thought through, and with, commonalities and contradictions emerging across their disparate approaches to studying urban infrastructure. Interdisciplinary dialogue, both within and between chapters, foregrounds the variegated infrastructural arenas where time comes into play, whether in the restructuring on multiscalar governance dynamics in Egypt, in the formation and flow of planning knowledge determining infrastructural lives in Venezuela and Laos, or in marshalling cross-sectoral risk profiles in an era of infrastructure-led development. Furthermore, bringing together a multiplicity of temporalities and cases from the global North and South compels further comparative reflection surrounding the conceptual and practical challenges of working with infrastructural times in specific geographic and historical contexts.

Following anthropological and ethnographic traditions, juxtaposition as a form of comparison illuminates what is distinct and provocative in given empirical instances and – by thinking *with* difference as a mode of analysis – 'destabilizes unexamined views and generalizations and opens up new possibilities of understanding' (Caldeira, 2017: 5). Taken collectively, our chapters belie the notion of time as a singular universal abstract measure that irreversibility ticks forward. Instead, these studies reveal how the heterodox nature of infrastructure time necessarily incorporates the material and the imagined, the technical and the organic, the planned and the affective, and how time can be accelerated, slowed, or suspended for different communities at differing junctures. The disciplinary logics of abstract time may oppose us as an external alienating force, drawing economic, political, ecological, social, cultural, and biological life towards the (illusion of a) simultaneous experience of quantified temporality (Nowotny, 1994; Lefebvre, 2004). Yet in the face of the creeping commodification of society, time itself remains a multiplicity, something that is qualitatively understood and lived on a deeply personal level in terms of our subjective perceptions and the political demands for 'temporal sovereignty' (Nowotny, 1994: 18–19).

If juxtaposition foregrounds the diversity of infrastructural temporality, the next step towards a comparative study of infrastructure time is to draw the lines of intersection that bring interdisciplinary research into deeper conversation. Connections appear via 'repeated instances' across empirical cases that move us from idiographic specificities towards the identification of some nomothetic regularities in the face of 'overcoded explanatory frameworks' (Jacobs, 2012: 906). For example, tracing the adoption of financial de-risking practices from Jakarta to Cairo reveals how an emerging infrastructural asset class materializes in the concrete and institutional remaking of urban space. We can further connect repeated instances of infrastructural knowledges (the knowledge that makes infrastructure possible) as they circulate across time and space: whether from the Harvard–MIT Joint Center for Urban Studies to Ciudad Guayana and back; from military applications to US military bases; or across the possible pasts (lived and bypassed) that continue to remake Berlin. Comparative lessons in speed politics are readily apparent in the contrasting experiences of West Papuans, persons living with dementia in suburban Toronto, and transport activists in San Francisco. Each case documents how marginalized communities are imbricated into hegemonic temporal orders while illustrating their capacity to refuse, resist, and remake time on their own terms. We encourage our readers to make connections across these cases to promote 'genetic' (Robinson, 2022) forms of comparison. Such comparative approaches tease out connections and commonalities and can expose how context-specific infrastructural temporalities are assembled in contingent ways and how things might have been – and could be – different.

On the one hand, the infrastructural times showcased in this book provide objects of analysis for comparative investigation. On the other hand, time can also foster conceptual innovation via 'generative' comparative tactics when deployed as an analytical or methodological framework (Robinson, 2022). In linking the temporalities of infrastructural lifetimes, social practices, and imaginaries, Coutard (this volume) illustrates how we might conceptually and methodologically integrate the necessary relations between time and infrastructure in future urban studies. Addie's (this volume) account of temporal repetition presents an alternative reading of Jacobs's (2012) 'repeated instances' (not just *where* instances are repeated, but *when*). In this sense, rhythmanalysis can be used as a comparative method to assess the production of difference and the dynamics of geo-historical continuity and discontinuity. Moss (this volume) and Ekman (this volume) both build from the conceptual and methodological practices of urban history to offer incisive interventions that contextualize the empirical and analytical utility of the past. Moss's call to *use* usable infrastructural pasts, in particular, gives researchers a robust means to understand how diverse histories can inform the present, and how comparing multifaceted pasts can help presage future infrastructural conditions across geographic contexts. The point of such comparative analysis is not just to identify nomothetic regularities of infrastructural times (nor is it to arrive at a singular grand theory). Such comparative strategies also help to recognize the temporal complexity of our infrastructural lives and begin to problematize these as deeply as – and weave them into – spatial perspectives on infrastructure. Infrastructure knowledge and the ideologies informing the planning and development of socio-technical systems circulate between institutions and cities, but mobile urban policies are assembled in place in differing and often unintended ways at specific temporal junctures. Interrogating the paradoxes, tensions, and multiplicity of infrastructure time via emergent modes of transdisciplinary (Coutard, this volume) or postcolonial (Simone, this volume) investigation can allow us to further orient ourselves towards more inclusive, equitable, and sustainable urban futures.

Infrastructural time as a political problematic

Extending this argument – and reflecting a key element of the critical infrastructure turn (McFarlane and Rutherford, 2008) – multiple chapters directly confront infrastructure time as a political problematic. On a fundamental level we cannot escape time, its passage, or the temporal rhythms of existence, even in the instant connectivity and splintered premium infrastructures of networked society. As infrastructural systems differentially connect and bypass networked space-time, unequal social relations are continually inscribed into the urban fabric (Graham and Marvin, 2001). A key social consequence of infrastructure's uneven temporalities is that some people have time to kill while others can only owe it. Examples including the racialized West Papuans subjugated by the colonial state and the essential workers compelled to work in the just-in-time economy during the COVID-19 pandemic illustrate the inequities of 'temporal arbitrage', where marginalized communities and exploited labour surrender their experience of time to the benefit of others (Chen and Sun, 2020). It is by paying concerted attention to the problematic of infrastructure time that we can 'politicize hitherto hidden aspects of temporal domination [as temporalities] enable and constrain, include or exclude, and produce or reproduce urban inequalities' (Besedovsky et al, 2019: 584).

Our contributors demonstrate how the temporalities of infrastructure can be reworked to reproduce hegemonic social orders, for instance, through strategies of state-backed de-risking or privileging the operation of critical infrastructures over equity concerns. Yet many cases also expose fissures, opportunities, and concrete practices through which hegemonic times can be contested and remade, whether through the tactical disruption of DIY (do-it-yourself) interventions (Thorpe, this volume), refusals of 'crip time' (Biglieri and Keil, this volume), or utilization of an open toolkit to study infrastructure-based futuring (Coutard, this volume). Such disruptive practices constitute moments of what Sharma (2014) terms 'temporal insurgency'. Many of this book's interventions support Sharma's assertion that 'a temporal politics is not about doing nothing, slowing down, or just taking leave of the institutions that exploit time. Not many people can merely exit and bask in the glory of free time. The first step is a time politics oriented towards dismantling the temporal order' (2014: 13).

What lessons can we draw from infrastructural disruptions and their implications for urban and regional decision-making? Urban infrastructures open multiple temporal horizons, but realizing progressive infrastructure futures 'require[s] a deep understanding of existing infrastructure institutional practices and how they are embedded in the preferences and aspirations of urban residents' (Simone and Pieterse, 2017: 138). New infrastructures are, as Anand et al put it, 'promises made in the present about our future' (2018: 27). Nevertheless, the materiality and spatial structure of infrastructural systems crystallize the ideology, knowledge, and needs of present and past eras and may therefore rise as barriers to alternative accumulation regimes or social values of different times.

Shifting our temporal horizons can open alternative ways of seeing, analysing, and validating other articulations of infrastructural practice and political transformation. If we reject privileging the teleological timelines of 'project time' and position incompleteness, adaptation, and decay as essential characteristics of infrastructure, the importance of reparative 'temporal fixes' actualized through the everyday labour of filling potholes, tightening leaky pipes, or prying fatbergs from sewer walls come into focus (Graham and Thrift, 2007; Denis and Pontille, 2015; Addie, 2021). Infrastructural promises made by politicians are commonly attached to electoral and budget cycles, whereas the quotidian rhythms of life across city-regions are mediated by different senses of 'time', 'tempo', and 'the temporal' (Sharma, 2011). In general, we are better able to understand the dynamic character of urbanism and urbanization when we recognize the varied and complex temporalities that underscore their construction. It is also possible to view the timing of infrastructural creation, maintenance, and repair less as acts of resilience and more as part of the performative, choreographed interaction between governance and the governed (Glass, 2018).

Time, space, and the scaling of infrastructural worlds

The temporal dynamics involved in making global urban worlds has been a central concern across this volume. Chapters have explored the urban across geographic contexts, forms, and levels of granularity. These range from global metropolises transforming their hinterlands and networked infrastructures reworking connections between military bases and adjacent towns to struggles over the right to the street and everyday social practices carried out in the shadows of infrastructural mega-projects. An obvious insight, then, is that a multidimensional understanding of urban infrastructure's temporalities must unfold across, and connect, uneven and multi-scalar terrains. These encompass mechanisms that control the circadian rhythms which help regulate individuals' behaviour and metabolism at a cellular level and the epochal transformations of anthropogenic climate change and their attendant visions of utopian and catastrophic futurity. In reading across these chapters, we encounter distinct epistemic and scalar perspectives, but these are not ontologically separate. They are mutually constitutive: small-scale lived experiences establish the groundwork upon which broader socio-spatial structures and forms of meaning-making are laid (Angelo and Hentschel, 2015).

Different temporalities and axes of social contestation come to the fore as we shift our scalar vantage point. Space changes within differing temporal systems. Moss (this volume) and Schindler and Kanai (this volume) both illustrate in different ways how utilizing historians' conceptions of time (with scales incorporating the *longue durée* of history and short run-time of events) gives us a sense of time that attunes us to the dramatic transformation and gradual accretions that (re)make infrastructural space. Institutions that appear to have a degree of permanence often change substantively over time as socio-political contexts evolve and technological developments arise, a process evident in post-Mubarak Egypt (Wahdan and Elshayal, this volume). This, however, raises questions about who has the capacity and privilege to see over what spatial scales and temporal horizons and what, if anything, is analytically distinct about an urban perspective on infrastructure time.

Cities and urban infrastructure have featured prominently in the contemporary 'infrastructure turn'. This renewed attention on infrastructure's material and discursive effects has done much to advance the study of cities by examining how urban inhabitants, institutions, and ecologies build and reshape socio-technical configurations (Wiig et al, 2023). In considering temporality and the making of global urban worlds, the urban *as a scale* draws us into the localized, experiential, and affective nature of infrastructure space and time, whether via a Berlin street, a Brampton neighbourhood, or a sprawling metropolitan setting such as Jayapura. Moreover, *as an analytic*, the urban in this volume has attuned us to questions of inequality, power, and networked relations between cities: in Brenner and Schmid's (2015: 178) terms, the urban is best understood as 'a collective project ... produced through collective action, negotiation, imagination, experimentation and struggle'. Collectively, the chapters in this book illustrate how urban infrastructures operate as a vital setting and stake for such social struggle, fostering, as they do, deep inequities and articulations of uneven development. Finally, as a *mediatory* level, the 'urban' in urban infrastructure reveals interconnections between a global level of abstract relations, institutional knowledges, and distant orders and a private level of inhabiting and everyday experience (Lefebvre, 2003: 79–81). It is through urban infrastructure that we encounter and understand general, abstract, and linear temporal orders and subjective, experiential, cyclical times. This is not a matter of scale, but of intersecting aspects of social reality; it is where the structural forces of capital, the state, and 'infrastructure fundamentalism' meet the everyday lived urbanisms of Papuan traders, Cairo commuters, and Canada's essential workers.

Yet the urban is not an all-encompassing problematic with which to examine infrastructure time. We see alternative epistemic vantage points emerging where urban questions abut the temporal logics of military requirements, provincial/state politics, or the nation-state. In our own collaborative research, we argue that reframing infrastructural questions through the scalar and analytic lens of the region prompts infrastructure researchers to ask different questions and results in alternative readings of socio-technical configurations (Addie et al, 2020; Glass et al, 2023). Indeed, institutional, legal, and regulatory contexts of infrastructure governance often elevate the region as a privileged scale of infrastructure provision. Multiplier effects for infrastructural investment are calculated using a region as the denominator while the 'operational landscapes' of large technical systems necessitate governance dynamics that transcend place-based city politics. There are inevitable overlaps and interchanges between urban and regional perspectives, but foregrounding 'the regional' compels us to consider multiple jurisdictions and cross-boundary governance realities. These concerns, along with the need to reflect profound differences between metropolitan and non-metropolitan regionalism, also require balancing competitive and collaborative stakeholder imperatives articulated through differing temporal horizons and institutional time frames (Gansauer and Haggerty, 2021).

'Project time' within a regional envelope is not singular but is negotiated in a variety of institutional spaces and times. This is a problematic that warrants further attention. Additionally, differing political constituencies are activated at the regional scale, as illustrated in the roll-out of responses to COVID-19 in Ontario and in the presence of regional geopolitical ambitions and concrete infrastructural spaces in Indonesia and Laos. Scaling up the politics of street infrastructure to the regional scale would introduce a different set of interests and actors and muddy the possibilities for realizing procedural and distributive equity around local urban transport. This is not simply a question of expanding our urban political frame. We would not only encounter the institutional realities of inter-regional geo-politics in metropolitan space but also need to confront the issues of who is forced to live auto-centric lives (out of necessity rather than choice) in varying metropolitan settings, and what the temporal implications and social consequences are for those faced with unavoidable hours-long cross-regional commutes. Labour and housing markets work at regional scales that reframe more localized claims of infrastructural citizenship. Local interventions remain significant, but regionalizing such struggles situates them as one of many contestations operating across myriad intersecting spatial and temporal scales.

Off the clock: Future trajectories for infrastructure time

This book has provided an expansive yet by no means exhaustive exploration of infrastructure time. One of our key objectives in closing this volume is to articulate how *Infrastructural Times* can inform a continuing research agenda – a 'temporal turn' – at the intersection of urban, infrastructure, and time studies. These are opportune moments to examine the production and experience of temporality through infrastructure. Emerging scholarship on maintenance and care, infrastructural imaginaries, green transitions, 'smart' digital governance technologies, automation, and technological disruptions all offer fertile grounds to infuse the question of time into critical infrastructure studies. In this concluding section, we open discussion on some exciting areas for further exploration (either touched upon by our contributors or beyond the scope of this volume) and present what we see as several compelling avenues for future temporal investigations of urban infrastructural planning, policy, and politics.

Accounting for urban futures

Accounting spreadsheets and software are a powerful if often overlooked conditioning force behind the timing and tempo of infrastructural provision. The construction of urban and regional futures through new transportation infrastructure can only occur if the utility of that project is justified via a nominally neutral and quantitative methodology such as cost–benefit analysis, which enumerates a set of values to evaluate the economic feasibility of a project. Cost–benefit calculations involve profoundly spatio-temporal assumptions, including the appropriate geographic scale for assessing the utility of the project, and the appropriate temporal horizons for understanding the funding and amortization. Both technical parameters (space and time) are highly malleable and can shape decisions about urban futures. The analysts who conduct cost–benefit analyses are hence responsible for shaping infrastructure times through their expertise on the appropriate discount rate to employ (calculating how future costs and benefits relate to present values), which in turn expresses how the future will be calibrated within the model. Benefit–cost ratios, internal rates of return, and geographic sensitivity analysis are all measured, and cost–benefit analyses are themselves aggregated into capital allocation software to evaluate the optimal tranche of infrastructure projects to approve in given budget cycles. Once infrastructures are built, the calculus shifts to optimal replacement time methodologies that use age to replace models to calculate the probability of infrastructural failure for actuarial decisions about when to replace or repair assets such as buried pipes and cables.

The socio-technical practice of allocating value and risk to infrastructural futures demands more attention (see Schindler and Kanai, this volume). As Weber's (2021) research on the time value of money shows, the calculative techniques used to determine project value are employed by networks of analysts trained in the language and presumptions of these methods. Because time and temporality are such profound features that underscore the justification of new infrastructural realities, the critical analysis of forecasting and budgeting tools beckons as a fruitful field for future research.

Infrastructure at night

Work in the field of 'night studies' offers another productive arena for research on infrastructure time. During the night, the city is animated by a distinct set of material infrastructures and 'dispositions' (Easterling, 2014) that differ from those of the daytime (Shaw, 2018). Urban transportation illustrates the differing infrastructural logics animating the 24-hour city. Many transit systems remain behind the times, slow to recalibrate in the face of shifts to the daily rhythms of consumer demand. This is due in part to the immutability of transportation corridors: roads and railbeds are difficult to relocate, meaning that these infrastructural components of the transit city do not change as populations move and different areas wax and wane in popularity throughout the day. The night-time economy poses challenges to the anticipation of transit providers. Even the London Underground did not run a round-the-clock schedule until August 2016, when service was launched on a limited number of 'Night Tube' lines over Friday and Saturday nights. Such a night service (even if limited) can safely transport revellers home once the evening is over but is still only a partial reflection of how cities work in the twenty-first century. For instance, failing to adequately plan for the mobility and safety needs of night-shift workers across sectors from construction and logistics to healthcare raises important questions regarding the temporal equity of our urban mobility systems (McArthur et al, 2019). These include the profoundly gendered experience of time fostered by urban infrastructures at night (Farina et al, 2022) and their susceptibility to un- or under-regulated disruptions from rideshare platforms such as Uber.

While regulatory interventions that are sensitive to the rhythms of the 24-hour city offer a means to pursue inclusive transport policies (Acuto et al, 2021), researchers should recognize that the city at night also provides important spaces for transgressive social practices and forms of infrastructural appropriation. Graffiti artists can take advantage of the night to tag bridges, tunnels, and trains, marking their physical and symbolic place in the city. In more extreme terms, the cover of darkness offers 'urban explorers' the chance to hack derelict and emergent infrastructural spaces, accessing sites and sights that are typically off limits (Garrett, 2013). Elsewhere, unhoused individuals (re)appropriate urban infrastructure (a park bench, a flyover, a subway car) to meet their basic need for shelter and a place to lay their head. The diurnal–nocturnal rhythms of infrastructure therefore challenge us to examine the creativity, transgression, and resiliency engendered in the city at night and compels a critique of the temporal privileges and exclusions that reframe infrastructure's varying temporal values.

Indigenous temporalities

There are always limits to the reach of hegemonic temporal orders. In foregrounding infrastructural life in a state of becoming, postcolonial work in the 'infrastructure turn' has disrupted monistic readings of socio-technical systems. The co-presence of 'heterogeneous infrastructural regimes' and epistemologies (Lawhon et al, 2018) invokes an associated amalgam of complex, contested, and overlapping temporalities that ferment in the gaps between the precarity of living on others' time and the possibility of reclaiming time for yourself (Simone, 2020). As multiple temporalities collide in the fissures of the planned city, informal sites, liminal spaces, and contested zones generate new temporal rhythms and opportunities to claim the right to produce urban space-time.

While colonial infrastructural violence may impose elements of 'settler time' into the temporal practices of marginalized subjects, indigenous understandings of time present a diverse set of temporal ontologies that cannot be reduced to a pre-modern 'Other' (Rifkin, 2017). Building upon Simone's (this volume) account of 'Papuan Time', thinking with non-Western experiences of time both challenges the binaries of 'settler time' (modern/pre-modern, progress/backwardness) and re-inscribes 'static' communities written out of time in the face of social and technological advancement. Many indigenous communities run counter to the generalized hegemony of Western time by embracing multiple temporalities rooted in ways of knowing connected to the land, relational rhythms of nature, and intra-generational kinship (Iparraguirre, 2016). For the Māori, time is not an arrow, but a spiral of multilayered times with 'no finality, no endings, no discrete historic phases' (Winter, 2020: 286). Awâsis (2020) validates comparable temporal logics in North American First Nations' 'Anishinaabe time', stressing the significance of intergenerational temporal frames and the importance of centring non-humans and their spiritual relations in community decision-making.

How might indigenous temporalities inform the study of urban infrastructure? On the one hand, engaging diverse epistemic communities can challenge, reframe, and restructure the technocratic governance and engineering knowledge that tends to shape modern infrastructures. Hoefsloot et al (2022) assess how technocratic planning has been opened to indigenous knowledge and approaches to water governance in Lima, albeit in fitful ways. In the face of climate change and urban expansion, Lima's municipal water utility agency has shifted towards a more pluralistic water knowledge system that appropriates both alternative epistemologies and material technologies through the restoration of pre-Hispanic *amunas*: small channels that slow the flow of rainwater so the soil can absorb it (Hoefsloot et al, 2022: 5). The resultant hybridized 'Andean water knowledge model' builds place-based resilience while partially integrating indigenous communities and knowledge into the process of infrastructure-based futuring. On the other hand, studies of North American pipeline reviews and indigenous resistance indicate that the planning regimes and time horizons of 'modern' infrastructure frequently exclude indigenous political and economic systems (Estes, 2019). In part, this reflects the fact that knowledge encoded in indigenous languages, cultural rhythms, and temporal formations often cannot be fully expressed in English (Awâsis, 2020: 846). McCreary and Milligan (2014) thus caution against the instrumental incorporation of indigenous ways of knowing into modern environmental and infrastructural governance. Instead, they expose the role of infrastructure systems in reproducing exploitative socio-ecological relations *and* advocate for indigenous communities' capacity to resist and reshape global geographies. Engaging infrastructure through alternative temporal ontologies may be generative then, not only because this validates heterodox ways of being-in-time but also because it expresses claims for self-determination in the face of colonial violence. Extending ethical obligations into deep time can further rework notions of 'temporal justice' (Goodin, 2009) beyond the limiting parameters of modernity.

Closing Time

This volume has presented urban and regional infrastructures as multifaceted 'timescapes' (Adam, 2004) that disclose both the material rhythms and operational logics of infrastructure time, and the possibility of creating more equitable collective provision, meaning, and urban solidarity in the present and into the future. Neither infrastructure nor the city, though, are fully knowable. The 'temporal incompleteness' of both means their outcomes are emergent (Guma, 2022). Amin and Thrift (2017: 89) have called for us to 'change our infrastructures so that they do not just act as tramlines but provide much greater senses of possibility'. There is much conceptual and applied work on infrastructure time that remains to be done to open such lines of flight. As a research problematic, infrastructure time foregrounds the importance of cyclical and hierarchical planning processes that are nested in different scales of the future, and the competing moral frameworks on which these processes are based. In the face of the next global infrastructure scramble, the neo-colonizing logics of network time, and the ongoing acceleration and commodification of urban life, we need to claim time for humbler and more sustainable urban futures, one capable of embracing rather than overriding place-specific histories, temporalities, geographies, ecologies, and epistemologies. Such futures may emerge, for instance, in the more-than-human temporalities of urban infrastructure (Wakefield and Braun, 2019; Taufen et al, 2022) or in a carefully decelerated urbanism that can reclaim time to 'enrich (rather than bypass) processes of democracy, citizenship, sustainability and belonging in the making of cities' (Shaban and Datta, 2017: 208). The richness of this book's empirical cases and theoretical contributions, and the generative sparks emerging between their pluralistic approaches to the temporalities and temporal politics of infrastructure, should help illuminate this path.

References

Acuto, M., Seijas, A., McArthur, J., and Robin, E. (2021) *Managing Cities at Night: A Practitioners Guide to the Urban Governance of the Night*, Bristol: Bristol University Press.

Adam, B. (2004) *Time*, Cambridge: Polity Press.

Addie, J.-P.D. (2021) 'Urban life in the shadows of infrastructural death: From people as infrastructure to dead labor and back again', *Urban Geography*, 42(9): 1349–61.

Addie, J.-P.D., Glass, M.R., and Nelles, J. (2020) 'Regionalizing the infrastructure turn: A research agenda', *Regional Studies, Regional Science*, 7(1): 10–26.

Amin, A., and Thrift, N. (2017) *Seeing Like a City*, Cambridge: Polity Press.

Angelo, H., and Hentschel, C. (2015) 'Interactions with infrastructure as windows into social worlds: A method for critical urban studies', *City*, 19(2–3): 306–12.

Appel, H., Anand, N., and Gupta, A. (2018) 'Temporality, politics, and the promise of infrastructure', in N. Anand, A. Gupta, and H. Appel (eds) *The Promise of Infrastructure*, Durham, NC: Duke University Press, pp 1–38.

Awâsis, S. (2020) '"Anishinaabe time": Temporalities and impact assessment in pipeline reviews', *Journal of Political Ecology*, 27(1): 830–52.

Besedovsky, N., Grafe, F.-J., Hilbrandt, H., and Langguth, H. (2019) 'Time as infrastructure: For an analysis of contemporary urbanization', *City*, 23(4–5): 580–8.

Brenner, N., and Schmid, C. (2015) 'Towards a new epistemology of the urban?', *City*, 19(2–3): 151–82.

Caldeira, T.P.R. (2017) 'Peripheral urbanization: Autoconstruction, transversal logics, and politics in cities of the global south', *Environment and Planning D: Society and Space*, 35(1): 3–20.

Chen, J.Y., and Sun, P. (2020) 'Temporal arbitrage, fragmented rush, and opportunistic behaviours: The labour politics of time in the platform economy', *New Media & Society*, 22(9): 1680–98.

Denis, J., and Pontille, D. (2015) 'Material ordering and the care of things', *Science, Technology, and Human Values*, 40(3): 338–67.

Easterling, K. (2014) *Extrastatecraft: The Power of Infrastructure Space*, London: Verso.

Estes, N. (2019) *Our History in the Future: Standing Rock versus the Dakota Access Pipeline and the Long Tradition of Indigenous Resistance*, London: Verso.

Farina, L., Boussaux, K., and Plyushteva, A. (2022) 'Moving safely at night? Women's nocturnal mobilities in Recife, Brazil and Brussels, Belgium', *Gender, Place and Culture*, 29(9): 1229–50.

Gansauer, G., and Haggerty, J. (2021) 'Beyond city limits: Infrastructural regionalism in rural Montana, USA', *Territory, Politics, Governance*, https://doi.org/10.1080/21622671.2021.1980428.

Garrett, B.L. (2013) *Explore Everything: Place-Hacking the City*, London: Verso.

Glass, M.R. (2018) 'Seeing like a city through the Singapore City Gallery', *City*, 22(2): 236–56.

Glass, M.R., Nelles, J., and Addie, J.-P.D. (2023) 'On fetishes, fragments, and future: Regionalizing infrastructural lives', in A. Wiig, K.G. Ward, T. Enright, M. Hodson, H. Pearsall, and J. Silver (eds) *Infrastructuring Urban Futures: The Politics of Remaking Cities*, Bristol: Bristol University Press, pp 188–98.

Goodin, R. (2009) 'Temporal justice', *Journal of Social Policy*, 39(1): 1–16.

Graham, S., and Marvin, S. (2001) *Splintering Urbanism: Networked Infrastructures, Technological Mobilities and the Urban Condition*, New York: Routledge.

Graham, S., and Thrift, N. (2007) 'Out of order: Understanding repair and maintenance', *Theory, Culture & Society*, 24(3): 1–25.

Guma, P.K. (2022) 'The temporal incompleteness of infrastructure and the urban', *Journal of Urban Technology*, 29(1): 59–67.

Hoefsloot, F., Martinez, J., and Pfeffer, K. (2022) 'An emerging knowledge system for future water governance: Sowing water for Lima', *Territory, Politics, Governance*, https://doi.org/10.1080/21622671.2021.2023365.

Iparraguirre, G. (2016) 'Time, temporality and cultural rhythmics: An anthropological case study', *Time & Society*, 25(3): 613–33.

Jacobs, J.M. (2012) 'Commentary: Comparing comparative urbanisms', *Urban Geography*, 33(6): 904–14.

Lawhon, M., Nilsson, D., Silver, J., Ernstson, H., and Lwasa, S. (2018) 'Thinking through heterogeneous infrastructure configurations', *Urban Studies*, 55(4): 720–32.

Lefebvre, H. (2003) *The Urban Revolution*, Minneapolis, MN: University of Minnesota Press.

Lefebvre, H. (2004) *Rhythmanalysis: Space, Time and Everyday Life*, London: Bloomsbury.

McArthur, J., Robin, E., and Smeds, E. (2019) 'Socio-spatial and temporal dimensions of transport equity for London's night time economy', *Transport Research Part A: Policy and Practice*, 121(March): 433–43.

McCreary, T.A., and Milligan, R.C. (2014) 'Pipelines, permits, and protests: Carrier Sekani encounters with the Enbridge Northern Gateway Project', *Cultural Geographies*, 21(1): 115–29.

McFarlane, C., and Rutherford, J. (2008) 'Political infrastructures: Governing and experiencing the fabric of the city', *International Journal of Urban and Regional Research*, 32(2): 363–74.

Nowotny, H. (1994) *Time: The Modern and Postmodern Experience*, Cambridge: Polity Press.

Rifkin, M. (2017) *Beyond Settler Time: Temporal Sovereignty and Indigenous Self-Determination*, Durham, NC: Duke University Press.

Robinson, J. (2022) *Comparative Urbanism: Tactics for Global Urban Studies*, Hoboken, NJ: Wiley.

Shaban, A., and Datta, A. (2017) 'Slow: Toward a decelerated urbanism', in A. Datta and A. Shaban (eds) *Mega-Urbanization in the Global South: Fast Cities and New Urban Utopias of the Postcolonial State*, London: Routledge, pp 205–20.

Sharma, S. (2011) 'The biological economy of time', *Journal of Communication Inquiry*, 35(4): 439–44.

Sharma, S. (2014) 'Because the night belongs to lovers: Occupying the time of precarity', *Communication and Critical/Cultural Studies*, 11(1): 5–14.

Shaw, R. (2018) *The Nocturnal City*, Abingdon: Routledge.

Simone, A.M. (2020) 'The complicity and interdependencies of temporalities', *Urban Geography*, 41(10): 1274–6.

Simone, A.M., and Pieterse, E. (2017) *New Urban Worlds: Inhabiting Dissonant Times*, Cambridge: Polity Press.

Taufen, A., Hoffman, L.M., and Yocom, K.P. (2022) 'Assemblage as heuristic: Unveiling infrastructures or port city waterfronts', *Territory, Politics, Governance*, https://doi.org/10.1080/21622671.2022.2055631.

Wakefield, S., and Braun, B. (2019) 'Oystertecture: Infrastructure, profanation, and the sacred figure of the human', in K. Hetherington (ed) *Infrastructure, Environment, and Life in the Anthropocene*, Durham, NC: Duke University Press, pp 193–215.

Weber, R. (2021) 'Embedding futurity in urban governance: Redevelopment schemes and the time value of money', *Environment and Planning A: Economy and Space*, 53(3): 503–24.

Wiig, A., Ward, K.G., Enright, T., Hodson, M., Pearsall, H., and Silver J. (eds) *Infrastructuring Urban Futures: The Politics of Remaking Cities*, Bristol: Bristol University Press.

Winter, C.J. (2020) 'Does time colonise intergenerational environmental justice theory?', *Environmental Politics*, 29(2): 278–96.

Index

Note: References to figures appear in *italic* type.

A

Aalbers, M.B. 164
ableism 238, 240–1, 242
Abram, Simone 35, 252
Abrams, Charles 126, 135
activism, in San Francisco 18, 253–66
actor-network theory (ANT) 56–7
Adam, B. 2, 5, 8, 10, 77, 209, 281
adaptation 85–6
adapted pasts 59–60
Administrative Capital for Urban Development (ACUD)/Egypt 169, 172
Africa, South
  bus rapid transit (BRT) initiatives 35
  mega-projects 36
African Union 150
ageism 242
agency 217, 219, 220, 244
Agenda 2063 150
aircraft control systems 187, 190
alcohol consumption, in Jayapura 106
always-on power 202
Amin, A. 3, 31, 281
Amin, Massoud 190, 193
amunas 280
Anagos, J. 163
Anand, N. 31
Angkasa district, Jayapura 108–9
Anishinaabe time 280
annoyance, and waiting 215
Anthropocene 16, 73, 85–8, 271
Appleyard, Donald 125, 126–7, 128, 129–30, 131–3
Argentina Productiva 2030 150
Arican, Alize 12, 251–2
Armed Forces Land Projects Agency (Egypt) 169
Armitage, David 54, 55
arrhythmia 29, 32, 40 *see also* disruption, rhythmic; disruption, temporal; dissonance, rhythmic; dissonance, temporal

Asdal, Kristin 56–7
Asia, South 165, 232–3
assemblage theory 57
asset class 14, 161, 163, 165, 177, 178, 272
  and Cairo Monorail 172
  and de-risking 176
asset management firms 163
Association of Defense Communities (ADC) 198, *200*
asynchronous modes of resilience 200–2
automobility 112, 133, 249, 250–1, 265
autonomic computing (AC) 188
'autonomy–resources trade-off' 164
Avenida Guayana 12, 13, 119, 120, 125, 127–8, 129, 130
Awâsis, S. 280

B

Bacon, Edmund 125
Bakker, K. 57
Bandak, A. 211
Banfield, Edward 132
Bank for Construction and Housing (Egypt) 168
banking system, Egypt 166
Baschet, J. 84, 87, 89, 90, 91
Basel III 162–3
behavioural learning 65
Belt and Road Initiative (BRI) 110, 112
Berlin 49, 50, *51*, 57, 58, 59–60, 61–2, 63–4
Berliners fetch water from a public pump during the general strike opposing the Kapp Putsch, March 1920 *50*
Besedovsky et al 4, 227, 274
Betancourt, President Rómulo 119, 122, 129–30
Biak 107
'big man' syndrome 105–6
bike lane, and death of cyclist *255*
BIPOC (black, indigenous, and other people of colour) communities 235, 242
Bissell, D. 17, 32, 210, 211

Black Brothers 96
blackness 11, 101, 102, 107, 113
Black Pacific 102
blended finance 145, 147–8
boarding houses 104–5
Boggs, Carl 256
Bombardier Transportation 172
Bond, P. 36
bond buyers 164
Bonneuil, C. 86
Boston, Massachusetts 120, 121, 122, 126–7, 198
Bourdieu, P. 219, 220
Bowker, G. 77
Brampton, Canada 231–7
Breed, London 253, 264
Brenner, N. 142, 143, 276
Bridge, G. 57
broken time 97, 98, 113
Brooks, Van Wyck 120
Brown, Patrick 235
Brun, C. 217, 222
Building Institutions for Markets (World Development Report) 143
Bush, R. 173
bus rapid transit (BRT) initiatives 35
Buton, Bugis, and Makassar (BBM) migrants 109–10

C

Cairo Monorail (CM) 161, 167, 169–73, 176, 177, 178
Caldeira, T.P.R. 272
Calhoun, C. 73
California Environmental Quality Act 264
campur 107
Canada 34, 231–7
Canal du Midi 74
capital, private 140, 142, 144, 145
capital accumulation 141, 144, 155, 157, 232
capitalism
 contemporary 87, 142, 155
 and crisis 1, 6, 155, 173
 everyday rhythms of 8, 29, 252
 financial 163, 173
capital markets 163, 164, 178
Caribbean
 and clay deposits and bauxite 121
 and infrastructure investment 165
cars 49, 64, 129, 216, 240–1, 250, 258–9, 260–1, 266
 and JAMs 262, 265
 and PLWD 240–1
 and SFMTrA 255
 and street infrastructure 249
Carse, A. 59, 61, 67, 208, 210, 251
'Cascade Objective and Algorithm' 146
Castells, Manuel 2, 5
Castree, N. 6

CBC News 234
CBRE investment firm 163
central business district of Egypt in the New Administrative Capital, Cairo *169*
Chakrabarti, Dr Sumon 236
Chauvel, R. 96, 101, 102
China 110–11, 150, 209
China–Pakistan Economic Corridor (CPEC) 150
Christophers, B. 6
'chronopolitics' 35
churches 105, 106
Cicero 79
cities
 desert 167, 170
 smart 82, 83, 85, 87, 89–90
citizenship, infrastructural 5, 277
city at night 31, 34, 278–9
Ciudad Guayana 12, 13, 119, 120, 121–36
class, and the COVID-19 pandemic 233
Clay, Grady 135
climate change 37, 152, 155
climate crisis 10, 37, 152
Cohen, A.J. 256–7
Coletta, C. 31, 201
Coletta et al 28, 38
Collier, Stephen 57, 191
Colson et al 193
colonization 31, 105, 252
 time as a colonizing force 10, 14, 40, 223
 Indonesia 96
commodity frontiers 155–6
communities of anticipation 89
community-based organizations 236
Connecticut Municipal Electricity Energy Cooperative 198
Consumer credit law 18/2020 (Egypt) 166
contextual learning 65
Convergence 146, 154
Corporacion Venezolana de Guayana (CVG) 121–2, 129, 134
corvee 76
cost–benefit analysis 278
counterfactual history 90
Coutard et al 90
Coventry, and street infrastructure 252
COVID-19 pandemic 31–2, 36, 227, 228, 232–7, 242–3
 and class 233
 infection rates 235
CPEC Authority 150
creditworthiness 177, 178
crip near-futures 244
crip time 229, 238, 240, 243
Critical Mass 253, 254
'critical mission' assets 196–7
crossing at the median in the Region of Waterloo, Ontario *241*
culture jamming 260

INDEX

cyberphysical attacks 191
cycle, and rhythm 32–6, 40
cycle lanes 258–9, 260–1, 263, 265
  and death of cyclist 255
cycling 250, 254–5, 257, 258–9
cyclists 250, 253, 254, 255, *255*, 262, 265–6

D

Datta, A. 91, 281
Davoudi, S. 6, 185
deaths, traffic 250, 254, 255, *255*, 257
debt instruments 175–6
decentralized rainwater percolation, Berlin 60
Defense Authorization Act, 2019 (US) 197
Defense Science Board (US) 196
DeLaure, M. 260
Delta variant, COVID-19 233, 236
delay 18, 78, 208, 209, 223
demand risk 147
dementia 227, 237–42, 243
dependency, and waiting 221
de-risking 166, 175–6, 272
desert cities 167, 170
desynchronization 17, 87, 230, 233, 243
  see also arrhythmia
digital infrastructure and control systems 83–5, 87, 186–8, 190, 199
digital presentism 11, 82
disability acceptance 238
disabled people 240, 241
discarded pasts 62
discordance, rhythmic 31
disposition 17, 83, 230
  and the city at night 278
  in the suburbs 230, 232, 236, 243–4
  in West Papua 95, 101, 105, 108, 111, 112
disruption
  and COVID-19 pandemic 31–2
  and energy systems/grids 163, 186, 190–3, 196, 199, 200
  rhythmic 32, 34, 78
  temporal 16, 17, 18, 32, 211, 260–1, 265, 274
dissonance
  rhythmic 29, 31
  scalar 177–8
  temporal 89, 170, 175–8
  urban 176–7
DIY (do-it-yourself) infrastructure 252–3, 254–5, 256, 262–3, 265, 266
Dock IX 109–10
drug use, in Jayapura 106
Dunne, A. 90
Dupuy, Gabriel D. 73
Dutch Public Works and Water Management Agency, Rijkswaterstaat 65

E

Easterling, K. 17, 230–1, 278
Eastern Economic Corridor Office (EECO) 149
Eastern Indonesia 101–2
economic agencies 172, 174
economic authorities (*hay'at iqtisadia*) 167
economic decline 143
Economic Reform and Structural Adjustment Programs (ERSAPs) 165–6, 167
Economist Intelligence Unit 161
Edensor, T. 25, 27, 28, 31
Edgerton, David 63
Edwards, P.N. 38, 73–4, 78
Egypt 160–2, 165–78
Egypt Economic Development Conference, 2015 160, 170
Egypt, Government of (GoE) 166, 170, 172
Egyptian Armed Forces 177
Egyptian National Bank 168
electricity
  blackouts, Texas 199
  grid system 190–1
  supply 61–2
  systems 78
  utility privatization, Berlin 63–4
electromagnetic events 191
Elektrissima 61–2
Elsner et al 3, 36, 40
embedded pasts 57–9
emergency diesel generators (EDGs) 191–2, 200
emergency generation 191–3
eminent domain 172, 175, 177
energy
  power systems 190
  resilience planning 198
  security 195–6
  storage technologies 62
  supply 195, 196
  transition strategies 36, 85
entrepreneurs 75, 105, 155, 156
entrepreneurship 109, 111
environmental change 154, 155, 157
Ericksen et al 237
essential workers 233, 235, 242, 243
Estache, A. 164–5
eurhythmia 29, 40
everyday life, experience of time in 28–9, 31–3, 40, 102, 105, 112, 119, 211, 228, 233, 239, 244, 276
extensions, as infrastructure 10, 97, 98, 99, 103–6

F

F-15 fighter 187, 190
Factoring and Leasing law 176/2018 (Egypt) 166

fail-safe energy supplies 198
fail-safe systems 188
failures, infrastructure 78
familiarity 17, 239, 243
feedback (cybernetics) 129, 134
Fernandez, R. 164
finance
  blended 145, 147–8
  infrastructure 6
financial de-risking 166, 175–6, 272
financialization 13, 163, 174, 178, 270
financial leasing companies 166–7
Financial Regulatory Authority (FRA) 166–7
financier-entrepreneurs 75
Fink, M. 260
Fischer, C. 197
flooding 34
force majeure 148, 153, 157
Ford Foundation 120, 122
foreign direct investment 149, 170
'forever present' 228, 231, 237
'forever time' 227
Fort Bliss, El Paso, Texas 196–7
France, roads 76–7
Friedmann, John 122, 130–1, 133
Fumihiko Maki 123
fundamentalism, infrastructure 141, 142, 143–4, 152, 154, 157
futured pasts 61–2
The Future Metropolis (Rodwin) 120
future-proofing 79, 80, 83, 88, 142
  of carbon-related financial interests 88
  the grid 16, 201
  profits 13, 151, 154, 155, 156, 157
futures 9, 11, 26, 35, 53, 54
  and accounting 278
  and climate crisis 10, 37
  energy 85
  and futured pasts 61
  and history 52
  infrastructure-based 72–3, 80, 85–6, 87–91
  and Peattie 134
  and re-membering 64
  and the suburbs 229
  see also urban futures
futuring, infrastructure-based 80, 85–6, 87–8
futurism 10, 73, 74, 79, 82, 83–4
futurist regime 79, 84, 85

G

G20 163
Gabor, Daniela 145, 147, 163, 166
games, serious 90
Gans, Herbert 121
garuda bird 152
gas, sewage, as a vehicle fuel 62
gas storage facility 59–60
gatherings, importance of in West Papua 106

genocide, slow 96
Gerda Henkel Foundation 65
Ghosh et al 187
giga-projects 149
global development policy 154
global environmental change 154–5, 157
Global Financial Crisis, 2008 35, 140, 144, 154, 162, 163
Global Infrastructure Hub (GIH) 146–7, 148, 152–3, 163, 165
global South 83, 144, 162, 175
global supply chains 170
global value chains 141, 142, 156
good governance 140, 141, 143, 173
Goodyear et al 261
Graham, S. 37
Granjou, C. 89
Great Garuda *151*, 152, 153–4, 155
Great Western Railway, England 209
greenfield infrastructure projects 142
greenhouse gases, and transport 250
grids 16, 185–6, 188–202
Groton Utilities 198
groundwater 60, 63, 64, 151
growth-pole theory 130–1, 133
Guayana 119, 120, 121–36
Guldi, Jo 54, 55
Gupta, Akhil 26, 209, 210, 251, 252

H

Hage, G. 217
Hall, T. 197
Harrison-Caldwell, M. 264
Hartog, Francois 78–9, 82, 83, 86, 87, 90
Harvard–MIT Joint Center for Urban Studies 120–5, 126, 128, 129, 131, 133, 136
  and Clay 135
  and Peattie 134
Harvey, David 5, 6, 26
Harvey, P. 18, 252
Hassan, Robert 5, 202
healthcare inequalities 235–6
health emergency 233–5
heating systems, Berlin 60
heckling 18, 249, 260–1, 265
Henke, Christopher 58
heroic regime 79
Heßler, M. 55
Hetherington, K. 5, 11, 28
hippocampus 237
historicity, regime of 78–80, 82, 83, 85
history, counterfactual 90
The History Manifesto (Guldi and Armitage) 54–5
Hitler, Adolf 64
Hoefsloot et al 280
a home razed below the new Vang Vieng railway tunnel, Vientiane province *216*

INDEX

Honnold Foundation 198–9
hope, and waiting 214, 217, 219, 220, 223
horse posthouse infrastructure 76
housing market, US 140
Hubbard, P. 252
Huber, R. 187
Hughes, Thomas 58, 59, 75
Humphrey, C. 164
Huyssen, Andreas 55, 57

I

ice storm in north-eastern North America, 1998 34
Ignagni et al 244
The Image of the City (Lynch) 128
immigrants 99, 109–10, 165, 232–3, 242
impersonal rule 74
impossible publics 18, 252, 260
impoverished imaginations 91
indigenous communities 11, 99, 107, 110, 280, 281
indigenous temporalities 280
Indonesia 106, 107, 111, 151–2, 154
  colonization/annexation 96
  and migrants 99
  and occupation 98
  and race 101–2
industrial capitalism 5
inequalities
  healthcare 235–6
  and infrastructure time 220, 242
  (sub)urban 227–8, 229
  and temporal insecurity 220
inequities, and time 243
infection rates, COVID-19 235
infrastructural
  agency 244
  citizenship 5, 277
  fixes 6, 7, 12, 35
  futures 11, 13, 14, 87–8, 278
  imaginaries 6–7, 13, 14, 15, 80, 277
  knowledge 12, 272, 273
  modernization 12
  pasts 9, 13, 17, 244, 273
  power 73
  regionalism 170
infrastructural temporalities 18, 201, 209, 210, 223, 273
  3 main registers 74–5
  and Bowker 77
  in the Toronto suburbs 229, 235–7
infrastructure-based futuring 72–3, 80, 85–6, 87–91
infrastructure deficit 140, 144, 162
infrastructure failures 78
infrastructure finance 6
infrastructure fundamentalism 13, 141, 142, 143–4, 152, 154, 157
infrastructure gap 140, 155, 164–5

infrastructure-led development (ILD) 13, 16, 141, 142, 143–4, 155, 156
infrastructure projects, long gestation periods for 12
infrastructure space 6, 37, 230, 231, 276
infrastructure time 7–8, 10, 11, 16, 17, 18, 142, 201, 209–11, 270–2
  and comparative urbanism 272–3
  and familiarity and memory 239
  and frustration and worry 215
  future directions 277–81
  and inequality 17, 220, 242
  and infrastructure-led development 140, 142, 145, 156
  and infrastructure space 231
  as lived 35
  and power 249
  as a political problematic 273–5
  as a temporal analytic 25–7, 34, 39–40, 223
  and waiting, suspension and stasis 208, 211, 219, 223
'infrastructure turn' 1, 2, 19, 271, 276, 279
  and rhythm 41
innovation 17, 41, 55, 59, 79, 273
  phases 75
insecurity, temporal 220
institutional racialization 235
International Monetary Fund (IMF) 166
international value chains 170
intersectionality 29, 41
inventor-entrepreneurs 75
investment portfolios 176
Invisible Berlin (film series) 65
Israeli F-15 fighter 187
Istanbul, construction projects 252

J

Jacobs, J.M. 272
Jakarta 151–2, 153–4, 155
Jalas et al 33
JAM (just a minute) 253, 254, 258–62, 263, 265, 266
Janeja, M.K. 211
Jasanoff, Sheila 56, 61
Jayapura 95–6, 97, 99, *100*, 111–12
  Angkasa district 108–9
  and blackness 102, 113
  morphological extensions 103–6
Jessop, B. 38
JFK Drive in Golden Gate Park 263
Joniak-Lüthi, A. 210
Jordan, Mel 260, 261
J.P. Morgan 172
Judt, Tony 54
Jüni, Dr Peter 236

K

Kaeng Sua Ten Dam, Thailand 210
Kalimantan 155–6

Kanai, J.M. 162–3, 174
Keil, R. 231–2
Kenya, national development plan 149
Kepes, György 126
Khan, Imran 150
Kitchin, R. 16, 31, 82, 83, 87, 201
Kneas, D. 59, 61, 67, 208, 210, 251
Knox, H. 18, 252
König, W. 55
kontraken 104–5
kosan 104–5
Kosseleck, Reinhard 59, 79, 119

L

Lamu Port–South Sudan–Ethiopia Transport Corridor 149
land auctioning 167–8
land banks 175
land–infrastructure–finance nexus 14, 161–2, 166, 170, 174–5, 176–7
Lander, Luis 121
land markets 175
land use 108–9
Lao 212, 221, 222
Laos–China Railway (LCR) 207–8, 209, 212
large technical systems (LTSs) 58–9, 75, 76
Latin America 119, 120, 121–36, 165
Lefebvre, Henri 8, 25–9, 36–7, 40, 77, 272, 276
  and cycle 32–3
  and linear time 37
  and repetition 30
  and space 27
  see also *Rhythmanalysis*
Levine, R. 220–1
life cycles of infrastructures 75–7
lifetimes of infrastructures 75–7
Lilley, K. 252
Lima 280
Lin, Justin 141–2
linear rhythms 34
Ljuslunder et al 238
logistical power 74
Luang Namtha province 211
Lynch, Kevin 126, 128–9, 130

M

MacGillis, A. 232
Madbouly, Mostafa 160
Madinaty 168
maintenance 7, 15, 34, 36, 77, 275
  and electricity systems 78
  and the grid 202
  and infrastructural temporality 75
  and repair 58
  in West Papua 103
Malaysia 150
Malhotra, Gurpreet 233
Manen, Max van 230

Manila 34
Mann, M. 73
Māori time 280
maps, sequential and 'spatial' 132
Marcel, G. 217
market fundamentalism 143
Marqusee et al 191, 192
Marvin, S. 37
Material Adverse Government Action (MAGA) 148
Mattern, Shannon 7
Maximizing Finance for Development (MFD) 144–5, 146
McCreary, T.A. 280–1
McCulloch, B. 187
McKinsey 163
  Global Institute 165
McNally, R. 147–8, 154
McQuade, W. 121
mega-projects 36, 160, 161–2, 170, 174, 177
Melanesian Spearhead Group 111
memories 238–9, 243
memory-as-infrastructure 239, 244
Meyerson, Martin 123
micro-enterprise law (Egypt) 166
microfinancing 166
microgrids 185–6, 188–202
Middle East and North Africa (MENA) 165, 176
migrants 99, 109–10, 242
militarization of urban space 102
military
  bases 196–8, 199, 201
  officials 102–3
  security 185
Miller, Heather 255
Milligan, R.C. 280–1
Mitchell, Timothy 2, 79–80, 84, 88
Mitchell et al 238
mixed parentage 107–8
mobility 36, 50, 60, 63, 84, 88, 106, 120, 163, 230, 238–40, 250, 279
  infrastructures of 32, 229, 232, 236
  transitions 163
modernist settlement 74
modernity 5, 10, 40, 73–5, 79, 101, 129, 132, 207, 209, 210, 219, 222, 238
modernization 5, 12
Moltke, Willo von 123, 124, 127–8, 129–30, 133
Mongolia, and development plan in 2022 150
monorail system 161, 167, 169–73, 176, 177, 178
Moore, J. 155
Morgan, B. 256–7
Morin, Karen 54
morphological extensions 103–6
morphological interruptions 103

INDEX

mosques 98, 105
'Motion, Sequence and the City' (Appleyard) 126–7
Mubarak, Hosni 160
Mukerji, C. 74, 84
multigenerational housing 233
multilateral development banks (MDBs) 164, 166
Multi-Level Perspective 56
Murphy, R. 34
Myer, John 126

N

National Authority for Tunnels (NAT)/ Egypt 167, 172
National Development Fund (Saudi Arabia) 149–50
national development plans 149, 150–1, 154
nationalization 175, 177
national self-determination 96
National Service Projects Organization (Egypt) 169
nation-time 96
The Nature and Art of Motion (Kepes) 126–7
Naval Submarine Base, New London (SUBASE) 198
neoliberal policy 140, 141, 143
networked infrastructure 15–16, 72, 83, 275
network society 5, 11
New Administrative Capital (NAC) 161, 167, 168–9, 170, 172
'newness' 111, 112, 113
New Orleans 199
New Towns 123–4, 125, 133, 168
New Urban Communities Authority (NUCA) 167, 168, 169
New York City, and blackouts 190–1
New York Transformation Department 258
'night studies' 278–9
night-time economy 279
Nixon, R. 142
Nkula-Wenz, L. 35
nocturnal city 31, 34
non-banking financial services and institutions (NBFIs) 166–7
non-governmental organizations (NGOs) 166
North America 34, 229, 231–7, 280
First Nations 280
North Jakarta 151–2, 153–4, 155
Nowotny, H. 4, 270, 272
Nusantara associations 108

O

OECD, on infrastructure investment 165
Office of Military Affairs (OMA)/ Connecticut 198
Offner, Jean-Marc 76, 77
Olmstead, N.A. 89–90

Olsen, Bjørnar 64
'operational landscapes' 142, 155, 156, 276–7
ordenamiento 122
order of growth 124–5
Osborne, P. 33
othering, temporal 19
Otsus Law 21/2001 (West Papua) 101
Al Oula for Non-Banking Financial Services 168
out of place 8, 102, 232

P

painted lines 251, 255
Pakistan, and the China–Pakistan Economic Corridor 150
pandemic, COVID-19 31–2, 36, 227, 228, 232–7, 242–3
Papua New Guinea (PNG) 110, 111, 150
Papuans 95–113
'Papuan time' 11, 96, 97, 99, 102
parallel pasts 60–1
Paris-centred star network 77
PARK(ing) Day 253, 254
participatory planning 173
pasts
  infrastructural 9, 13, 17, 244, 273
  usable 50, 53–67, 120
path dependence 2, 55, 56, 57–8, 162
Peattie, Lisa 122, 123, 134, 135
Peck, J. 143
pedestrians 250, 253, 262, 265–6
  deaths 250, 254, 255, 257
  disabled 240–1
pedestrian safety 'pilot' 256
Peel Region 231–7
Penfold, A.H. 125, 134–5
people living with dementia (PLWD) 227, 228, 231, 237–42, 243, 244
periodization 37–9
Persico, Maureen 260
Peru, and road infrastructure 252
Petit, P. 221
Phnom Penh Post 207
Pieterse, E. 274
Planning a Pluralist City (Appleyard) 131
Planning: Rethinking Ciudad Guayana (Peattie) 134
pluralizing times 86–7
Plyushteva, A. 34, 40
political risk 145, 148–51
polyrhythmia 29, 31, 32, 40
pop-up healthcare infrastructure 235, 236, 242–3
portfolio investment 145, 163, 164, 175, 176
postmetropolis 232
power 223, 251–2
  and automobility 265
  infrastructural 73
  logistical 74

291

power grids 185–6, 188–202
power industry 190
powerlessness 213–14, 221
power of waiting 220–2
power outages 191, 198, 199
precarity 221
  precarious employment 233, 235
prefiguration 256
present, perpetual 11, 82, 97, 110–1
present, suspended 208, 210
presentism 10, 73, 78, 82, 83–4
  and the Anthropocene 86
  and COVID-19 pandemic 227
  and history 52, 54
private capital 140, 142, 144, 145
private funds *(Sanadeeq Khasa)* 167
privatization 63, 163, 167, 177
The Production of Space (Lefebvre) 26
profits, future-proofing 13, 151, 154, 155, 156, 157
project time 15, 36, 208, 209, 210, 223, 275, 277
  and suspension and stasis 16, 211
project timelines 12, 35
The Promise of Infrastructure (Anand et al) 51, 56, 61, 119, 209, 274
public health infrastructure, underfunding 233, 235
Public Investment Fund (Saudi Arabia) 150
public–private partnerships (PPPs) 165, 167, 170
publics, impossible 18, 252, 260
Pulido, D. 146

Q

Quick Build 264
Quinby, R. 229, 232

R

Rabwa Real Estate 168
Raby, F. 90
race
  and the COVID-19 pandemic 233
  in Eastern Indonesia 101–2
racialization
  in Brampton 231
  institutional 235
racialized communities 242, 251
racism 6, 242
Raco et al 35
railroads/railways 207–24
railway pylons *218*
rainwater percolation, decentralized, Berlin 60
Ravard, Rafael Alfonzo 121
regimes of historicity 78–80, 82, 83, 85
Regional Development Policy: A Case Study of Venezuela (Friedmann) 130–1
regionalism, infrastructural 170

Regulier, Catherine 27
Reid-Musson, E. 29
re-iterating pasts 64–5, 66
religious institutions 105
re-membering pasts 64, 66
renewable energies 60
repair 3, 7, 34, 244, 275, 278
  and maintenance 58
  in West Papua 103
'repeated instances' 272, 273
repetition 29–32, 39–40
representations of time 26
re-presenting pasts 63–4, 66
repurposing 50, 59, 64, 209
resilience 193, 202
reuse technologies, 1930s Berlin 63
rhythmanalysis 25, 28, 29, 31, 41, 272
Rhythmanalysis (Lefebvre) 25, 27, 29
rhythmic discordance 29, 31
rhythm 3, 8, 25, 27–9, 39–41, 210, 253, 257, 275, 279
  bodily 4, 31, 239–42
  of capitalism 29
  and everyday life 16, 17, 18, 27, 77–8, 85, 97, 119, 217, 233, 237, 244
  as cycle 32–6, 40
  linear 34
  natural 5, 27, 280
  as period 36–9
  as repetition 29–32
  suburban 232
  urban 25, 40, 82, 130
  see also arrythmia, eurhythmia, polyrhythmia
Rickerson et al 196, 198
risk 13, 144, 145, 155
  economic 146–8
  environmental 151–5
  mitigation strategies 157
  political 145, 148–51
roads
  infrastuctures 7, 76, 252 *see also* street infrastructure
  regulation of 76
Robin, E. 35
Rodrik, D. 143
Rodwin, Lloyd 121, 123, 134
Ronneberger, K. 231–2
Rosa, H. 230, 238, 244
Rotterdam, energy transitions 36
rule, impersonal 74
Rundell, J. 222
Rwanda, and development plan in 2020 150

S

'sacrifice zones' 112–13
Safe Street Rebel 260, 261–2
Salazar, J.F. 89
Salehie, M. 188

INDEX

San Francisco 250, 251, 252–66
San Francisco Bicycle Coalition 253, 254
San Francisco Municipal Transformation Agency (SFMTrA) 254–6, 257–8, 259–60, 263
San Francisco Municipal Transportation Agency (SFMTA) 258, 263, 264
Saudi Arabia, and *Vision 2030* 149–50
Sayre, N. 6
Schindler, S. 162–3, 174
Schipper et al 60, 63
Schivelbusch, W. 85, 209
Schmid, C. 27, 37, 276
Schorske, Carl 66
Schwanen, T. 34, 40
self, sense of 238
self-determination 11, 96, 111, 281
self-financing 167
self-healing systems 15, 187–94
sequence, and urban growth 124–5, 127, 128, 129, 130, 133
sequential map 132
serious games 90
sewage gas as a vehicle fuel 62
Shaban, A. 281
Shared Prosperity Vision 2030 150
Sharma, Sara 6, 19, 274
sharrows 251
Shaw, R. 31, 34, 278
Sheller, M. 230
Shove et al 80
'shrinking world' effect 240
Simone, A.M. 7, 28, 91, 228, 236, 274, 280
Sims, Benjamin 58
Siphandone, Sonexay 207
al-Sisi, President Abdel Fattah 14, 160
Slattery, Kate 254–5
slow genocide 96
slowness 259, 262, 265–6
slow operations 142, 155–7
'slow violence' 142
smart cities 82, 83, 85, 87, 89–90
smart microgrids 15, 16, 59, 185–6, 188–202
Smith, M.L. 2
Smith, R.J. 5, 28
social futures 72, 80, 85, 87, 88, 90–1
social temporalities 10, 72, 78, 80
socio-ecological systems 188
socio-technical assemblages 64, 66
socio-technical imaginaries 61
socio-technical trajectories 62
Solomon Islands, security agreement with China 110
South Africa
  bus rapid transit (BRT) initiatives 35
  mega-projects 36
South Asian immigration 165, 232–3
sovereign debt instruments 176
sovereign green bonds 172

space, and Lefebvre 27
space–time 19, 25–7, 31, 39, 240–1
  and COVID-19 pandemic 32, 243
  and everyday rhythms of capitalism 29
  extending 106–10
spatial fixes 6, 13, 88
'spatial' maps 132
spatio-temporal fixes 6
Special Autonomy Law, West Papua 111
special economic zones 141, 149, 170
speculative design 90
speed 208, 211, 219, 222, 223, 266
  'China speed' 16, 208, 209, 210, 212, 223
  Laos–China Railway (LCR) 209
  and Vision Zero 265
speed politics, in San Francisco 253–4, 262–5
Splintering Urbanism (Graham and Marvin) 37
Spoorenberg, F. 147–8, 154
standby capacity 191–3
Star, Susan Leigh 1
stasis 16, 208, 210, 211, 221, 222, 223
State Ownership Policy Document (Egypt) 177
Steinberg, M. 187
stigma, and dementia 238
storm in north-eastern North America, 1998 34
Stratton, Julius 122
Straughan et al 211, 220
street infrastructure 249–53
street water pumps 49, *50, 51, 52*, 59, 64
'structure of time,' and infrastructure 230
student protests, West Papua 103–4
SUBASE, Groton, Connecticut 198
subordination, and waiting 221
sub-Saharan Africa, and infrastructure investment 165
suburb-as-disposition 230
suburbs 227–8, 229–37, 239, 240–4
Supreme Council for Planning and Urban Development (Egypt) 173, 174
'suspended present' 208, 210
suspension 16, 208, 210, 211, 221, 222, 223, 251
  and hope 219
Sustainable Development Goals (SDGs) 163, 164, 173
Swaan, A. de 73
system builders 58, 75

T

Taameer for Securitization 168
Tahvildari, L. 188
Tarr, Joel 53, 55, 73
tempo 6, 7, 222, 275, 278
temporal
  alignment/misalignment 13, 14, 19, 32–5
  arbitrage 274

fixes 6, 275
imaginaries 6–7
insecurity 220
insurgency 274
justice 281
othering 19
readjustments 186–7
violence 29, 34, 40
temporality 2–4, 10, 12, 26, 80, 112, 119, 135, 201–2, 223, 272, 278
　of form 125–30
　of infrastructure-led development 142
　pandemic 243
　and power 251
territorial moment 161, 170, 173
Texas, electricity blackouts 199
Thailand
　and Eastern Economic Corridor Office (EECO) 149
　Kaeng Sua Ten Dam 210
Thailand 4.0 149
theft, in Jayapura 106
Thiel, Philip 128
thought experiments 90
Thrift, N. 3, 31, 281
time
　abstract 40, 272
　as broken 11, 97, 98, 113, 231, 244
　clock 5, 32
　cyclical 32, 34–5, 36, 40, 276
　dilation 12
　and inequities 243
　linear 32, 33, 37
　lived 36, 223, 230, 237–8
　network 5, 16, 202
　perceived 17, 26
　railroad/railway 208, 209
　representational 26
　water 31
　see also infrastructure time; project time
time dilation 12
time horizons 13, 14, 19, 34, 36, 121, 149, 280
　and Banfield 132
　and Brampton 233
　and project stability 150
timelines, project 12, 35
time–space
　compression 5, 82–3, 209
　contraction 12
　matrix, of the suburbs 229, 230, 233
　see also space–time
timescape 8, 77, 281
　of smart cities 82, 87
time to heal (TTH) 188
Tonkiss, F. 16
Toronto suburbs 231–44
Tosh, John 54, 55
Toussaint, Bert 65

traffic deaths 250, 254, 255, *255*, 257
transition strategies 72
transit systems 15, 279
transport officials cool off during a heatwave, Berlin, 1931 *51*
Treitel, J. 163
Trejo-Mathys, J. 230
Trentmann, Frank 64
Tsing, Anna 155–6
Tumlin, Jeffrey 264

U

Uekotter, Frank 53
UN (United Nations)
　Sustainable Development Goals (SDGs) 163, 164, 173
　UNCTAD 144, 173
uncertainty 219, 220, 223
underground gas storage facility 59–60
The Unheavenly City (Banfield) 132
urban accumulation 101
urban extensions of Jayapura 104–5
urban futures 31, 83, 84, 90–1, 120, 281
　and smart cities 85
　and smart grids 201, 202
urban inequalities 227–8
urbanism 6, 121, 278
　decelerated 281
　experimental 83
　networked 26, 29, 39
　post-war 124
urbanization 6, 28, 39, 119, 122, 142, 156, 170, 275
　extended 98, 227
　frontier 153
　of Papuans 100
'urban knowledge' 131
Urban Renewal 120–1, 123
urban resilience 185, 186
The Urban Revolution (Lefebvre) 37
urban rhythms 25, 40, 130
The Urban Villagers (Gans) 121
US (United States)
　housing market 140
　military 185
　national electricity grid system 190–1
usable infrastructure pasts 50, 272
　adapted 59–60
　discarded 62
　embedded 57–9
　futured 61–2
　parallel 60–1
usable pasts 50, 53–67, 120

V

vaccine roll-out, COVID-19 235, 236, 242
value chains 170
Vang Vieng railway tunnel, Vientiane province *216*

INDEX

Venezuela 119, 121–36
'view from nowhere' 135
The View from the Barrio (Peattie) 134
View from the Road (Appleyard, Lynch, and Myer) 126
violence
  of imagination 91
  slow 142
Vision 2030 (Kenya) 149
Vision 2030 (Saudi Arabia) 149–50
Vision 2050 (Papua New Guinea) 150
'vision in motion' 126, *127*
Vision Zero 250, 251, 265
Vohra-Miller et al 231
vulnerability 221, 240

W

waiting 16–17, 18, 208, 210–11, 212–17, 218–24
  and annoyance 215
  and dependency 221
  and hope 214, 217, 219, 220, 223
  and power 220–2
  and subordination 221
  suspension and stasis 208, 211, 223
Walker et al 28–9
walking 250, 256, 257
Walk San Francisco 253, 254
Wall Street Consensus 142, 145, 148
Walter Post Theological College 97
'want-it-in-my-backyard' (WIMBY) land 197
Washington Consensus 140, 143, 163, 164
water
  consumption scheme, Berlin 61
  governance 280
  pumps 49, *50*, *51*, *52*, 59, 64
  reuse 62
  supply 49, 64
'water time' 31
weather events, extreme 191, 199
Weaver, C. 131, 133
Weber, H. 55
Weber, R. 278
West Papua 95–113
Why History Matters (Tosh) 54–5
Winter, C.J. 280–1
Wollenberg, Bruce 190
a woman washes materials from a wedding festival in her village's stream, alongside which railway pylons have been constructed *218*
Wood, A. 35
workers, essential 233, 235, 242, 243
World Bank 144–5, 146
Wright, E.O. 89

www.ingramcontent.com/pod-product-compliance
Lightning Source LLC
Chambersburg PA
CBHW051529020426
42333CB00016B/1839